Ancient Origins of the Mexican Plaza

Roger Fullington Series in Architecture

ANCIENT ORIGINS OF THE MEXICAN PLAZA

FROM PRIMORDIAL SEA TO PUBLIC SPACE

LOGAN WAGNER

HAL BOX

SUSAN KLINE MOREHEAD

University of Texas Press ⌁ Austin

Publication of this book was made possible in part by the Program for
Cultural Cooperation between Spain's Ministry of Culture and United States'
Universities, as well as support from Roger Fullington and a challenge grant
from the National Endowment for the Humanities.

Requests for permission to reproduce material from this work should
be sent to:
Permissions
    University of Texas Press
    P.O. Box 7819
    Austin, TX 78713-7819
    www.utexas.edu/utpress/about/bpermission.html

The paper used in this book meets the minimum requirements of
ANSI/NISO Z39.48-1992 (R1997) (Permanence of Paper). ∞

Library of Congress Cataloging-in-Publication Data

Wagner, Logan.
    Ancient origins of the Mexican plaza : from primordial sea
to public space / by Logan Wagner, Hal Box, and Susan Kline
Morehead.—First [edition].
        pages   cm—(Roger Fullington series in architecture)
    Includes bibliographical references and index.
    ISBN 978-0-292-71916-3 (hardback)
    1. Plazas—Mexico—History. 2. Public spaces—Mexico—
History. 3. Architecture and society—Mexico—History. I. Box, Hal.
II. Morehead, Susan Kline. III. Title.

NA9070.W34 2013
711'.550972—dc23   2012024685
doi:10.7560/19163

To Hal, our friend, mentor, colleague, and coauthor, who left us on May 8, 2011, after the manuscript was completed but before he saw it in print.

CONTENTS

AUTHORS' NOTE

Our enthusiasm for plazas began differently for each of us.

Logan Wagner grew up in Mexico with a plaza at the heart of his world. Speaking Spanish and a bit of Nahuatl and Mayan, and having studied anthropology and earned degrees in architecture and Latin American Studies, Logan also knew the ways of modern Mexico and could fly an airplane over it for a special look. After we found ourselves deeply involved in the idea of communal open space, Logan completed a Ph.D. on Mesoamerican sacred open spaces with one of its leading scholars, Linda Schele. Logan once said, "When you grow up in Latin America, plazas are in every town and city; they are part and parcel of daily life. Plazas were taken for granted in my world; I thought everyone had one."

Hal Box, an architect, professor, and dean of the School of Architecture at the University of Texas at Austin for sixteen years, grew up around an active Texas town square, which had recollections of the Mexican plaza. His architectural experience had been not in Mexico but in urban design and architecture influenced by Camillo Sitte, where most designs centered on a plaza or patio. He and his wife, Eden, loved Mexico and had just bought a house in Cuernavaca in 1985 when this project started.

Susan Kline Morehead, a lecturer, arts advocate, and nonprofit organization executive director, joined Hal and Logan in many of the field research adventures, and on entering the architectural history graduate program at UT Austin, participated in Studio Mexico, a program of the School of Architecture designed by her husband, Sinclair Black, and Logan in 1991, and begun with Hal's blessing as dean in 1992. Sinclair and Logan conducted Studio Mexico for eight years, with Susan involved in many of the sessions. Her master's thesis on the iconography of sixteenth-century Mexican churches contributed to her experience, which was also informed by her travels to many plazas in Europe, Japan, India, Africa, South America, and the Middle East.

Architect J. B. Johnson, a friend and longtime resident of Mexico, took Hal on a tour of sixteenth-century *conventos* and set the hook in his soul. J.B. joined us on all of our following field research, and with Carmen Cusi de García-Pimentel has written the definitive monograph, *Churches of the Mayas*.

Soon after Hal's enlightening experience in Mexico with J. B. Johnson, Brian Rosbrough of Earthwatch, an organization that provides volunteers for scholarly enterprises, came by Hal's office to inquire if Earthwatch might conduct a project with the School of Architecture. Hal knew just which project to suggest. Within an hour a project was conceived to measure, photograph, and otherwise document the art of Mexican building and the phenomenon of its communal open spaces: the sacred patios and plazas where the life of the towns was centered.

0.1.   Hal Box

The partnership began when Hal realized that he had the audacity to accept the job of principal investigator on a project in Mexico when he spoke no more than tourist Spanish. So he called his former student and friend Logan Wagner to persuade him to get involved as coinvestigator, and got assurances from J.B. that he would help. Starting almost instantly and continuing over the next twelve summers, Hal, Logan, and J.B. organized the investigations—with maps, surveying equipment, large-format cameras, drawing boards, and field teams of volunteers. Ground transportation was an old red Cherokee, a borrowed Dodge Dart, and a Ram pickup; lodging was picturesque; meals came from convents we measured, townspeople we found to fix lunch for twenty people, and local cafés, all making delightful experiences. Operating in this manner, we explored, documented, and recorded our findings on over ninety towns, many previously unconsidered by historians.

We realized that the plaza had a vitality and substance that should be documented and studied, and that its historic, architectural, social, and economic qualities might contribute to the mainstream of urban design and architecture today. As we learned more about plazas and sacred spaces, we wanted to know how they might have grown in importance from their Mesoamerican origins. We also wanted to know what happened as communal open space was modified by Spanish intervention. This led Logan into several years of graduate study and a Ph.D. with a dissertation on the subject. Hal developed a graduate seminar on the subject in which students studied and refined the field drawings.

From field research and study we offer our ideas on how these sacred communal spaces began and how their form developed into the Mexican plaza. Over the twelve summers, 287 Earthwatch volunteers assisted by providing two weeks of their time, their own transportation, and a portion of the field cost. The volunteers learned to measure, sketch, use a plane table and alidade, and prepare scale drawings from their field notes—all while experiencing life for a day or more in each town we documented, enjoying the special life in Mexico. The volunteers were teachers, doctors, priests, businessmen and women, and students—the youngest was eighteen and the oldest eighty-five—and some came summer after summer. Architecture students in Hal's seminar on Mexican architecture redrew the field drawings for study and publication. The measured plans, all to the same scale, are the heart of the documentation and individuation of each space and place. Our drawings seek to describe the town fabric as a spatial setting for the open spaces. The towns are presented here in various levels of detail. We hope that our descriptions and documentation can give you the sense of being in these exceptional spaces.

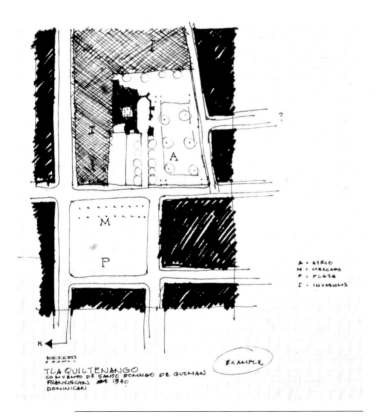

0.2. Prototype of survey drawing. Sketch by Hal Box.

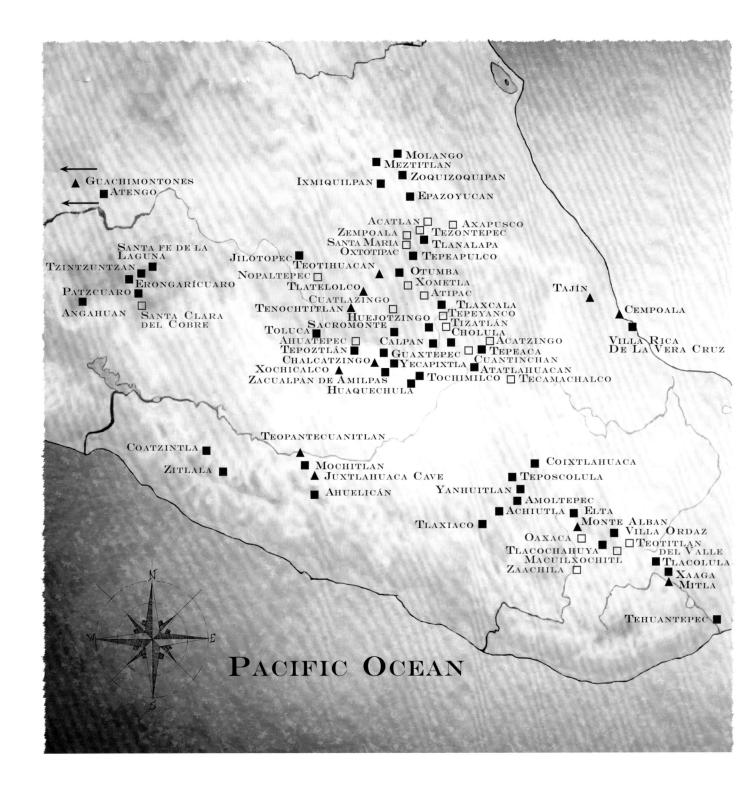

MOLANGO
MEZTITLAN
ZOQUIZOQUIPAN
IXMIQUILPAN
EPAZOYUCAN

GUACHIMONTONES
ATENGO

ACATLAN ☐   ☐ AXAPUSCO
ZEMPOALA ☐   ☐ TEZONTEPEC
SANTA MARIA ☐ ☐ TLANALAPA
OXTOTIPAC   ☐ TEPEAPULCO

SANTA FE DE LA
LAGUNA
TZINTZUNTZAN
ERONGARÍCUARO
PATZCUARO
ANGAHUAN   SANTA CLARA
            DEL COBRE

JILOTOPEC
TEOTIHUACAN
NOPALTEPEC   OTUMBA ▲
TLATELOLCO   XOMETLA ☐
CUATLAZINGO   ATIPAC ☐
TENOCHTITLAN ▲   TLAXCALA
HUEJOTZINGO ☐   TEPEYANCO
SACROMONTE   TIZATLÁN ☐
TOLUCA   CHOLULA
AHUATEPEC ☐ CALPAN ☐   ACATZINGO ☐
TEPOZTLÁN   TEPEACA ☐
CHALCATZINGO ▲ GUAXTEPEC   CUANTINCHAN
XOCHICALCO ▲   YECAPIXTLA   ATATLAHUACAN
ZACUALPAN DE AMILPAS   TOCHIMILCO ☐ TECAMACHALCO ☐
            HUAQUECHULA

TAJÍN ▲
CEMPOALA ▲
VILLA RICA
DE LA VERA CRUZ

TEOPANTECUANITLAN

COATZINTLA
ZITLALA
MOCHITLAN
JUXTLAHUACA CAVE ▲
AHUELICÁN
YANHUITLAN
ACHIUTLA
TLAXIACO

COIXTLAHUACA
TEPOSCOLULA
AMOLTEPEC
ELTA
MONTE ALBAN ▲   VILLA ORDAZ
OAXACA ☐   TEOTITLAN
TLACOCHAHUYA ☐   DEL VALLE
MACUILXOCHITL   TLACOLULA
ZAACHILA ☐   XAAGA ▲
                  MITLA

TEHUANTEPEC

N
W   E
S

PACIFIC OCEAN

GULF OF MEXICO

▲ MESOAMERICAN SITES
■ 16TH CENTURY SITES
□ 16TH CENTURY SITES IN APPENDIX

CABO CATOCHE ▲

EK BALAM ▲

▲ TIHOO
■ MÉRIDA
■ IZAMAL
■ SUDZAL

COZUMEL

■ VALLADOLID

▲

■ YOTHOLÍN

TULUM ▲

■ TIBOLON

▲ UXMAL

▲ CHAMPOTÓN

LA VENTA ▲

UAXACTUN
▲

TIKAL
▲

ROCKY POINT ▲

▲ PALENQUE

PIEDRAS
NEGRAS ▲

MACHAQUILÁ ▲

YAXCHILAN ▲

TONINÁ
▲

BONAMPAK ▲

▲ LA BLANCA

COPÁN ▲

[Map 1.]   Map of New Spain.
            Drawing by David Bowers, Black & Vernooy Architects.

ACKNOWLEDGMENTS

The measured drawings and field notes on ninety Mexican town centers are housed in the Alexander Architectural Archive of the University of Texas at Austin, findable with the marvelous help, formerly of Beth Dodd, and now of Nancy Sparrow. Over 100,000 digital images and 250,000 slides are housed in the Visual Resource Collection of the School of Architecture and can be located with the expert help of Elizabeth Schaub. Many of the images can be seen online at ARTstor.org, among them the 5,722 images included in the Hal Box and Logan Wagner Collection of Mexican Architecture and Urban Design.

We secured the help of the Instituto Nacional de Antropología e Historia in visiting the sites through Logan's colleagues in Mexico, such as Jaime Cama Villafranca, who also provided the use of his car and drafting tables.

Bill Glade, director of the Institute for Latin American Studies at the University of Texas (now the Long Institute for Latin American Studies, or LILAS), and his successor, Richard Adams, gave us encouragement, a reading list, and some start-up funds. Architect Ricardo Legorreta provided poetic insights into the Mexican spirit and Mexican ways of building, gave us personal tours of buildings whose spaces and proportions he admired, and instructed us in the connoisseurship of tequila.

Here we acknowledge others who participated in producing the book: Theresa May, Jim Burr, Lynne Chapman, Nancy Warrington, Ayham Ghraowi, Regina Fuentes, Nancy Bryan, and others at the University of Texas Press; the unknown readers of the manuscript; J. B. Johnson, Sinclair Black, Eden Box, Patricia Tweedy, Jill Nokes, Aurora McClain, Manuel Serrano Cabrera, Luis Millet Cámara, Jaime Cama Villafranca, Ramón Carrasco, Alfonso Morales, Leticia Roche Cano, Kent Reilly, Ed Barnhardt, Carolyn Tate, Julia Guernsey, Bob Renfro, Michael Hironymous, Macduff Everton, Brian Lang, Laura Raymond, Danelle Briscoe, Eve Beckwith, David Bowers, Juan Fenton, Jorge Loyzaga, Carrie Strahan, Patrick Eugene Jones Wagner, Guillaume Smith, Anne Robertson, Jennifer Gromam, Gillette Griffin, and Richard Cleary. The University of Texas School of Architecture provided film, processing, equipment, and other support. Grants were provided by the University of Texas at Austin Graduate School and LLILAS, and by the government of Spain.

The following volunteers gave their time and talent during the fieldwork conducted on "The Art of Mexican Building" Earthwatch expeditions over twelve summers: Kathleen MacLeod, Sylvia Campbell, Lita Elvers, Margaret Hodder, Jane Robbins, Roberta C. Heyer, Anita Anderson, William Steele, Ardella Kemmler, Kathryn Nonnennmann, Sara Kimball, Virginia Sturrock, Raquel Kramer, Edgar Dixon, Kathie Van Hoven, Rae Ragland, Patricia Kule, Mark Freeman, John Hittell, Cecile Rosser, Elaine Adler,

Lorraine Kapakjian, Kristi Wessenberg, Walter Ogilvie III, Virginia Church, Walter Elvers, Adriane Mayko, Virginia Steinhauer, Nadine Holder, Judy Schmidt, Tommy Shaw, Anne Rumsey, Kirby Hall, Meredith Rode, Suzanne Murphy-Larronde, Roberta Huber, Richard Huber, Cassandra Meyers, Patricia Gallup, John Phillipp, Claire Nelson, Joseph Battaglini, Patricia Oertley, Marcella Hill, Robert Oertley, Norma Becker, Betty Vizzini, Brigid O'Hanrahan, James Duncanson, Anne Perkins, Amelia Van Itallie, Kathleen Woodruff, M. Catherine Beamer, Alan Baird, Mary Lawrence, Anne Stewart, Elizabeth Dion, Wilfred Rousseau, Clarence Egan, Virginia Chase, Cletis Roy Foley, Gerald Fleming, Jane Beswick, Claude McLean Jr., Warren Heyer, Lee Bretz, Stephanie Bourgeois, Annmarie Adreani, Yolanda Calvo, Margaret Gerring, Raymond Stewart, Cecily Diness, A. Stuart Bay, Dorothea Cavanagh, Vanessa Cao, Sandra Acosta, Nicolas Zorotovich, Scott Stewart, Anthony Campbell, Hillary Ingram, Claudia McLaughlin, Marjorie Smuts, Kristen Woiwode, Joe Vetrano, Lee Andrews, Patricia Broehl, Juan Gomez-Novy, Mary Bell, Kenneth Sprayberry, Rebecca Kinney, Judith Ellisen, Seth Weissman, Jennifer Spoon, Cathleen Thorrez, Gwendolyn Andrey, Marilyn Bodek, Myrna Horton, Joyce Clark, Dan Epperson, Susan Lynch, Maria Hope, Trudy Scott, Laura Raymond, Nina Allen, Erica Seidman, John Maniscalco, Brooke Bartholomew, Sheila Wells, Antje Wilkes, Sara Chapman, Alicia Snyder, Kenneth Lowstetter, Barbara Harrison, Jo Marsh, Stephen Sears, Maureen Clark, Mary Corey March, Kit Sutherland, Dorothy Ann Altwarg, Barbara MacDonald, Bertha Ugalde, Monique Lopez, Jean Hammond, Dorothy Gerring, Susan Kempler, Gladyce Stais, Sonja Stobie, Charles Broehl, Joyce Frederick, Janet David, Ruthann Wilson, Joseph Schwarzenbach, Carla Henebry Branscombe, Jane Jervey, Tom Hofmaier, Jane Stone, Patricia A. Harmon, Kathy Willens, Mark Gura, Muriel Fujii, Penny Bay, Cathy Lehman, Karen Gilg, Lisa Zhito, James Fraerman, Edward Colacion, Anita Majetich, Sarah Newick, Ruth Steele, Judith Wolfe, Nancy Eisenman, Robert Harker, Phyllis Schmitt, Michael Durand, Deborah Maynard, Paula Flinn, Patricia Fitzpatrick, Madeleine Charron, Myrna Phelps, Regina Dorian, Andrew Arbury, Anne-Lise Lemche, Brian Dunbar, Milena Smith, Jonathan Racek, Amy Harfeld, James Kisiel, Sherry Sands, June Tiley, Diana Jones, Elizabeth deNiord, Stephanie Sharis, Rachel Delgado, Margaret Ponzio, Virginia Hall, Cindy Bugarin, Lan Nguyen, Barbara Bates, Carrol Betz, Traci Rustin, Evelyn Virshup, Rosana Rossi, Kerri Lorigan, Margaret Goff, Alexander Phelps, Kara Galli, Lois McCubbin, Virginia Soffa, Craig Levine, Aaron Virshup, Muriel Goldblatt, Kim Barrington, Sharen McLean, Pascal Ouimet, Mike McBride, Kristina Contreras, Sheldon Altwarg, Martha McMahon, Katherine Preston, David Phillips, Laurie Pessah, Jacob Menn, Melyn Roberson, Christopher Neale, Eva Johnson, Betty Schumacher, Yvonne Daizadeh, Sarah Verity, Andrea McEvoy, Jacob Hernandez, Carla Reiber, Kyle Dieters, Joel Carda, Laura Kogan, Sarabeth Guyon, Remy Vincent, and Skye Chapman.

Ancient Origins of the Mexican Plaza

INTRODUCTION

The Mexican plaza is the most complete expression of Mexico's rich four-thousand-year-old multifaceted heritage. It is the open-air heart of every Mexican neighborhood, town, and city—its communal living room. The plaza is part of an ensemble of secular and sacred communal open spaces that include the cloister; the sacred patio, or *atrio*, of the church; and sometimes a civic or market plaza. The evolution and comparison of these dynamic spaces shaped by the architecture around them and activated by the life of the community are the objects of our study and presentation.

Communal open spaces fascinate us because they are where things happen—where new friends and old meet, where one goes to see what's new, and where personal and communal rituals and celebrations happen, where history and sense of place are ever present. The great urban places formed by buildings over time: plazas, piazzas, squares, courts, Middle Eastern maidans, Chinese *guang changs*—our communal open spaces—center the world's towns and cities. They show us the central and most visible architectural feature of the town or city. Such communal open spaces provide the physical settings for the high points of human activity and some of the world's most celebrated architecture. One can learn much about a place and its people just by looking around its plaza.

The most visible feature of the Mexican plaza is almost always a church and its *atrio*. The sixteenth-century *atrio* was the initial communal space of the town, built by the friars for Christianizing the natives before a church structure could be built. Later, the secular plaza was formed outside the *atrio* for nonsacred communal activities such as civic events, markets, social interchange, and the local government housed in a Palacio Municipal. Plazas and *atrios* have many variations and additions, such as bullrings or, in Michoacán, *hospitales* with patios to serve natives in need.[1]

More inclusive than other aesthetic experiences like *looking* at a painting, *listening* to a piece of music, *touching* a sculpture, *reading* a book, *tasting* and *smelling* food, the perception of space involves all of these senses plus the awareness of the *three-dimensional space* itself. A poet described experiencing space as "being cut up by the space as I move through it."[2] High excitement indeed, when one can see it; smell it; taste it; hear it; touch it; find adventure, friends, and rituals in it; and be cut up by it all at the same time. The drama can build to that of an operatic stage. The communal open spaces of Mexico delight all of our senses. When we sense also the layers of Mesoamerican and European history creating the place, the passion in the iconography, and the human art and labor of building the place along with the lives of people moving around us, the space can consume us with its spiritual and sensual qualities. In its totality, it makes a place that is ultimately unique to its specific culture, to its geography, and to its particular moment.

All one has to do to get deeply engaged in a plaza is to sit in it for a while: read, get a shoe shine, watch a couple in love, buy a trinket, have lunch, listen to the sound of music and conversation, and wait for the parade — there will soon be one — for a saint's day, a national holiday, or simply a family escorting a young bride to her wedding.

All the delights of these communal open spaces are available to tourists as they travel, but when one lives in Mexico, the central plaza becomes part of the daily ritual. Just as the plaza and the *atrio* of the church are the urban centers, the open patios of individual houses are the centers of family life.

This book describes the phenomenon of the Mexican plaza, concentrating on the Mesoamerican sacred sites overlaid by Spanish new towns, and how plazas have persisted as the most important places for religious rituals, parades, and civic ceremonies; trade and commerce; socializing and contemplation. It introduces the idea of place-making via the formation of communal open spaces and explores how these spaces function in different scales, from residential patios to major plazas. Some of the churches and *atrios* of this period have been well documented by George Kubler, John McAndrew, and others; our contribution is to add the *ensemble* of communal open spaces that form the heart of the towns, the sacred space as well as the secular: the plazas, *mercados*, and street spaces that form the core of the town. We also expand the number of churches and towns previously documented to include additional examples. We describe our findings from field research and libraries, give interpretations to help the reader get a sense of the presence and life of the plaza, and give a brief history of the forces that caused the plazas to be significant and sacred in their particular places. Our survey could not be all-inclusive. The plazas of major cities in Mexico have had such extensive redevelopment since their formation that we chose to examine only plazas closer to their original form in the smaller towns that have seen few basic changes since the sixteenth century. We have chosen thirty-four town centers to discuss here, and we present in the appendix twenty additional measured drawings of the seventy town centers that we have completed.

In the details of the documentation we hope that the magic of the Mexican plaza can be understood and perhaps imported into today's urban design initiatives. We invite you to imagine the individual spaces using the scale plans, the eye-level photographs, aerial photographs, our interpretation of the formative forces, and the human dimension of the plaza to help you obtain a vivid sense of these special places.

In addition to documenting these spaces for their urban design example and use in preservation, one purpose of this study and fieldwork was to determine if Mesoamerican communal open spaces were incorporated into the open spaces the Spaniards created when founding new towns in the New World. To understand the nature and origins of the Mesoamerican open spaces, we undertook a review of the existing scholarship. We analyzed some known pre-Hispanic sites in order to identify, illustrate, and summarize concepts that created the design and use of planned urban open spaces in Mesoamerica. We point out how certain design directives were followed in the creation of urban centers and the open spaces within them, from the initial urban settlements of the latter half of the second millennium BCE to the settlements built on the eve of the arrival of the invading European culture at the start of the sixteenth century, a span of three thousand years. We address those issues in Chapter One.

In Chapter Two we present the principles and urban design experience that Europeans would bring with them as they re-formed the vast number of settlements in the Americas at the beginning of the sixteenth century. We also describe the creation of Mexican towns in the sixteenth century when European-based urban concepts are laid over preexisting Mesoamerican sacred urban centers to Christianize them. A syncretism of open space occurs in the resulting new towns.

In Chapter Three, after the discussion of Mesoamerican and European antecedents and the fusion of cultures involved in the building in New Spain as historical background, we describe the sites as we found them almost five hundred years later. We present specific cases from our field surveys where we believe this unique blending of European and native use of planned urban open space is palpably evident. Native open spaces are transformed to incorporate the European concepts and standards, resulting in new forms of urban open spaces with characteristics emanating from distinct cultural traditions.

Finally, we present in Chapter Four our understanding of the integration of Mesoamerican and Spanish concepts of space, and we follow in the epilogue with the concepts of communal urban spaces from the distant past as they might be used in addressing urban design issues of today.

CHAPTER ONE

THE PRIMORDIAL SEA
FORMING OPEN SPACE IN MESOAMERICA

The American architect was restricted by technology to the assembling of solid masses, but in the operations of design, he was infinitely more attentive to their harmonious combination than the Europeans. This special field in which the Americans excelled was the achievement of large rhythmically ordered open volumes.

George Kubler, "The Design of Space in Maya Architecture"

The concept of the *plaza* might have been created when hunter-gatherers selected a stopping place in their wilderness world and marked it, perhaps by laying three stones, to identify it as a place known to them, a place to which they could return, a place that could center their group for the task of finding food. That three-stone place, or some other place marked by a natural feature in the landscape, would become their axis mundi. In the thousands of years that hunter-gatherers on all the earth's continents searched for food, they centered their short stays at places that had significance to them, usually based on some aspect of the landscape: a topographic feature with which they identified, a sheltering cave, a source of water, or an unusual mountain shape—something that gave meaning to the place.

It is evident that in Mesoamerica,[1] the *place* had a mystic or spiritual meaning. As agriculture developed, groups also searched for the soil, water, and climate that would foster their new food source, but these conditions would typically be sought in the area surrounding their chosen spiritual place rather than in the place itself. They could settle, grow crops, and build permanent shelters around this center, while some of the group would still travel to hunt and gather but would return to the place. The place, of course, had a central open space where the community could come together for fire, food, safety, and trade. That communal open space was the embryonic form of the plaza, a portion of which was eventually set aside for

spiritual expression. The two open spaces that resulted, the sacred open space and the communal open space, evolved to become the sacred patio and the plaza.

The development of the Mesoamerican plaza into an urban form of architectural significance took thousands of years, during which the desire to create sacred space for spiritual rites and rituals was the driving force. That space was joined closely with a place to gather and trade. A thousand years before the Roman Forum and on a different continent, the plaza had one of its most dynamic beginnings in Mesoamerica.

MESOAMERICAN CONCEPT OF SPACE

With the advent of agriculture, life became more sedentary for the people of Mesoamerica. Population centers began to appear on the landscape; urban life emerged. At the core of Mesoamerican urban settlements were sacred ceremonial precincts, open spaces formed by architecture. Created "as setting[s] for the ritual to unfold,"[2] ceremonial centers in Mesoamerica are based on the shaping of open space or volumes by architectural monuments that use religious symbolism to reinforce the creation myths and other sacred rituals being enacted within the ceremonial precincts. Planned open urban space lies at the very origin and purpose of Mesoamerican population centers (Fig. 1.1).

The roots of communal open space in Mesoamerica date back to the origins of human settlements themselves. Open urban spaces, now commonly

1.1.   Palenque, aerial view. Courtesy of the School of Architecture
        Visual Resources Collection, The University of Texas at
        Austin (Hal Box and Logan Wagner Collection of Mexican
        Architecture and Urban Design [hereafter "Box-Wagner
        Collection"], VRC 96-04005).

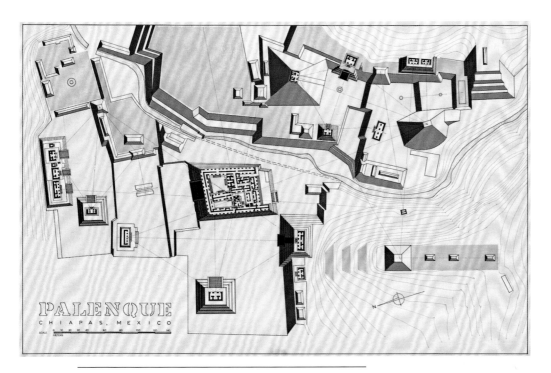

1.2.   Palenque, plan by George Andrews. George F. and Geraldine
       D. Andrews Collection, The Alexander Architectural Archive,
       University of Texas Libraries, The University of Texas at Austin.

known as plazas and courts, played a seminal role in the conception and building of the ceremonial core of Mesoamerican urban centers, from 1200 BCE at Teopantecuanitlán, one of the earliest known sites, to 1521 CE at Tenochtitlan, the Aztec capital conquered when Europeans arrived.

Several noted scholars have made observations about Mesoamerican open space, its characteristics, and how it was used. Linda Schele, the renowned Maya epigrapher, summarized the importance of open space in Maya ceremonial centers when she stated, "Experiencing Maya architecture can be disconcerting for people who grew up with the European tradition all around them. European architecture focuses for the most part on interior space. In Maya public architecture, the operational spaces are the plazas and courtyards that are surrounded by buildings."[3]

George Andrews, an architect, scholar, and professor who spent the latter half of his life documenting Maya architecture, sums up the concept of streetless Maya urban centers when he says, "It cannot be overemphasized that the open space of the plaza is one of the essential ingredients of Maya cities. [Plazas] are public spaces above all and must have served as a focus of community life" (Fig. 1.2).[4]

Schele and Mathews dwell on the function of the plaza as a theatrical setting for the enactment of rituals: "The Maya created complex patterns of space not by constructing buildings with a great many rooms, but by assembling discrete buildings around open spaces."[5] They elaborate further on the roles of open spaces and architecture when they state, "Unlike the European tradition of architecture, the Maya did not create their structures with the primary aim of creating interior space. Instead, public architecture functioned like a gigantic stage set to serve as the backdrop for huge processional rituals, dances and public dramas."[6]

Processions and dancing were major components of the ritual performances that took place in the open plazas and courts of Mesoamerica. Nikolai Grube, renowned Maya epigrapher, was the first scholar to decipher the glyph attributed to dance.[7] Whenever this glyph appears in the Maya hieroglyphic corpus, be it on stone sculpture, painted on skins, or on ceramic vessels, it is likely the dancing took place in an open space, either in the plazas or in the more intimate private setting of elite palace courts.

Mary Ellen Miller has interpreted the famous murals of Bonampak in the modern-day Mexican state of Chiapas as depictions of the scenes that would have played out in the plaza.[8] Beautifully manifested in three tiers on each of the four walls in all three temple rooms, the murals portray events as if they were seen from the plaza in front of the temple. Depicted are processions and dancing of pompously dressed celebrants, musicians in procession passing through the plaza, presentations of tribute, and the seating of a new ruler. Sacrificed captives still in bonds sprawl on the lower tiered platforms that face the plaza below the triad of temples, confirming the practice of human blood sacrifice (Fig. 1.3).

Mesoamerican ceremonial spaces served to reinforce the myths and religious concepts that were enacted in the rituals performed within them. The work of many scholars, especially archaeologists, epigraphers, and art historians, indicates that these ceremonial spaces formed the central cores of population centers in Mesoamerica.[9] Mesoamerican builders and planners were symbolically re-creating the natural world in the design of sacred spaces: pyramids represent mountains, plazas symbolize the primordial sea, and the ubiquitous stelae, called *te tun* in Mayan, are literally "stone trees." More recent interpretations consider stelae to be *lakamtun*, or stone banners, stone versions of vertical standards that once stood in prominent places in Maya city centers, as depicted in ancient Maya graffiti (Fig. 1.4).[10]

The Maya myth of creation, as expressed in the sacred book *Popol Vuh*, states that before the universe existed, there was a primordial sea. The sky was lifted from this sea, and then the earth, the mountains, and the rest of nature came forth from it as well.[11] Mesoamericans believed that the entire earth floated on the primordial sea, and they imagined the earth's crust as a caiman (*Caiman crocodilus*) swimming in that sea,

1.3. Bonampak, mural showing stair into plaza. Nettie Lee Benson Latin American Collection, University of Texas Libraries, The University of Texas at Austin; courtesy of Carnegie Institution of Washington.

1.4. Copán, stelae in plaza. © Macduff Everton.

its ridges representing mountain ranges.[12] An example of this myth mirrored in a ceremonial center can be found at Yaxchilán, a Classic period Maya site on the Mexican side of the Usumacinta River, where a stone caiman, or crocodile, floats in the primordial sea of the Grand Plaza (Fig. 1.5).

One could infer that Mesoamericans reenacted the creation process in sequence when constructing the ceremonial center, starting first with the plaza, symbol of the watery vastness. Temples, palaces, pyramids, and other monuments or elements of the natural landscape would then rise from the plaza, engendered by it in the same way that the earth was drawn from the primordial sea. Thus open space would be created and populated with temples, altars, and stelae. The equation of "plaza" with "body of water" is linguistically reinforced by the Mayan word for lake or lagoon, *naab*, which is also the Mayan word for plaza.[13]

The Mesoamerican world was documented by the Franciscan Fray Bernardino de Sahagún, known as the "father of modern ethnology." Sahagún's description of the main plaza precinct of Tenochtitlan evokes the perception of a body of water dotted by mountainous islands when he states that the temples are located *within* the plaza rather than around it:

> The patio of the great temple was very large, it had 200 fathoms in square, all covered by pavers and within it there were many buildings and towers. The main one was in the center and it was the tallest and was divided into two chapels, each with different insignia.[14]

Corroboration of the engendering qualities of the planned open space is found in archaeological reports describing the earliest stages of construction of ceremonial centers. George Andrews describes this early construction in detail, noting that the ceremonial center's earliest form is "a single small plaza and its associated structures." He defines the plaza as "open space, cleared of trees and artificially leveled . . . paved with limestone cement." He notes its difference from a natural open space:

> By its visible negation of soil and plants, [the plaza] creates a specific, manmade domain. It must be emphasized that the leveling and paving of the plaza is an architectural conceptualization of the greatest importance. It represents a giant step beyond the crude clearing of the forest which is predicated solely on physical

survival. The paved plaza is neither forest nor farmstead—the very act of removal from fortuitous nature makes it unique and self-conscious, a fitting response to the need of self-determination which characterizes civilized man throughout the world.[15]

Whether the final project is intended to be a series of enormous elevated platforms supporting entire ceremonial centers, or a housing cluster of individual platform mounds for single-family residences, the initial act of building is to create a symbolic body of water, the primordial sea.

Andrews classifies one such type of open space as a terrace and describes it as "an open space, leveled and paved and in many ways similar to a plaza, but built up artificially above the natural ground level." Its uniqueness, he states, is in its being marked as different from the ground level by being elevated. At building sites with irregular topography, cutting and filling was used to create terraces with the same special spatial qualities as those that were artificially built up. Like plazas, he adds, terraces may have their edges reinforced with buildings, and some buildings may be situated within the open space of the terrace itself.[16]

Sometimes, a particular plaza may be elevated above a main plaza, creating a platform plaza, which in turn engenders the pyramid temple, the palace, or another sacred building type. Such is the case with many platform temples built in the Maya area, including the platforms supporting the Kinich Kak Mo temple in Izamal and the Nunnery Quadrangle and the Governor's Palace in Uxmal, all in Yucatán (Figs. 1.6–1.7).

In her rendering and description of Structure A-V of Uaxactún in *An Album of Maya Architecture*,

1.5: Yaxchilán, stone caiman in the Great Plaza. Courtesy of Carolyn Tate.

1.6. Izamal, Kinich Kak Mo pyramid illustrating plaza platforms. Logan Wagner.

1.7. Uxmal, Governor's Palace and Nunnery Quadrangle sited on platforms. Courtesy of the School of Architecture Visual Resources Collection, The University of Texas at Austin (Box-Wagner Collection, VRC 92-12645).

Tatiana Proskouriakoff illustrates cut-and-fill activities that create platforms on which temples and other architecture are built (Fig. 1.8).[17]

Tikal's main urban complex, consisting of the main plaza, the main temples, and the many buildings of the Central Acropolis, was built on a gigantic artificial platform. Peter D. Harrison, one of the excavators of Tikal, describes how the overall platform raises the plaza and North Acropolis above the surrounding terrain.[18] Other examples at Tikal of large, high platforms are those that hold Complex Q and Complex R, the largest twin-pyramid groups at Tikal.[19] The exorbitant investment of material and human energy expended in building massive platform plazas from which the monumental pyramids surrounding them could then sprout highlights the important symbolism of the open space or plaza, the creation medium. This communal investment of human labor, especially without the use of wheels or draft animals, is enormous.

At mountainous sites, one often encounters ceremonial centers that present a series of escalating courts and plazas terraced into the mountain at different levels of the rising slope. Xochicalco, Monte Albán, and Toniná are but three magnificent examples from the Central Highlands and the Oaxaca and Maya areas respectively. The mountain is terraced into ever-ascending plazas, shaped and framed by temples. Each plaza level is connected by monumental stairways, culminating at the top in a sacred temple precinct court (Figs. 1.9–1.11).

1.8.   Uaxactún, terraced platforms showing cut-and-fill activity. Drawing by Tatiana Proskouriakoff. Nettie Lee Benson Latin American Collection, University of Texas Libraries, The University of Texas at Austin; courtesy of Carnegie Institution of Washington.

1.9. Xochicalco, sited on terraced platforms. Courtesy of the School of Architecture Visual Resources Collection, The University of Texas at Austin (Box-Wagner Collection, VRC 2007-4916).

1.10. Monte Albán, sited on platform, being documented by UT Studio Mexico students. Logan Wagner.

1.11. Toniná, sited on terraced platforms. Courtesy of Sinclair Black.

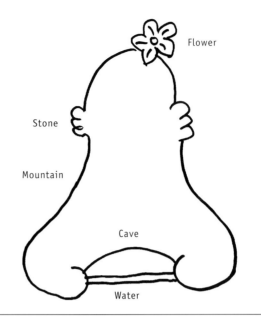

Flower

Stone

Mountain

Cave

Water

1.12. *Altepetl* prototype. Drawing by Logan Wagner.

MOUNTAINS AND *ALTEPETL*S

There is no aspect of Mesoamerican life that is not linked to the belief in a living world, the central features of which are the powerful symbols of mountains, water, and caves.

James E. Brady and Keith M. Prufer,
In the Maw of the Earth Monster

As mentioned above, pyramids in Mesoamerican sites represent mountains. At each site was constructed a principal pyramid that served as the symbolic sustenance mountain: a mountain at whose base is a source of water, the precious liquid, the provider of life depicted within a cave in the mountain.[20] In the Central Highlands as well as the Oaxaca area, each community is identified by its sustenance mountain. At times referred to as "snake mountain," or *coatepetl* in Nahuatl, each image of this mountain would have an added graphic feature to distinguish it from the mountains of other communities. Native pictorial documents provide many examples of this stylized mountain, along with its graphically specific identifier. Each of these is known as an *altepetl*, literally "water mountain" (*al* = water + *tepetl* = mountain). In codices, stone carvings, and other artistic manifestations, each community is identified by its individual *altepetl*. In addition to its graphic meaning, *altepetl* refers to

the political organization of the community and the boundaries of its territory. As James Lockhart puts it, "At the heart of the organization of the Nahua world, both before the Spaniards came and long after, lay the *altepetl* or ethnic state."[21]

The graphic symbol for the *altepetl* as water mountain is represented throughout Mesoamerican art and iconography. From codices to inscriptions in stone to tributary scrolls, *altepetl*s in the Mexican highlands name settlements much as emblem glyphs identify communities in Maya writing (Fig. 1.12). Nahuatl dictionaries invariably translate *altepetl* as "village" or "town."[22]

David Carrasco offers a description of *altepetl*s when he states:

> The crucial role played by mountains in Aztec religion is reflected by the Nahuatl term for village, city or community, *altepetl*, meaning "mountain filled with water." The human community with its various ceremonial centers was defined in terms of its landscape, the Mountain of Sustenance, which provided the resources for life. The many mountains surrounding the Valley of Mexico were conceived as huge hollow vessels or "houses" filled with water that came from the subterranean streams that filled the space beneath the earth. This underworld realm was called Tlalocan, considered the paradise of the great water deity Tlaloc. In this way

the mountains were also *axis mundis* linking the watery underworld with the terrestrial level of the city to the celestial realms.[23]

The pan-Mesoamerican universal symbols for towns or communities, *altepetl* signs, are in effect toponyms or place-names (Fig. 1.13). Every community has its water mountain; what distinguishes one from another is the unique graphic element that identifies each particular community. Chapultepec, or Grasshopper Hill, for instance, is graphically represented by the *altepetl* sign with a grasshopper (*chapulín* in Mexican Spanish) climbing the side of the hill or mountain. Xochiteptl has a flower on its hill, Citlatepetl, a star. The hill or mountain element of each *altepetl* has a lobed pyramidal shape, and at the base of each hill is a sideways C or inverted U shape representing the cave that shelters the water source. We propose that the flat horizontal line at the bottom represents the primordial sea, the plaza. The flatness of the straight line, in contrast to the organic form of the *tepetl*, or mountain, alludes to the flat nature of the surface of a body of water, the void of the primordial sea, the plaza.

CAVES, QUATREFOILS, AND SUNKEN COURTS

Many Mesoamerican scholars have reaffirmed the symbolic importance of caves, canyons, crevices, and other openings in the earth's crust as natural portals to the supernatural realm. Doris Heyden, in her groundbreaking analysis of the urban origins of Teotihuacan, posits that the cave discovered under the Pyramid of the Sun was the natural feature in the terrain that prompted the choice of site in founding the city that was to become the grandest Mesoamerican urban center.[24] In Mesoamerica we find site after site founded at particular spots on the landscape that offered natural "portals" to the supernatural world, a universe inhabited by gods, ancestors, and other supernatural beings.[25] The cave of Juxtlahuaca in Guerrero is the site of perhaps the earliest Olmec murals found to date, nearly a mile deep inside the cave and consisting of a feathered serpent, a red jaguar, and a large human figure in jaguar costume looming ominously over a smaller human figure (Fig. 1.14). The cave also contains a small lake beyond the murals.[26]

Ceremonial centers have human-made portal counterparts. To re-create the natural landscape, the

1.13.   Three Mesoamerican toponyms: (1) From the Central Highlands, *altepetl* of Guaxtepec, "Hill of Gourds," detail of Relación Geográfica of Guaxtepec. Nettie Lee Benson Latin American Collection, University of Texas Libraries, The University of Texas at Austin. (2) From the Oaxaca area, *altepetl* of Tehuantepec, "Hill of the Jaguar," detail from Codex Nuttall. (3) From the Maya area, emblem glyph of Tikal. © Foundation for the Advancement of Mesoamerican Studies, Inc., www.famsi.org.

1.14. Juxtlahuaca Cave, Olmec image of plumed serpent. Courtesy of the School of Architecture Visual Resources Collection, The University of Texas at Austin (Box-Wagner Collection, VRC 90-9333).

pyramid-mountains of the Mesoamerican ceremonial centers were formed with cave portals as well. The temples atop the pyramids symbolically represent cave entrances, and many doorways in temples literally portray the gaping mouth of the earth deity through sculpture, stucco relief, or painting. The various subcultures of Mesoamerica—from Olmec, Maya, Zapotec, Mixtec, and Toltec to Aztec—offer examples that assure us that this symbolism is prevalent in the ceremonial centers of Mesoamerica (Figs. 1.15–1.17).

Carolyn E. Tate first identified a specific shape associated with supernatural portals, the shape of the quatrefoil, and she associates it with the cleft on the Cauac Earth Monster, a portal to the Maya Underworld.[27]

At the highland Olmec site of Chalcatzingo, analyzed and interpreted by F. Kent Reilly III, the ruler is portrayed at the mouth of the cave, a half quatrefoil, with access through the portal to the spiritual world inhabited by deities.[28] The ruler justifies his or her power through this access to the supernatural world that gives him or her the ability to intercede with the gods and thereby secure the sustenance-providing rains (Fig. 1.18). Reilly has proposed that this half-quatrefoil shape depicted in Monument 1, also called El Rey, has the same meaning as the full quatrefoil depicted in Monument 9, an instance of pars pro toto.[29] Monument 9 depicts a frontal view of the Earth Monster, its large mouth being the quatrefoil portal. It has been sug-

gested that the smoothing of the edges of the mouth was caused during rituals as priests or rulers emerged from the monster's mouth.[30]

The shape of this portal is a quatrefoil, and this four-lobed symbol is found throughout the Mesoamerican iconographic and artistic corpus. Known in Mayan as *ol*, the quatrefoil, scholars agree, is synonymous with that most important portal to the supernatural world. Used to frame ballcourt markers, sacrificial bowls, and ornamental ritual garments of the bloodletting royalty, the quatrefoil invariably invokes supernatural access. In Mesoamerican art, beings depicted within the quatrefoil boundaries are living in the supernatural realm.[31] The quatrefoil serves as a window into that supernatural realm of the gods and ancestors.

Quatrefoils are also found in plazas, the primordial waters. Linguistically there is a link between quatrefoil/*ol* and plaza/*naab*. The logographic Maya glyph for plaza, also called *naab* (lagoon), is a quatrefoil.[32] By constructing quatrefoil portals in the plazas and engaging with these portals during religious rituals, rulers and priests reinforced the spiritual power publicly assigned to the quatrefoil shape.

1.15. Malinalco, doorway of El Cuauhcalli temple dedicated to Aztec eagle and jaguar warriors. Courtesy of the School of Architecture Visual Resources Collection, The University of Texas at Austin (Box-Wagner Collection, VRC 95-05114).

1.17. Ek' Balam, doorway of Structure 1. © Macduff Everton.

1.16. Uxmal, doorway of El Adivino, Temple of the Magician. Susan Kline Morehead.

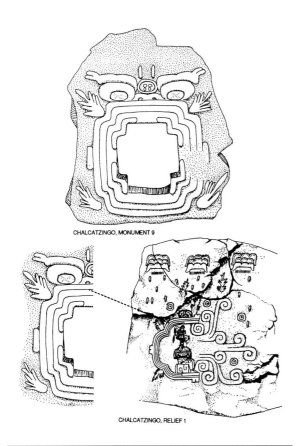

CHALCATZINGO, MONUMENT 9

CHALCATZINGO, RELIEF 1

1.18. Chalcatzingo, Monument 9: quatrefoil maw of Earth Monster
       (above), Monument 1: ruler seated in half-quatrefoil maw of
       Earth Monster. Courtesy of F. Kent Reilly III.

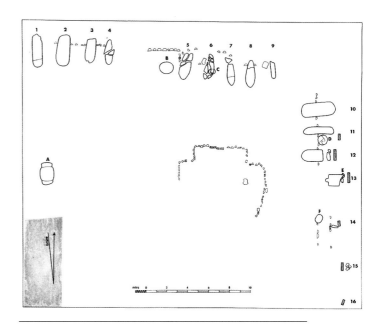

1.19. Machaquilá, Plaza A with quatrefoil shape. Drawing by Ian
       Graham, courtesy of Middle American Research Institute,
       Tulane.

An *ol* can form the outline of a court or plaza so that the shape of the void is the quatrefoil. The excavated plaza at the Classic Maya site of Machaquilá, Guatemala, is a case in point (Fig. 1.19). At the Maya site of Seibal, hieroglyphic text on the side of Stela 8 describes ceremonies taking place in the plaza, denoting "plaza" by the quatrefoil-shaped glyph.[33]

Stelae found at Machaquilá as well as at the Zapotec capital of Monte Albán, in the modern Mexican state of Oaxaca, depict rulers standing on half-quatrefoil shapes (Figs. 1.20–1.21).[34] This public art testifies to the legitimacy and credibility of the rulers by showing they have access to the supernatural portal, the mountain's cave.[35]

One of the most pristine and intact examples of a sunken quatrefoil discovered to date is the basin at the Middle Formative site of La Blanca on the Pacific slopes of Guatemala. Here, the beautiful quatrefoil sunken basin, in the main plaza, consists of the four petal shapes modeled in high relief into a basin

(Fig. 1.22).[36] The quatrefoil shape is outlined by a shallow canal, presumably to carry water during rituals, thus underlining the association of the portal with water, the source of life.[37] It has also been suggested that this quatrefoil basin might have been intentionally filled with water, turning it into a pool that could act as a mirror, another form of portal in Mesoamerican cultures.[38]

Sunken courts are a recurring type of sacred precinct in Mesoamerican sites. They are based on the belief that the realm of the sacred lies beneath the surface of the earth. Sunken courts allow rituals to take place below the earth's surface in the sacred realm.[39] About 800 BCE, the Olmecs of La Venta expended enormous effort to dig several meters below the surface, carefully lay out scores of greenstone plaques in mosaics, and then bury this offering under layers of different-colored soils to create the ultimate offering of their most precious material to the gods.

Chalcatzingo and Teopantecuanitlán, two of the oldest examples of sunken courts, both display architectural representations of an element known in Olmec iconography as a "double merlon." The double merlon motif is prevalent in Olmec art and is often depicted as a headdress on statues and paintings of rulers and gods. Similar in form and meaning to the Olmec

1.21. Monte Albán, stela of Zapotec ruler standing on partial quatrefoil. Drawing by Logan Wagner.

1.22. La Blanca Monument 3, quatrefoil basin. Courtesy of Michael Love.

1.20. Machaquilá, Stela 4 of ruler standing on partial quatrefoil. Drawing by Ian Graham, courtesy of Middle American Research Institute, Tulane.

cleft from which corn plants emerge, the double merlon represents a crevice portal to the supernatural world. When the topography of the landscape presented a naturally formed double merlon, as is the case of Chalcatzingo's iconic pair of hills, Mesoamericans saw a natural sacred portal (Fig. 1.23).[40] Similarly, at the north end of the Avenue of the Dead at Teotihuacan, the Pyramid of the Moon mimics the hill behind it, called Cerro Gordo, and aligns with the "double merlon" cleft on the mountain's profile (Fig. 1.24). A similar mimicking occurs at Guachimontones in Jalisco (Fig. 1.25). The two double merlons at Teopantecuanitlán are created by four huge travertine blocks carved into inverted T shapes depicting maize deities that rise from the east and west walls of the sunken court (Fig. 1.26). The court itself is entered by a clay staircase with a stair rail ending in a volute (Fig. 1.27). A small canal located at the court's northwest corner had a large stone stopper that could be raised or lowered to control the flow of water through the canal, making it possible to create an actual lake, or primordial sea, by flooding the sunken court.

TYPES OF OPEN SPACE IN MESOAMERICA

In an attempt to identify the different types and shapes of open spaces that are present in Mesoamerican sites, what follows is a listing, description, and analysis of possible symbolism of open spaces. It is not meant to be an all-encompassing list, for surely scholars will identify other types of open spaces. Supported and inspired by the work of earlier scholars and observers, we find that the shaping of open spaces or voids by Mesoamerican designers and builders was deliberate and intentional.

Triad Centering

"Triad centering" is a term first coined by Linda Schele to describe a particular arrangement of three temples. It alludes to the three stones of creation, where the gods met to commence the creation process. According to Freidel, Schele, and Parker, these three stones are represented in the sky by the three stars that form a triangle in the constellation Orion.[41] Schele elaborates, "The most sacred and ancient of arrangements was the triangular form that echoed the three stones of the Cosmic Hearth constructed by the Gods to center the world."[42]

1.23. Chalcatzingo, hills forming double merlon. Courtesy of the School of Architecture Visual Resources Collection, The University of Texas at Austin (Box-Wagner Collection, VRC 91-4815 corrected).

1.24. Teotihuacan, Avenue of the Dead aligned with Pyramid of the Moon and cleft in Cerro Gordo peak.
Courtesy of Sinclair Black.

1.25. Guachimontones, pyramid mimicking the hill behind it.
Susan Kline Morehead.

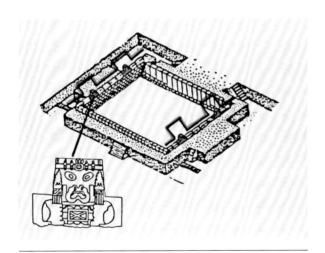

1.26. Teopantecuanitlán, double merlon formed by monoliths in
sunken court. Courtesy of F. Kent Reilly III.

1.27. Teopantecuanitlán, stair with volute. Susan Kline Morehead.

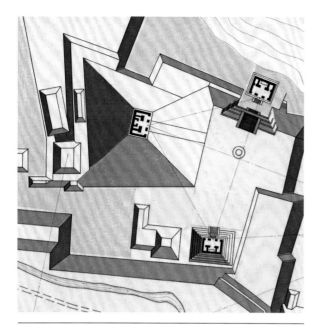

1.28. Palenque, Group of the Cross illustrating triad centering. George F. and Geraldine D. Andrews Collection, The Alexander Architectural Archive, University of Texas Libraries, The University of Texas at Austin.

1.29. Triad centering at house scale in three-stone hearth. Courtesy of Michael Hironymous.

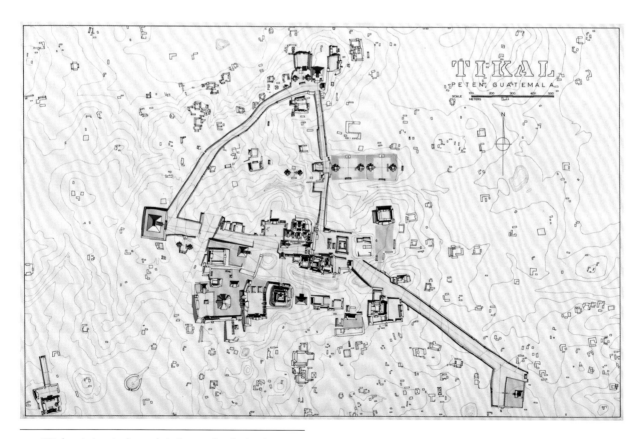

1.30. Triad centering at urban scale in three nodes of urban layout of Tikal. George F. and Geraldine D. Andrews Collection, The Alexander Architectural Archive, University of Texas Libraries, The University of Texas at Austin.

Examples of triad centering are numerous and manifested at different scales. A well-known example of triad centering is the Group of the Cross at Palenque, a Classic Maya site in the state of Chiapas, Mexico (Fig. 1.28). Commissioned by Cham Bahlum, the son of the famous ruler Pakal, in mid-seventh century CE, the Group of the Cross is composed of the Temple of the Cross, the Temple of the Foliated Cross, and the Temple of the Sun. In the middle of this architectural triangulation is an altar, an obvious focal point from atop all three temples. As part of the ritual of termination following Cham Bahlum's death, his brother, who succeeded him, built Temple XIV next to the Temple of the Sun and directly in front of the Temple of the Foliated Cross. This action unbalanced the centering of the triad, terminating its power.[43]

Another example of architectural triad centering can be seen at the unexcavated site of Rocky Point on the central coast of Belize, where three mounds form a triangle. Triad centering is also manifested at a personal, individual, more intimate scale by hamlets and other small groupings of individual peasant dwellings arranged in a triadic form. Archaeological and ethnographic evidence indicates that the individual house, as well, has at its center a three-stone hearth (Fig. 1.29). The three-stone cosmic hearth mentioned by Schele is re-created and therefore "centered" at individual dwellings.[44]

Finally, at the macro urban scale, one cannot miss the triad centering exhibited by the urban layout of Tikal. Three original urban nodes built on elevated human-made platforms are connected by raised artificial causeways that form an urban-sized triangle. The human effort required to create and connect the platforms in just this triangular relationship can be measured in millions of cubic feet of material moved and plastered (Fig. 1.30). Peter Harrison makes a strong case for the placing, alignment, and orientation of important buildings in Tikal into triangulations involving right triangles.[45]

U-shaped Courts

A variation of the three-temple arrangement of buildings is the grouping of a higher pyramid temple flanked by two parallel lower platform temples. This arrangement forms a U-shaped court or plaza open on one side. In most cases of the U-shaped court groupings, the two side temples are skewed in plan to create an open-sided trapezoid with the open side being the widest. It is interesting to note that U-shaped courts formed by a three-temple arrangement are ubiquitous in Mesoamerican sites. Tatiana Proskouriakoff was the first to recognize and present the triadic architectural arrangement in her 1946 treatise on the sequential construction of Structure A-V of Uaxactún (Fig. 1.31).[46]

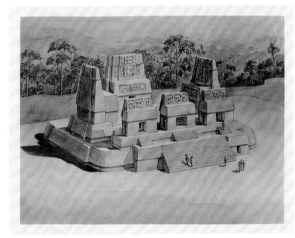

1.31. Triad centering at Uaxactún: Stages 1, 4, and 8. Drawings by Tatiana Proskouriakoff. Nettie Lee Benson Latin American Collection, University of Texas Libraries, The University of Texas at Austin; courtesy of Carnegie Institution of Washington.

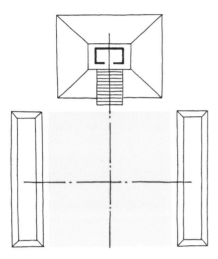

George Andrews illustrates site plans in his book *Maya Cities* by graphically highlighting the open space in a striking yellow. Andrews concludes in his study that there was a basic architectural grouping, which he calls "Basic Plaza Grouping," the same form we here term "U-shaped court" (Fig. 1.32). Curiously enough, preceramic sites on the Andean coast of South America also depict a basic architectural grouping of U-shaped courts, thousands of miles away and appearing a millennium before they appear in Mesoamerica.[47] To determine if this is a case of cultural diffusion or independent invention is beyond the scope of this book; nevertheless, the similarity is intriguing.

Turned on its side, the U shape of a court becomes interior space in many Mesoamerican images. U- or C-shaped forms of the void, seen in art as the "ground" left open by the "figure," seem to have special resonance for Mesoamerican cultures. Examples are evident in the artistic depictions of architecture. Rulers are often portrayed in the interior space of their palaces, where they are receiving dignitaries or conducting other activities. On many painted vases from the Maya area, this interior space is framed in what amounts to an architectural section shaped like a C or a U on its side (Fig. 1.33). Similar representations

1.34. Mixtec temple shown in architectural section. Codex Nuttall.

1.35. Metaphorical plaza depicting the primordial sea or Underworld. Note that the base of the *altepetl*, with its water-filled cave, is immersed in the water, and its mountain rises above the plaza/primordial sea level, where three visiting dignitaries approach the C-shaped temple. Codex Nuttall.

of interior space can be observed throughout Mixtec codices (Fig. 1.34).

Frequently in Mixtec codices we find that the image traditionally interpreted as a body of water—a lake or lagoon—is a shallow U-shaped vessel containing the precious liquid. We propose here that the body of water in its container, as rendered artistically in Mixtec codices, is in fact a metaphorical graphic manifestation of a Mixtec plaza (Fig. 1.35).

Finally, the element we suggest is water in the "water mountain," the *al* of *altepetl*, is enclosed by an inverted C shape. We have proposed that this C shape

is a cave within the mountain. The preponderance of C and U shapes in Mesoamerican art suggests that this shape be interpreted as both a portal to the supernatural and the source of life-sustaining water.

Quadrangles

Another architectural or plaza grouping that archaeologists have identified in Mesoamerica is a quadrangle consisting of four buildings, generally on platforms. As the name implies, a quadrangle creates a square-shaped court, sometimes open at the corners. Quadrangles have a relationship with the four cardinal directions and were associated with the Tzuc partition god in the Maya area.[48]

The square is the other form besides the triad that the Maya tied to creation, since it is the shape that resulted when the creator gods arranged the *kan tzuk, kan xuc*, "the four sides, the four corners," to give shape and order to the cosmos. The gods then raised the great center tree called *wakah-chan*, the "raised-up sky."[49]

Generally associated with rituals of a more private nature that involved an elite segment of society, quadrangle courts seem to have evolved when U-shaped courts were enclosed with a structure built at the open side. As noted, Tatiana Proskouriakoff reenacts the sequence of construction for architectural groupings in Structure A-V at Uaxactún (see Fig. 1.31); she does the same for the acropolis of the Classic period site of Piedras Negras, Guatemala.[50] The first phase includes a triad-centering group characteristic of a U-shaped court. This first phase is followed by the closing of the U-shaped court with a subsequent structure perpendicular to the arms formed by the platform structures. The sequence continues to become more elaborate and complex, culminating in an eighth phase; nevertheless, the initial configuration of the quadrangular court is maintained.

An analysis of Tikal's overall site plan indicates two different configurations for residential layouts. One is the three-structure U-shaped court layout, the other, the four- structure quadrangle court shape, leading to the conclusion that the builders followed the expected sequence: after they had built the three-structure court, they would eventually enclose the resulting U-shaped court to form a quadrangle court (Fig. 1.36).

After the quadrangle was formed, the plaza group continued to grow and transform via the creation of a new U-shaped court. The new court was formed by adding parallel mound structures to the quadrangular

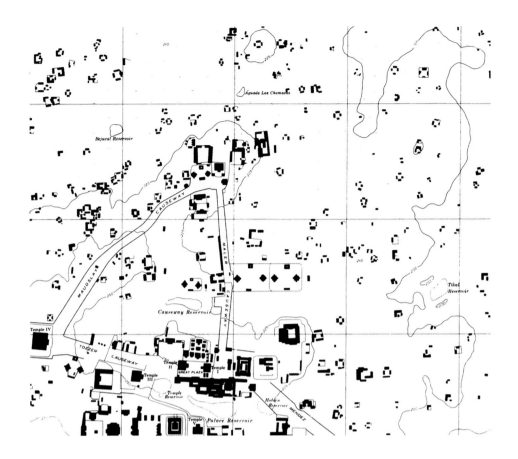

1.36. Tikal, site plan of outlying residential mounds showing triad and quadrangular centering of houses. Courtesy of The University of Texas Mesoamerican Center.

1.37. Basic quadrangle sequence. George F. and Geraldine D. Andrews Collection, The Alexander Architectural Archive, University of Texas Libraries, The University of Texas at Austin.

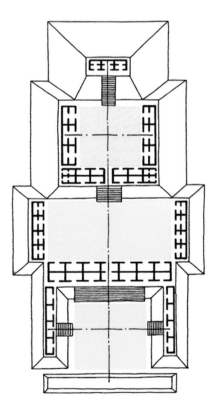

court (Fig. 1.37). This sequence could conceivably be continued ad infinitum.

A quintessential example of the quadrangle and U-shaped court architectural grouping can be found at the Zapotec site of Mitla in the modern state of Oaxaca (Fig. 1.38). As if to underline the private, elite nature of the quadrangle-shaped court, the Mitla architects devised a circuitous passage leading from the open U-shaped outer court to the inner quadrangular courts rather than allowing direct access.

Mastery of architecturally shaped open ritual space is in evidence at the Nunnery Quadrangle at the Puuc Maya site of Uxmal. During ritual processions, participants who had dressed in colorful costume regalia and entered a trance from dancing and music proceeded from the ballcourt to the Nunnery Quadrangle court, entering through the monumental corbelled vault of the south building. As the procession entered the court, the higher east and west buildings would enhance the ever-ascending perceptual experience of the ritual procession, leading to a spatial crescendo that culminated at the highest structure on the north side (Fig. 1.39). Looming overhead and to the east is the gaping maw of the Temple of the Magician. The open space is shaped by the architecture and the art of the ceremonial center, which serves to support and enhance the ritual.

1.38. Mitla, U-shaped and quadrangular courts in the same building. Courtesy of the School of Architecture Visual Resources Collection, The University of Texas at Austin (Box-Wagner Collection, VRC 2007-4827).

1.39. Uxmal, quadrangle sequence illustrating processional space. © Macduff Everton.

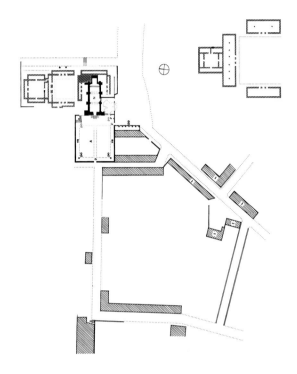

QUINCUNX: SYMBOL OF THE COSMOS

Maya repeated these world-making activities by placing an altar or a tree in the center of the four-cornered, four-sided plaza. The resulting form with its four corners and a center is called a "quincunx" by modern researchers. This quincunx symbol of the cosmos also appeared in inscriptions as the sign for *beh*, "road."

Linda Schele and Peter Mathews, *The Code of Kings*

Mesoamericans believed that the horizontal plane of the universe had four directions, each associated with a color and a bird. At the center of this quadrangle was the axis mundi connecting the terrestrial plane to the heavens above and the Underworld below.[51] The ordering and centering of a building or place in a symbolic quincunx shape was another strong architectural expression of Mesoamerican belief. The quincunx symbol is found throughout the Mesoamerican iconographic corpus. Olmec scholars Peter David Joralemon and F. Kent Reilly III give us examples of quincunx symbolism dating back at least to the Middle Formative period. In many instances, the center of the quincunx is represented by the World Tree, its roots penetrating the nine levels of the Underworld, its branches extending skyward to reach the thirteen levels of the heavens. As Reilly has proven, the ruler of a community was the personification of the axis mundi (Fig. 1.40). The power invested by the community in the ruler rested on his ability to act as an intercessor between the reality plane inhabited by mortals and the supernatural worlds populated with gods, ancestors, and other supernaturals.[52]

The connection between the quincunx symbol as cosmos and the Mayan word for road, *beh* (sometimes spelled *be*), lies in the interpretation of "road" as one's calling, way, talent, profession, or work, as in the biblical quotation "I am the way." The Mayan term *sacbe*, which literally means "white road," refers in archaeology to the monumental, elevated, lustrously plastered white masonry roads that link temples and sites in the northern lowland Maya area. It also refers to the great white cosmic road of the Milky Way, which serves symbolically as the axis mundi in the quincunx of the four-cornered cosmos. The Maya glyph *beh* can be traced back to the Olmec symbol known as "bar and four dots" motif that various scholars have argued represents the cosmos and the central axis mundi.[53]

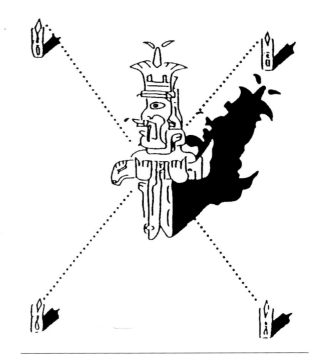

1.40. Ruler as axis mundi in center of quincunx. Drawing by F. Kent Reilly III.

We propose here that the pathways know as *sacbeob* (plural of *sacbe*) are, in effect, architectural stage sets for ritual, the monumental path being a representation of the axis mundi of quincunxial centering. Scholars agree that the monumentality of the Maya *sacbeob* suggests a deeper significance than simply expediting pedestrian mobility. In terms of costs, the volume of material is staggering; the labor involved, overwhelming; the care and detail, reverential. In addition, their straightness and astronomical alignments suggest their role is more religious than practical. We believe that they are cosmic, spiritual pathways that center and anchor communal and personal life.

The concept of quincunx is linked to the quatrefoil by their function as portals. Dancing in ritual procession on the *sacbe* is equivalent to rituals performed in quatrefoils. In some instances, quatrefoil and quincunx overlap.

When quadrangular courts have a central altar, they are invariably invoking a quincunxial symbolism, as at the Zapotec site near Villa de Etla (see Fig. 3.146). At the personal dwelling level, the four corner posts that hold up the roof structure are centered with the three stones of the hearth in the middle of the dwelling, thus creating a family quincunxial centering.

Quincunx arrangements and ceremonies exist in

indigenous communities to this day. Anthropologist Evon Vogt, who conducted substantial fieldwork on the Tzetzal indigenous group's relationship to space in the highland Maya area of Chiapas, describes how, when selecting a field to begin planting corn, the farmer will make offerings at each corner of the quadrangular field that culminate with the main offering in the center.[54] In Valladolid, Yucatán, during the recent restoration project of an early-nineteenth-century government building, restorers discovered caches at the four corners and in the middle of the central patio, a vivid testimony to the fact that quincunxial ceremonies to bless a new building survived well into colonial times.

One of the most colorful and exciting rituals of Mesoamerica's ancient past to survive into modern times is the famous *voladores* (flyers) ceremony. The *volador* ritual is still performed on special feast days among indigenous groups such as those in the Nahuatl-speaking villages of the Sierra Norte, in Puebla, and in Totonac villages in western Veracruz. After extensive offerings to the forest spirits, a carefully selected tree from the forest is felled. Stripped of its bark and branches, the tall trunk is erected in the town's plaza. A rope spiraling up the pole forms the rungs of a makeshift ladder. At the top, a small square platform is secured with a frame that supports a long rope extending from each corner (Fig. 1.41).

The *volador* troupe consists of five people: four flyers, each of whom has his or her ankles tied to one of the four corner ropes, and a central, fifth participant who dances in circles on the square platform while playing a drum and a flute. As the central figure turns to the rhythm of the flute and cadence of the drumbeat on his tiny platform, the four *voladores* descend, hanging by their ankles, in thirteen spiraling turns until they reach the ground.[55] The four *voladores* and the central axis mundi troupe master/musician form a human quincunx.

Another ubiquitous symbol in Mesoamerican art is the so-called cross-bands sky motif. Because of its shape, this cross is sometimes referred to as St. Andrew's Cross. The cross-bands sky motif, as its name implies, is associated with the celestial world.[56] The X of the cross-bands motif is another form of quincunxial symbolism. An ancient map of Tenochtitlan, the Aztec capital, shows the city as the axis mundi located at the crossing of the bands that describe a four-cornered universe (Fig. 1.42).

1.41. *Voladores*, four flyers and a musician creating a human quincunx. Courtesy of Sinclair Black.

1.42. Tenochtitlan, map showing city as axis mundi, with cross bands describing four-cornered universe. Codex Mendoza.

From architectural arrangements to flying *volador* rituals, quincunx symbolism is at the core of the Mesoamerican politico-religious symbolic charter. The use of symbolic architectural shaping of open space to reinforce processional rituals plays an essential role in the creation of a uniquely Mexican ceremonial open space during the "contact period."[57] Spanish mendicant friars incorporated native ceremonial open spaces into their building programs during the early part of the sixteenth century, establishing what is known as the "architecture of conversion." The use of quincunxial forms in open space continued into the viceregal era and is addressed in Chapter Three.

BALLCOURTS

When the Maize Gods arrived at the place of the new Creation, they sprang from the crack of the Cosmic Turtle. The Maya saw this turtle as the three stars we call Orion's belt and they also saw the crack in the turtle's back as the ball court.

Schele and Mathews, *The Code of Kings*

One of the traits that define Mesoamerican culture is the practice of the ritual ball game, which was enacted in the ballcourts found in ceremonial centers.[58] Like the quatrefoil shape, ballcourts act as portals, in this case to the Underworld of Xibalba, land of the dead. The ball game ritual is at the core of Mesoamerican religious and mystical belief, charged with the symbolism of creation, cosmic motion, death, rebirth, and ultimately human sacrifice.

Mesoamerican ballcourts generally form an I shape when viewed in plan.[59] The earliest forms of the Mesoamerican ballcourt consist of twin parallel mounds that create a symbolic crevice, canyon, or gash in the earth's crust, associated with the mythological crack in the turtle's shell, and therefore a portal to Xibalba and the world of the supernatural. As Schele and Mathews note, "The word 'crevice' is the word for 'ballcourt' in the Popol Vuh of the K'iche' Maya." They continue, "As a crevice into the surface of the earth, the ballcourt gives human beings access to the Otherworld where the Gods and ancestors live."[60] Many ballcourts have markers that portray the quatrefoil shape, confirming their status as portals to the Underworld.[61]

Some ballcourt structures are parallel dirt mounds, often faced with dressed stone. The more

1.43. Glyph for ballcourt, *pitz*, in the form of a half quatrefoil. Drawing by Linda Schele, © David Schele, courtesy of Foundation for the Advancement of Mesoamerican Studies, Inc., www.famsi.org.

elaborate ones are veritable stone architectural monuments inscribed with public art in stone sculpture and painted murals. The largest ballcourt yet found in Mesoamerica is located in Chichén Itzá. One of the smallest and earliest is the "false" or "effigy" ballcourt within the sunken court at Teopantecuanitlán. Many sites have several ballcourts, such as Tajín, a Totonac site in central Veracruz, where at least ten have been excavated.[62]

Seen in section, the profile shape of a ballcourt is that of a half quatrefoil, not unlike Monument 1 of Chalcatzingo, making it a cleft in the earth and a portal to the Underworld. We propose that the half-quatrefoil shape of the Mesoamerican ballcourt as depicted in cross section is designed, not coincidental. Reinforcing this view is the logographic representation, in Classic period Maya hieroglyphic writing, of the word for ballcourt, *pitz* (Fig. 1.43).[63] Adding a mirror image to the ballcourt glyph constructs a full quatrefoil, echoing the quatrefoils and half quatrefoils of the Mesoamerican Formative period. Many ballcourt markers found in the Maya area are full quatrefoil shapes (Fig. 1.44). The shape of the ballcourt as a gash in the earth's crust creates an architectural setting for ritual passage into the Underworld. Passage is achieved when the ball game culminates in human sacrifice and bloodletting. Further, the typical profile of the ballcourt is an inversion of the basic pyramid form, creating a symbolic valley in counterpart to the pyramid's symbolic mountain. While the pyramid was intended to connect earth to the heavens, the ballcourt served as a connection to the Underworld, providing an appropriate setting for rituals related to death and rebirth (Fig. 1.45).[64]

1.44. Copán, ballcourt marker, full-quatrefoil shape.
© Foundation for the Advancement of Mesoamerican Studies,
Inc., www.famsi.org.

1.45. Ballcourt-pyramid interchange of solid and void shape.
Courtesy of Aurora McClain.

THE SUNKEN COURT OF TEOPANTECUANITLÁN

We were fortunate to see the ruins of the ancient Olmec
site soon after its discovery in the early 1980s in the
company of archaeologist Guadalupe Martínez Donjuán,
a visit that culminated in a *Washington Post* article
heralding its discovery. Soon after, we were able to fly
over the site and photograph it from the air with Gillett
Griffin, curator of the pre-Columbian art collection at
Princeton and an avid proponent of establishing Olmec
origins in the Guerrero area of Mexico. Indeed a timely
event because soon thereafter, a protective roof was
built over the sunken court that obliterated the court's
alignments to the surrounding terrain, the cycles of the
sun, and the movement of the stars. During the first
session of Studio Mexico in 1992, students under our
direction conducted measured drawings of the court, and
Susan Morehead's photo documentation, presented in
Linda Schele's class, inspired Linda to visit the site soon
thereafter.

Logan Wagner, 1992

The archaeological site of Teopantecuanitlán is located in a remote area of the state of Guerrero. Within
the vicinity of the modern town of Copalillo, near the
confluence of the Mescala and Amacuzac Rivers, Teopantecuanitlán comprises an area of about 150 acres.
The first official excavations of the site began in the
early 1980s. To date, three pyramid-shaped structures,
two ballcourts, an elaborate aqueduct system, and a
ceremonial compound have been uncovered. Several
burials, a small Olmec-style monumental head, and
perhaps one of the earliest examples of a corbelled
vault have also been detected.[65]

Since it possesses several topographic features that
relate to specific issues and concepts mentioned in this
writing, we have selected the sunken ceremonial court
at Teopantecuanitlán for our analysis. With radiocar-
bon dating setting the earliest portions at 1200 BCE,
the sunken court represents the beginnings of Mesoamerica's long tradition of built ceremonial centers.[66]

The court, as depicted in site plans and seen in
aerial photos, was placed at the crux of two ridges that
descend from the mountain, reinforcing the concept
that crevices are portals to the supernatural world
(Fig. 1.46). The sidewalls of the sunken court are lined
with dry-stacked blocks of dressed travertine stone
(Fig. 1.47). On top of the east and west walls sit four
monoliths carved with images identified by Karl Taube

1.46. Teopantecuanitlán, aerial photo showing mountain crevice as portal to supernatural world. Courtesy of the School of Architecture Visual Resources Collection, The University of Texas at Austin (Box-Wagner Collection, VRC 2008–1020).

1.47. Teopantecuanitlán, Studio Mexico students working with alidade inside the court. Susan Kline Morehead.

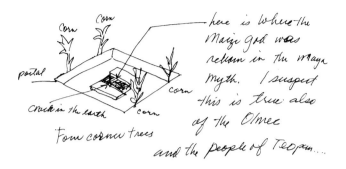

But here is what you have in full explanation

Corn *Corn*

Corn

here is where the Maize god was reborn in the Maya myth. I suspect this is true also of the Olmec

portal

corn

crack in the earth *corn*

Four corner trees

and the people of Teopan . . .

1.48. Teopantecuanitlán, diagrammatic sketch by Linda Schele. "But here is what you have in full explanation. Here is where the maize god was reborn in the Maya myth. I suspect this is true also of the Olmec and the people of Teopan . . ." Labels: portal on left, four corner trees labeled "corn," crack in the earth in center of ballcourt. Logan Wagner.

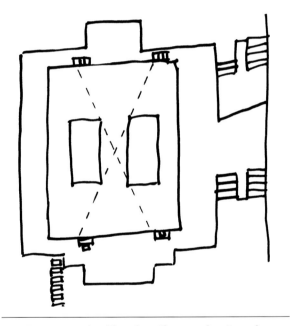

1.49. Teopantecuanitlán, Floor plan with proposed conjectural alignments. Drawing by Logan Wagner.

as aspects of the Olmec maize god.[67] The maize deity at each monolith is holding a pair of ears of corn. The profile of these four monoliths, two on the east wall, two on the west, present the "double merlon" motif referred to earlier. Within the court, a stone aqueduct was uncovered, suggesting that water was used as a principal element in rituals performed within the precinct. One descends into the court on symmetrical staircases made of clay.

At the center of the sunken court, two small parallel mounds have been located. Termed an *effigy ballcourt* by archaeologists, these mounds could be the earliest example of a ballcourt in Mesoamerica. Toward the end of her life, Linda Schele summarized her interpretation of Teopantecuanitlán's sunken-court maize-deity symbolism in a simple pencil sketch (Fig. 1.48).

At the core of her interpretation, and the basis of Mesoamerican culture, is the cult of maize deities. The four monolithic maize god figures grasping ears of corn center the axis mundi—the ballcourt—in the middle of the sunken court. Together they form the Mesoamerican quincunx. If imaginary lines are drawn from each monolith to the one diagonally opposite it, they form an X (Fig. 1.49). The proportions of this imaginary X are very similar to the cross-bands motif prevalent in Olmec iconography. This common symbol of Mesoamerican art, as mentioned earlier, is associated with the celestial realm.[68] During a solstice, the shadows of the maize deity monoliths project the cross-band onto the floor of the sunken court, announcing the solar alignment. Astronomical simulations tend to suggest alignments with the constellations Ursa Major and Cassiopeia, the North Cross, and the iconic mountain, Jaguar Mountain, west of the court.

Embodying many of the urban design concepts that subsequent sites manifest throughout Mesoamerica, Teopantecuanitlán's sunken court serves as an urban design prototype for Mesoamerican ceremonial centers. We propose that Teopantecuanitlán's sunken court embodies the symbolism that eventually surfaces in the church forecourts built in the sixteenth century by Spanish friars to facilitate the conversion process. This theme is addressed in the following chapter.

THE DALLAS PLAQUE: A COSMOGRAM

Sacred objects, when transported, were and still are carefully placed and wrapped in cloth bundles. These highly symbolic and religiously charged objects were meticulously arranged in a precise order as represented in the Dallas Plaque.

Located in the Dallas Museum of Art, the 3.5-inch-square incised greenstone plaque, named for the city that houses it, is believed to come from Ahuelicán in the mountainous Río Balsas area of the state of Guerrero, Mexico.[69] First mentioned by Carlo Gay, this small object of Formative period art has generated much scholarly interest.[70] The relevance of the piece to this study is the apparent symbolism interpreted from the incised design on one of the faces of the plaque. Essentially, it depicts a summary of symbols mentioned above (Fig 1.50).

The composition of the plaque completes a Mesoamerican cosmogram in vertical arrangement. Starting at the base, the monument begins with the three stones of creation. Above the middle stone is a seed of corn. The seed of corn is located within a U- or C-shaped water vessel placed at the base of a mountain or pyramid, perhaps one of the earliest examples of the symbol for *altepetl*, or water mountain. Sprouting from the top of the mountain is a World Tree in the form of a corn plant; four seeds mark the corners of a quincunx centered by the corn plant as axis mundi. Above the corn quincunx the cross-bands sky motif representing the heavens is surrounded by thirteen leaves or feathers that symbolize the thirteen layers of the Mesoamerican sky.[71] The vertical assembly of the cosmogram of symbols itself acts as an axis mundi for the plaza etched on the face of the plaque. The plaza is centered within the four corners of the quadrangle, with its four sides marked by platforms.

In a 2008 conference on Olmec culture held at UT-Austin, David Freidel explained how the object symbols on the Dallas Plaque represent objects within a sacred *bundle*, placed in a carefully designed order.[72] Based on Freidel's interpretation, we suggest that the order of the symbols represents the sacred sequence of the act of creation. The symbols are sacred elements of the community, bundled in a four-cornered sacred cloth representing the plaza, which is also depicted as the primordial sea, that all-engendering creation medium. Linda Schele alludes to this interpretation when she states, "The plaque is framed with a device that may refer either to a plaza space or the four sides of the earth."[73]

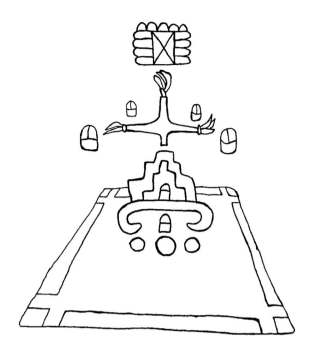

1.50. Dallas Plaque, a cosmogram with elements shown vertically. Courtesy of F. Kent Reilly III.

FORMING SPANISH TOWNS IN MESOAMERICAN CULTURE

PEOPLE AND IDEAS

As Mesoamerica flourished during the fifteenth century, with cities as large as those in Europe,[1] the cultures of the two continents had no idea that the other existed or that they would make dramatic contact. Two distinct peoples with completely different and proud backgrounds meeting in the Americas would create a third culture.

To aid in understanding the mind-set of the sixteenth-century Europeans who would come to Mesoamerica, let us consider some of the people and ideas active in Europe in the late fifteenth and early sixteenth centuries, just before the two civilizations met.

- Filippo Brunelleschi (1377–1446) studied the ruins of Rome and the first-century architectural treatise of Vitruvius,[2] incorporating columns and arches into his designs; in 1413, he established the geometric linear perspective still used today.
- Leon Battista Alberti (1404–1472) also studied Rome; wrote *De re aedificatoria* (*On the Art of Building in Ten Books*) based on Vitruvius, a treatise on perspective in painting, and another on sculpture; and with Brunelleschi, ushered in the Renaissance in Italian architecture and planning.
- Johannes Gutenberg (c. 1400–1468) invented the mechanical printing press that used movable type,

facilitating the spread of knowledge through printed books.
- Thomas More (1478–1535) wrote *Utopia*, in which he described an ideal society: a community of religious tolerance, communal ownership of land, equal education of men and women, and an urban form designed to promote humanitarian ideals.
- Leonardo da Vinci (1452–1519), painter, scientist, and inventor, and Michelangelo (1475–1564), painter, architect, and engineer, both consummate Renaissance men, advanced art and invention.
- Medieval Spain, barely touched by the Italian Renaissance, had just ended almost eight hundred years of Moorish occupation of the Iberian Peninsula.
- Martin Luther (1483–1546) initiated the Protestant Reformation in 1517.

Other important events that occurred in or around the sixteenth century would have an impact on the perspectives of the Europeans coming to the New World during the early part of the conquest.

- Bernardo Rossellino (1409–1464) designed Pienza's Renaissance plaza and town center for Pope Pius II from 1460 to 1463.
- Pedro Machuca (1485?–1550) started work on the Palace of Charles V inside the Alhambra in 1527.
- Juan de Herrera (1530–1597) began the Escorial in 1563.

2.1. "The Great City of Tenochtitlán," by Diego Rivera, showing Tlatelolco Market in foreground, main temple, Lake Texcoco, and volcanoes in background; part of the mural cycle Rivera painted in 1945 at the Palacio Nacional in Mexico City. Nettie Lee Benson Latin American Collection, University of Texas Libraries, The University of Texas at Austin.

- Andrea Palladio (1508–1580) reenvisioned architectural form according to classical Roman principles, wrote *The Four Books of Architecture*, and dramatically affected the history of Western architecture.

This concentration of significant events in human history was the background for the European thrust into the Americas.

During this same period in Mesoamerica, the Maya were in decline, but the Mexica much farther north had been migrating to the lake area of the Central Plateau. They settled in this area and eventually created the Aztec Empire, formed from a Triple Alliance of the allied city-states of Tenochtitlan, Texcoco, and Tlacopan. This relatively new culture of the Aztecs became dominant by conquering most of the tribes in the Central Plateau except for the Chichimecas to the north, the Tarascans to the northwest, and the Tlaxcalans to the east. By the early sixteenth century, the Aztec Empire was about the same size as Spain, but with three times the population and speaking Nahuatl as their primary language.[3] Their capital city, Tenochtitlan, embodied the Mesoamerican myths and traditions, although they had been rewritten slightly to present an Aztec-centered history. The Aztecs did not extend southward to conquer the Maya, yet by the sixteenth century they had built one of the largest cities in the world, as large as any in Europe at that time (Fig. 2.1).

Spain, the major power in Europe, had extended its domain to include Naples, Sicily, Milan, the Netherlands, Flanders, Luxembourg, Burgundy, and Austrian territories during the fifteenth century and, under Charles V (1500–1558), sought further expansion. Spain had financed the explorations of Christopher Columbus (1451–1506) and had helped establish settlements on the newly found islands thought to be off the coast of Asia. From those islands, Spain invaded Mesoamerica with two broad objectives. First was the individual quest for free land, noble titles, and great riches of precious metals extracted from the free land by the free labor they found. These Spanish conquistadors carried the morals, religious values, and traditions of their Spanish culture into the new land. Second was the quest for souls. The mendicant friars of the Franciscan Order, and later the Augustinian and Dominican Orders, would do the actual colonizing of the conquered as they organized and began the conversion of an estimated 25 million Mesoamericans. These friars sought to convert the people of a three-thousand-year-old (or more) civilization to Christianity, a new religion imported from Europe and only half as old.

THE INVASION

The first Europeans to set foot in Mesoamerica were shipwrecked near the island of Cozumel off the Caribbean coast of Yucatán in 1511. The two survivors,

Gonzalo Guerrero and Fray Gerónimo de Aguilar, made friends with the Maya and learned their language. Guerrero married a Maya, and they had the first mestizo children. Aguilar later became one of the two translators who enabled Hernán Cortés to communicate with the Mesoamericans. When Francisco Hernández de Córdoba sailed from Cuba in 1517 with an expedition of three ships and 110 settlers, he was surprised to find a civilized people wearing clothes and living amid monumental cut-stone architecture (Fig. 2.2). Guerrero, the shipwreck survivor, led Maya warriors against them, and they found the Maya to be generally hostile. They retreated with many dead and injured, which caused the colonization effort to be abandoned. The next year, Juan de Grijalva made contact along the Gulf Coast and had many encounters with the Mesoamericans, causing news of strange men with beards and white faces to be sent inland to Tenochtitlan and Moctezuma. Bernal Díaz del Castillo, one of the men who had accompanied Hernández de Córdoba, joined the expedition from Cuba led by Cortés two years later. From this firsthand perspective, he chronicled the conquest of Mesoamerica.

Cortés's journey started in Cuba; his first stop was the island of Cozumel. It was at Cozumel that Cortés sent for Fray Gerónimo de Aguilar, who agreed to join his now famous trek to Tenochtitlan. From Cozumel, Cortés and his men sailed around the Yucatán Peninsula, making landfall at several points. When they arrived at Champotón, he met Malinche, a native noblewoman who joined the voyage, contributing her knowledge of Mayan and Nahuatl. Thus began Cortés's complex mode of communication, with Fray Gerónimo, who spoke Spanish and had become conversant in Mayan, translating from Spanish to Mayan, and then Malinche translating from Mayan to Nahuatl. Through this method, Cortés was able to converse face-to-face with Moctezuma, the Aztec emperor, a few weeks later—with every word translated from Spanish to Mayan to Nahuatl and back again.

Near what is now known as Cape Catoche, on the northeast point of the Yucatán Peninsula, Bernal Díaz del Castillo made what is possibly the first European report of a Maya U-shaped court: "Un poco más adelante de donde nos dieron aquella refriega estaba una placeta y tres casas de cal y canto" (A little farther ahead from where we had that skirmish was a court and three dressed-stone masonry houses).[4] From Champotón, Cortés and crew proceeded along

2.2.   Tulum, Mesoamerican city on the coast of Yucatán. Courtesy of the School of Architecture Visual Resources Collection, The University of Texas at Austin (Box-Wagner Collection, VRC 95-06120).

the coast of what we now call the Gulf of Mexico and made landfall in central Veracruz, where he founded the town of Villa Rica de la Vera Cruz.

In the summer of 1519, after burning the ships on which they had sailed from Cuba so that his men could not retreat, Hernán Cortés began his historic trek into the interior of the American continent with men, guns, weapons, horses, and attack dogs. After journeying through wilderness and villages large and small, he was welcomed in Tenochtitlan by Moctezuma II (c. 1466–1520), head of the Nahuatl-speaking Aztec nation, the largest power in Mesoamerica. He was received warmly because ancient legend had foretold that Quetzalcóatl, the bearded, fair-skinned Toltec ruler-god, would return from the east to reclaim his kingdom at the same time that Cortés arrived. While the encounter was initially amicable, it soon turned bloody, leading to the death of Moctezuma. He was succeeded by his nephew Cuauhtémoc (c. 1495–1525), who took the throne at age eighteen while Tenochtitlan was besieged by the Spaniards and devastated by the smallpox they brought to the continent.[5] He was the last of the Aztec rulers, later executed by Cortés.

The eventual Spanish Conquest in 1521 brought Charles V of Spain vast new lands and enormous wealth that would finance his empire's European expansion and defense as well as fund further exploration into new territories. The Mesoamericans would

2.3. Tenochtitlan, model set into pavement of Zócalo.
Courtesy of Sinclair Black.

be decimated by epidemic disease,[6] overwhelmed by superior arms, forced into labor, brought into a new spiritual world, and led into building extraordinary towns and churches.

Admiration and fascination with open space in Mesoamerican cities began with some of the earliest European witnesses at the time of the conquest. A fascination with these spaces has continued through history, reinforced by exploration and travel reports,[7] and supported by the research and scholarship current to this day. This admiration for the ability of Mesoamerican urban planners to shape, orient, and architecturally orchestrate open urban space was manifested from the very first Spanish eyewitness reports.

It is evident that the newly arrived Spaniards were accustomed to, and took pride in, the plazas and open spaces they had known in Spain. Most of these were small, irregularly shaped open spaces forming the parvis of a church.[8] So when they witnessed, discovered, and experienced the grand urban centers of the New World, Spaniards were able to compare them to the plazas they had back home. The fact that Spaniards even had specific words for urban open spaces attests to the appreciation for these forms that they brought with them from their homeland. One can imagine

their wonderment on encountering the New World urban centers with their huge open spaces—spaces they encountered for the first time as Cortés's troops advanced inland—culminating in the grandest open space of Mesoamerica, the seat of power, Tenochtitlan's sacred walled precinct (Fig. 2.3). Cortés described the city in a letter to Charles V:

> This city has many squares where trading is done and markets are held continuously. There is also one square twice as big as that of Salamanca, with arcades all around, where more than sixty thousand people come each day to buy and sell, and where every kind of merchandise produced in these lands is found. . . . Amongst these temples there is one, the principal one, whose great size and magnificence no human tongue could describe, for it is so large that within the precincts, which are surrounded by a very high wall, a town of some five hundred inhabitants could easily be built.[9]

THE EUROPEANS MAKING CONTACT

While the fighting would be carried out by the *conquistadores*, and the land and people would be exploited by the *encomenderos*, the mendicant friars would be the ones to bring the Mesoamerican natives into the protective care of the church—making the real conquest by building the churches and establishing the new towns atop the existing Mesoamerican towns.

The first individuals involved, bringing their European experiences to the new continent, are introduced here to provide a sense of how their backgrounds might have affected their mission.

- Hernán Cortés (1485–1547), born of lower nobility in Extremadura, Spain, arrived in Santo Domingo, Hispaniola, in 1504 at the age of eighteen, became a landowner and then mayor of the capital of Cuba. After fifteen years in the islands, he led the expedition that made the conquest of Mesoamerica, landing in 1519 with 508 men, an additional one hundred seamen, eleven ships, ten brass guns, thirty-two crossbowmen, thirteen musketeers, much powder and shot, and the first sixteen horses on the continent.[10] He proclaimed victory over the Aztecs in 1521. As both a conquistador and a carrier of the faith who said Mass for his troops, Cortés valued the friars and their mission as strongly as his own. Along with Cortés came a surveyor, Luis de Alonso, who would lay out Mexico City on the ruins of Tenochtitlan in 1522;[11] Francisco de Montejo (c. 1479–c. 1553), who sought to conquer the Yucatán; and Bernal Díaz del Castillo (1492–1585) from Valladolid, Spain, who became the chronicler of the conquest, accompanying both Hernández de Córdoba and Cortés.
- Fray Pedro de Gante (1486–1572) of Ghent in Flanders, now Belgium, a relative of King Charles V, was the most effective of the first friars in educating and converting the natives. Arriving in 1523 as the first Christian missionary to New Spain,[12] he learned to communicate with the Mesoamericans in their Nahuatl and Otomi languages and founded an effective new education system.
- Fray Martín de Valencia (c. 1466–1534), an intellectual, led the significantly numbered group of twelve Franciscan friars that Cortés requested. After their selection by Charles V and appointment by Pope Hadrian VI to create the missions in the "New World," they arrived in 1524, a year after Pedro de Gante, walking 400 kilometers from Veracruz to Mexico City. When their shoes wore out, they walked in their bare feet. We know that Fray Martín grew up in Valencia de Don Juan, León, Spain, that he is alleged to have had some experience in architecture as a builder in Spain,[13] and that he visited Rome at least once.
- Fray Juan de Zumárraga (c. 1468–1548), from the Basque region of Spain, became the first archbishop of Mexico, 1528–1548, and was known as the "Protector of the Indians."

- Fray Toribio de Benavente "Motolinía" (c. 1482–c. 1569), from Zamora in northwestern Spain, wrote *Historia de los indios de la Nueva España* (*History of the Indians of New Spain*) describing the Franciscan missions from 1530 to 1570, at which time the secular church assumed power over the mendicants' missions.
- Vasco de Quiroga (c. 1470–1565), from Castile, Spain, a follower of Thomas More's teachings on utopias, became bishop of Michoacán, bringing human rights to the conquered and creating successful, productive towns with churches and *hospitales* in the new villages he founded.
- Fray Bartolomé de Las Casas (1484–1566), a Dominican bishop from Seville, Spain, brought missions to Chiapas, defended the natives from torture, and recorded their religious rites.
- Fray Bernardino de Sahagún (1499–1590), from León, Spain, recorded pre-Columbian history, compiling the *Florentine Codex*.

Among the friar-builders of note are these:

- Augustinians Diego de Chávez (–c. 1572), who came to Mexico as a boy before 1535 and built *conventos* at Tiripetio, Tacámbaro, and Yuriria, and Andrés de Mata (–c. 1574), who built those at Actopan and Ixmiquilpan.[14]
- Dominican Francisco Marín, who built at Teposcolula, Yanhuitlán, Coixtlahuaca, and Santo Domingo Oaxaca.[15]
- Franciscan Juan de Mérida, who built at Mérida, Maní, Izamal, and Valladolid in Yucatán.
- Another Franciscan, Juan de Alameda (–c. 1570), from Concepción, Spain, who arrived in Mexico in 1528, one of the few alleged architects among the early friars. He worked at Huejotzingo starting in 1529, at Tula in 1539, and at Huaquechula, where he died in 1570.[16] He may also have worked at Calpan, a few miles from Huejotzingo, and completed about the same time (1548–1550).
- Hernando Toribio de Alcaraz (–c. 1570), who was the first known professional architect in New Spain. He arrived in 1544 and worked for Bishop Quiroga on the cathedral in Pátzcuaro.[17]
- Claudio de Arciniega (1520–1593), who arrived in 1545 at age eighteen and was trained as a designer in Mexico, becoming "the most remarkable civilian architect of the epoch." He is credited with advising on the rebuilding of Puebla Cathedral in 1555 and contributing significantly to the cathedral in Mexico City.[18]

- Francisco Becerra (c. 1545–1605) came to Mexico in 1573 after training in Spain and laid the foundation of Puebla Cathedral as well as being associated with its design after 1575. He is thought to have been associated with numerous other projects as a consultant.[19]

The conquistadors with Cortés were mainly from Spain's poorest region, Extremadura, where life was extremely harsh with little education and less hope for improvement. It is no wonder they came in search of riches. The friars, on the other hand, came in quest of souls.

These early friars were nearly all observants, that is, followers of reform movements to purify the clergy by strengthening the preaching mission and austerity of the mendicant orders. Among Spanish Franciscans, these reforms were instituted by Cardinal Francisco Ximénez de Cisneros, confessor for Queen Isabella after 1492, who urged the friars to give up worldly goods and return to emulation of the life of Christ. The result of the reforms among mendicant orders was the creation of what Kubler has called "a spiritual militia in the New World."[20]

In addition to the reform movement for observance and, to a lesser extent, the concerns of the Counter-Reformation, the friars were influenced by humanism, which had moved from Italy to the established universities of Salamanca and Valladolid, as well as to the new university of Alcalá de Henares, founded near Madrid by Ximénez in 1508.[21] The tenets of humanism, with its shift in focus from medieval contemplation of the divine to active pursuit of secular goals, included concern for the public good of individual citizens; the exercise of reason; accurate observation of nature; and the full development of one's intellectual, cultural, and material potential. The new learning was embraced at the highest levels, with Isabella and her daughter setting an example by mastering Latin. Humanism spread throughout Spanish intellectual life; for example, Renaissance scholar Antonio de Nebrija returned from ten years of humanist study in Italy to teach at Salamanca and Alcalá. His work included preparation of a Latin grammar, a Latin-Spanish dictionary, the first modern Spanish grammar, and editing of the Complutensian Polyglot Bible (1514–1517) in Latin, Greek, and Hebrew.

Charles Gibson points out that the friars who later studied Nahuatl in Mexico were greatly indebted to these humanistic language studies.[22] After the Mexican friars learned to speak the local languages, they transcribed them from their unwritten form using Spanish phonetics and orthography and taught the natives to read and write in their own tongues, transliterated through Spanish.[23] In 1539, they began printing books in Nahuatl, the most widely spoken indigenous language, to expedite their teaching. The first book was a catechism in Nahuatl and Spanish, and by 1580 over one hundred texts in nine different languages had been printed in Mexico.[24] The Franciscans in particular, led by Zumárraga and his humanist ideals, founded schools everywhere, teaching literacy and Hispanic values along with Christianity. Their earliest model was Pedro de Gante's school for the sons of noble natives in Tenochtitlan. At the Franciscan Colegio de Santa Cruz in Tlatelolco, natives studied various disciplines, including Latin; and the model community of Santa Fe, founded by Vasco de Quiroga on the western edge of the Valley of Mexico in the 1530s, was based on Thomas More's description of utopia.[25]

The friars who came eagerly to the New World were knowledgeable about European cities. Many of those from Spain had been educated at universities in Salamanca and Alcalá, and some had traveled to Paris to the Sorbonne. Others came from Flanders, Portugal, France, Italy, Denmark, and Scotland.[26] Influenced by Erasmus and the doctrine of Christian humanism, they believed in the potential of the pagan natives to become a great, civilized people, especially with the help of the purified Christianity. And they believed that the New World was an earthly paradise whose settlement would renew and transform Europe for the good, as imagined by Thomas More in *Utopia* and by Shakespeare in *The Tempest*:

> Miranda: O Wonder!
> How many goodly creatures are there here!
> How beauteous mankind is! O, brave new world,
> That has such people in't.[27]

Filled with zeal for their mission by the promise of untainted souls to be saved in the new earthly paradise; armed with commitments to poverty, teaching, and active service by the reforms of the fifteenth century; and enlightened by the spirit of humanism spreading throughout Europe, the mendicant friars from Europe were well equipped for their work. While their architectural experience was scant, they were well educated, and some were of noble birth. In addition to their knowledge of cities and their familiarity with monastic buildings, they brought with them illustrated books and printed images that served as guides for much of the architecture and its ornamentation.[28] Their building program was informed by these newly published European books, products of the Renaissance, that not only came with the early friars but also were included in shipments of books from Seville beginning early in the sixteenth century.[29] Some of these books may have influenced development of the standard scheme and the design of individual monasteries, but their wider impact was on the Indian artisans who used the illustrations as models for details.

Among the illustrated architectural books that would have been available to the friars were various editions of Vitruvius beginning in 1511, a Spanish treatise on Vitruvius from 1526, an edition of Alberti in 1550, and works by Sebastiano Serlio available from 1537, with a widely available Spanish edition in 1552.[30] Of these, Serlio's work was the most influential in Mexico, because, as McAndrew points out, it offered "the most picture with the least theory."[31]

The earliest architectural treatise to be written in the New World was the manuscript of Andrés de San Miguel (1577–1644).[32] This treatise probably dates from the beginning of the seventeenth century and is therefore too late for the early building campaigns. Widespread use of architectural treatises, particularly their illustrations, in the design and construction of religious buildings in Mexico became codified by 1589, when guilds of carpenters and masons began requiring masters to pass an exam in drawing the five Roman orders.[33]

The friars coming to the New World would have known the irregular streets and plazas of medieval European towns and some of the ideas about plazas coming from the Renaissance, and probably the example of Pope Pius II's plaza in Pienza (Fig. 2.4). In 1459, Pius II, a Renaissance humanist, had architect Bernardo Rossellino, pupil of Alberti, rebuild his childhood village as an ideal Renaissance town with a grid plan centered on a plaza.[34] The first of its sort, this urban design concept, blessed and promoted by the pope, served as an urban planning example for many other cities in Italy and Europe.[35]

The friars, especially those from Spain, would have known Moorish walled gardens, courts, and patios. These gardens, also known as paradise gardens, date from Persia in the time of Cyrus the Great

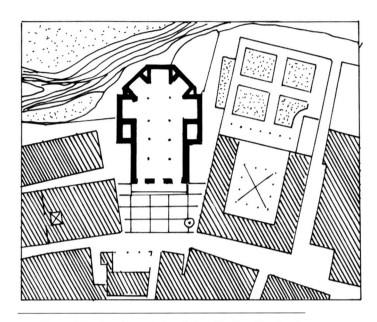

2.4.   Pienza, Italy, plan of central plaza designed by Pope Pius II and Bernardo Rossellino 1460–1463. Redrawn by Logan Wagner.

(559–530 BCE), who brought water in underground channels called *qanats* from the foothills of the Zagros Mountains to his four-square garden at Pasargadae, demonstrating his right to rule by his ability to grow fruits and flowers in the desert.[36] Islam continued the practice of walled gardens divided axially by water channels, and along with courtyards, patios, and fountains, these were established in Spain by the Moors, notably at the Alhambra and the mosque at Córdoba.[37]

Some friars may even have been aware of the thirteenth-century French bastides, or the Florentine new towns of the fourteenth century, towns built on grid plans to concentrate populations for their protection and governance.[38] The one grid plan town that might have had influence on the Spanish friars was the military camp of Santa Fe de Granada, built on the old Roman *castrum* grid plan with a *cardo*, the north-south main street, and *decumanus*, the secondary east-west perpendicular cross street. However, most of them would not have been aware of the use of sacred open space in early Christian rites in Rome,[39] although they would have known of the *hortus conclusus*, literally "enclosed garden" of the Bible, and its evolution into the cloister. Nor would they have known of the even earlier outdoor sacred spaces such as Stonehenge.

The well-educated early friars knew the arts and ideas active in much of Europe. They were equipped to bring a new religion to the New World, along with a new way of expressing it in words, art, and architecture that would present a whole new way of life. In the next fifty years, they would establish some four hundred communities with grand new churches and cause new towns to evolve around them to concentrate the natives. The first work was in and around Tenochtitlan in the region controlled by the Triple Alliance. In building churches and towns in this unknown land, they would have an unusual and extraordinary opportunity: free land on which to build, free material, free labor, excellent native craftsmanship, and the European building technology of stone arch and vault systems that could create large interior spaces previously unknown in Mesoamerica. What an exciting time to build! They brought draft animals and the wheel for use in agriculture and industry along with their guns, steel, horses, and religious zeal; they also brought their collective memory of the European cities and architecture of the fifteenth and early sixteenth centuries.

Even though many of the early Spaniards considered the natives to be subhuman savages, a status that did not officially change until 1537, sixteen years after the conquest,[40] native skill and dedication built the great churches we know today.

The friars had the opportunity to build new towns as well as churches influenced by the civic and architectural ideals growing out of the Renaissance. It would have been clear to them that town founding and church building would become a major enterprise—essential for their mission to Christianize the natives. They could use a temporary altar or build a temporary chapel to celebrate Mass, but how would they build significant churches to serve the people they would find on this new continent? How would they attract natives from their individual homes in the wilderness and concentrate them into communities where they could be Christianized by friars and exploited by landowners? How could they begin to accommodate as many as 25 million converts?

Imagine the challenge. What knowledge, images, and ideas would they bring from Europe to help build new towns? To understand their thinking, we must know something about the towns and cities they had visited and what those places were like when the friars left for Mesoamerica in the early sixteenth century—places quite different from European cities today and significantly different from those same cities after the plazas of medieval towns became formalized in the late sixteenth and seventeenth centuries. We will look

at images the friars understood before they began the fusion of the two disparate cultures to create a new kind of town and a new kind of plaza.

EUROPEAN PLAZAS IN THE EARLY SIXTEENTH CENTURY

Historians have often posited that European traditions alone formed Americans' ideas of community and shaped our towns and plazas. The distinguished scholar John W. Reps, for example, makes no mention of the influence of existing Mesoamerican cities in his encyclopedic *Making of Urban America*. This Eurocentric view is disputed by our current understanding of history, as we now know that Mesoamerica had strong traditions of town planning, described in Chapter One.[41] We know that the conquistadors and friars came from a medieval Spain of irregular streets and small, irregularly shaped plazas bearing little resemblance to the new forms they would build in the Americas. We know that the open space in front of the European churches, the parvis, was used for gathering congregations and for sheltering pilgrims, but not for worship services, since it had no altar. Europeans, with their focus on liturgy, worshipped inside buildings because tradition and climate required it and because they possessed the technology to build large indoor spaces. The Mesoamericans made sacred spaces outdoors primarily because of their focus on the natural world, especially the topography and the skies, but also due to the hospitable climate and their lack of technology to build large interior spaces. One purpose of this examination is to describe the way these spaces evolved in Mesoamerican culture from primitive outdoor gathering place to paved and bounded sacred space before leading to the vital three-part ensemble of Mexican *atrio*, church, and plaza, as well as to the new town form designed on top of the existing Mesoamerican towns.

While historians typically discuss the European influences that shaped building in the New World, it is conceivable that planning ideas eventually flowed from New Spain to Europe as well, like the produce and precious metals that the conquistadors sent back to Spain. Mesoamericans gave to Europeans their first taste of tomatoes, potatoes, corn, pumpkin, squash, beans, avocados, pineapple, peanuts, sweet potatoes, vanilla, bell peppers, chiles, manioc, and chocolate, and introduced them to tobacco and rubber, all new to Europeans.[42] Imagine Europe without tomatoes or potatoes.

Mesoamerican and New Spanish town forms could have influenced the creation of large rectangular urban plazas in Europe such as the Plaza Mayor in Madrid that Philip II hired Juan de Herrera to formalize from the old, chaotic Plaza del Arrabal in the 1560s, or later, the plaza in Salamanca that Philip V hired Alberto de Churriguera and Andrés García de Quiñones to enlarge and improve in the mid-eighteenth century. The large cities of preconquest Mesoamerica that had grand plazas, especially Tenochtitlan, Cholula, and Teotihuacan, were similar in size to Paris and larger than London and Rome.[43] The conquistadors described Tenochtitlan as cleaner and safer than these cities, benefiting as it did from city sewers and piped drinking water. With archaeological evidence of Mesoamerican cities comparable in age and size to European cities, it is engaging to visualize more cultural equality between the "Old World" and the "New World" than the story taught us in the third grade about the civilized peoples of Europe discovering the savages in the "wilderness" of the American continent.

ORIGINS OF THE PLAZA

To understand the plaza, its form, and the life within it, one must consider how towns and cities have been shaped through time on most continents. Plazas, or communal open spaces of some kind, have been at the core of every town and city in every culture on every continent. In Mesoamerica, the "three-stone" centering settlements mentioned in Chapter One gave a physical and sacred place for hunter-gatherers traveling in *bands*; they grew to center larger *tribes*, then developed politically into *chiefdoms*, and perhaps grew larger into *states*.[44] All the while, the powerful mystery of the sacred primordial sea brought cohesion and hierarchy to the community and to the place. The town form and the power structure were strengthened by the central space being sacred space, the place of primitive altars, temples, and churches, the space that was the awesome paradise where one stood in the presence of a god.

Family shelters that clustered around a central open space for intimate communal activities and rituals appear in most archaeological digs and still exist in the rural developing world. These are often placed on earthen platforms, as were sacred communal spaces. This instinct of centering, for the purpose of cohering a community, has continued as a human desire in many physical forms: *forum*, *atrio*, *court*, *piazza*, *square*, *plaza*, *place*, *platz*, *town common*, *maidan* or *musallá* in the Middle East, or *guang chang* in China. At smaller scales in residences and on campuses, the central open space was a *patio*, *cortile*, *quadrangle*, English *courtyard*, French *cour*, or Chinese *siheyuan*.[45]

A hierarchy of communal open spaces can be seen in the towns of many cultures where the smallest open space is the patio of a family house, a small plaza is the focus of a neighborhood, and a larger plaza surrounded by such neighborhoods centers the town. The pattern of arrangement around a central open space extended itself in various ways as growth demanded. Building of residences and other facilities followed pathways leading to food-producing areas and to other towns for trade.

The sense of space that the Europeans carried with them to the Americas developed from many sources. They may have been aware of the immense open spaces of Egypt, where significant objects sit in infinite space.[46] In his *City Square: A Historical Evolution*, Michael Webb offers two examples of architectural masses in infinite space that developed into the centers of civic life in ancient Athens: the Parthenon and temples of the Acropolis formed the highly sacred space, while a separate rectangular agora, enclosed by the long lines of shops in stoae on three sides, formed a space for buying and selling, assemblies, and government—the center of civic life.[47]

2.5. Mirepoix, France, plaza of bastide town founded in early thirteenth century. Susan Kline Morehead.

2.6. Isfahan, Iran, Maidan Naqsh-e-Jahan, the royal plaza built by
Shah Abbas c. 1600. Susan Kline Morehead.

Webb also describes the earlier fifth-century BCE town of Miletus, where Hippodamus is said to have originated the Hippodamian grid and designed the first agora, a perfectly rectangular space measuring 400 by 540 feet. A high degree of order could be applied with the grid plan, which was composed of more or less straight streets, running more or less perpendicular to each other, forming blocks of land where families could build shelters. The grid, sometimes irregular for reasons of topography, became an easy way to divide communal land for individual use. It typically offered an area near the middle that could become the town center, its genius loci, a communal gathering place suitable for meeting, marketing, and staging rituals. The town's significant buildings—shops, businesses, town houses, palaces, and sacred places—were located adjacent to or near the plaza, causing the surrounding area to grow in density naturally.

The grid plan was used in the bastides, new agricultural towns of southern France just across the Pyrenees from Spain, such as Mirepoix (Fig. 2.5), as well as in military towns such as Santa Fe de Granada, based on ancient Roman *castra*.[48] The builders of Islamic towns preferred smaller, more irregular streets and spaces. When they conquered a city based on an ordered plan, they remodeled it over the years to fit their cultural patterns, with streets that had numerous twists and turns, as did the entrances to individual houses, for reasons of security and defense.[49] The grid

plan has ancient roots, but most European towns of the late fifteenth century were more laissez-faire arrangements.[50] We believe that the friars had limited experience with grid-formed cities before coming to the New World, but they were influenced by Renaissance ideas that they began implementing in Hispaniola and Cuba before arriving in Mesoamerica.

Nearly eight hundred years of Moorish occupation had formed the cities that were known to the Spaniards who went to the Americas. While the towns were composed of twisting streets and irregular open spaces, the medieval Moorish Alhambra of Granada offered an idealized model of the patio to which the friars could have referred. It was not until nearly 1600 that Shah Abbas moved the Safavid capital to Isfahan and created his grand maidan as the city's heart and the setting for two mosques, the bazaar, and his palace (Fig. 2.6).[51] Likewise, medieval Rome, where the ruins of the ancient city were overlaid by settlements without apparent order, offered a very different kind of experience than it does today, after being remodeled according to Pope Sixtus V's sixteenth-century baroque plan.

The streets of medieval European cities began as random paths that eventually evolved for available transportation—walking, horses, or carriages—with little formal order except that dictated by topography. At the same time, Mesoamerican towns and cities had no need for roads or streets because, in part, they had no draft animals or wheels for carriages, and more

FORMING SPANISH TOWNS IN MESOAMERICAN CULTURE

2.7.   Montevarchi, plan of a Florentine new town.

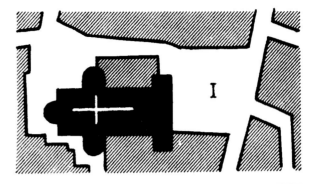

2.8.   Padua, medieval city plan detail of plaza by Camillo Sitte.

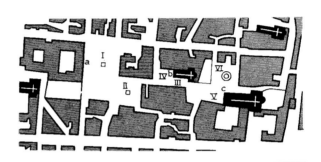

2.9.   Lucca, medieval city plan with plaza by Camillo Sitte.

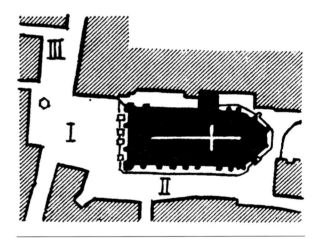

2.10.   Regensburg, medieval city plan plaza by Camillo Sitte.

importantly, all the buildings were situated in the open space. The exception was ritual paths known as *sacbeob*. Medieval European towns formed and maintained some kind of central open space as they grew.[52] As larger churches were erected near the town centers, space was cleared out in front of the churches to provide a forecourt, a parvis, for the dominating edifice. Those churches, with their plazas, *places*, or *platz*, became the magnetic, concentrating force that created the town's major meeting place for ritual processions, celebrations, and markets.

New towns that were planned for a growing population in locations near the city of Florence in the mid-thirteenth century provide some record of ideas about urban design in that era. These new towns were consciously conceived as a whole rather than growing organically and naturally from the needs of a grouping of people. The Florentine towns utilized and adapted the grid to their purposes, providing a hierarchy to the organization of the town that was centered on the main plaza, which was typically the site for the major church (Fig. 2.7).

We can see the medieval shape of many open spaces in Camillo Sitte's nineteenth-century documentation of plazas in major European cities.[53] He made drawings that show the infinitely varying shape

of the spaces formed by the surrounding building masses, in his effort to understand how to design new cities for the next century (Figs. 2.8–2.10). Sitte's work gave rise to the mid-twentieth-century field of Urban Design as a formal discipline. Our own interest in the plazas of Mexico is informed by Sitte's investigation. The plazas built in Mexico, with their high degree of order, are much different from the medieval European plazas sketched by Sitte, but the uses of plazas and the

2.11. Cholula, Plaza Mayor with costumed dancers reenacting the Battle of the Christians and the Moors. Courtesy of Sinclair Black.

buildings that form them are very similar. He sought the principles of composition that supported communal life in old cities and found them in the plazas:

> In the Middle Ages and the Renaissance there still existed a vital and functional use of the town square for community life and also, in connection with this, a rapport between square and surrounding public buildings.[54]

By custom, these plazas served practical purposes as well as making symbolic distinctions between ecclesiastical and secular authorities; that is, they focused on the market, the cathedral, and the government buildings.

The friars would not have expected to find a limited ability to span large interior spaces in Mesoamerica, where the arch and vault were unknown. Nor would they have expected to find that they would not have draft animals or the wheel for use in transportation. European use of the arch and vault to span large distances was able to create magical interior spaces larger than any the Mesoamericans had ever seen before, spaces similar in some ways to the caves that they revered. The friars entered the Americas with such strong faith and found such abundant natural resources that they became a powerful force — more effective in conquering the people of Mesoamerica than the soldiers, horses, armor, and weapons of the conquistadors. The friars won over the Mesoamericans by the special care they gave to the natives; by their seductive spirituality; and to some extent by the magic

of the new spaces, structures, and iconography that they created.

Some of the first friars had visited cities in Italy, Spain, France, and Flanders and might have had those plazas in mind along with the ideals of the Vitruvian city and Thomas More's utopia. In the early sixteenth century, they would have known of the main plaza of Madrid, but they would not have seen what we see today after the extensive remodeling that began in the 1560s. Madrid's Plaza Mayor was not finished until 1621. Salamanca's Plaza Mayor, though famed for its size, was irregular until rebuilt in the 1700s.[55] The first regular, unified major plaza in Spain was laid out in the Castilian city of Valladolid in 1561 on the orders of Phillip II, after many such plazas had been built in Nueva España.[56]

Fray Martín de Valencia knew his hometown of Valencia de Don Juan, in the northwestern kingdom of León, as a medieval town of narrow, irregular streets with small, plaza-like open spaces. When he visited Rome, he might have seen the rectangular Campo de'Fiori much as it is today, but he could have observed only the beginnings of the Piazza Navona or Michelangelo's Piazza del Campidoglio under construction. Other friars might have visited the Piazza della Signoria and Piazza San Lorenzo of Florence. They could have seen the Piazza del Campo built over a Roman amphitheater in Siena, or the Piazza San Marco in Venice, looking much as they do today. They would not have seen the Place de la Concorde (1755) in Paris, because at that time the most important plaza in Paris, which had a population of about 200,000, was only a small parvis in front of Notre Dame. If they visited London, they could not have seen Trafalgar Square, because it came into being three hundred years later. The large town squares had not yet been built; Rome's Piazza San Pietro (1656–1667) and Piazza del Popolo (1811), Bordeaux's Place des Quinconces (1820), and St. Petersburg Square (1703) would come along much later. It could be that the large Mesoamerican plazas, such as those in Tenochtitlan, Cholula (Fig. 2.11), and the ruins of Monte Albán, influenced the scale of these later squares in Europe and the East. The Renaissance plaza that would have been familiar to them and a strong influence, if for no other reason than its association with the pope, was the fifteenth-century plaza in Pienza.

The mendicant friars, using the labor and skill

of the conquered Mesoamericans, founded and built *conventos* and churches of substantial and innovative architecture, causing the creation of four hundred towns in their first fifty years in the Americas—the world's largest and most extensive building enterprise before the industrial revolution.

BUILDING NEW WORLD TOWNS

The crowds of laborers were so thick that one could hardly move in the wide streets. . . . Many died from being crushed by beams or falling from high places, or in tearing down old buildings for new ones . . . The laborers carry everything on their backs; they drag great stones and beams with ropes, and in the absence of skill but abundance of hands, four hundred men are used to move the stone or beam for which only one hundred are necessary. It is their custom, when moving materials, that the crowds sing and shout, and these voices continued by night and day, with the great fervor of building.

Motolinía (1482–1568),
History of the Indians of New Spain

Spanish settlements in New Spain have been classified into categories according to their ethnic makeup, location, or economic function. Five types of urban settlements and layouts were created during the sixteenth century in what was by then being called Nueva España, or New Spain, although of course some towns grew without any perceptible deliberate design.[57]

Types of Towns

1. Indian towns: Settlements refounded on top of preexisting native urban centers, such as Mexico-Tenochtitlan, Mérida, Izamal, Atlatlahuacan, Molango.
2. Spanish towns: New towns founded by the Spaniards for their own inhabitation, such as Puebla, Oaxaca, and Guadalajara.
3. *Reducciones*: Also inhabited primarily by indigenous populations, *reducciones* are new towns for the resettlement of dispersed native groups. These occur mainly in remote areas in the modern states of Michoacán and Yucatán, such as Santa Fe de la Laguna, Michoacán.
4. Mining towns: Usually found in the mountains where extreme topography resists the grid plan, such as Guanajuato, Pachuca, and Zacatecas.
5. Coastal towns: Here the coast acts as the dominant focal point of the town rather than the plaza, such as

in Antigua, Veracruz; Huatulco, Oaxaca; and San Blas, Nayarit.

To assess whether any of the sacred open spaces of pre-Columbian origin survived into the postconquest and viceregal eras, we focused our field research on communities that were in existence at the time of Spanish contact. For the sake of comparison, we also studied some examples of new towns for relocated native communities, or *reducciones*.

The origins of Spanish urban layouts in the New World can perhaps be traced to urban design principles established by the celebrated Roman architect Vitruvius in the first century BCE; or possibly to ideas being discussed by the urban designers of the Italian Renaissance, especially Alberti;[58] or even to the French bastides of the thirteenth century; or to the need to have a town layout that was expedient for military actions. The official policy of the Spanish Crown to design new towns in a grid or "checkerboard square" pattern emanating from a central open space or plaza did not become official until well into the latter quarter of the first century of Spanish colonization, when grid layouts were finally made official in 1573 during the reign of Phillip II. The document in which these instructions were decreed is known as "The Laws of the Indies" and will be addressed later.

First Acts and Encounters

When Spaniards founded a town, their first official act was to place a stone pillar in the space that would become the plaza. Bernal Díaz del Castillo reports the first such action to take place on the American continent, the founding of the Villa Rica de la Veracruz: "A pillar was placed in the plaza, and outside the village, a gallows."[59]

On the Spaniards' trek toward Tenochtitlan, one of the first large communities they encountered was Cempoala on the coast of the Gulf of Mexico. Díaz del Castillo describes the open spaces of this site in what is now the state of Veracruz: "Our field scouts who were on horseback arrived at the plaza and patios where the temples were located."[60]

He also supplies the first account of Mesoamerican plaza furnishings, describing what archaeologists now refer to as a *tzompantli*, or skullrack: "I remembered they had a plaza, where some altars were located, there were reams of dead skulls" (Fig. 2.12).[61]

In chronicling the conquest of Tenochtitlan,

2.12. *Tzompantli*, skullrack carved in stone at Chichén Itzá, Yucatán. Courtesy of the School of Architecture Visual Resources Collection, The University of Texas at Austin (Box-Wagner Collection, VRC 91-4855).

Bernal Díaz del Castillo describes the city's spaces, temples, and buildings, marveling at the magnificence of the Aztecs' plazas, the height of their buildings, and their great population. He gives particular attention to their stone craftsmanship, comparing the Aztec Empire's capital to the Plaza of Salamanca in his description.[62] He and others also mention both the huge scale and the orderliness of the Aztecs' plaza before Spanish reconstruction and afterward. The market plaza of Tlatelolco and the main plaza of Tenochtitlan "were said to be able to hold crowds of 50,000 to 60,000 each—some said 100,000."[63] In 1554, the Spaniard who would become rector of the new University in Mexico City exclaimed in his *Dialogues*:

> Now here is the plaza. Look carefully please, and note whether you have seen another which could equal it in size and grandeur. None that I can remember. Nor do I believe that its equal can be found in either hemisphere. Good heavens! how level it is! and how spacious! How gay! How greatly embellished by the superb and magnificent buildings that surround it on all sides! What order! What beauty! What a situation and location![64]

Other early Spaniards, mainly mendicant friars, also expressed their admiration for those Mesoamerican plazas and open spaces. Fray Toribio de Benavente, otherwise known by his Indian name, Motolinía,

wrote in his *Memoriales* (Memoirs) about many aspects of the native cultures he was encountering. In describing the characteristics of the temple precincts throughout the Mexican highlands, he refers to the plazas and open spaces with admiration, even as he expresses his horror and shock at the human sacrifices made to "devil gods" in those places:

> In all this land we find that they would make a big square in the best part of town, close to a crossbow shot from corner to corner in the biggest towns, and in the smaller towns, it was the length of a bow shot. The smaller the town, the smaller the court. They would enclose them with walls, keeping openings to the principal streets and roads, which they would build so they would lead to the court of the demon; and to give more honor to the temples, the roads would be laid out, one or two leagues, very straight by cord. It was a thing to see, from above, how the roads would come from the minor towns and neighborhoods straight to the court.[65]

One of the early official acts when establishing a new town or building over a native settlement was to construct an altar and then to erect a cross. Starting with Cortés's expedition, we learn from his chronicler Díaz del Castillo of the first instances where altars were built and crosses erected.[66] After the fall of Tenochtitlan, when the mendicant friars were sent out to the hinterlands to convert the native population, the process of re-urbanization occurs. Upon arriving at an existing settlement, the friars' first act was to erect a Christian cross at the summit of the main pyramid. Then the open space in front of the pyramid temples would be adapted for continued use for religious processions and rituals, this time Christian rather than Mesoamerican. In most cases, the dressed and artistically carved stone of the native temples was reused to build the new religious architecture, in which the Christian god was substituted for the native gods and the cross replaced the World Tree. Many rituals and their elements remained in continuous use. Once a primitive altar had been built, usually just a table under a thatched-roof structure, the friars were able to hold Mass until a more permanent altar and chapel were erected to protect the sacrament.

After erecting a cross and building an altar atop the sacred space—the primordial sea of Mesoamerican belief—but long before beginning construction of a church and convent, the friars would direct their new followers to build a wall around the sacred space to create a walled garden, a sacred patio, a paradise. The next development was to build small *posa* chapels at the four corners, which combined with the central cross to create the traditional quincunx form inherent in Mesoamerican religions, thereby reinforcing the sacredness of the space. This walled enclosure, referred to as a sacred patio by the friars and later termed an *atrio* by historians, became an outdoor church for the multitude of new converts. This was the space where teaching was done, where thousands were eventually baptized, and where religious services were held. Because a building would be too small to contain the many followers, and because the Mesoamerican tradition involved worshipping under the sky, not under a roof, the *atrio* provided the best setting for the new ritual. In the new form of liturgy created to fit this outdoor space, the clergy conducting the service would form a procession along the *via sacra*, which followed the perimeter of the *atrio*, pausing at the four corner *posa* chapels to address the crowds. Their route was counterclockwise, conveniently reinforcing the Mesoamerican preference for a counterclockwise movement around the four directions.[67] The altar and thatched roof gave rise to the open-air chapel, which to the natives symbolized the mouth of the cave, the maw of the Earth Monster god, the portal to the supernatural. Along with the four corner *posa* chapels and the axis mundi of the Christian cross, this quincunxial sacred space continued to be used in the postconquest era and still forms the geographical and spiritual center of most communities today.

As the open chapels, walled sacred patio, cross, and *posa* chapels became the center of the settlement, a secular patio or plaza developed just outside the new *atrio* walls. This became the market, the public gathering place, and the social center of the community as the town fused a new form, and in the early stages, it served as a *plaza de armas* for assembling troops. Mesoamerican settlements had been arranged around platforms and plazas, so the plaza was a natural setting—a sacred grouping of buildings and formation of space as discussed in Chapter One.

This secular plaza became the heart of the town where the Spanish concept of the new town layout began and generated a grid street plan for organization and division of private property, a change in the concept of land use for the Mesoamericans, who held agrarian land in common and lived on land often allo-cated by town authorities and by custom.[68] European-style streets to accommodate the wheeled carts and draft animals brought by the Spaniards were also new, unlike the native footpaths, causeways, and ceremonial paved roads called *sacbeob*.

The Spanish desire, eventually mandated by law, to place a wall around every piece of private property was quick to create streets and define outdoor open spaces, as Spanish settlers came and natives built in the new way. The churches and convents, as well as the *atrio*, served to create a rectilinear pattern on the land as the populace rebuilt its towns.

At the same time, permanent housing for the friars was created through the building of cloister convents. The cloister, another form of communal open space, became the patio for the friars, used for their private worship, with its passageways for movement and altars for contemplation. The cloister was the most sacred and private space in the hierarchy of communal open spaces in the town, which ranged from the secular plaza, *mercado*, and *plaza de armas* to the sacred *atrio* and the multitude of private family patios. After the cloister was finished, the church nave was finally built. This process and sequence was repeated at every settlement. The final church nave was the last building to be erected within the monastery complexes that were built in New Spain; in some cases, this construction sequence would take a century or more to complete.

The urban design and planning of Indian towns was executed by the friars, who made sure, for the most part, that the religious monastery-*atrio*-church complex dominated the newly crafted open space overlaid on the original ceremonial center.[69]

In the mid-sixteenth century, Fray Diego de Landa, the controversial Franciscan friar, marveled at the vast architectural inventory he was finding in Yucatán, particularly the open spaces in the center of each community. Landa talks almost gushingly about the beauty of the plazas:

> . . . and in the town's center . . . beautiful plazas. . . . And the grouping of their buildings, temples, palaces and pyramids . . . were not set along streets and avenues as in European cities . . . but rather around plazas and courts.[70]

Besides admiring their beauty, Landa makes a very important observation that alludes to a fundamental difference between European and Mesoamerican open spaces. Streets as we know them in the Western world were nonexistent in Mesoamerica except for a few examples: the highly ceremonial walkway found at Maya sites, known as the *sacbe*, literally "white road"; the ceremonial causeways that connected architectural groupings, as at Tikal; the causeways over water needed to reach the sacred island precinct of Tenochtitlan; and the long, narrow, multilevel string of rectangular plazas known, erroneously, as the Avenue of the Dead at Teotihuacan.[71] One might be tempted to attribute this fundamental difference to the fact that pack animals and wheeled vehicles were unknown in Mesoamerica, which might eliminate the need for streets.

In European towns, one moves around by way of streets; in Mesoamerican urban centers, open space is traversed to reach an urban destination. Urban centers in Mesoamerica attempt to re-create the world on a smaller scale. A grand plaza or platform is formed from a series of interconnected, seemingly amorphous widespread open spaces that include within them other specifically shaped open volumes. These open volumes are given shape by solid masses with little or no interior space. As noted, the Mesoamerican metaphor—a crocodile swimming in a lake, with the ridges on his back symbolizing the mountain ranges of the earth, and the plaza, a lake, sea, or lagoon studded with hilly islands that are temple pyramids and other buildings—is re-created at every site. In Mesoamerica, plazas were shaped and punctuated by sacred buildings, and together they formed the setting for ritual. Streets as we know them came with the Spaniards.

Within a handful of years after the fall of Tenochtitlan, the Spanish Crown embarked on an unprecedented campaign to conquer, settle, and colonize the newfound territories of New Spain and beyond, mainly in South America and the Philippines. Even before founding settlements on the mainland of the American continent, the Spaniards implemented a specific urban design plan for the foundation of settlements on some of the recently discovered and settled islands in the Caribbean. The plan consisted of laying out streets in a grid pattern emanating from a central open space known by the Spanish term *plaza*.[72]

Starting with Tenochtitlan, the defeated capital of the Aztec Empire, and soon spreading to other Mesoamerican population centers in central and southern Mexico, the Spanish colonization effort began in earnest. The largest campaign of town founding the world would ever experience had begun.

LAWS OF THE INDIES

The size of the plaza should be proportionate to the number of inhabitants, keeping in mind that in native settlements, since they are new, the intention is that they will grow, and therefore the plaza should be planned for population growth. The plaza shall be no less than 200 feet wide by 300 feet long, nor larger than 800 feet long by 530 feet wide. A medium-size plaza with good proportions is 600 feet long by 400 feet wide.

Laws of the Indies, Ordinance 113[73]

The royal decree that eventually delineated the policy and practices for Spanish colonization of the New World, published and made official in 1573, was a document known as the Laws of the Indies. In the section that established the physical parameters for urban layouts, the shape, dimensions, and orientations of the open space or plaza and the surrounding street grid were clearly specified. The desired proportion for the central plaza was that the length be twice the width. If one were to follow layout instructions in the Laws of the Indies to the letter, towns would look like the prototype shown in Fig. 2.13. However, our field research indicated that, early on, the overlay, or superimposition, of the Spanish urban design for colonization in the New World differed from the rigid formality established in the Laws of the Indies in cases where preexisting towns were refounded by the Spanish. Our documentation indicates that many of these town layouts did incorporate, or adapt to, the existing open spaces of native ceremonial centers and

2.13. Laws of the Indies prototype town. Drawing by Logan Wagner.

therefore became implicitly tied to features of the natural landscapes. To understand more clearly the founding of towns in the New World by the Spanish, we must look at the basic mission that motivated them: Christianizing the Mesoamericans.

CONVERSION

With the discovery of America, the growing Spanish Empire was faced with an unprecedented opportunity to exploit the riches of these newfound lands, and indeed they did. Unlimited material and human resources were readily available. In the Age of Discovery, Spain and Portugal became the two military and economic superpowers that controlled the newly discovered world in its spherical totality. Both Christian-based monarchies adhered to papal decrees from the Vatican.

The charter mission, besides conquest, wealth, and power, was to convert the indigenous population, bringing it into the Spanish Catholic fold. Perhaps this served to justify the plunder of conquest and colonization in the minds of the Spaniards. To this end, the Spanish royalty selected the mendicant orders to convert and protect the native indigenous population from the Spanish civil population and practices.[74]

Although several military battles occurred after the initial fall of Tenochtitlan in 1521, the conquest of New Spain was for the most part a spiritual conquest. Believing they were on a sacred quest to spread the life of Christianity, to build the New Jerusalem, mendicant friars made personal contact with the indigenous population.

Hernán Cortés soon realized, after defeating the Aztec emperor, that missionaries were desperately needed to convert the vast multitudes of the indigenous population. In 1524, Cortés knelt reverently on the Tacubaya causeway leading into Tenochtitlan to welcome the first symbolic twelve friars of the Franciscan Order, led by Martín de Valencia. In addition to missionaries, tools were needed for the conversion. Utilizing the existing ceremonial centers of the conquered as a tool in converting them to the religion of the conquerors was a common practice throughout ancient history. Evidence of Christianity employing these practices can be traced to Roman times: the Romans themselves had built temples over Greek sacred shrines as well. In the seventh century, Pope

2.14. Coatzintla, Veracruz, celebration of the Festival of St. James the Greater, July 1991, in the *atrio*.
Courtesy of George O. Jackson, Jr.

Gregory I decreed that the pagan temples of the newly conquered British Isles be remodeled into Christian churches and shrines.[75]

In Mesoamerica it was common for rulers to build their new temples over existing temples. Linda Schele referred to the process of uncovering these superimposed temples through archaeological digs as "peeling layers of onion skins."[76] When the Mesoamericans lost the battle against the invading Spanish conquerors, they must have expected the Spanish friars who took over administration of towns to build their own shrines and churches atop the native temples and pyramids. Incorporating native religious ceremonial open space into the architectural setting of the new Christian temple served the friars well in the effort to convert the Native American population.

In describing the process of acculturation that occurred at the beginning of the colonial period, anthropologist Klor de Alva states that the crucial first decades after the Spanish invasion involved the continued use of ceremonial open space. In his analysis, Klor de Alva establishes three phases of Indian acculturation to Spanish and Western reign. The first, from 1521 to 1560, can be characterized by a dominant labor force provided by the *encomienda* system, a lack of word borrowing, and extensive participation in public Christian ceremonies. In describing the first phase, he emphasizes this continuity in the ceremonial use of open space:

2.15. Mochitlan, Guerrero, ceremony with bull masks in the open space of the *atrio*. Courtesy of George O. Jackson, Jr.

2.16. Ixmiquilpan, mural of battle between Aztec jaguar and eagle warriors in the nave of San Miguel Arcángel; an example of native art and ritual used to support the conversion effort. Susan Kline Morehead.

I propose, then, that the first "triumphant" decades registered by Fray Toribio (de Benavente) Motolinía (1971, 1973), Fray Pedro de Gante, and others represented the continuation of precontact patterns of state-level religious rationalization, organization, and extensive use of public ceremonial space.[77]

As stated in the Mesoamerican chapter, outdoor ritual formed the essential core of Mesoamerican religion. To facilitate conversion efforts, the mendicant friars allowed the continued integration of native customs of open-air processions and dancing ceremonies as part of the religious ceremony. Usually deemed harmless, or even helpful in the conversion effort, many of the native rituals were allowed to continue as a way of ameliorating the impact of the new imposed religion on the defeated native inhabitants.[78] Such rituals have continued into the present time (Figs. 2.14–2.15).

It is now becoming more evident that the mendicant friars deliberately used similarities and coincidences to aid in the effort of conversion, especially when it came to religious dates, symbols, and rituals (Fig. 2.16). This phenomenon has recently been termed "expedient selection" by Sam Edgerton.[79]

QUINCUNX PATIOS

With Spain having just reconquered its homeland after eight hundred years of Moorish dominance, the Spanish friars erroneously believed that all infidels were alike, used to worshipping in the architectural setting of an Islamic mosque. The Spanish demonstrated this thinking when they built the first structures for taking care of the native population's spiritual needs in Mexico-Tenochtitlan and the sacred city of Cholula. These first "open chapels" were uncannily similar to the mosques they had left behind in Spain. The chapel San José de los Naturales at the Franciscan base in what is now downtown Mexico City has unfortunately long been lost. The Capilla Real in Cholula, Puebla, on the other hand, still exists and is in active use to this day (Fig. 2.17). Both were built with a plan consisting of an array of columns and arches that form bays. McAndrew reports two other mosque-type chapels at Jilotepec and Toluca.[80]

Once they realized that Mesoamerican culture, religion, and art were very different from the Islamic

2.17. Cholula, Capilla Real interior reminiscent of the mosque of Córdoba, Spain. Courtesy of the School of Architecture Visual Resources Collection, The University of Texas at Austin (Box-Wagner Collection, VRC 92-3968).

religion and culture of the Moors that they had left behind in Spain, Spanish friars began incorporating Mesoamerican ceremonial open space, rituals, and processions into the otherwise rigid architectural format of convents and churches. The Mesoamericans had worshipped in open sacred spaces because their gods were rooted in the natural world and, to a lesser extent, because they lived in a hospitable climate and lacked the technology to build large covered spaces. While the friars possessed the technology required to build these large structures, they were attempting to convert such large numbers of natives that they needed to use the open, sacred patios to accommodate the vast crowds. The natives did not want to leave their sacred ground, their primordial sea, for nonsacred ground, so it made the most sense for the friars to locate their sacred patios or *atrios* on the ground that the natives already held sacred.

As noted in the Mesoamerican chapter, recent advances in the fields of Mesoamerican archaeology, art history, epigraphy, and linguistics seem to suggest that the concept that the world is divided into the four cardinal directions or intercardinal points at the earthly level of reality lies at the core of Mesoamerican religious thinking and philosophy.[81] At the center of this quadrangular arrangement stands a World Tree, or axis mundi, connecting the earth-level reality with the supernatural reality of the heavens above and the Underworld below. This concept, when manifested in

2.18. Pedro de Gante at the center of a quincunx, from the Codex Osuna. Nettie Lee Benson Latin American Collection, University of Texas Libraries, The University of Texas at Austin.

2.19. Engraving of the ideal *atrio* in *Rhetorica Christiana* by Diego Valadés, 1579. Nettie Lee Benson Latin American Collection, University of Texas Libraries, The University of Texas at Austin.

to the unique combination of architectural elements and open space that included the *atrio* quincunx, open chapels, *atrio* walls, and triumphal arched entries as the "architecture of conversion." The creation of sixteenth-century church patios is arguably the most palpable evidence of the incorporation of native Mesoamerican open space into the prescribed Spanish urban layouts. To whom should we attribute this conversion strategy, which proved so successful? Archival evidence tends to point to Fray Pedro de Gante (Peter of Ghent), half brother to King Charles V, as the person responsible for this approach. One of the original three missionaries to arrive following the conquest of Tenochtitlan, Pedro de Gante took on the conversion task with characteristic missionary zeal. He quickly taught himself the native languages of highland Mexico like Nahuatl and Otomi and then set out to learn as much as possible about the native culture and customs. Pedro de Gante, along with other dedicated early friars, sought to convert the native peoples by adapting his teaching method to the culture, incorporating native rituals and sacred space into the Catholic setting and ritual.

The Codex Osuna, created soon after the conquest, depicts Pedro de Gante himself at the center of a quincunxial arrangement (Fig. 2.18). Each of the *posa* chapels represented was cared for by members of the town's four neighborhoods, or *calpullis*. This corroborated, perhaps, Gante's identification of quincunx beliefs and their reimplementation as a successful ritualistic symbolism in the aid of the conversion effort. In 1579, an Indian student of Fray Pedro de Gante, Diego de Valadés, published an engraving of the prototype for the layout of church patios and their suggested uses (Fig. 2.19).[82] By midcentury, the architectural prototype for church patios was circulating among all three mendicant orders working in New Spain. Each order experimented with this new arrangement of known architectural elements. Examples of this layout are also found in South America and even occasionally in the Philippines, but never in the numbers to be found in New Spain.

A good example of a quincunxial *atrio* with all the elements of the architecture of conversion extant is found in the Franciscan house in Atlatlahuacan, Morelos (see Fig. 3.31, next chapter). The Relación Geográfica of Atlatlahuacan reinforces the importance of the quincunxial centering of each community: each town in the vicinity is represented as a quincunxial

the artistic corpus throughout Mesoamerican culture and history, is known as quincunx. When the three initial mendicant orders came to the New World to undertake the epic conversion of a whole new race, sacred patios became the postconquest version of the pre-Hispanic quincunx court.

The quadrangular open forecourts found in the sixteenth-century churches of Mexico, usually called *atrios*, but also sometimes *patios* or even *corrals* in the early colonial period, tend to indicate that the mendicant friars intentionally incorporated the quincunx ritual space and ceremonies into the missionary monastery complexes through the combination of the requisite corner chapels, known as *posas*, and the central *atrio* cross. Architectural historians often refer

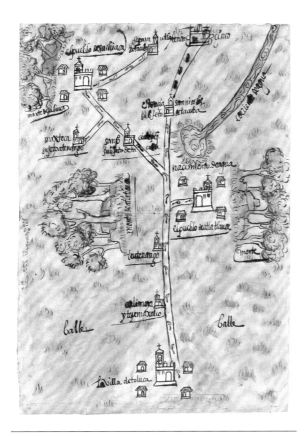

2.20. Relación Geográfica of Atlatlahuacan. Nettie Lee Benson Latin American Collection, University of Texas Libraries, The University of Texas at Austin.

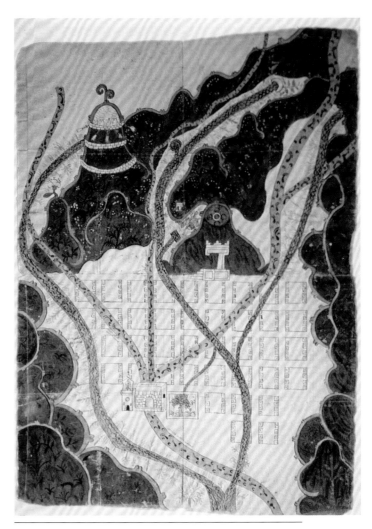

2.21. Relación Geográfica of Texupan. Collection of the Real Academia de la Historia, Madrid.

whole with four *calpullis*, or neighborhood chapels, around the central main church of the community (Fig. 2.20).

RELACIONES GEOGRÁFICAS

To understand the nature and aspects of his territories in the New World, which he was never able to visit, in the 1570s King Philip II ordered surveys and questionnaires to be circulated throughout New Spain. The questionnaire, consisting of twenty questions, delved into aspects of the economic, political, and social makeup of each area of New Spain. To accompany the questionnaires, informants were asked to develop maps of each of the areas in question. Created using a combination of European and Native American cartographic practices, the Relaciones Geográficas (RGs) are a treasure trove of information about the communities described and their surrounding landscapes. They literally present a culture's view of its settlements. Close observation of some of the maps reveals a prolif-

eration of Mesoamerican concepts that continued to survive well into the colonial period.

Altepetl representations abound, just as in pre-Columbian times; communities are depicted by *altepetl* symbols, each with a unique logograph defining the community. Also of interest is the continued use of native graphic symbols for rivers, bodies of water, and other topographic features. Paths, as in Mesoamerican art and documents, are shown as ribbons with footsteps. In some cases, and in an apparent concession to new ways of locomotion brought by the colonizers, they are shown with horseshoe prints. In many instances, towns are depicted with the checkerboard grid of the Spanish urban layout overlaying the existing native communities. Particularly interesting is the continuation of quincunx symbolism as a necessary reality of the confirmation of the existence and center-

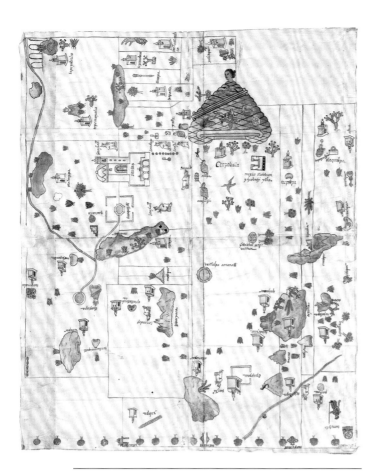

2.22. Relación Geográfica of Cempoala. Note plaza shown as source of water. Nettie Lee Benson Latin American Collection, University of Texas Libraries, The University of Texas at Austin.

ing of every community. The quincunx is present on the summit of the hill beside the main community in the RG of Texupan, Oaxaca (Fig. 2.21).

Perhaps most telling in our study of open space is the evidence that the open spaces of each community—the plazas and church *atrios*—are the symbols necessary to acknowledge the existence of each community. The evidence is overwhelming. Most of the Relaciones Geográficas we studied show each community as a combination of church and court, the colonial continuation of the *altepetl* concept and symbolism. Confirming the importance of open spaces, we find that many of the RGs present either the *atrio* or the plaza as the source of water and abundance, be it in the form of the Mesoamerican symbol for a water spring or the European drawing of a fountain or well. Such is the case in the RGs of Yuririapundaro (Yuriria), Cempoala (Fig. 2.22), Iztapalapa (Fig. 2.23), Texupan, Zacatlan, and Acapistla (Yecapixtla) (Fig. 2.24). The *altepetls*, or native toponyms, in many

cases are also located in the town's open spaces, such as the *atrio* or plaza, as in Guaxtepec (Fig. 2.25) and Culhuacan (Fig. 2.26). The correlation between native and European understanding is maintained in that the *altepetl*, or water mountain, of each pre-Hispanic community is represented in the ceremonial center with the pyramid as mountain and the plaza as water source; when transposed into viceregal or colonial times, the church becomes the mountain, the colonial plaza the water source. The inclusion of fountains or water spouts in the colonial plazas seems to corroborate the "watery nature" of the plaza/open space of the community.

In many cases, the RGs, in an apparent concession to power sharing, indicate Spanish churches and/or civil government buildings sharing the plaza with native temples, such as in Culhuacan, Iztapalapa, and Amoltepec (Fig. 2.27). This occurs most notably in the *Relación de Tlaxcala* (or Tlaxcala Codex), where

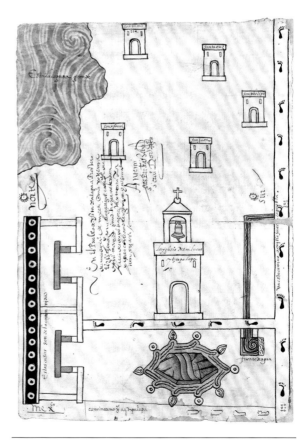

2.23. Relación Geográfica of Iztapalapa. Note plaza shown as source of water. Nettie Lee Benson Latin American Collection, University of Texas Libraries, The University of Texas at Austin.

2.24. Relación Geográfica of Acapistla [Yecapixtla]. Nettie Lee Benson Latin American Collection, University of Texas Libraries, The University of Texas at Austin.

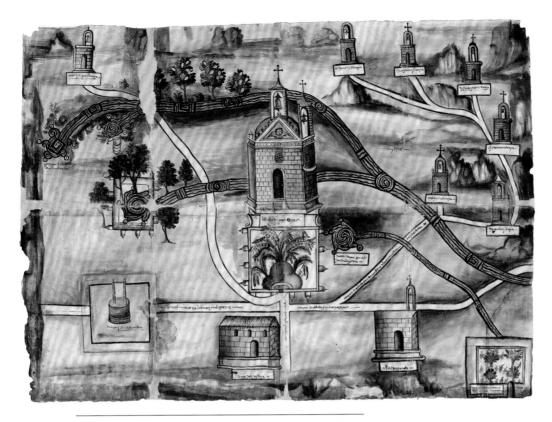

2.25. Relación Geográfica of Guaxtepec. Note *altepetl* in plaza. Nettie Lee Benson Latin American Collection, University of Texas Libraries, The University of Texas at Austin.

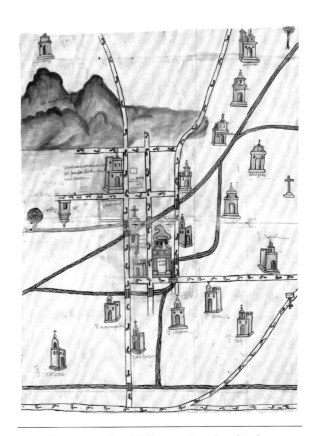

2.26. Relación Geográfica of Culhuacan. Note *altepetl* in plaza. Nettie Lee Benson Latin American Collection, University of Texas Libraries, The University of Texas at Austin.

two sides of the rectangular *plaza mayor* are bordered by European buildings and the other two sides by decidedly native architecture (Fig. 2.28). In the case of the Misquiahuala (Atengo) RG, three native temples form the classic U-shaped court referenced earlier (Fig. 2.29).

One of the most informative and beautiful of the Relaciones Geográficas is the one created for the sacred city of Cholula, a strongly indigenous city in the modern state of Puebla. The Cholula RG (Fig. 2.30) is a rich combination of both European and indigenous architectural, topographic, and urban symbols. The Spanish orthogonal urban grid is immediately obvious, a perfect checkerboard consisting of a grid of five-by-five city blocks. The main temple of Cholula is located in the upper right-hand city block. The pre-Hispanic *altepetl* for Cholula is presented in the block to the left of the temple, in the center of what must have been the Mesoamerican plaza. On top of the *altepetl* is the horn representing Saint Gabriel, the patron saint of Cholula. The Spanish plaza without an *altepetl*, at the center of the RG, is surrounded by European architecture, with the convent church of San Gabriel taking the principal role.

If we isolate the hills that represent the native temples, it is obvious that the resulting native urban open space was vast. The Spanish urban grid that was overlaid adapted to the existing structures; the more elongated blocks are presumably shaped to contain an existing native temple. The Spanish urban designer who laid out the grid in Cholula was left with ample urban open space, allowing for the uncharacteristically large main plaza comprising two full city blocks. The monastery church of San Gabriel enjoys a small rectangular *atrio*, and the open chapel of the Capilla Real next to it a much larger *atrio*. Finally, the typical layout of residential lots within a Spanish New World town allows each long, thin lot to have the residence fronting the street while the open spaces of patios and orchards extend toward the center of each block. These open spaces are not evident when walking the streets of typical Spanish towns in the New World, but site plans like the Cholula RG or aerial photographs show that, in essence, each city block is a large open space enclosed by the structures of the contiguous residences.

With this background, an understanding of the Mesoamerican sense of communal open space, and access to the ethnohistorical documents, we can proceed to an analysis of the open spaces that we were able to document in our field study.

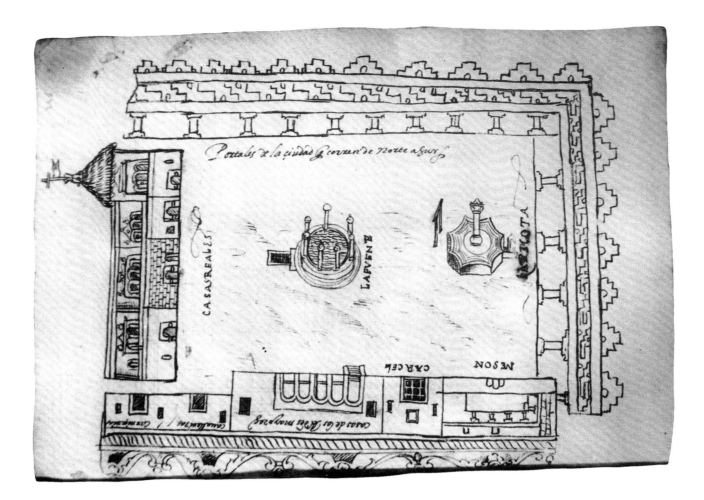

Portales de la ciudad ق corren de norte a sur

CASAS REALES

LA FUENTE

PICOTA

MESON

CARCEL

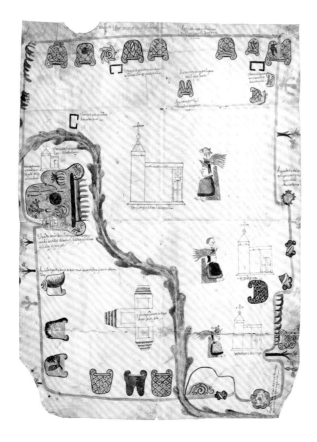

2.28. Tlaxcala, from *Descripción de la ciudad y provincia de Tlaxcala* by Diego Muñoz Camargo. Note buildings depicted in indigenous style on one side of plaza and in Spanish style on the other. Nettie Lee Benson Latin American Collection, University of Texas Libraries, The University of Texas at Austin; Bridgeman Art Library.

2.29. Relación Geográfica of Misquiahuala (Atengo). Nettie Lee Benson Latin American Collection, University of Texas Libraries, The University of Texas at Austin.

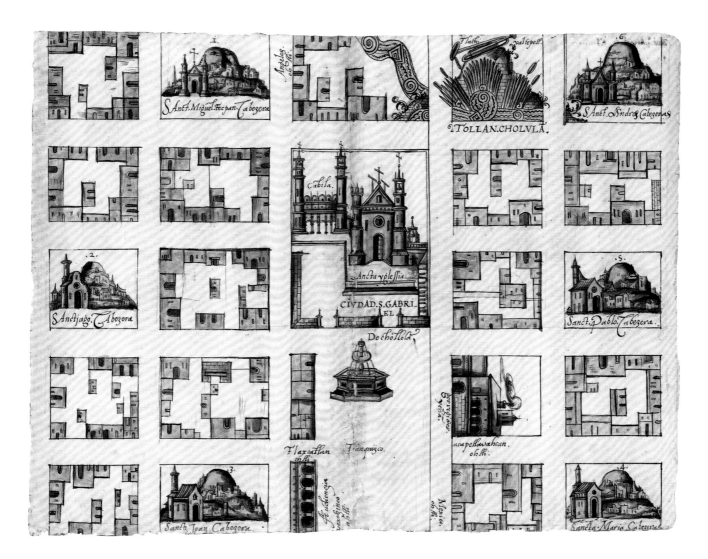

2.30. Relación Geográfica of Cholula. Nettie Lee Benson Latin
American Collection, University of Texas Libraries, The
University of Texas at Austin.

CHAPTER THREE

SIXTEENTH-CENTURY COMMUNAL OPEN SPACES
(FIVE HUNDRED YEARS LATER)

Arriving at a site always had its surprises. There were no prior arrangements possible, we were usually welcomed, but occasionally we startled a community by arriving unannounced. One time, the town's loudspeaker, mounted on a pole in their plaza, announced that everyone should come to the church to protect it from strangers invading the *atrio*. Another time, people threw our equipment back into our truck thinking we were going to build a road through their church, though the next day their mayor sought us out in a neighboring village to apologize and invite us back. On yet another occasion, a cautious crowd was won over when I showed them movies I had just taken of their children. The encounter that scared us most was in a Maya village deep in the jungle where we were greeted with a street full of residents waving machetes. Yet each day was a marvelous experience, appreciating the architecture and getting to know the town and a few of its people.

Hal Box, 1990

With the scholarship and field observations of earlier generations in hand, such as work done by Manuel Toussaint, George Kubler, John McAndrew, Elizabeth Wilder Weisman, and others, we organized our teams to examine sixteenth-century towns formed by the fusion of Mesoamerican and Spanish planning concepts. It seemed appropriate to expand the previous scholarship by considering the interior of the church and the public plaza as two extensions of the sacred open space, the primordial sea. We did so by making measured architectural drawings and taking photographs, while absorbing the experience of being in those special places and understanding the history as well as we could. We also sought to discover other sites of note in our field research to broaden the knowledge of these phenomena of urban design and provide information to aid in their preservation.

As has previously been discussed, the actual fusion of the two disparate civilizations manifested itself in the friars' building of Spanish towns superimposed on established Mesoamerican towns with a conceptual base in both cultures. After the military conquest, these friars made the actual conquest of the Mesoamericans as they sought to convert the native population to Christianity and protect them from exploitation by Spanish settlers. The friars found that in order to establish places for Christian worship, they had to build on existing sacred ground—the symbolic primordial

sea where the Mesoamerican gods and ancestors lived, where their temples stood. This need to respect and maintain the Mesoamericans' spiritual values in the process of conversion produced a certain amount of fusion between the two belief systems that is evident in the art and architecture created during the early period of Spanish occupation.

Respect for spiritual values did not extend to the preservation of existing religious buildings. Reusing the stones of the temples to build new churches was not only a tradition of conquerors but also decreed by Charles V. To understand what happened to Mesoamerican spaces as Europeans remade them, we set out to document the central areas of towns and communities known to have been founded in sixteenth-century New Spain. As expected, we discovered that the more remote and less economically developed communities were the least altered from their original layouts, allowing us to imagine more clearly what they would have been like in the sixteenth century. Using simple surveying instruments such as compass, alidade, plane table, and measuring tapes, students and Earthwatch volunteers under our supervision and instruction produced urban plans to scale.[1] The plans that we produced are much more accurate than the published drawings that we encountered along the way, which were often idealized, yet our plans are intended to offer accurate observations for study purposes and are not

3.1. Legend for measured drawings

Major Spaces	Upper Case Letters		Secondary Spaces	Lower Case Letters		North Arrow
Atrio	A		Atrio Cross	ac		
Cloister	C		Capilla Abierta	ca		
Huerta	H		Capilla	c		
Jardín	J		Cantina	ct		
Mercado	M		Fountain	f		
Nave	N		Kiosko	k		
Plaza	PL		Palacio Municipal	pm		
			Posa	po		0 10m
			Portales	pp		10 meters or
			Portal	p		32.81 feet
			Stations of the Cross	sc		diameter
			Tienda	t		
			Via Sacra	vs		

intended as legal surveys in any way. The plan elements are shown in the legend (Fig. 3.1). Centered on the plaza, the urban plans include the blocks around the plaza, along with any other open spaces, to help us understand the shapes of the architectural spaces and the street patterns. We also sought to detect any changes that had been made to the friars' layouts over time. Scale urban plans were complemented with photographs of the architecture shaping these spaces, mainly churches and government buildings. On some rare occasions, when budget would allow, we were able to take aerial photographs. The completed surveys are included here in Chapter Three and in the appendix. These and additional surveys are housed in the Visual Resources Collection of the School of Architecture at the University of Texas at Austin. The communities we will present in this publication are those that we believe best illustrate a possible continued use of open space from Mesoamerican ceremonial centers to modern times.

The towns described in this chapter provide a sampling of the ninety towns that we surveyed with measured drawings over twelve summers. We chose three sites to illustrate certain design issues in detail: Sacromonte to explain the significance of the cave and illustrate the passion of building, Calpan to underscore the profound symbolism of the sunken court coupled with the indigenous iconography embedded in the Christian art used in teaching the new religion, and

Izamal to illustrate the ways in which the Spaniards capitalized on the monumental Mesoamerican setting to enhance the conversion process. We present them here with descriptions of our encounters and our architectural analysis of the individual towns that were formed during the active fusion of cultures in the sixteenth century.

CAVES AND CREVICES

As noted in Chapter One, caves and other openings in the earth's crust were viewed as highly sacred spots on the landscape, natural portals to the supernatural world. It is no coincidence that some of the most prominent pilgrimage churches in Mexico were built over preexisting temples and ceremonial centers located in caves, canyons, or other natural openings on the earth's surface.

Perhaps the most famous example of a church built over a cave is found on the Hill of Tepeyac, northeast of Mexico City, site of the shrine dedicated to the patroness of Mexico, the Virgin of Guadalupe. Legend states that Guadalupe appeared several times to the Indian Juan Diego in December of 1531, and on the last appearance, she manifested as an image on his white cape.[2] Viewing and honoring this shroud image is the ultimate goal of hundreds of thousands of pilgrims who visit the now-expanded shrine complex each year. Built on top of a temple dedicated to the cave-dwelling Mesoamerican earth goddess Tonantzin, this site, known to locals and foreigners as "La Villa," has become the most important religious pilgrimage site in the Americas.[3]

The church of Señor de Chalma in the modern state of Mexico draws enormous crowds of devotees as well (Fig. 3.2). The church we find today at Chalma is located over a cave. The town built around the shrine is at the bottom of a topographic bowl formed by the hills that surround it. To arrive at the shrine, remodeled in the neoclassic style, one must descend steep pedestrian streets culminating at the bottom in a large court in front of the church. Flanking one side of the quadrangle is a three-story building housing rooms for pilgrims. Opposite this flank and protected by a guard-rail wall is a precipice. The waters of the Chalma River running below are believed to be sacred, and like the sacred Ganges River in Calcutta, India, the Chalma attracts pilgrims seeking to bathe in these miraculously curative waters. Rather than document these popular pilgrimage sites, we chose a little-known but very special site that began with a cave.

Sacromonte, the first site we documented, is a hilltop pilgrimage site with a spiritual history that spans over five hundred years. It began as a preconquest Chichimeca temple site, became the meditation cave of the one of the first Franciscan friars, and was later elaborated into a series of buildings that exemplify the art of architecture without architects, an art that we seek to describe in this example.

3.2. Pilgrimage site of Señor de Chalma. Courtesy of the School of Architecture Visual Resources Collection, The University of Texas at Austin (Box-Wagner Collection, VRC 89-2366).

Amecameca, State of México: El Señor de Sacromonte

J.B. Johnson led me to Sacromonte for my first experience in sixteenth-century Nueva España, where, overlooking the ancient town of Amecameca, eating a blue-corn taco and drinking a cold beer, I fell in love with the place and its history. A few months later, I arrived with Logan, J.B., and a team of fifteen Earthwatch volunteers to document the site, starting with a temple and cave that had been sacred to the Mesoamericans before being adapted as a meditation place by one of the first friars, Fray Martín de Valencia. It became sanctified by the locals as a pilgrimage site built in stages over a period of four centuries.

The documentation of Sacromonte was special to us for many reasons, not only because it was the first of nearly one hundred sites that we examined, or because it had a spectacular view of the snow-capped volcano Popocatépetl, but also because we made arrangements with the nuns to have them prepare our lunch for each day of our ten-day stay. The mundane activity of having lunch became an almost mystical experience in the penumbra of the dimly lit refectory in the nunnery. As the nuns in their flowing habits entered the refectory carrying plates of food, we could almost hear Gregorian chants in the background. Adding to the mystique of the place was an unforgettable character, a young man who rang the church bells. He climbed up the dome into a small space without a floor near the top of the bell tower. He would swing the enormous half-ton cast bronze bells by hand. After starting the seemingly perpetual swing on the first bell, he would jump out of the way, as nimbly as a cat, onto the ledge of the arched opening in the bell tower to initiate the swing of another, adjacent bell. Then, after he had carefully synchronized the tolling of all three bells while avoiding being hit by any of them, his efforts would treat the townspeople of Amecameca to an exciting cacophony of bells announcing Mass. Reminiscent of Victor Hugo's novel about the cathedral of Notre Dame, our star performer was also a hunchback. I climbed the dome and tower once to ring the bells, but was only able to ring two bells faintly at a time.

Hal Box, 1986

The group of sacred structures and artifacts located on the hill overlooking the town of Amecameca, called Cerro de Sacromonte, forms a composite expression of over five hundred years of religious ritual in the central plateau of Mesoamerica. Shaped over time by forces from disparate cultures, this architecture, developed by the hands and minds of both Native Americans and Europeans, creates dramatic settings of communal open space for evolving rituals.

Mesoamerican and Mexican architecture, which lies outside the mainstream of Western architectural history, confounds the casual observer with apparently unrelated forms that are either entirely alien or only indirectly attributable to the familiar Greco-Roman tradition. In addition to forms born in Mesoamerica's rich ancient culture, three Mexican ideas are added to the tradition: *conjunto*, *mestizo*, and *anastilo*. The term *conjunto* refers to a joined ensemble of parts formed from ideas happening at the same time and place, often drawn from vastly different, contrasting, or conflicting forms, colors, styles, or sounds. *Mestizo* describes an impure hybrid of ideas and forms, a mixture that transforms the original parts into something different. *Anastilo* describes an absence of style or an unidentifiable style, often referring to something that is out of stylistic progression and particular to a place. These three ideas present an architecture that will become apparent as we explore Sacromonte.[4]

An analysis of the way the unpretentious site of Sacromonte developed over an extended period of time will help provide insight into the intentions of the builders as they developed physical designs for metaphysical ritual space. The architecture of Mexico presents powerful examples of how indigenous culture was fused with the advanced technology of the Europeans. While skilled artisans executed some of the architecture handsomely, with glorious stylistic interpretations, much of the building simply gives form to the intentions of the friars or priests responsible, who were instructing the available workmen. While the early friars were well educated and knowledgeable about architecture, and sometimes achieved works of incredible skill and daring, the majority of the buildings in Nueva España were peripheral works in small villages or special *santuarios* such as those on Sacromonte. We propose that the study of church building at this level can enable an intimate understanding of architecture that is just as rewarding as the study of cathedrals.

In Mesoamerica, evolution and revolution generated architectural form and space for ritual, creating layers of meaning. Spaces for ceremonies in paths, clearings, platforms, and caves evolved into causeways, pyramids, and temples, which then developed into sacred ways, *atrios*, *posas*, and open chapels. Revolutions in culture, style, iconography, and technology from the advanced civilizations of Mesoamerica to those of Europe dramatically imposed new beliefs and capabilities. Most significantly, the large enclosed spaces that Europeans could build presented spectacular new opportunities for rituals with enormous visual power and acoustics never before heard outside of large caves.

This architectural undertaking can be examined in three types of progressions: chronological, cultural, and spatial. The chronological progression concerns people and ideas changing through time: from Formative to Late Postclassic Mesoamerican, to European influences, to the present. Parallel to the chronological, the cultural progression concerns the cultural needs for ritual space generated by custom and enabled by technology, a process of development that moves from open clearings and sacred caves to vaulted edifices. The third function, spatial progression, is the progression of movement through ritual sequences, ascending from the village in the valley to the top of Cerro de Sacromonte, and then extending in space to a distant alignment with an Aztec solstice stone placed on the western slope of Volcán Iztaccíhuatl, thirty miles away.

Chronological Progression

The chronological progression of Cerro de Sacromonte begins with its creation from volcanic activity, as the hill is a cinder cone formed from ash. It is likely that Cerro de Sacromonte began to be used for ritual because of its location on the plain below Iztaccíhuatl, its gentle slopes that allow ascension, and its commanding view of the valley below. Furthermore, Sacromonte, 400 feet above the plain, completes a mystical triangle with the two snow-capped volcanoes Iztaccíhuatl and Popocatépetl, a topographic triad centering.

The first type of ritualistic use of the hill may have involved simply a clearing in the woods used for ceremonies to invoke the gods, enhanced perhaps by music, dancing, chanting, stimulants, and hallucinogens. These rituals still happen on the back of the hill.[5]

In addition, caves (Fig. 3.3), easily formed by the action of water in the volcanic ash of the hill, offered shelter as well as ritual space for nomads and early inhabitants of the village of Amequemecan (Amecameca) established in 1268 by the Chichimecas.[6] One such *chalchiumomozco*, Nahuatl for "cave on a hill," forms the continuing central element of the complex at Sacromonte.

3.3. Sacromonte; cave formations in the volcanic ash can be read as sacred portals to the Underworld. Hal Box.

A Toltec, then later Aztec, temple, Teteoinán, allegedly occupied the top of the hill.[7] This temple would have been accompanied by a causeway from the village to the temple, perhaps along the path of the later *via sacra*.

The temple, if there was one, could have been destroyed by direct order of Hernán Cortés himself in 1519. Cortés, with his small band of Spanish forces and allied Indian armies, spent more than a little time in the village of Amequemecan, mostly at the base of Cerro de Sacromonte, during his first march into the Valley of Mexico toward Tenochtitlan.[8] Since it was Cortés's custom to destroy old religious icons in the temples and replace them with new Christian icons,[9] any temple on Sacromonte could have been partially destroyed on Cortés's first visit.

The second significant Spanish visitor to Sacromonte found a cave to use for meditation, just as his mentor, Saint Francis of Assisi, had done in Italy.[10] This Franciscan, Fray Martín de Valencia (1474–1534),[11] was the central figure in the history of Sacromonte and the leader of that extraordinary group of friars known as "the Twelve" who arrived upon orders of Charles V in 1524.[12] Pope Hadrian VI had authorized the Franciscans to handle the conversion of Nueva España.[13] So important was Fray Martín de Valencia that when the Twelve arrived at Tenochtitlan in 1524, Cortés went to welcome them, accompanied by his most important officials and by scores of conquistadors and Indian lords, all carrying wooden crosses. Cortés advanced five hundred paces on his knees, took off his hat, and threw down his cape for Fray Martín de Valencia to walk upon, in symbolic imitation of Christ's entry into Jerusalem on the first Palm Sunday.[14] During the time that he lived in the cave on Sacromonte, Fray Martín de Valencia became beloved by the Indians for his miracle-working powers.

A legend about a mule forms the next chronological step in the building of Sacromonte. In the legend, a mule carrying a life-size reclining image of Christ ran away from a pack train in Sacromonte to the mouth of the sacred cave used by Fray Martín de Valencia. The mule refused to budge until the image was removed. The Indians took this as a sign that they should build a chapel there at the mouth of the cave for the reclining Christ image.[15] The chapel at the mouth of the cave was completed in 1527 (Fig. 3.4).[16] Fray Martín de Valencia used both chapel and cave regularly and planted olive trees on the hill.[17] The Christ figure of the legend remains there to this day, housed in a nineteenth-century glass-and-wood case fitted for carrying in processions and clothed in fabric, with a black face appearing as if in death or sleep.[18] The main church down in the town was established later, in 1534.[19]

There is evidence that a cult developed around Fray Martín de Valencia that affected the Indians and their buildings at both Sacromonte and Tlalmanalco.[20] In 1534, he was buried in the church founded at nearby Tlalmanalco, 30 kilometers away.[21] In 1567, his stolen body was found and allegedly reburied outside the Capilla de la Cueva (Cave Chapel) of Sacromonte. Indians stood guard over the grave.[22] Fray Martín de Valencia's tunics were kept in a box at the foot of the Christ figure during the nineteenth century.[23]

The Capilla de la Cueva attracted Indians from distant villages and, in the nineteenth century, attracted faithful for Ash Wednesday celebrations from as far away as San Luis Potosí. A 1584 earthquake destroyed all or part of the Capilla de la Cueva,[24] which was also known as El Santuario del Sacromonte and

3.4. Sacromonte, aerial photo. Courtesy of the School of
Architecture Visual Resources Collection, The University of
Texas at Austin (Box-Wagner Collection, VRC 91-4745).

La Capilla de la Santa Cruz.[25] It may also have been affected earlier by the 1540 eruption of Popocatépetl.[26] Fray Juan Páez, Padre de Parroquia 1584–1588, was a devoted follower of Fray Martín de Valencia and was involved with the rebuilding of the chapel after the earthquake.[27] The chapel has been restored many times, as recently as between the authors' visits of 1986 and 1987. The original chapel of 1527 would not have had a dome. The cave may have collapsed during the earthquake of 1554, after which the relic would have been retrieved from the rubble and the cave rebuilt with a dome to represent the friar's original cave.

The popularity of the site for rituals created a need to expand the ceremonial and worship spaces. It would have been difficult to enlarge either the cave or the Capilla de la Cueva on the edge of the hill (Figs. 3.5–3.8). A solution was developed that required tunneling through from the opposite side of the hill. In the end, a large part of the hill was excavated and replaced by the new structure, a domed sanctuary known as Capilla del Señor de Sacromonte. This new structure connected directly to the cave, revealing the reclining Christ figure behind the new altar. The two chapels interconnect spatially; however, there is no passageway between them.

The construction of the Capilla del Señor de Sacromonte appears to have begun in the late seventeenth century and continued well into the eighteenth. The baroque stairs ascending the outside of the build-

ing, the central organization of the atypical hexagonal domed nave, and the typical eighteenth-century tower indicate that most of the construction occurred in the eighteenth century. Elizabeth Wilder Weismann describes the dilemma of dating and explaining Mexican architecture by means of style progressions:

> When you begin to talk—in a situation at once provincial and primitive—of setting up an Early Christian mission, and you use amateur designers and builders who are more or less familiar with Classical, Romanesque, Gothic, Renaissance, Mudéjar, Isabelline, Manueline, and the earliest Baroque styles in half a dozen European countries—working with craftsmen trained in alien and exotic forms—it is obvious that the resulting artifact cannot be described by any one of these names. If it is to be called a style at all, it will have to dodge the issue by denying the great styles, by calling itself hybrid or mongrel or "mestizo." For the concept of style is essentially one of purity, and a proper style should change only progressively in time.[28]

Continued attraction of pilgrims to Sacromonte led to the construction of an *hospedería* in 1835 for the purpose of housing visiting clergy.[29] The *hospedería*

ANCIENT ORIGINS OF THE MEXICAN PLAZA   66

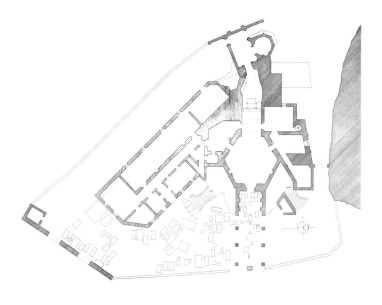

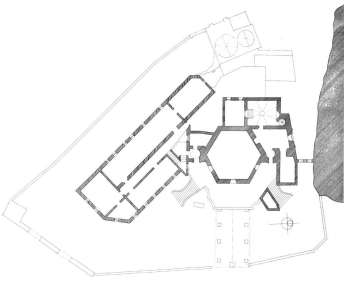

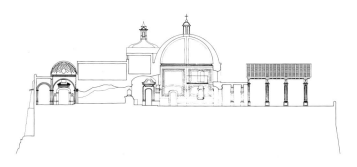

3.5. Sacromonte, ground floor plan, Capilla del Señor. Courtesy of the School of Architecture Visual Resources Collection, The University of Texas at Austin (Box-Wagner Collection).

3.6. Sacromonte, upper-level plan, Capilla del Señor. Courtesy of the School of Architecture Visual Resources Collection, The University of Texas at Austin (Box-Wagner Collection).

3.7. Sacromonte, elevation, Capilla del Señor. Courtesy of the School of Architecture Visual Resources Collection, The University of Texas at Austin (Box-Wagner Collection).

3.8. Sacromonte, lateral section, Capilla del Señor. Courtesy of the School of Architecture Visual Resources Collection, The University of Texas at Austin (Box-Wagner Collection).

contains a long refectory with handsomely painted wainscoting, a kitchen, and living accommodations.

The last addition to the structure is the portico that extends the main nave outside to provide cover for the worshippers and pilgrims (Fig. 3.9). This unique space forms a monumental but friendly front porch for the chapel and provides a dramatic view of the town and the volcanoes. The gable roof formed by slender wood trusses has extensions of lesser slope at the overhangs, yielding an unusual shape that is a local vernacular roof form (Fig. 3.10). This elegant roof shape, expressive of the rainy weather of the region, covers the majority of the buildings in the town of Amecameca, yet is not used in the surrounding towns that have the same climate. A nineteenth-century painting of the portico shows a flat roof in place of the sloped, vernacular roof.[30] The decoration of the brick columns, executed in two colors of plaster, is in the manner of eighteenth-century plaster decoration.

3.9. Sacromonte, Capilla del Señor, view from the portico overlooking the town of Amecameca. Hal Box.

SIXTEENTH-CENTURY COMMUNAL OPEN SPACES (FIVE HUNDRED YEARS LATER)

3.10. Sacromonte, Capilla del Señor, overall view showing the vernacular portico roof and bell tower. Hal Box.

Cultural Progression

The cultural progression can best be examined by a look at the evolution of rituals and ritual spaces in Mesoamerica and how that might apply to Cerro de Sacromonte. The spaces for outdoor ritual in Mesoamerica started in primitive clearings at special places long before they developed into the spectacular pageantry presented by Teotihuacan, Monte Albán, Xochicalco, and thousands of lesser complexes of temple structures, plazas, ballcourts, and causeways. Comfortable climate, limited technology for spanning interior space, and strong belief in gods of nature led to a reliance on outdoor ritual that was quite different from the practice of contemporary Europeans. Sacromonte utilizes both the open spaces of Mesoamerican tradition and another type of primal ritual space, the closed inner spaces of a cave.

The cave, *cueva,* or *gruta* affords an entrance into the Underworld, the home of gods. While less known and less architectural, underground rituals were important to Mesoamericans for getting in touch with the gods of the Underworld through hallucinogens, heat, sweating, and actual entry into the Underworld of the cave. The European experience with caves was further in the past, yet for the mendicant friars following Saint Francis, the cave was symbolic of the meditative life of their patron saint. Vows of poverty had been taken, possessions were minimal, shelter and sense of place were primitively economical. Natives and Europeans held caves to be important for different reasons, yet both revered the notion of the cave.

A description of the cultural progression at Cerro de Sacromonte in terms of ritual spaces follows. Sacromonte has two caves with active legends: the one adopted by Fray Martín de Valencia, which was made into the chapel, and another cave nearby, which leads straight down into the earth. Julio, the sacristan of Sacromonte when we visited, described this cave as being "30 kilometers deep and full of serpents with bodies like snakes and heads like humans."[31] Our field research team descended about 8 meters and found a passage blocked with rubble. The revered cave of Fray Martín de Valencia has now been built over and around to become a human-made pastiche of the original cave, yet it is still convincing as a cave with its place in the spatial assemblage.

The Capilla de la Cueva, built to celebrate and preserve the cave entrance in the soft volcanic soil, provided more room for followers and pilgrims. The

3.11. Sacromonte, Capilla de la Cueva. Located at the mouth of Fray Martín de Valencia's Cave, this chapel was rebuilt many times. Inside the cave rests a Christ figure in a nineteenth-century vitrine used for processions. Hal Box.

chapel's simple vaulted masonry structure forms three spaces. The first is an entry space supported by a high retaining wall on the edge of the hill, obviously an addition to the original chapel due to the effort needed to build such a retaining wall. Next is a domed space 15 feet square, with gilded plaster ornamentation in a pattern of serpents. The pendentives contain icons of the crucifixion: hammer, nails, ladder, spear, pliers, and cross. Paintings on the piers depict the Virgin and Saint Francis (Fig. 3.11). To one side is an octagonal baptistery space with shallow niches. The cave is presented as a dark, mysterious, but inviting place that attracts many visitors.

The main chapel was built in the seventeenth century. A dome and thick load-bearing walls contain all of the appurtenances of a worship space of today, but in an unusual form and with a few extra spaces. The hexagonal shape of the central nave is extremely rare, and it is by no means clear if it was built as a sophistication of form or as the result of a misunderstanding. The side vestibule created to accommodate overflow crowds and the narthex and chancel formed from deep extensions of two sides of the hexagon do little to enliven the static space; the excitement comes from looking through the extensions, into the cave past the reclining Christ figure, or out the front door through the portico and on to the snow-capped volcanoes.

The portico and the symmetrical baroque stairs are both unique to Sacromonte and serve similar functions as appendages to the chapel structure, offering platforms for viewing. From both, views can be had of the town below, of the ceremony inside, and of the processions outside. The front porch, a very desirable space for congregating before and after church services, has few precedents but many modern prospects for emulation.

Christendom presents the Stations of the Cross in many different ways, yet few are as compelling as the *via sacra* in the design at Sacromonte, an outdoor path that winds up the hill, like the Sacred Way of Christ in Jerusalem. The *via sacra* of Sacromonte dramatizes the events of the Passion with numerous architectural devices along a path 6 meters wide and 433 meters long. The observer is first introduced to the Passion by a stage formed of steps and a proscenium created by the initial portal piers. Beyond, a diorama of Christ carrying the cross is displayed in a small chapel (Fig. 3.12). The ritual space presents the Stations of

3.12.   Sacromonte; this flight of nine steps leading to a chapel off a major street in Amecameca marks the beginning of the Sacred Way. Hal Box.

3.13.   Sacromonte, termination of the Sacred Way as it enters the patio of the church. Courtesy of the School of Architecture Visual Resources Collection, The University of Texas at Austin (Box-Wagner Collection, VRC 91-4620).

the Cross (Fig. 3.13) then continues through portals and *atrio* to the sepulcher, the cave with the reclining Christ figure, before entering the main chapel. From there it continues up through an additional Mexican sacred way with monuments describing Juan Diego's four visions of the Virgen de Guadalupe, finally leading into the chapel in her name at the top of the hill.

Ash Wednesday is the time of the main celebration at Sacromonte. In the 1880s this holiday attracted up to 200,000 people,[32] as many as it attracts today in the form of a *feria*. At other times the *via sacra* serves the primitive rituals that linger into the present day, such as the practice of placing the umbilical cords of newborn children on the branches of olive trees planted by Fray Martín de Valencia.

The Capilla de la Virgen de Guadalupe at the top of Cerro de Sacromonte is a simple, handsomely proportioned, single-nave, pedimented structure with the rare feature of three equally sized arched doors in the east front. A sacristy projects to the north, and the surrounding unwalled space contains many tombs, mainly from the nineteenth century. It may have been built on top of the alleged temple of Teteoinán or perhaps to the side. There is no evidence of date and no mention in any of the histories we have found so far—although it was likely built in the eighteenth century. The building's simplicity and lack of particular stylization give it the timeless quality of *anastilo*.

Spatial Progression

The architectural phenomenon is best expressed in the spatial progression. Try to visualize the experience of moving through a progression of spaces below in the town of Amecameca, based on the foregoing descriptions of chronology, setting, culture, technology, and sequence (Fig. 3.14). Distant views display the snow of Iztaccíhuatl and Popocatépetl, and a near view of Cerro de Sacromonte shows both chapels visible from below. On festival days, a brightly colored procession forms in the *atrio* of the *parroquia* (parish church). Once assembled, it passes through the orderly rectangular plaza, into the narrow streets shaded by the unique vernacular roof overhangs of Amecameca, and out into an open space at the foot of Cerro de Sacromonte (Fig. 3.15). The central programmatic feature of this open space is the initial portal in front, which is elevated to act as a stage and proscenium for the play that is to follow. The first chapel graphically describes the Passion, and at the time of the *feria* on Ash Wednesday, the Christ figure from the cave is brought down by bearers on its glass-enclosed litter for the crowds to see. "'Dust you are and to dust you will return,' are the first terrible words said at the bottom

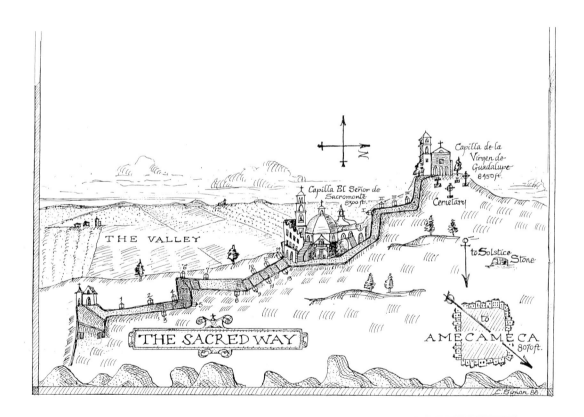

3.14. Sacromonte, the Sacred Way. A pilgrimage path lined with Stations of the Cross leads from the town of Amecameca in the valley up to the Capilla de Sacromonte, with an extension up to the Capilla de la Virgen de Guadalupe on the top of the hill. "The Sacred Way" © Earthwatch Institute. Courtesy of Earthwatch Institute.

3.15. Amecameca, view of urban center showing Plaza Mayor, market building, church, and *atrio*. Courtesy of the School of Architecture Visual Resources Collection, The University of Texas at Austin (Box-Wagner Collection, VRC 91-4631).

of the hill."[33] As the wide, tree-enclosed walk ascends, pilgrims encounter fourteen Stations of the Cross set among the trees like side chapels in a nave.

During the *feria*, the walk is also lined with food vendors whose offerings enliven the spiritual experience with a sensual intensity of smells, sounds, tastes, and visual delights, as well as fostering a feeling of closeness with friends, community, and God. Visual contrasts are active in light and dark, low and high, natural and human-made, textures, bright colors, sparkles of light, and movement of people. Sounds of talking, singing, chanting, guitars, trumpets, flutes, birds, and bells combine with smells of food, smoke, candles, incense, and people—all adding to the words and icons that enrich the architectural experience both visually and aurally. This Aztec poem might still be appropriate today on the sacred way:

> Take, reach for, arrive at the truth,
> For it is said, and is true,
> That you are the substitute,
> The surrogate of the Lord of All,
> The Supreme Lord.
> You are his dream,
> You are his flute;
> From within you he speaks.[34]

After an ascent of 230 feet, the equivalent of climbing the stairs of a seventeen-story office build-

ing, the breathless participant approaches the double portal that leads to the *atrio* of Capilla del Señor de Sacromonte and goes first to the cave, then to the main chapel. The sense of arrival at a place is emphasized by the portal, the entry into the walled *cementerio-atrio* space; the shelter of the portico; the coolness and reverberant sound of the enclosed vestibule; the awareness of the domed space; and finally arrival at the altar. Leaving, a decompression takes place, as one comes out into the bright sunlight and the vast space of the encircling mountains.

As a communal open space, the complex at Sacromonte is an example of a linear set of spaces arranged not in a straight line, as in a baroque composition, but in a meandering and discontinuous progression in which choices are made at different times and for different purposes. Cerro de Sacromonte is not an important architectural accomplishment, yet in its stones and spaces one can sense a lively passion for building architecture that fulfills a way of life (Fig. 3.16).

3.16. Sacromonte, Capilla del Señor viewed through the *atrio* portal of Asunción de Nuestra Señora. Hal Box.

Zoquizoquipan, Hidalgo:
La Virgen de la Asunción

While examining topographic maps of the state of Hidalgo, J.B. noticed a town nestled in the arms of two hills facing west, and because of its prominence in the landscape, he sensed that we would find there both an early sacred site and a sixteenth-century church built atop it. Kubler had not mentioned this place in his encyclopedic inventory of sixteenth-century churches, and McAndrew had only a brief mention of it. The map showed the site at the end of a dotted-line road, so we bought some tow rope to help get all our cars through—only one had four-wheel drive. From the hill above, the church and sacred patio seemed to be in just the right place in the world. Looking at the steps and the terrace, it was clear that they had been built up and leveled as part of an Otomi sacred site years before and built over by the mendicant friars. We navigated the water on the rutted dirt road and discovered the town of Zoquizoquipan seemingly deserted, gleaming in the sun. It wasn't deserted for long. Twenty people swarming all over the place with equipment drew considerable attention. As we got hungry, we wondered where we would eat, because we saw no stores or cafés in town. We asked one of the local boys hanging around where we might eat, and he said, "Come to my house and my mother will fix you something." We had a delightful lunch of tortillas and eggs cooked over charcoal on the open porch of a good-size adobe house with at least four generations of the family going in and out, along with lots of chickens (Fig. 3.17). The white-haired matriarch sat in a dark room by herself, receiving family members, some of whom seemed to accept money from her. On our return trip, the church portal and interior had been elaborately decorated with designs in reeds and colored fabric, and the town was filled with pilgrims celebrating the day of their patroness, the Virgen de la Asunción (Virgin of the Assumption). We were unable to make measured drawings because of the crowd.

Hal Box, 1987

Several features make the parish church of La Virgen de la Asunción in Zoquizoquipan worthy of note. Most striking of all is the location of the church, and especially the *atrio* perched on the edge of a deep and magnificent crevice (Figs. 3.18–3.19). Standing on the west end of the *atrio* produces a peculiar type of vertigo, an overwhelming, exhilarating sense of awe

3.17. Zoquizoquipan, prize rooster examines the author's view camera outside a home. Courtesy of the School of Architecture Visual Resources Collection, The University of Texas at Austin (Box-Wagner Collection, VRC 90-10932).

3.18. Zoquizoquipan, its grand siting between two mountain ridges, as seen from the east. Courtesy of the School of Architecture Visual Resources Collection, The University of Texas at Austin (Box-Wagner Collection, VRC 89-1430).

and respectful trepidation. If we try to empathize with a Mesoamerican mind-set, we can feel we are standing at the edge of the gaping maw of the Earth Monster, as swirling winds announce its heaving breaths. We encountered several *atrios* that exhibited this condition; San Juan Teposcolula in Oaxaca is another example that produces the same vivid sense of vertigo at the edge of the cliff.

All the elements of the architecture of conversion—the *posa* chapels, the open chapel, the *atrio* wall, and the *atrio* cross—are still intact, a rare and delightful sight to encounter when searching out sixteenth-century mendicant churches and *atrios* (Fig. 3.20). Upon closer inspection, we found that the inside *atrio* walls were replete with filled-in niches. This could provide evidence that early friars placed a variety of Catholic saints in the niches for veneration, as a way to continue the polytheism of the native religion. The merlons atop the *atrio* wall punctuate the sky rhythmically, emphasizing the horizon (Fig. 3.21). The stairway up to the *atrio* platform is more welcoming than the pyramid steps that it replaced (Fig. 3.22).

As if we were being rewarded for having stumbled on such a pristine, age-old ceremonial center, we were advised on the day that we surveyed that the town would celebrate the day of their patroness, La Virgen

3.19. Zoquizoquipan, aerial view. Courtesy of J. B. Johnson.

3.20. Zoquizoquipan, windswept *atrio* of La Virgen de la Asunción, up in the clouds. Hal Box.

3.21. Zoquizoquipan, view to the west through the merlons of the *atrio* wall. Courtesy of the School of Architecture Visual Resources Collection, The University of Texas at Austin (Box-Wagner Collection, VRC 89-774).

3.22. Zoquizoquipan, steps ascending to the *atrio* platform of La Virgen de la Asunción. Courtesy of the School of Architecture Visual Resources Collection, The University of Texas at Austin (Box-Wagner Collection, VRC 89-799).

3.23. Zoquizoquipan, *atrio* filled with celebrants as the vitrine with the statue of the Virgin is moved through the decorated portal of the church on festival day. Courtesy of the School of Architecture Visual Resources Collection, The University of Texas at Austin (Box-Wagner Collection, VRC 90-11028).

3.24. Zoquizoquipan, sixteenth-century *atrio* cross surrounded by the crowd on festival day. Courtesy of the School of Architecture Visual Resources Collection, The University of Texas at Austin (Box-Wagner Collection, VRC 90-9883).

de la Asunción, in two days. As is customary in Mexico and Central America when celebrating patron saints, the church was festooned with strings of colorful triangular banners that extended from the parapet of the main façade to the far west wall of the *atrio*. Standing under these fluttering banners gave a sensation of light airiness, as if one were flying on a kite in the sky above.

On August 15, 1988, a cold, rainy day, Zoquizoquipan's *atrio* was packed with people, some fortunate enough to have brought along their umbrellas or sheets of plastic (Figs. 3.23–3.24). During Mass, the town's faithful responded in unison when prompted by the priest, overseen by the glass-enclosed statue of the Virgin of the Assumption on her yearly removal outside to attend the celebration. This was a sight to behold, appearing as a reenactment of traditional outdoor worship in the sixteenth century.

In all, the *atrio*-church complex at Zoquizoquipan, with its quincunxial arrangement of the *atrio*, *posa* chapels, and *atrio* cross located at the edge of a precipice, denotes a strong pre-Columbian connection to the landscape that is still palpable today.

REFLECTED CEILING PLAN
NAVE

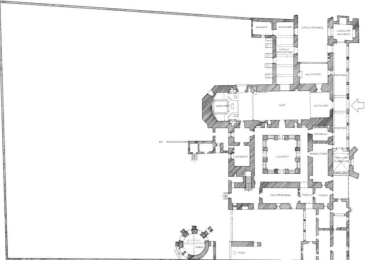

3.25. Valladolid, plan of San Bernardino de Siena de Sisal. Courtesy of the School of Architecture Visual Resources Collection, The University of Texas at Austin (Box-Wagner Collection).

Valladolid, Yucatán: San Bernardino de Siena de Sisal

The Studio Mexico group from U.T. Austin visited the Yucatán for five weeks. We stayed for two or three days in Valladolid in an interesting hotel that served the best soup any of us had ever encountered, called Caldo Tlalpeño. During the day, we visited various sites, including Sisal. I assigned a two-hour drawing project for the students, to make sketches of the complex and the numerous architectural monuments of interest. While the students were busy exploring and sketching the complex, I decided to document the plan by walking through, slowly observing and recording each space and how it related to the whole. The special places, i.e., the entry, the apse, the chapel, the stair, and, of course, the *noria*—probably the best surviving example of a dome-covered water well in Mexico—were all represented in plan oblique to indicate the three-dimensionality of those special architectural events.

Sinclair Black, 1993

Valladolid is the second-largest city in the state of Yucatán, after the capital, Mérida. It was founded by the Spanish in 1545, following an attempt by Spanish conquistadors to establish a base in the eastern part of the Yucatán Peninsula three years earlier at a different location.

Originally the site of the Cupul Maya settlement of Zaci ("white hawk" in Mayan), Valladolid was founded over the existing Maya ceremonial center by the nephew of the conqueror of Yucatán, Francisco de Montejo. The Franciscan friars had been selected by the Spanish Crown to establish convents throughout the peninsula, with their central base in Mérida. In addition, four major convents served as bases for converting the native population in Izamal, Motul, Maní, and Sisal, also called Valladolid.

The Franciscan convent in Valladolid was founded in 1552 and finished in 1560. Dedicated to San Bernardino de Siena, it is one of the most massive viceregal convent structures in the Yucatán (Fig. 3.25). The complex was designed by Fray Juan de Mérida, who also designed the convent at Izamal.

Fearing insurrection from the Maya, the Franciscan friars built the convent to withstand an attack and survive a siege. It was purposely designed to be self-sufficient, with ample land for plant cultivation and, more importantly, an underground water source. The convent sits squarely on top of a cavernous cenote. In the orchard behind the convent, a circular, dome-covered *noria*, or well, with an animal-powered water-wheel still exists in remarkable condition (Fig. 3.26). Anecdotal accounts tell of congregation members hearing the sounds of water sloshing below them dur-

3.26. Valladolid, dome over the sacred cenote in the early *atrio* of
San Bernardino. Courtesy of the School of Architecture Visual
Resources Collection, The University of Texas at Austin (Box-
Wagner Collection, VRC 95-06043).

3.27. Valladolid, façade of San Bernardino with *portales* opening to a
grand civic plaza. Courtesy of Sinclair Black.

3.28. Valladolid, temporary bullring in the *atrio* of San Bernardino.
Logan Wagner.

ing celebrations of Mass. The mystical and religious importance of this cenote notwithstanding, the reason for the convent's location over an underground river probably had more to do with the friars' need to feel secure and self-sustainable in case of an indigenous uprising. This was a well-founded fear, for in the nineteenth century a nearly successful uprising for native independence had its origins in native communities in the forest just east of Valladolid's Franciscan convent, at that time the edge of the Spanish frontier (Fig. 3.27).

Seen in plan, the urban layout of Valladolid is a dramatic example of two conflicting urban grids. The plan of San Bernadino de Siena and the grid it established came first, followed a few decades later by a different grid emanating from the central plaza and San Gervasio Cathedral, founded in 1570. Today, the oldest buildings in Valladolid are those along a street of the original grid that connects the convent to the downtown grid established later. The cathedral building you see today was built in 1702, replacing the original.

The convent cloister is located on the shady north side of the nave, rather than on the south as is customary in Central Mexico, a typical layout response for Franciscan convents in the extreme hot climate of Yucatán. The massive complex is fronted on the west façade by an extended arcade, or *portería*, with the entrance to the church nave through the central arch.

The convent is flanked on its east and west sides by very generous open spaces. On the east, behind the apse and cloister, is an extensive area dedicated as a *huerta*, or orchard, and as grazing land for cattle. The *noria* is on the north-central edge of the *huerta*.

To the west is a large open space that originally served as the church *atrio* but is now dedicated as a city park, Parque Sisal. The extensive open space originally included a proposed town plaza that does not exist now, due to the imposition of the newer downtown grid and central plaza next to San Gervasio Cathedral. Until recently, a temporary bullring would be built in the old *atrio*, and bullfights would be held during the celebrations honoring the patron saint San Bernardino (Fig. 3.28). Now the open space is covered in grass.

A small chapel south of the convent church nave, built for the native indigenous population, leads one to believe that the open space to the south was originally used as a small *atrio*. A smaller courtyard sits directly north of the cloister but still lies within the convent complex.

Even though the original layout initiated by the Franciscan friars was superseded by the imposition of the urban grid dictated by the secular church and the Spanish civil population, in the end this alteration of the grid orientation adds more interest to the urban layout. The fact that both layouts include spaces for plazas increases the open space allotted to the inhabitants of Valladolid, a twist of urban design fate we can all enjoy and appreciate today.

QUINCUNXIAL ARRANGEMENTS

Quincunxial centering and the rituals surrounding it are at the core of Mesoamerican belief, and the early friars, spearheaded by Fray Pedro de Gante, soon realized its value as a conversion tool, arguably the most effective one in the mendicant toolbox. A typical quincunxial arrangement is manifested at the Franciscan site of Yecapixtla in the state of Morelos, seen here from the air (Fig. 3.29); compare it with the Yecapixtla Relación Geográfica at Fig. 2.24.

The friars created the essential architectural formula to begin the widespread spiritual conquest throughout New Spain by centering open spaces, highlighting the four directions with chapels at the corners of a quadrangular space, placing a Christian cross in the center of the space, and allowing the ritual processions from Mesoamerican antiquity to continue. A telling sign of early church layouts, the quincunxial *atrio* courts were continued in the northern frontier well into the seventeenth and eighteenth centuries by the Jesuits, long after the secular church had systematically supplanted and dominated the churches of the early mendicants.

As has been illustrated earlier in the example of the Olmec site of Teopantecuanitlán, and as Sam Edgerton has pointed out in his discussion of the processional sequence of *posa* chapels within the *atrio*,[35] the four-cornered *atrios* characteristic of mendicant conventual complexes in early New Spain were symbolically tied to the movement of the sun, even though the friars were most probably unaware of the mythical and celestial origins of the Mesoamerican quincunxial ritual.

3.29. Yecapixtla, aerial view showing quincunx formed by *posa* chapels and cross in *atrio*. Courtesy of the School of Architecture Visual Resources Collection, The University of Texas at Austin (Box-Wagner Collection, VRC 91-5306).

Richard Phillips, in his exhaustive dissertation, proves very convincingly that the quincunxial ritual was continued even further into secondary open spaces, the convent cloisters, which were the friars' private domain.[36] His work reinforces the importance mendicant friars invested in continuing the quincunxial ritual.

Although the quincunxial open space of mendicant churches was in evidence in nearly all the towns we documented, the examples that follow have unique qualities and characteristics that we deemed strong enough to mention under this subtitle. Following are descriptions of a handful of such quincunxial open spaces, as well as the other communal open spaces nearby.

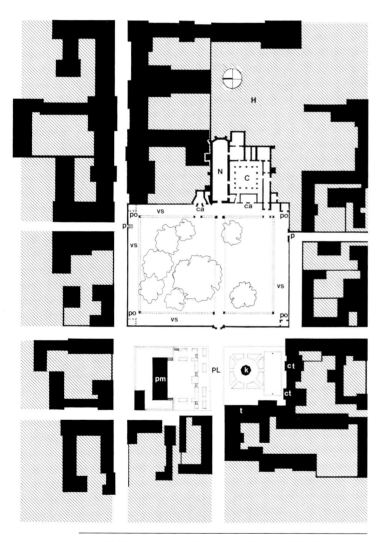

3.30. Atlatlahuacan, plan of town center. Courtesy of the School of Architecture Visual Resources Collection, The University of Texas at Austin (Box-Wagner Collection).

Atlatlahuacan, Morelos: La Concepción (now San Mateo)

Heading into the sun rising around snow-capped Popocatépetl, I drove from our house in Cuernavaca to Hacienda Cocoyoc to join Logan and our second Earthwatch team of the summer, just arrived the night before—most seeing Mexico for the first time. We gathered the fifteen-person team, cameras, and surveying equipment into cars and headed for the sixteenth-century town of Atlatlahuacan on the slopes of Popo to document its communal open spaces. We had a good head start on this town. The church and *atrio* had been well described by Kubler and McAndrew, so our objective was to understand and document it, along with the secular plaza and the core of the town. Logan had rented a small airplane the week before to take aerial photographs, and we have an extraordinary map of the town, known as a Relación Geográfica, drawn around 1570 by an indigenous artist, or *tlacuilo*, for King Philip II's inventory of his lands in New Spain. Our sense of time was warped by what we were seeing, by the realization that this monumental work of architecture had been built 86 years before the founding of Harvard and 226 years before the founding of the United States of America. After Logan showed the team how to use the surveying equipment, they set up the plane table and alidade to measure the spaces formed by the church and central buildings of the village. I moved the big 4 × 5 view camera around in the hope of capturing the sense of the plaza and sacred patio in photographs. Young boys shot baskets on the plaza ballcourt as a few old men sat in the shade and watched.

Hal Box, 1986

Atlatlahuacan, like the other towns in this survey, was an active town before the arrival of the Europeans. Augustinian friars founded the *convento* in the existing native settlement between 1531 and 1540, building an open chapel and large *atrio* (Figs. 3.30–3.31, and see the RG at Fig. 2.20). These towns, *pueblos de indios*, were intended to concentrate the natives for conversion and exploitation, and the Spanish colonists were not allowed to live in them. According to Kubler, the church nave and façade we see now were built around 1570, but dates are difficult to confirm, since some are the dates of official founding and others the dates of either beginning or completion of construction. The *atrio*, or sacred patio, is intact, with excellent examples of *posa* chapels in the four corners and an open chapel

3.32. Atlatlahuacan, early open chapel and façade of later sanctuary. Courtesy of the School of Architecture Visual Resources Collection, The University of Texas at Austin (Box-Wagner Collection, VRC 2007-5055).

3.33. Atlatlahuacan, *posa* with merlons and no iconographic carvings. Courtesy of the School of Architecture Visual Resources Collection, The University of Texas at Austin (Box-Wagner Collection, VRC 91-11762).

3.31. Atlatlahuacan, aerial view of convent and *atrio*, showing open chapel on left, *posa* chapel on right, and *portería* in the center. Courtesy of the School of Architecture Visual Resources Collection, The University of Texas at Austin (Box-Wagner Collection, VRC 91-11756).

with altar for saying Mass for the outdoor congregation (Fig. 3.32). The *posa* chapels are handsome structures with domed roofs and merlons but without the descriptive religious carving of contemporary *posas* at Calpan and Huejotzingo (Fig. 3.33). A wide *via sacra*, or sacred way, demarked by a low wall, connects the *posa* chapels. Only extensive archaeology could determine whether this walled *atrio* was identical to the symbolic primordial sea of the previous civilization, but it is safe to assume that it was, since spiritual ritual took place in the historically sacred space. It would

have been difficult for the friars to use a different space, as the ancestors and gods could not be moved.

We must remember that the Mesoamerican tradition held its religious rituals outdoors on the primordial sea rather than inside a building, as in Europe. Further, the friars' goal of converting large numbers of natives could not be accommodated inside a building, so the *atrio*/Mesoamerican sacred platform served the purposes of maintaining the kind of space used for earlier rituals and accommodating large crowds for services. The concept of the church nave as a sacred cave is reinforced visually by the portal to the church serving as a maw or opening into the Underworld and the massive interior creating a cool, resonant space (Figs. 3.34–3.35).

Beyond the *atrio*, one sees the civic plaza formed by the walls of small *tiendas* and dwellings centered on a fountain. A quincunxial plaza in the French

3.34. Atlatlahuacan, church portal viewed from the *atrio*. Courtesy of the School of Architecture Visual Resources Collection, The University of Texas at Austin (Box-Wagner Collection, VRC 2007-5053).

3.35. Atlatlahuacan, worshipper just inside the portal to the cavelike nave. Courtesy of the School of Architecture Visual Resources Collection, The University of Texas at Austin (Box-Wagner Collection, VRC 2007-5051).

manner was built in part of the original long, rectangular open space, of the type that was popular in the nineteenth-century era of the Porfiriato, and more recently a municipal building has invaded the other end. The plaza is active, with modern basketball courts and some modern landscape forms that are visually out of place, yet bring new life to the small plaza. This open space is still the center of town, raising the question of historical authenticity versus social and economic vitality for the community.

Huejotzingo, Puebla: San Miguel

On the day I left the city of Churultecal [Cholula], I traveled four leagues to some villages of the state of Guasucingo [Huejotzingo], where I was very well received by the natives, who gave me some female slaves and clothing and some small pieces of gold, which in all was very little, because they own very little on account of their being allies of the Tascaltecans and surrounded on all sides by Mutezuma's land, so they have no trade save with the people of their own province; because of this they live very poorly.

Hernán Cortés, *Letters from Mexico*

In the first decades after the conquest, mendicant friars founded, designed, and supervised the building of monasteries because there were no professional architects available until after 1544.[37] Only a handful of the friar-architects are known, chief among them Juan de Alameda, a Franciscan from the province of Concepción in Spain.[38] It is thought that he designed San Andrés Calpan as well as San Miguel Huejotzingo, where he began his work in New Spain, and San Martín Huaquechula, where he is buried.[39] He may also have helped with the work begun by Motolinía at Santa María de Jesús Atlixco.[40] These four Franciscan monasteries are within a day's walk of each other, and they were built between 1529 and 1570 when Fray Juan was active. They are similar in sculptural style and iconographic program as well as uniform in their adherence to the typical plan for Mexican convents invented by the early friars.

Contemporary chronicles of the Franciscan Order report that Juan de Alameda left Seville with the newly appointed bishop of Mexico, Juan de Zumárraga, who was not only Mexico's first bishop but also a humanist influenced by Erasmus. They sailed in August 1528, arriving in Mexico in December. One of Fray Juan's first accomplishments was to follow the advice given to all Franciscan friars on arrival: learn the native language

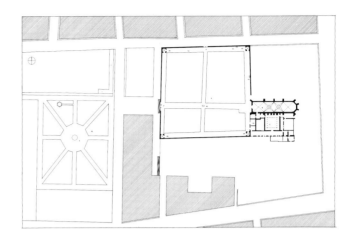

3.36. Huejotzingo, plan of San Miguel and communal open spaces. Courtesy of the School of Architecture Visual Resources Collection, The University of Texas at Austin (Box-Wagner Collection).

3.37. Huejotzingo, steps from public plaza up to portal of sacred *atrio*. Courtesy of the School of Architecture Visual Resources Collection, The University of Texas at Austin (Box-Wagner Collection, VRC 2007-4917).

because it is indispensable preparation for the work of conversion and guidance of the Indians. The record says that he learned Nahuatl and spoke it very well.[41] By that time, the Franciscans had established missions in the preconquest urban centers of Tlaxcala and Huejotzingo; these two missions were among the first four founded in New Spain in 1524.[42] Within a year of Fray Juan's arrival, he moved the town of Huejotzingo, with its 40,000 inhabitants, from an unhealthy arroyo at the foot of the volcano Iztaccíhuatl to a nearby flat site, laid out the new town, and built a monastery there (Fig. 3.36).

3.38. Huejotzingo, looking west from the *atrio*.
Susan Kline Morehead.

3.39. Huejotzingo, costumed participants in reenactment of the Battle
of the Christians and the Moors in the Plaza Mayor.
Susan Kline Morehead.

3.40. Huejotzingo, kiosk and children's ride in Plaza Mayor.
Susan Kline Morehead.

The complex, dedicated to San Miguel, sits above the town's generous central *plaza mayor* on a high rubble platform. The enormity of the task of building such a platform, especially where no cut-and-fill work was required to level the site, suggests it existed before the Spaniards arrived. The church and monastery face a grand walled *atrio* that is entered through a triumphal arch at the top of a broad stone stair (Fig. 3.37).[43] Below the stair, a small court, framed on both sides with shops, buffers the monastery complex from the main road. At the foot of the stairs, the court extends laterally, forming a T that connects to streets on both sides of the monastery complex (Fig. 3.38). The main road runs north–south through Huejotzingo, dividing the *convento* from the *plaza mayor*; until its recent widening, it was lined for miles toward Cholula with giant eucalyptus trees brought to the Puebla area by construction workers in the late nineteenth century.

The plaza, shaded by more tall eucalyptus trees, is quite spacious, the same width as the monastery grounds, which are roughly square, and two-thirds as deep. Together they cover five elongated blocks at the center of town, except for the incursions made into the monastery's orchard by a school and a row of shops. The western third of the plaza is paved, without trees, and is used for various purposes, including markets and festivals. One- and two-story shops and civic buildings surround the plaza on three sides, with a church and the only section of *portales* on the western block. Angled parking is available on three of the plaza's edges, with a few more spaces along the main road.

The furnishings of the plaza include the *convento*'s original large stone *atrio* cross carved as a cactus and decorated with emblems of the stigmata and a crown of thorns at the crossing of the arms. In addition, a nineteenth-century kiosk sits in the center, and a recent monument to the first evangelizers is to one side. The plaza is the scene of numerous festivals and celebrations, including the reenactment of the Battle of the Christians and the Moors, complete with costumes and gunfire (Fig. 3.39). During festivals, the plaza is filled with tented *tiendas* selling seasonal and local food specialties and handicrafts, a merry-go-round full of laughing and shouting children, and horse and donkey rides, while people in costumes spill over into the surrounding streets, many walking or riding in parades, often to the sounds from loudspeakers (Fig. 3.40). Especially favored treats are the local honey and the cider from apple orchards planted by the early friars.

The *atrio*, at the top level of the sequence of open spaces, is the site of quieter activities today but was once a scene of ritual and pageant like the plaza below. The sacred way follows the walls of the *atrio*, creating a square that is bisected in both directions. Along the path from *atrio* gate to church portal, traffic is arrested by the stone-carved *atrio* cross (Fig. 3.41).[44] It sits in the center of the path and at the center of the *atrio*, where it acts as an axis mundi. Together, the corner *posas* and the central cross form a quincunx.

The four *posas* are renowned for the elegantly carved pairs of winged angels carrying the instruments of the Passion that remain on both doorways of the first three *posas*. Unfortunately, the angels on the fourth *posa* were lost to French soldiers' target practice sometime during the nineteenth century. Processions leaving the church turn right toward the first *posa*, in the northeast corner of the *atrio*, and are greeted by angels in the spandrels of the arched opening. An *alfiz*

of knotted cord, a symbol of the Franciscan Order, outlines the space they occupy, marked at the center by the crown of the Virgin Mary above a cartouche emblazoned with her initials AV (Ave Maria) that is surmounted by a cross. Each *posa* façade varies only in the instruments carried by the angels and the insignia on the cartouche, where the insignia of the Virgin alternates with that of Christ (Fig. 3.42). Most of the instruments are the traditional Christian ones—nails, hammer, pincers, lance, crown of thorns, ewer and basin, lantern, sponge of vinegar, bag of money—but the second *posa*'s angels sound the Last Judgment on trombones whose sounds appear as flowers in an indigenous artist's use of the preconquest technique of showing sound, often called a speech glyph.

Above the *alfiz* is a rectangular frame holding a row of four additional shields, each with the Franciscan symbol of the stigmata, the five wounds of Christ, in its peculiarly Mexican version. The bleed-

3.41. Huejotzingo, *atrio* cross and façade of San Miguel. Courtesy of the School of Architecture Visual Resources Collection, The University of Texas at Austin (Box-Wagner Collection, VRC 92-4145).

3.42. Huejotzingo, *posa* chapel in the northwest corner of the *atrio*. Courtesy of the School of Architecture Visual Resources Collection, The University of Texas at Austin (Box-Wagner Collection, VRC 92-4120).

ing wounds not only form a quincunx, but they also embed a familiar Mesoamerican symbol into the Christian iconography (Fig. 3.43). The circular or oval wounds themselves are represented by the widely used Mesoamerican symbol for jade, valued above all else, even gold. Several meanings adhere to this powerful jade symbol, called *chalchihuitl*. It is the symbol for precious water, the generative liquid of the primordial sea from which life originates in Mesoamerican cosmology.[45] It is also the symbol for another precious liquid: blood, particularly the human blood that the Aztecs believed was required by the sun as nourishment to sustain its daily movement across the sky.[46] Accustomed as they were to human sacrifice as a daily necessity for warding off the end of the world, these artisans would have instinctively, if not deliberately, linked Christ's wounds, with their cascading droplets of blood, to the *chalchihuitl* form. For the Indians, the concept of Christ's precious blood being shed to save

Christians from eternal damnation would have been informed by their own tradition of sacrificial blood, shed to save the world from darkness and destruction. It is further enriched by the *chalchihuitl*'s association with the generative power of water, symbolism that ties new life to blood sacrifice, much like Christ's sacrifice promises eternal life to humans.[47] Jade beads masquerading as Isabelline gothic pearls also decorate the capitals and bases of the colonnettes supporting the *posa* arches.

The counterclockwise procession around the sacred way, with pauses at *posa* altars, is reminiscent of the procession with pauses for prayer at the Stations of the Cross that can be conducted inside or outside a church. It is also similar to the procession along the meditational walkway of the monastery cloister, where friars and perhaps their students paused at the corner *testera* niches containing sacred murals or sculpture, which face those walking counterclockwise.[48] The cloister, like the *atrio*, forms a quincunx with its corner niches and central fountain, and would have been recognized as a re-creation of the world by native students and their families.

Huaquechula, Puebla: San Martín

This city of Guacachulla [*sic*] is situated in a plain bounded on the one side by some high and rugged mountains and on the others by two rivers about two crossbowshots apart which run through large and deep ravines. Thus the approaches to the city are few, and all of them are so steep that the horses can barely pass either up or down them. The city is surrounded by a very strong wall built of stone and mortar which is as high as twenty-four feet on the outside and almost level with the ground on the inside. All along the top of this wall runs a battlement three feet high to protect them while fighting. And there are four gateways wide enough for a man to enter on horseback. At each entrance there are three or four bends in the wall, doubling back on one another; and there are also battlements on each of these bends. On this wall they keep a number of stones, both small and large and of various shapes, which they use for fighting. This city has some five or six thousand inhabitants, and there are as many more in the hamlets which are subject to it. It occupies a very large area, for within the city are many gardens with fruit and sweet-smelling flowers as is their custom.

Hernán Cortés, *Letters from Mexico*

3.43. Huejotzingo, detail of Five Wounds of Christ motif on *posa* chapel. Courtesy of the School of Architecture Visual Resources Collection, The University of Texas at Austin (Box-Wagner Collection, VRC 92-4123).

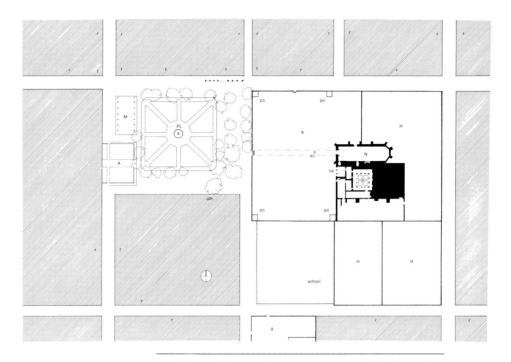

3.44. Huaquechula, plan of town center. Courtesy of the School of Architecture Visual Resources Collection, The University of Texas at Austin (Box-Wagner Collection).

Cortés described preconquest Huaquechula to Charles V in his letter of 1520. Later chroniclers of the conquest century tell of the "sumptuous church" and monastery at Huaquechula, on the southern slopes of Popocatépetl in the Atlixco Valley, built by Juan de Alameda, the Franciscan friar whose craftsmen earlier built Huejotzingo and probably Calpan.[49] Fray Juan was buried at Huaquechula in 1570. Today the town has about 34,000 inhabitants.

As in Alameda's other works, Huaquechula's *atrio* re-created the Mesoamerican universe as a quincunx, with *posas* and a central cross (Fig. 3.44). Here, as at Calpan, one walks through an arched gate in the crenellated *atrio* wall and down a stair into the *atrio*, reinforcing its role as primordial sea (Fig. 3.45). Today, the original *atrio* cross is gone from its pedestal and only one *posa* remains, the others reduced to their foundations. A flimsy wooden frame with cubic form and a pyramidal roof like the *posas* at Huejotzingo has been added to the foundation of the southeast *posa* (Fig. 3.46). In addition to building the convent complex, Fray Juan "reformed the urban plan" and planted many fruit trees.[50] The grid plan of the town remains intact, with the blocks divided by cobblestone streets. Each block is edged by houses that surround an interior space filled with trees, creating private, shady green spaces, just the reverse of the North American practice of filling the blocks with houses and leaving the open space at the street edge.

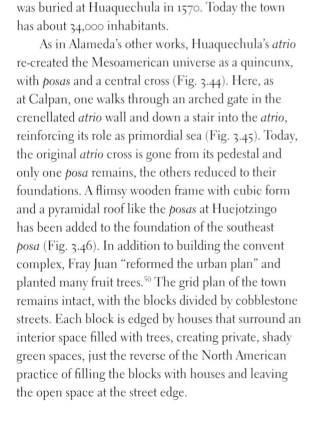

3.45. Huaquechula, *atrio* with replacement *atrio* cross and *atrio* portal. Courtesy of the School of Architecture Visual Resources Collection, The University of Texas at Austin (Box-Wagner Collection, VRC 92-13323).

3.46. Huaquechula, façade of church and monastery in *atrio*, showing recently added stick *posa*. Courtesy of Sinclair Black.

3.48. Huaquechula, town viewed past north gate of *atrio* from roof of church, with Popocatépetl in background. Courtesy of the School of Architecture Visual Resources Collection, The University of Texas at Austin (Box-Wagner Collection, VRC 92-12570).

3.47. Huaquechula, cloister of San Martín. Courtesy of the School of Architecture Visual Resources Collection, The University of Texas at Austin (Box-Wagner Collection VRC, 92-12569).

The tree-filled *plaza mayor*, immediately west of the *atrio*, has an eighteenth-century kiosk in the center, benches in and around the plaza on a sidewalk of paving stones, and a display of archaeological artifacts, including a calendar stone. The plaza fills the northern half block across from the *atrio*, and a concession stand and civic building take up part of the adjacent southern half. Opposite the plaza to the north, the Presidencia Municipal provides shady *portales*. The buildings lining the streets around the plaza and *convento* are one-story, some with colonial ogive-arched windows with grills, and in typical Mexican fashion, painted in bright colors.

Early in the conversion period, natives of Huaquechula had to go to Huejotzingo to worship, as they had no church, but in 1533 or 1534, the Franciscans came and built a rudimentary but serviceable *convento*, followed by the buildings we see today. The whole complex is built of red-streaked golden limestone. The large, rib-vaulted open chapel was built above the arcaded *portería* on the south side of the church, allowing the friars a view of everyone in the *atrio* during services. The cloister has two stories, as was the norm at that time, and today is entered through a courtyard on the south rather than through the *portería* on the front (Fig. 3.47). If one is fortunate, the custodian will lead the way to the roof, where the views are magnificent (Fig. 3.48) and one can inspect the single-bell *espadaña*, or bell wall.

The church is dedicated to San Martín, named for Martin of Tours, who cut his cloak in two, gave half to a beggar, and was rewarded by a vision of Christ. In a similar act of charity, when the first tired and bedraggled friars arrived at Huaquechula after their long walk from Huejotzingo, the cacique welcomed them with clothing. He and the townspeople were soon baptized.

The decorated portal of the church draws the viewer between the welcoming embrace of tall, diagonal buttresses. Two large shields emblazoned with the stigmata, each held by an angel, are set into the spandrels of the arch in the midst of elaborate vegetative relief. In this instance, the Five Wounds motif is a secondary element in the larger, plateresque decorative scheme. Above the door inside an *alfiz* is a relief of a smiling San Martín on his horse, both man and beast turning to look at the beggar while Martín's sword cuts through his cloak (Fig. 3.49).

Zacualpan de Amilpas, Morelos: La Concepción

The church of La Concepción, founded in 1535, was built in the mid-sixteenth century by Fray Juan Cruzat.[51] Zacualpan is Nahuatl for "that which is covered." *Milpa* is Nahuatl for an agricultural field of several crops. Without archaeology on the site, it is unknown what was covered, yet one could imagine that below the *atrio* lay the elevated sacred platform of the previous culture and that it had been covered by the new (Fig. 3.50). The Augustinian church has the seventeenth-century addition of an attached baroque-style chapel and exuberant rebuilt *posas* on a diagonal—one of many forms of *posas* that can be found (Fig. 3.51). The public plaza is well shaped, with three sets of *portales*, active *tiendas*, a market building, and a Palacio Municipal. The plaza is bounded by the walls of surrounding buildings, including a reentrant corner toward the church and dynamic street entry points rather than a grid (Fig. 3.52). The cluster of *portales* at the northwest corner is important enough to have a portal into the *atrio* with a diagonal walkway (Fig. 3.53). A *via sacra* is not apparent. The early open chapel of the *atrio* and the late baroque *posas* seem to give shape to time, stretching it from the sixteenth century into the eighteenth.

TERRACED MOUNTAINS

When Hernán Cortés returned to Spain, King Charles V asked him to describe what was soon to become New Spain. Cortés crumpled a sheet of paper in his hand, saying, "That is what Mexico looks like," in an allusion to the abrupt and broken terrain this mountainous land is known for.[52]

In Chapter One, we delved into the important role mountains play in Mesoamerican origin myths and religion. We also described the symbolism of the elements in the built environment of Mesoamerican ceremonial centers, wherein plazas represent the primordial sea and pyramid temple structures become the mountains in a symbolic re-creation of the natural world.

Where the terrain is flat, as it is in Yucatán and other lowland areas of Mesoamerica, pyramid temple

3.49. Huaquechula, detail of San Martín on façade of church. Courtesy of the School of Architecture Visual Resources Collection, The University of Texas at Austin (Box-Wagner Collection, VRC 92-12587).

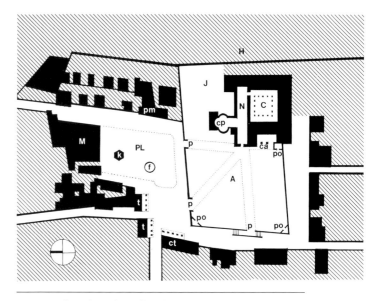

3.50. Zacualpan de Amilpas, plan of town center. Courtesy of the School of Architecture Visual Resources Collection, The University of Texas at Austin (Box-Wagner Collection).

structures become the only mountains, albeit human-made. In mountainous areas, however, the abruptness of the terrain provides magnificent natural platforms for the plazas and pyramid temple structures that form the ceremonial centers of Mesoamerican settlements. In some cases, contiguous and ever-ascending elevations of the hilly landscape are terraced. These serve as

3.51. Zacualpan de Amilpas, Convento de Concepción, view from the *atrio* showing façade, *portería*, and baroque chapel addition. Courtesy of the School of Architecture Visual Resources Collection, The University of Texas at Austin (Box-Wagner Collection).

3.53. Zacualpan de Amilpas, steps from the plaza up to the baroque portal of the *atrio*. Courtesy of the School of Architecture Visual Resources Collection, The University of Texas at Austin (Box-Wagner Collection, VRC 91-12130).

3.52. Zacualpan de Amilpas, vendor fixing lunch in one of the *portales* adjacent to the plaza. Courtesy of the School of Architecture Visual Resources Collection, The University of Texas at Austin (Box-Wagner Collection, VRC 91-12133).

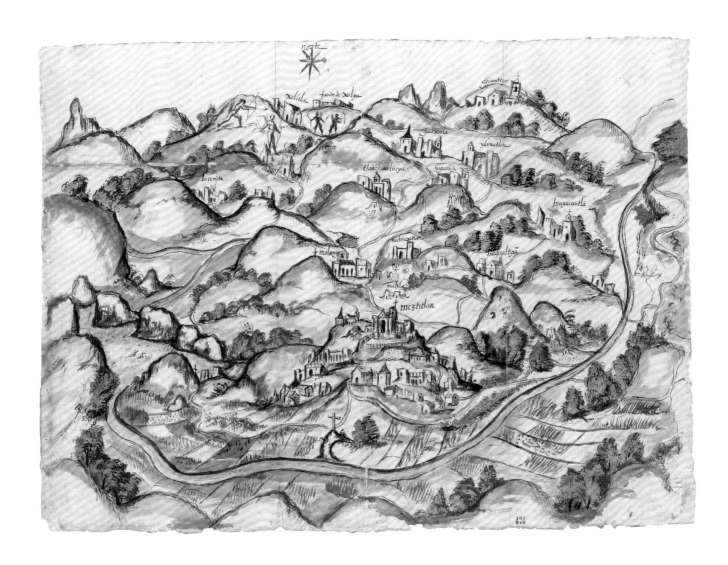

3.54. Relación Geográfica of Meztitlan. Nettie Lee Benson Latin
American Collection, University of Texas Libraries, The
University of Texas at Austin.

3.55. Meztitlan, view from church roof of town below and distant mountains. Susan Kline Morehead.

pedestals on which to present and enhance the built plazas and structures, creating a spectacular setting for the centers. Among Mesoamerican sites, we mention Xochicalco, Toniná, and Monte Albán as formidable examples of the Mesoamerican expertise in creating this symbiotic relationship between the built environment and the natural terrain.

Fortunately, several Mesoamerican settlements with natural settings like those mentioned above were still inhabited at the time of arrival of the Spaniards. These native centers were transformed by the superimposition of Spanish urban layouts, becoming towns during viceregal times. Today they are modern urban entities. Among them is Meztitlan, in the mountains not far from Molango, where the monastic complex was moved up the terraced hill from its original siting at the lower level where the town remains (Fig. 3.54). One level above the town is the plaza, surrounded by hotels, restaurants, and small *tiendas*. On a level above that plaza are the large *atrio*, monastery, and church dedicated to Los Santos Reyes with its magnificent seven-bell *espadaña* (Fig. 3.55).

The following examples that we surveyed are a mere handful of sites where this harmonious and magnificent relationship between natural landscape and urban layout is manifested.

Molango, Hidalgo: Santa María

Nestled in a valley of green mountains, Molango was our base for four weeks as we investigated sixteenth-century new towns in the state of Hidalgo. We stayed in a little hotel on the *plaza mayor*, which we rated minus two stars, but we overlooked the plaza-marketplace and became aware of its dramatically changing everyday activities, filling with stalls and people on market day, *día de plaza*.

Hal Box, 1989

The Augustinian convent of Santa María, like Zoquizoquipan, was clearly built atop an existing pyramid, which McAndrew identifies as a temple to the god Mola.[53] The sacred patio was carefully planted with trees that create a shaded sacred place with a sense of paradise, a parvis that looks majestically west over an extended prairie. The dramatic descent from this paradise platform, down many steps, pauses in the unusual architectural device of circular steps, concave and then convex, with a circle at the landing. At the bottom lies the real world, dusty and hot (Figs. 3.56–3.59).

Molango was the first base for the Augustinian friars working in these remote and abrupt mountains. Kubler describes it as the oldest in the sierras, founded in 1538 by Fray Antonio de Roa, with construction of the *convento* beginning around 1546. Besides the spectacular setting of the *atrio*, Molango's Santa María

3.56. Molango, aerial view. Courtesy of the School of Architecture
Visual Resources Collection, The University of Texas at Austin
(Box-Wagner Collection).

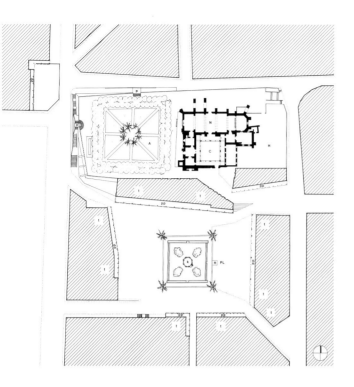

3.57. Molango, plan of Santa María and communal open spaces of the town center. Courtesy of the School of Architecture Visual Resources Collection, The University of Texas at Austin (Box-Wagner Collection).

3.58. Molango, circular stair into *atrio*. Courtesy of the School of Architecture Visual Resources Collection, The University of Texas at Austin (Box-Wagner Collection, VRC 89-843).

3.59. Molango, view of town center with church and plaza atop an ancient platform overlooking the valley and lake. Courtesy of the School of Architecture Visual Resources Collection, The University of Texas at Austin (Box-Wagner Collection, VRC 89-1423).

3.60. Molango, the *espadaña* of Santa María atop the ancient platform. Courtesy of the School of Architecture Visual Resources Collection, The University of Texas at Austin (Box-Wagner Collection, VRC 90-10844).

3.61. Molango, stairs leading up the side of the ancient sacred platform to the *atrio* gate of Santa María. Courtesy of the School of Architecture Visual Resources Collection, The University of Texas at Austin (Box-Wagner Collection VRC 89-1172).

includes a unique, structurally independent, and elaborate belfry wall, or *espadaña*, that emphasizes the drama of the platform's height (Fig 3.60).[54] Attesting to indigenous religious symbolism, some of the stone carvings on the jambs of the main doorway into the church's nave have obvious pre-Hispanic references in the form of *tequitqui*.[55] Some *tequitqui* carried extensive connotations. For example, one symbol carved on the jambs is a lazy-S shape reminiscent of the Olmec-style lazy S on the throne and scepter of the ruler of Chalcatzingo depicted on Monument 1 (see Fig. 1.18). In that context, the lazy S means clouds, an obvious connection to Molango's high mountain environment; in a Maya context much later, the form, called a blood scroll, suggests bloodletting. In combination, these symbols reflect the relationship between sacrifice and fertility.[56]

The unusually large *plaza mayor* is positioned to one side of the church and *atrio* platform ensemble, rather than on axis at the lower level (Fig. 3.61). It is enclosed by commercial buildings, most of which have *portales*. A nineteenth-century *kiosko* seeks to center the plaza, which currently lacks the shade of trees, as it is paved and devoid of landscaping to facilitate the temporary structures of market day.

Achiutla, Oaxaca: San Miguel

As our survey team headed through the long valley up to Achiutla for the first time from our base in nearby Tlaxiaco, we could feel the site's presence well before we arrived, even though we did not know precisely if that was our intended site until we saw the church surmounting the Mixtec platforms. It is so isolated that local inhabitants informed us that the first automobile arrived in Achiutla as late as the 1950s.

Logan Wagner, 1990

Remoteness, inaccessibility, and economic stagnation are factors that usually guarantee that a sixteenth-century site has undergone little or no transformation from its original creation. Another, sometimes overlooked, factor is found in situations where a community must be relocated due to extraneous physical circumstances, such as loss of the only water source, or the site proving too small to accommodate population growth through time. Such is the case of San Miguel Achiutla in the Mixteca Alta of Oaxaca.

A *visita* of Tlaxiaco, San Miguel Achiutla is located in extremely hilly and mountainous terrain.[57] Before the arrival of Europeans, this site was a Mixtec ceremonial center and is often mentioned in the famous Mixtec codices. It was also over this pre-Hispanic ceremonial center that Dominican Order friars decided to build their monastery, church, church patio, Calvary chapel, and town proper (Fig. 3.62).

As is the case at many a mountainous site, the

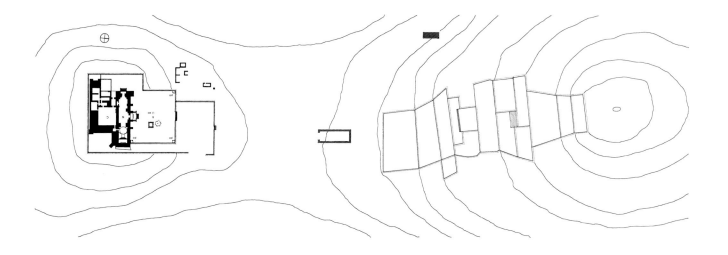

3.62. Achiutla, plan of sixteenth-century church of San Miguel and Mixtec terraced mountain platforms. Courtesy of the School of Architecture Visual Resources Collection, The University of Texas at Austin (Box-Wagner Collection, VRC 2007-4817).

3.63. Achiutla, view of church from Calvary chapel on platform on the opposite, terraced hill. Courtesy of the School of Architecture Visual Resources Collection, The University of Texas at Austin (Box-Wagner Collection, VRC 90-11631).

3.64. Achiutla, view of mountain terraces and Calvary chapel from church *atrio* on opposite hill. Courtesy of the School of Architecture Visual Resources Collection, The University of Texas at Austin (Box-Wagner Collection, VRC 90-8364).

3.65. Achiutla, view of nave toward the altar at the east end. Courtesy of the School of Architecture Visual Resources Collection, The University of Texas at Austin (Box-Wagner Collection, VRC 90-8380).

friars who were building the monastic complex over a native ceremonial center had to adapt their construction guidelines, orientation, and format to the physical constraints of the location. Many Mesoamerican sites are located at places on the landscape that provide a strong focal point for the distant viewer. Achiutla, built on a small twin-hill promontory in the valley of the same name, is an outstanding example of this phenomenon. As in the Olmec highland site of Chalcatzingo, the two mountain promontories at Achiutla create the "double merlon" of Olmec iconography that provides a portal to the Underworld manifested in the landscape. Temple platforms occupied the two hills at Achiutla, while the depression between them served as the pre-Hispanic plaza. Pre-Hispanic platforms provided the base on which Dominican friars built the monastic complex, replacing the pagan temples.

As the site plan indicates, Dominican friars founded the monastery and the town in a topographically restricted area. Since there were pre-Hispanic platforms on both of the twin hills, friars built the monastery complex on one hill and the cemetery, or *campo santo*, on the other. The Calvary chapel, also built on this platform, is on a perpendicular axis to the nave of the church on the opposing hill (Figs. 3.63–3.64). The small valley between the two hills became the site of the new town. Ruins of the civilian structures are still visible today, surrounding a necessarily small plaza. An increase in population forced the town to relocate about a kilometer away, down below the twin hills, but to this day the church dedicated to the patron saint San Miguel remains the principal house of worship for the town below.

3.66. Achiutla, north side of complex showing the church's apse, dome above transept and nave, with *atrio* wall in the foreground enclosing the one remaining *posa* chapel and the belfry. Courtesy of the School of Architecture Visual Resources Collection, The University of Texas at Austin (Box-Wagner Collection, VRC 90-8341).

Traditionally, sixteenth-century Mexican town centers were oriented so that the nave of the church would be on an east-west axis, with the altar at the east end toward the rising sun (Fig. 3.65). The west and main façade would face the sacred patio. In the case of Achiutla, the friars were able to build the nave on an east-west axis according to tradition, and the cloister that abuts the nave on the south side as well. Only ruins remain of the cloister. The *atrio*, which in 1990 still had one wood *posa* chapel, albeit dilapidated, had to be located on the north side of the nave, rather than on the traditional west side, to make it fit the site (Fig. 3.66).

Presumably, the processional ritual associated with the *atrio* and *posa* chapels would have been altered as

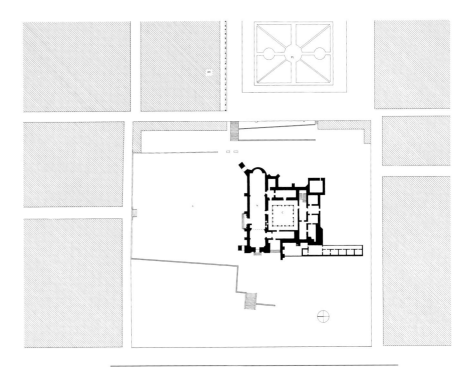

3.67. Yanhuitlán, plan of Santo Domingo and town center. Courtesy of the School of Architecture Visual Resources Collection, The University of Texas at Austin (Box-Wagner Collection).

well. Instead of beginning at the west door, the procession would shift ninety degrees, beginning at the north door, the side entry to the nave, and proceeding to the east, with pauses at the southeast and northeast *posa* chapels in the traditional counterclockwise sequence.

Yanhuitlán, Oaxaca: Santa Domingo

The church of Yanhuitlán is a monument of the first rank, which would not be out of place in any European city.

Manuel Toussaint, *Colonial Art in Mexico*

The monastery at Yanhuitlán, half a day's ride over the mountains, has the handsomest sixteenth-century church in Oaxaca if not in all Mexico.

John McAndrew, *Open-Air Churches*

It is one of the glories of sixteenth-century Mexican architecture.

Robert J. Mullen, *Architecture and Its Sculpture in Viceregal Mexico*

High in the steep mountains of the Mixteca Alta, Yanhuitlán was a thriving preconquest town in the sixteenth century, with a population of 20,000 married men, according to Father Bernabé Cobo in 1630.[58] His source was the company of Dominican friars at Yanhuitlán, where he visited for three days. By the time of his visit, the handsome church on its high *atrio* was just over fifty years old.

Like a similar Dominican monastery in the Mixteca at Coixtlahuaca, Yanhuitlán sits on a platform terrace that measures about 350 by 500 feet and is 20 feet high. Both platforms contain large amounts of Mesoamerican temple and pyramid shards, suggesting to McAndrew that they were constructed at the direction of friars.[59] He adds that there were pyramids next to the primitive church at the site, which were demolished before 1550, "and before deforestation had shriveled that once-great city to a village." Mullen, on the other hand, notes that the platform is clearly human-made and suggests it previously served as the base of a pre-Hispanic temple.[60]

The church *atrio* extends to the north, like the one at Coixtlahuaca, with a flight of stairs down to the street on axis with the north door and a smaller space in front of the west façade. Mullen calls the complex "staggering in size," the *atrio* extending just over 100 feet to the west, where another stair 20 feet wide with twenty-eight steps connects it with the road (now highway).[61] The main plaza of Yanhuitlán, like that at San Pedro y San Pablo Teposcolula, is behind the church, to the east, down yet another stairway (Fig. 3.67).

Although Dominican friars were sent to Yanhuitlán in 1538, the local *encomendero*, who was a relative

3.68. Yanhuitlán, west-facing façade on platform. Secular plaza and town are in the rear of the church. Courtesy of Sinclair Black.

3.69. Yanhuitlán, west front with Renaissance *retablo*. Courtesy of Sinclair Black.

of Cortés, and the local native lord refused to give them any assistance, and they retreated to Teposcolula, where they spent the next ten years building the monastery of San Pedro y San Pablo. The first church at Yanhuitlán was completed in 1541 but was of such poor quality that it was torn down on the return of the friars in 1548. In its place, they built the current complex, using funds left by the repentant *encomendero* and with the enthusiastic support of his devout son and heir.[62] Fray Antonio de Serna and Fray Francisco Marín, friar-architects of note, supervised the design and construction. Fray Marín is also credited with planning and early construction at both Coixtlahuaca and Teposcolula (Fig. 3.68).[63]

In the 1530s, the standard monastery plan in New Spain began to emerge. It took real form in the 1540s and was made mandatory in 1548. In 1550, Viceroy Mendoza asked his successor to follow his lead and approve the "moderate plan" he had used so as to avoid the errors of work done without architects. He recommended that Hernando Toribio de Alcaraz be appointed to oversee the building campaign. At that time, only the Dominicans were building enormous monasteries in Mexico.[64] Disregarding the instruction, they continued with Yanhuitlán until its completion in the 1570s. The Dominican chronicler Francisco de Burgoa wrote in the 1660s that Yanhuitlán took twenty-five years to complete and that an architect was involved. Another Dominican described Marín as someone who, "with the skill of an architect, drew plans for the community's churches and *conventos* and supervised their construction," confirming his identity.[65]

The church has a Renaissance *retablo* façade, divided vertically and horizontally into three parts, each side decorated with sculptures in niches, while the center panel contains the choir window, a relief sculpture of Mary with the Christ Child, and the west portal has a diamond-paneled arch (Fig. 3.69). The façade is set between two slightly protruding tower bases, only one of which has a belfry. In 1975, an earlier façade was discovered beneath the current one.[66] A small panel on the lower façade contains a symbol of the Dominican Order: a dog with a torch in its mouth, based on an image dreamed by Saint Dominic's mother before he was born of a dog lighting the world with the torch of Christianity held in his mouth. The dream is often retold with an accompanying play on words, *domini canis*, "dog of the lord."

The heavy stonework of the church walls and its

3.70. Yanhuitlán, buttresses, high windows, and plateresque north door seen across the green *atrio*. Courtesy of Sinclair Black.

3.71. Yanhuitlán, view west from the open chapel. Courtesy of Sinclair Black.

3.72. Yanhuitlán; sunlight from the cloister illuminates the walk and its rib vaulting. Courtesy of Sinclair Black.

huge semicircular apse are braced on the north by stepped buttresses pierced with arched doorways. The north nave wall has arched windows of gothic tracery and a handsome north door, called by Perry "the most sophisticated Plateresque doorway in Oaxaca" (Fig. 3.70).[67] The monastery complex braces the south side of the church. Inside, the huge nave is covered with ribbed vaulting and *retablos* in various styles. The sixteenth-century main *retablo* by Andrés de la Concha of Seville is a particularly rare treasure of the viceregal period, as so few from that century remain. The painter is thought to have worked on *retablos* at Coixtlahuaca and other missions in the area, along with Simon Pereyns, a Flemish artist.

The open chapel here was placed next to the bell tower at the top of a broad stair, creating a stage from which the friars could preach to their audience below (Fig. 3.71). The cloister is surrounded by vaulted walks, and the lower floor is accessed from the *portería* (Fig. 3.72). Sixteen brick cells, where the friars lived, are on the second floor along with a large latrine. Although only two, or perhaps three, friars lived at most monasteries, such a large number of facilities must have been necessary when the Dominican province of fifty friars met there in 1558.

SUNKEN COURTS

Natural openings into the earth's crust were held sacred by Mesoamericans. A variation is the human-made penetration that creates a sunken court, seeking the same sacred subterranean source of the supernatural. The sacred cave under the Pyramid of the Sun in Teotihuacan is both natural and modified by humans. In mountainous terrain, it may be necessary to terrace the land; sunken courts can be a result, and to the indigenous population, sacred *atrios* below grade would have alluded to the sacred Underworld of ancient Mesoamerica. In the corpus of Mesoamerican sites, we have many examples of both sunken courts and totally enclosed courts. As noted, the oldest sunken court found to date is Teopantecuanitlán, Guerrero, and among enclosed courts, we can cite La Ciudadela in Teotihuacan and the Nunnery Quadrangle at Uxmal.

Among the sixteenth-century mendicant order sites that we surveyed, we chose three to illustrate Mesoamerican continuity of sunken courts: Tepoztlán, Tochimilco, and Calpan; Huaquechula, described above, has one as well. Perhaps coincidentally, several

of the sites have a number of steps down into their *atrios* that correspond with sacred Mesoamerican numbers, one with nine steps and two with thirteen, numbers that suggest the nine levels of the Underworld and the thirteen of the heavens.

Tepoztlán, Morelos: Natividad de Nuestra Señora

Our ancestors taught us to bless the seed with copal, with incense. This is the aroma of sacredness in Mexico. So, this is a petition to Mother Earth and the blessing, the smudging, is done in the four directions in the form of a cross so that She helps nurture the seed and that it grows and gives fruit.

Tepoztlán farmer, Lamberto Chayo Guzmán, http:// www.gourmet.com/video?videoID=64378014001

The town of Tepoztlán nestles in a 5,500-foot-high valley surrounded by craggy volcanic mountains (Figs. 3.73–3.74). At the site of a mountain cleft above the town is the ancient temple dedicated to Tepoztecatl, one of the Aztec gods of pulque. Pulque is a milky alcoholic drink made of fermented maguey sap. Identified with mother's milk in Mesoamerican mythology,[68] it is still consumed, although in less quantity than of old, and it supplements the staple diet of corn and beans. In the 1930s, Stuart Chase noted its nutritional value:

> It is even fed to children. Far from doing them harm it now appears that they could hardly survive without it. Aztecs, and Mexicans after them, never ate enough fruit and vegetables to offset properly the high protein intake of corn and beans. Why did they persist so sturdily? Dr. Jose Zozaya, a brilliant young investigator who has been called Mexico's foremost scientist, tells me that the answer is pulque. It follows the law whereby all surviving primitive peoples, after long centuries of trial and error, balance their diet.[69]

The more obvious role of pulque as an intoxicant has deep roots in Mesoamerica, well into the colonial period. In *Drinking, Homicide, and Rebellion in Colonial Mexican Villages*, William Taylor describes preconquest drinking habits; the making of pulque; and the association of pulque-maguey with fertility, agriculture, feminism, and religion. He then goes on to document the continuation of pulque drinking in seventeenth-century Mexico, including ritual celebrations that measured devotion by the degree of

3.73. Tepoztlán, plan of town center. Courtesy of the School of Architecture Visual Resources Collection, The University of Texas at Austin (Box-Wagner Collection).

3.74. Tepoztlán, aerial view. Courtesy of the School of Architecture Visual Resources Collection, The University of Texas at Austin (Box-Wagner Collection, VRC 92-2496).

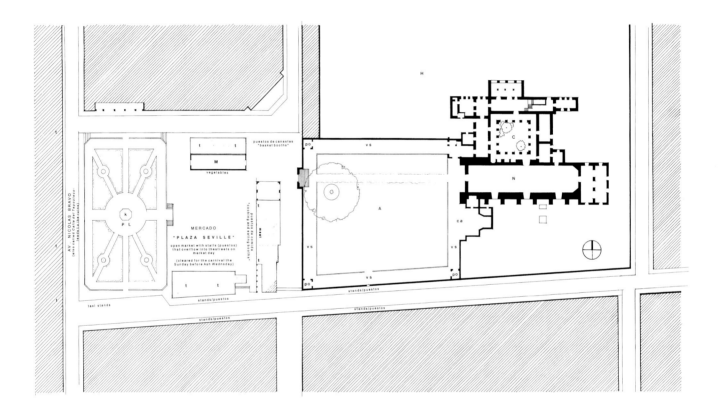

intoxication, condemned by the Spanish as drunken orgies and idolatry.[70]

Spaniards visited Tepoztlán even before the "conquest" was complete. Díaz del Castillo notes that when Cortés and his conquistadors came to Tepoztlán in early April 1521, before the fall of Tenochtitlan, they found there "some very pretty Indian women and much spoil." But, after summoning the caciques "to come and make peace," and receiving the reply that they would not come, Cortés had the town burned "to strike fear into the neighboring towns."[71] The date of the Dominican friars' arrival in Tepoztlán is not certain. Kubler says they arrived about 1559 but mentions that a sculpture of Ometochtli was sent from Tepoztlán in 1534 to be built into the foundation of the church at Oaxtepec.[72] Ricard says the parish was founded before 1556.[73] Perry says that the Dominicans succeeded in baptizing the old king and thus converting the natives to Catholicism in 1538.[74] That event is still reenacted each September during a festival known as Altepe-ilhuitl, which Ricard says was established by Fray Domingo de la Anunciación "as a substitute for a pre-Hispanic seasonal festival."[75] Once they had arrived, the Dominicans began to establish both the *convento* and the town as well as convert the local population (Fig. 3.75).

Tepoztlán's *atrio* is sunken, like the one at Calpan. McAndrew describes both sites by noting that the buildings are at the lower end of sloping land, so many yards of earth had to be cut out of the hillside and carried away to make the *atrio* level. As one walks down into them, it becomes clear that the *atrio* and the higher adjacent plaza are experienced sequentially rather than simultaneously.[76] At Tepoztlán, the plaza is west of the *atrio*, fourteen steps higher, and an arched gate separates them at the top (Fig. 3.76). One steps down from the bustling market plaza into the calm, quiet, regenerative atmosphere of the *atrio* and is reminded of its association with the primordial sea.

At the top of the steep stair is a marketplace where each vendor has covered his wares with a fabric awning, creating the impression that the whole market has been roofed (Fig. 3.77). The market plaza is the same width as the *atrio* and about half as wide as the original convent grounds, the other half of its block taken up by a school. A civic plaza with a central kiosk lies to the west of the market plaza, bounded by trees. Built-in benches provide places to rest or chat (Fig. 3.78). Together, the market and civic plazas are the

3.75. Tepoztlán, entry portal into *atrio* decorated with seeds and beans. Susan Kline Morehead.

same size and area as the school, and in combination, they are approximately equal in size to the walled *convento* grounds. A pedestrian street at the level of the market plaza marks the boundary of the original convent grounds, and another, perpendicular to it, extends from the convent's *atrio* wall and separates the plazas from the school. The main roads into and through Tepoztlán lead to the central plazas, bounding them on their northern, western, and southern edges with space to drive and park, and keeping cars out of the central blocks.

The elements of the architecture of conversion are all represented at Natividad de Nuestra Señora in Tepoztlán, although only two of the *posa* chapels remain intact. The large open chapel on the south of the church is a roofless ruin marked by its wide sanctuary arch and squared apse, behind a line of column bases that mark the once-arcaded space in front. The *atrio* is centered on the open chapel. The first *posa*, the northeastern one, is embedded in the *portería* of the

3.77. Tepoztlán, market vendors. Susan Kline Morehead.

3.78. Tepoztlán, civic plaza. Courtesy of the School of Architecture Visual Resources Collection, The University of Texas at Austin (Box-Wagner Collection).

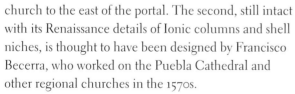

3.76. Tepoztlán, view from *atrio* stair up into plaza. Courtesy of Sinclair Black.

church to the east of the portal. The second, still intact with its Renaissance details of Ionic columns and shell niches, is thought to have been designed by Francisco Becerra, who worked on the Puebla Cathedral and other regional churches in the 1570s.

Kubler assigns the church façade to a class of "tall pedimented doorways" and associates it with the north façade at Coixtlahuaca, a Dominican establishment in Oaxaca (Fig. 3.79).[77] Tepoztlán's façade angels, like those at Calpan and Huaquechula, fly toward each other, here supporting an empty frame, their skirts and wings stiffly flapping. Like the figures who stand below them—the Virgin with her feathered halo, Saint Dominic, and Saint Catherine of Siena—the angels are examples of *tequitqui*, the flat, linear native execu-

tion of European forms with a sprinkling of native motifs.

Inside the monastery, the two levels of cloister bays are plain and unbuttressed, but the sixteenth-century murals have been restored and add life and color. Above the upper cloister are rows of capped merlons that echo the mountain crags, along with one single-bell *espadaña*. On the second level, a loggia looks out over the valley, where farmers still grow corn and magueys. One local farmer, who grows traditional, nonhybridized, indigenous corn, ceremonially blesses his sacks of seed corn over smoking copal incense by marking the four corners of the universe on the bags, making the sign of the cross.[78] The quincunx symbolism is alive and well today in Tepoztlán.

3.79. Tepoztlán, *atrio* and façade. Courtesy of Sinclair Black.

Tochimilco, Puebla ("The Place of the Field of Rabbits"): Santa María Asunción

This Franciscan monastery dedicated to the Assumption of the Virgin Mary is located on a promontory on the southwest piedmont of Popocatépetl Volcano, some fifteen miles west of Atlixco, Puebla, and just east of the border with the state of Morelos. Kubler attributes its foundation to the decade of 1550 to 1560, after an earlier attempt was made at a site closer to Atlixco.[79] Today the town of Tochimilco is a small village that provides a spectacular view of the volcanoes Popocatépetl and Iztaccíhuatl for its obviously dwindling population.

With large rectangular city blocks, Tochimilco's urban grid offers a remarkable orthogonal regularity, considering the abruptness of the surrounding terrain, prompting one to assume the original center of town was located on a small flat plateau at the top of the hill. At first glance, one can deduce that a whole city block was allotted to the conventual complex of nave,

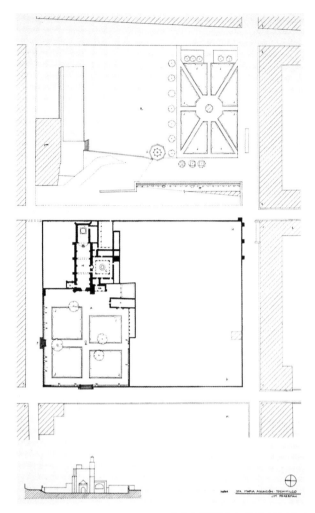

3.80. Tochimilco, plan and section of Santa María Asunción. Courtesy of the School of Architecture Visual Resources Collection, The University of Texas at Austin (Box-Wagner Collection, VRC 2007-4795).

3.81. Tochimilco, stair down into square *atrio* with central cross. Courtesy of the School of Architecture Visual Resources Collection, The University of Texas at Austin (Box-Wagner Collection, VRC 92-9329).

cloister, and *atrio*, and another complete city block was dedicated to the civic plaza and municipal government building (Fig. 3.80).

The convent and associated open land, comprising the original *huerta*, *atrio*, and north court, are completely surrounded by a wall separating them from the rest of the town. Over half of the city block dedicated to the convent constitutes the *huerta*, south of the *atrio* and convent.

The sunken *atrio* is enclosed by walls on three sides, with the convent and nave forming the fourth, east side. One can descend into the *atrio*, some 10 feet below street level, through openings on the west and north sides, whose walls are topped with merlons in accordance with sixteenth-century construction practices. Protruding from the *atrio* walls are niched shrines on square pedestals that form the processional sequence of the fourteen Stations of the Cross. Characteristic of the architecture of conversion, the *atrio* cross is located at the center of the *atrio* in alignment with the west *atrio* entry, the main doorway into the church nave, and the altar.

Capillas posas no longer exist, except for a small chapel structure with *portales* at the southeast corner

of the *atrio* that seems to have substituted for the customary *posa* chapel at this location. Currently, landscaping divides the *atrio* into four quadrants, neatly and geometrically aligning the walkways with the north and west entry stairs. The two south quadrants and the north–south pathway are out of alignment to accommodate the chapel at the southeast corner of the *atrio* (Fig. 3.81).

Completing the architecture of conversion is a magnificent second-story vaulted open chapel, perched over the three-arched *portería* of the convent, similar to the famous open chapel at the Augustinian convent of Acolman near the ruins of Teotihuacan. Closed until recently by a masonry wall, the open chapel once depicted polychrome mural painting; unfortunately, the murals were destroyed during the uncovering of the open chapel (Fig. 3.82).

A more restricted and intimate open space, the cloister patio, is surrounded on all four sides by an arcaded and rib-vaulted walkway at ground level that is repeated on the upper level to give access to friars' alcoves. Now paved with clay tile, the cloister patio has at its center a source of life, a fountain. The quadrangular geometry of the court punctuated by the fountain as axis mundi provides a setting for the continuation of quincunxial ritual processions of native origin (Fig. 3.83).

Perhaps the best-known architectural element of Tochimilco is the Gothic-style fountain that has miraculously survived and is located on the city block allocated to the civic plaza. An aqueduct was built to bring water to the fountain for the town from snow-capped Popocatépetl. Octagonal in plan, the fountain's corners are marked by short pillars with cone-shaped merlons, each surmounted by a Gothic Isabelline pearl. At the center, a taller pillar is decorated with a ring of similar pearls, followed by another cone-shaped merlon and topped with a crested shield depicting a rabbit, an eagle, and agave plants, all executed in *tequitqui* style. The crest is dated 1558, making this fountain one of the earliest extant colonial fountains.[80] The shape, crest, and date of the central pillar suggest that it was the *picota*, or foundation pillar, of Tochimilco, an essential element of plaza furnishings of the sixteenth century, making it, along with those in Cholula and Tlacochahuaya, among the last remaining colonial *picotas* (Fig. 3.84).

3.83. Tochimilco, view of cloister with central fountain from roof. Courtesy of the School of Architecture Visual Resources Collection, The University of Texas at Austin (Box-Wagner Collection, VRC 92-9328).

3.84. Tochimilco, fountain in civic plaza. Courtesy of the School of Architecture Visual Resources Collection, The University of Texas at Austin (Box-Wagner Collection, VRC 92-13204).

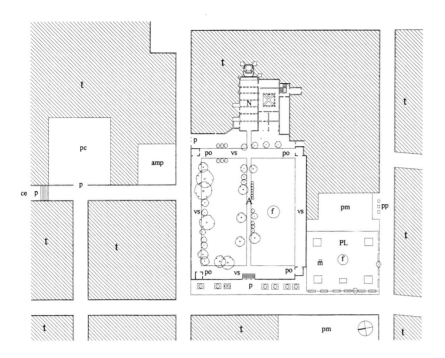

3.85. Calpan, plan of town center. Courtesy of the School of
Architecture Visual Resources Collection, The University of
Texas at Austin (Box-Wagner Collection).

Calpan, Puebla: San Andrés

A form that for the friars was nothing but purely
decorative had the power to embody a religious concept
for the Indian, thus attaining religious syncretism. In
this way, both friar and Indian were satisfied.

**Constantino Reyes-Valerio, *Arte indocristiana* (trans-
lation by Susan Kline Morehead)**

San Andrés Calpan is well known among aficio-
nados of sixteenth-century Mexican architecture for
being the indigenous counterpart of the nearby Franciscan monastery of Huejotzingo. As such, we use this
example to describe the iconography around the *atrio*
and what those symbols communicated to the indigenous population. In a visit to Calpan in 1585, Antonio
de Ciudad Real described it as located between some
ravines in the foothills of the volcanoes and as having
abundant water from a spring that fed the "splendid"
stone fountain in the center of the plaza.[81] The spring
and the ravines would have made this site attractive
to Mesoamericans seeking portals to the Underworld
of their gods. Calpan's sunken court, built by first- or
second-generation indigenous stonemasons about
1548,[82] echoes the ancient search for portals.

The town's *plaza mayor* is at street level, but
rather than extending west from the church, as it does
in most towns, it is located beside the *atrio*'s southwest
edge, taking up the corner of a large block that also
contains the walled *atrio*, the church and convent, and
grounds that were probably the convent's orchard (Fig.
3.85). A small Palacio Municipal sits on the east side of
the plaza, facing the same direction as the church. A
high adobe wall flanks the entire southern edge of the
long block, turning north behind the *convento* grounds
to enclose the east end of the block. It joins the stone
wall on the block's northern edge, a portion of which
forms the *atrio* wall, which wraps around to the west
edge of the block. On that side, the stone wall extends
only far enough to complete the enclosure of the *atrio*.

Two triple-arched gates lead into the *atrio*, one
from the west, on axis with the church façade (Fig.
3.86), and one plainer, older gate in the north wall
near the front of the church. Contemporaneous with
the church and monastery, this north gate stands at
the conjunction of a preconquest market square to the
north and a temple site to the south where the convent
complex now sits. Today a parish church is located on
the old market site, as can be seen in the plan of the
monastery and the blocks that surround it. The town
cemetery is on axis with the center of the *atrio* and lies
beyond the old market site on a rise, with views of the
two volcanoes to the west and another snow-capped
mountain to the southeast (Fig. 3.87).

The road that physically connects the ancient

3.86. Calpan, façade of San Andrés through triumphal arch at entry.
Susan Kline Morehead.

3.87. Calpan, view of church from the cemetery looking south.
Susan Kline Morehead.

3.88. Calpan, sunken court showing stair leading down into *atrio*. Courtesy of Sinclair Black.

ceremonial space, now *atrio*, with the cemetery also connects those spaces spiritually, as mourners walk from the church to the burying ground with their dead. Other ceremonies in the *atrio* today include celebrations of *quinceañeras* and weddings, first communions and saint's days.

Calpan is rich in examples of traditional Mesoamerican symbols that continue to carry meaning even after their incorporation into Christian church and monastery complexes, symbols located in ornament as well as in open space. The Mesoamerican form of the universe, a quincunx with four corners marking the cardinal directions and a central axis mundi joining the earth to the heavens and the Underworld, was re-created over and over in the *atrios* of New Spain churches, with their four corner *posas* and central *atrio* crosses. The fact that Calpan's *atrio* lies nine steps below street level emphasizes both its symbolic role as a point of entry to the nine levels of the Underworld and its function as the primordial sea, a place where the earth's crust has thinned, making entry easier. The space creates a theatrical backdrop for the iconography that was used as a teaching tool along with the spatial setting (Fig. 3.88).

The ornament on the church façade and on the four *posa* chapels was intended to teach the indigenous population about Christianity. This ornament reveals the doctrinal concerns of the European friars, and at the same time, the artistic techniques and motifs of the natives being converted. Their combination in art

reflects the syncretism of native and European ideals and beliefs that characterizes the spiritual conquest.

It is thought that Calpan was built by native craftsmen who may have worked with Fray Juan de Alameda, the Franciscan who moved the town of Huejotzingo and built the monastic complex there, then later built the complex at Huaquechula, where he is buried. The craftsmen that he had trained were in demand, as they were sent for by the citizens of Puebla to work on their first cathedral in 1536, and later, in 1576, six years after Fray Juan's death, natives that he had trained in making aqueducts were called from Huejotzingo. The mobility of craftsmen and the gaps in Fray Juan's known activities make it possible that Calpan was his design and his craftsmen's handiwork. Significant similarities in the iconographic themes of the three monasteries strengthen the possibility of Fray Juan's involvement, while their implementation argues for a high level of independence on the part of the native craftsmen.

The natives who actually built and decorated the monasteries in Mexico were at a significant disadvantage, since they were members of a conquered people under conversion to Christianity. However, they comprised a group of highly skilled artisans, trained in a richly developed, three-thousand-year-old architectural and artistic tradition. From the early Olmecs of c. 1200 BCE to the Aztec Empire conquered by Cortés in 1521 CE, Mesoamericans built pyramids that rival those of Egypt[83] on which to place their temples, palaces and apartment complexes with elaborate decoration to house their rulers and priests, and axial ceremonial centers oriented by sophisticated astronomical calculations.[84] Their sculpture is equally impressive: colossal portrait heads of basalt and finely detailed jade figurines of the Olmec period, elaborate narrative reliefs that ornament stelae and buildings in the Classic period, and Aztec wonders in stone, gold, and silver that astounded Europe after the conquest. The quality of craftsmanship is more remarkable because no metal tools were used; preconquest carving was accomplished by Stone Age methods of working the stone with tools of stone, bone, horn, wood, and reeds, then finishing it with water and sand.[85] When metal stoneworking tools were introduced from Europe, the already skilled natives increased production dramatically, despite having to learn new, Christian motifs.

Calpan is one of the best examples of sixteenth-century architecture providing lessons for the natives in architectural ornament. Several major Christian themes appear and overlap in the ornamental programs at the three monasteries designed by Fray Juan, reflecting the spiritual concerns of the Catholic Church in sixteenth-century Europe and particularly of the Franciscan Order. Chief among these themes is the coming of the end of the world, with Christ sitting in judgment.[86] The Last Judgment is depicted in relief at two of the three sites, Calpan and Huaquechula, and its corollary symbolism, the triumphal parading of the instruments of Christ's Passion to portray his power over death, dominates the relief program at Huejotzingo. In his study of medieval iconography, Emile Mâle identifies the trend of fifteenth-century religious literature and art toward an "overflowing of sensibility," expressed as a concern for the passion and suffering of Christ. Its source is Saint Francis, of whom Mâle says:

> St. Francis is like the second founder of Christianity. . . . he experienced the revelation of the Passion, suffering so deeply that from then on he bore its signs: a miracle of love that astonished all of Europe and gave birth to completely new forms of sensibility.[87]

Imagery depicting the Passion began to include the instruments of torture—the crown of thorns, the lance, the nails, the cross—as well as the wounds themselves. Mâle notes that the instruments were frequently carried by angels and that their number increased to include peripheral items, such as Pontius Pilate's ewer and basin or Christ's seamless garment.[88] Juan de Alameda programmed this Late Medieval theme of the Passion, particularly the imagery of angels bearing the instruments, at Calpan and on all the *posas* at Huejotzingo.

In addition to the major Christian themes portrayed in stone on the façades, which turned them into a kind of architectural picture book, a group of smaller motifs with significance in both European and native iconography appear in and around the larger images. These small motifs, especially in the bands that surround larger relief panels, provide specific information from native tradition that informs the Catholic themes of the reliefs and helps make them sacred to the local population. Similar bands of various motifs appear in the Mesoamerican codices that still exist, confirming

3.89. Calpan, principal façade. Courtesy of the School of Architecture Visual Resources Collection, The University of Texas at Austin (Box-Wagner Collection, VRC 92-12612).

the notion that the carvers were familiar with the concept. It seems likely that the native sculptors consciously used these small motifs as keys to the larger relief panels, explaining the Christian stories with small but highly symbolic indigenous motifs that held meaning for them and their own people. The Mesoamerican artistic tradition of allowing an abstracted part of an image to represent the whole, pars pro toto, makes this even more likely.

One frequently recurring motif appears prominently on the portals of all three churches, as well as on many other churches of the time. Mounted symmetrically on a heraldic shield, the Five Wounds of Christ, also called the stigmata, appear as circular or oval openings dripping blood (Fig. 3.89). The importance of this symbol in fifteenth-century European religious life is such that confraternities and cults were established in its name; studies were made of details

3.90. Calpan, façade detail of Five Wounds of Christ on shield held by angels. Susan Kline Morehead.

3.91. Calpan, northwest *posa* with angel holding shield with Five Wounds motif and Saint Francis at top right corner. Courtesy of the School of Architecture Visual Resources Collection, The University of Texas at Austin (Box-Wagner Collection, VRC 92-12627).

such as the central wound's exact dimensions; and in art, the wounds and the blood flowing from them began appearing in increasingly graphic elaborations.[89] It is a particularly appropriate symbol for Franciscan monasteries, because Saint Francis, the founder of the order, was marked by the stigmata. Placed at the entries, it announces that these monasteries belong to the Franciscan Order, first among the three mendicant orders to be charged with converting Mexico's natives, first to arrive in the New World, and first in their devotion to their vows of poverty. Its frequent and prominent placement on the monastic façades also illustrates the use made of sculptural ornament as visual texts for teaching Christian doctrine. The fact that native stone carvers rendered the wounds as *chalchihuitls*, or jade beads, the Mesoamerican symbol for blood, enhances the power of the symbol.[90]

At Calpan, the Five Wounds motif is the primary element on one *posa* façade as well as figuring prominently on the church façade (Fig. 3.90). On the northwest *posa*, dedicated to Saint Francis, the shield with the Five Wounds is held from above by an angel with outstretched wings, filling the space above the arch (Fig. 3.91). Its central wound is emphasized by increased size, and traces remain of the red with which it was once painted. Here the forms are rounder and fuller, with none of the overall patterning of Huejotzingo's "purer plateresque," giving the sculpture at Calpan "more vigor and personality."[91] Similarly, the motifs on the church portal assert themselves energetically. The central symbol of the Five Wounds is framed in an elaborate escutcheon, so large that it overlaps the extrados of the arch beneath. Like its mate on the *posa*, it is borne aloft, here by a pair of large, winged angels whose heavy draped skirts flap and curl in the wind. Two smaller stigmata in more sedate shields decorate the tall candelabra columns framing the door, marking the start of the choir window. They seem to serve as bases—or flower pots—for the tapering columns of maguey stalks that flank the window.[92] More wound motifs decorate the space between the columns and the Franciscan cord that forms an *alfiz*, framing the window.

The *chalchihuitl* motif also occurs as a decorative band at Calpan, in the crown that sits atop the *posa* dedicated to the Virgin Mary, as well as appearing at Huejotzingo, encircling the column capitals of the *posa* arches. Whether or not the friars were aware of the significance of the *chalchihuitl*, its circular form is so simple and so universal that it could easily have been overlooked as simply decorative in any attempt to purge native religious symbols.

When one walks the sacred way at Calpan, beginning at the front of the church and turning north along the path toward the first *posa*, the path leads out of the gate rather than into the arched doorway of the *posa*. The *posa* is offset slightly to the west along the *atrio* wall, providing a third façade for ornamentation in addition to the two usual ones. At Calpan, this *posa* is dedicated to the Virgin Mary and is decorated with bands of alternating roses and marigolds. Scenes from Mary's life decorate the three façades, one showing the annunciation, another her triumphal assumption into heaven as a pair of angels place a crown on her head (Fig. 3.92), while in the third she is pierced by seven enormous swords representing her seven sorrows. The sword handles terminate in large round medallions that have lost their original images, one for each sorrow. It has been suggested that the medallions contained obsidian or greenstone disks like those the Aztecs placed in their idols' chests to give them life; the sorrows would then be alive, inflicting boundless suffering and pain on Mary. Curiously, the number seven was as significant to Mesoamericans as it is to Christians, considered to be an omen of good luck. Moreover, calendar names with the number seven in them signify seeds; for example, "Seven Serpent" is the esoteric name for corn. The goddess Seven Serpent was the most important of the gods of vegetation, and her nickname was "seven ears of corn."[93]

Decorative banding with motifs from both cultures is evident in the alternation of roses and marigolds on the *posa* dedicated to the Virgin Mary (Fig. 3.93). In Christian iconography, the rose, which bloomed without thorns in paradise according to Saint Ambrose, is a symbol of the Virgin Mary because she is untainted by original sin.[94] The rose is also associated with Saint Francis. He threw himself into a thorn bush to repress the temptations of the flesh, and where the drops of his blood fell in the snow, roses grew.[95] It appears in Mexican Christianity in 1531, when the vision of the Virgin Mary seen by native convert Juan Diego was made manifest to Bishop Zumárraga by the miraculous blooming of roses in winter; this event established the cult of the Virgin of Guadalupe, patroness of Mexican Indians. The vision occurred at the site of a shrine to Tonantzin, the Aztec earth mother god-

3.92. Calpan, northeast *posa* relief of the Assumption of the Virgin banded by alternating marigolds and roses. Susan Kline Morehead.

dess, causing some subsequent confusion and concern among the community of friars.

Marigolds signify Mary in English because they recall her name, but there is no such correspondence with Spanish.[96] In preconquest Mexico, the Nahuatl word for marigolds, *cempoalxochitl*, means "flower of the dead," and even today, *cempoalxochitl* flowers decorate altars, tombs, and pathways in cemeteries on the eve of Día de los Muertos.[97] Day of the Dead home altars include an offering to the dead, the *ofrenda*, for which "the last and most crucial item to be picked or purchased are the *cempoalxochitl* flowers." The altars and *ofrenda* are sacred, representing ceremonial centers that recall the sacred Aztec "Mountain of Sustenance" and "symbolize the body of the life-giving earth with its forces of regeneration."[98] Everything is prepared to tempt the spirits back home and to nourish

3.93. Calpan, detail of marigold and rose banding on northeast *posa*. Susan Kline Morehead.

3.94. Example of a *sello*, a pre-Columbian stamp, of a marigold. Drawing by Jorge Enciso.

them during Día de los Muertos. Both the aromatic scent and brilliant colors of the *cempoalxochitl* are believed to attract the souls of the dead to the offerings. Paths of vivid orange and yellow *cempoalxochitl* flower petals are laid out to guide the souls to their feast. These altars and *ofrendas* are part of sacred ceremonial rites that recall Aztec celebrations of the dead.[99]

The marigolds on the *posa* of the Virgin Mary are depicted in the flat, outlined style of preconquest art, very different from the European style of roses. They resemble designs of *sellos*, seals or clay stamps used to imprint pottery or bark paper (Fig. 3.94).[100] Each *posa* marigold has two rings of petals around a circular center: an inner ring of eight petals and an outer ring

of thirteen. The pre-Columbian significance of these numbers relates the petals of the marigold to the layers of the cosmos: the thirteen petals correspond to the thirteen heavenly levels, and the eight petals plus the center correspond to the nine-level Underworld that counts the earthly plane as one of its levels. Moreover, the marigold's center is the axis mundi, and the petals in the inner ring locate the four corners of the world and their midpoints, creating a set of two quincunx forms. Numerically, the marigold is a symbol of the preconquest universe, symbolism that enriches its role as the flower of the dead souls who traverse levels of the cosmos to visit the earthly plane each year.

The biblical scenes carved on the spandrels, jambs, and arches of the *posas* are different at each one, and the roof shapes vary as well: the Virgin's is pyramidal, topped with a crown and cactus-stalk cross, while the second, dedicated to Saint Francis, has a bulging square dome divided in quadrants by the Franciscan cord and now topped with a globe and cross. The third *posa*'s crown is a tiara, the papal crown, more elaborate than Mary's, and this *posa* is dedicated to Saint Michael Archangel. He and his companions Gabriel and Raphael face the faithful who walk on the sacred way toward his *posa*. But the most celebrated image at Calpan, the Last Judgment, is carved on the east façade of this third *posa* (Fig. 3.95). Based on one of a number of woodcuts that were likely to have been in a friar's library, Christ sits majestically holding a lily and a sword, while Mary and John the Baptist plead for the souls of the dead who are rising from their graves below.

Framing the doorways of this *posa* are bands of alternating hearts and shells that reflect the cyclical rhythm of life, death, and rebirth, echoing or perhaps interpreting that same pattern in Christ's sacrifice for man's everlasting life that is central to the scene of Judgment Day (Fig. 3.96). It is the most flagrant display of native iconography at Calpan. These heart and shell motifs, seemingly innocuous decorative elements in European art, are integral to Mesoamerican cosmology and the rite of sacrifice. The hearts are depicted in section, much as they must have looked as they were ripped from live victims with the help of a curved obsidian "heart extractor" knife, before they were offered to the sun god.[101] Similar heart images can be found in murals at Atetelco, a suburb of Teotihuacan (c. 150–750 CE), and in sculptural reliefs at Chichén Itzá centuries later, as well as in Aztec art at the time of the

3.95. Calpan, Last Judgment scene on southwest *posa* with band of hearts and shells. Courtesy of the School of Architecture Visual Resources Collection, The University of Texas at Austin (Box-Wagner Collection, VRC 92-12596).

3.96. Calpan, detail of heart and shell banding motif. Susan Kline Morehead.

3.97. Calpan, southeast *posa* with medallions of the four evangelists and Saint John in the center forming a quincunx. Courtesy of Sinclair Black.

3.98. Calpan, detail of medallion of Saint John, "Sant Ivan" in mirror image, on southeast *posa*. Susan Kline Morehead.

conquest. Among those at Atetelco are ritual scenes depicting the heart held aloft on the point of the warrior-priest's heart extractor, and at Chichén Itzá, jaguars are eating hearts. Shells indicate a watery realm throughout preconquest art, most often the primordial sea that is the source of fertility and generation.[102] Implicit in images of this primordial sea is its function as transition space—a portal—between the human world and the Underworld inhabited by ancestor gods. Imbued with these Mesoamerican meanings, the alternating hearts and shells reflect the rhythm of life and death. With that interpretation, their placement bordering the Last Judgment seems an appropriate visual explication for the natives.

The fourth *posa* at Calpan, dedicated to Saint John, has a quincunx made of four medallions containing the evangelists depicted as their Christian symbols—lion, eagle, ox, and man—centered by a niche holding Saint John. This image confirms the use of woodcuts by native stonemasons, as the letters spelling out "SANT IVAN" (Saint John) are carved backward, in a mirror image (Figs. 3.97–3.98). The woodcut must have gotten damp, so the image bled through to the other side, unbeknownst to the mason, who didn't know the difference. One possible source of the image is the woodcut title page of an early work on the Inquisition, *Directorium inquisitorum* by Nicolaus Eymericus, printed in Barcelona by Johann Luschner in 1503, which shows the evangelistic angel, eagle, bull, and lion in roundels with inscribed streamers appearing near their mouths, all surrounding a figure

of Christ.[103] The pre-Columbian speech scroll and the inscribed ribbon fluttering near the mouths of the European evangelists' symbols both inform this new Mexican imagery.

The complex at Calpan is closely tied to Meso-american concepts and images through its form as sunken court and quincunx, its siting on axis with the indigenous market and cemetery, and its teaching program of iconographic notes carved in the stone banding to "translate" the Christian themes on the façades of the church and *posas*. Set in the open spaces of Mesoamerican courts or New Spain's *atrios*, art reinforces ritual; the combination of images, theater, and setting created a powerful tool for conversion.

BALLCOURTS AND BULLRINGS

In the Mesoamerican chapter, we discussed the significance of the ball game in Mesoamerican religion and its importance as a vital element of the architectural repertoire of a typical Mesoamerican ceremonial center. Symbolizing a gash in the earth's crust, and thus a portal to the Underworld, the ballcourt is diagnostic of Mesoamerican sacred ceremonial centers.

Soon after the fall of Tenochtitlan, mendicant friars opposed, condemned, and prohibited the ball game and its associated ballcourts because of the ball game's religious importance and its inevitable connection with human blood sacrifice. Although we often find remains of Mesoamerican temples and platforms today, most Mesoamerican ballcourts were systematically destroyed.

The existence of bullrings next to mendicant monasteries tends to suggest, perhaps, that Spanish friars used bullfights as a substitute for the native ball game. Both rituals, the ball game and the bullfight, involve blood sacrifice. Both rituals hark back to the mystical origins of their cultures.

Except for the small handful of Spanish friars assigned to each of the existing native communities, *pueblos de indios*, the Spanish population was practically nonexistent, so why the need for bullrings? Tlaxcala, which was home to an indigenous nation that allied with Cortés during the siege of Tenochtitlan, allowing their kingdoms and culture to continue virtually untouched by the Spanish, boasts perhaps the most beautiful colonial bullring in Mexico (Fig. 3.99). One can easily understand the need to hold bullfights, a most Spanish of mass entertainment activities, in the

3.99. Tlaxcala bullring viewed from the open chapel of the *convento* San Francisco. Susan Kline Morehead.

Spanish urban centers of Puebla, Morelia, Guadalajara, Oaxaca, and even the capital, Mexico-Tenochtitlan, but in the strictly indigenous communities where the friars were evangelizing, their presence seems rather odd. Several Indian communities with mendicant monasteries that we surveyed included a circular masonry arena for bullfights next to, or even within, the convent's grounds.

Many indigenous communities, even to this day, celebrate the culminating event of the weeklong festivities honoring the town's patron saint by holding bullfights in the plaza. Temporary bullrings are built to host this exciting event. Of interest to us here is that the bullfight occurs in the town's premier open space, the plaza, and not at the edge of town, where more space would be available and fewer obstructions would be present (Fig. 3.100).

In most rural towns in the state of Oaxaca, it is customary for the inhabitants to build primitive, temporary rectangular-shaped corrals in the plaza for bullfights and equestrian feats as part of the festivities for celebrations of their local patron saint. Locally, both the events and the corrals are known as *jaripeos*. Santo Domingo del Valle, Oaxaca, is typical of the way *jaripeos* are located in the local plaza.

A similar custom is prevalent even today in the Mayan-speaking villages of central Yucatán. There the bullrings are circular, often elaborate two-story structures. Built of wood poles lashed together by specialized teams using local henequen rope, these sophisticated temporary arenas usually take two weeks to erect. They are strong and large enough to support the entire village's population along with visitors. Welcome afternoon shade is provided by palm thatching to protect from Yucatán's scorching afternoon sun (Fig. 3.101).

When attending a bullfight in one of these structures, as in their masonry counterparts, one purchases a ticket, the price of which depends on the seat's

3.100. Reminiscent of a bullring's shape, the setting for this rain petition is the plaza of Zitlala Tecoaliztli. Courtesy of George O. Jackson, Jr.

a

b

c

d

e

3.101. Temporary bullring in Yucatán: (a) initial phase of construction, (b) in construction adjacent to the church, (c) detail of two-story construction, (d) detail of outer wall thatching, (e) ground-floor circulation below balcony seating, (f) advanced stage of construction, (g) detail of finished outer wall, (h) spectators in balcony seating during bullfight, (i) master builder.

g

f

h

i

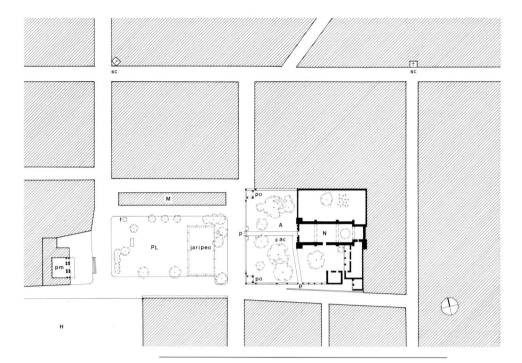

3.102. Villa Díaz Ordaz, plan of town center. Courtesy of the School of Architecture Visual Resources Collection, The University of Texas at Austin (Box-Wagner Collection).

location: first level or balcony. Refreshment and snack vendors patrol the aisles selling their wares. At the end of the town's festivities, the bullrings are disassembled, to be reassembled at some neighboring village when that village's yearly festival comes around.

Villa Díaz Ordaz, Oaxaca: Santo Domingo

The courtyards are very large and comely, for the people are many, and do not fit in the churches. For this reason their chapel is outdoors in the courtyard, because all hear Mass every Sunday and feastday, while the churches are used on weekdays.

Toribio Motolinía, quoted by George Kubler in *Mexican Architecture of the Sixteenth Century*

Villa Díaz Ordaz gets its name from General José María Díaz Ordaz, governor of the state of Oaxaca, who died from wounds suffered during a battle between Liberals and Conservatives that took place here in 1860. Archival records, however, indicate the settlement was founded by the Dominican friars in 1526, and the principal church is dutifully named in honor of Saint Dominic, its patron saint.

Before the arrival of Europeans, this Zapotec community had been conquered by Aztecs, so the settlement has had at least four names: the original Zapotec name; a Nahuatl translation of the original Zapotec name, following the Aztec conquest of the fifteenth century; the original Spanish name given by the Do-

minican friars in 1526, Santo Domingo del Valle; and its current name, Villa Díaz Ordaz, in honor of the Oaxacan hero of the War of Reform of 1860.

Located in the sacred Tlacolula Valley of the Central Valleys district of the modern state of Oaxaca, Villa Díaz Ordaz is located some 40 kilometers east of the capital city of Oaxaca (Fig. 3.102). As in many Mesoamerican indigenous communities, especially in the Oaxaca area, rulers are identified with mountains surrounding the settlement. In many cases, hills were physically modified to become pyramids within a sacred ceremonial center. Villa Díaz Ordaz's tutelary hill is a case in point and awaits archaeological excavation that may shed more light on this village's origins.

A first glance at Villa Díaz Ordaz's plan reveals the expected checkerboard grid established as the norm for Spanish settlements in the New World. Upon closer inspection, however, important anomalies can be detected, such as an unusually large city block surrounding the church. One can assume this land was once church property, probably dedicated to orchards and farm animals, and subsequently invaded and privatized following the War of Reform. A second anomaly is the diagonal street approaching and bisecting the orthogonal grid. Like other "off-grid" streets in

3.103. Villa Díaz Ordaz, façade of Santo Domingo.
Courtesy of the School of Architecture Visual Resources
Collection, The University of Texas at Austin (Box-Wagner
Collection, VRC 90-8904).

3.104. Villa Díaz Ordaz, *posa* chapel of Santo Domingo.
Courtesy of the School of Architecture Visual Resources
Collection, The University of Texas at Austin (Box-Wagner
Collection, VRC 90-9100).

Villa Díaz Ordaz, these roads existed before the grid
was laid out and have now been incorporated into the
street pattern.

The *atrio* is quadrangular, and two *posa* chapels
remain at its west side. Along with the central *atrio*
cross, these elements are all that remain of the original
architecture of conversion (Figs. 3.103–3.104). Instead

of the traditional convent cloister, a series of rooms
was constructed along a portico on the east side of the
atrio where visiting friars could stay. This is a typical arrangement for churches of smaller communities, known as *visita* churches, which rely on visiting
priests, hence the name. This architectural substitute
for the cloistered convents is known in Spanish as
curato or *casa cural.*

The town's plaza is fronted on the west side by
the Palacio Municipal, itself preceded by a small
open space. Civil government is located here, and the
nineteenth-century building has offices surrounding a
courtyard entered through the arcade facing the main
plaza. The original dimension of the plaza has been
sliced at the north edge into a slender rectangle that is
limited by the original north street of the plaza and a
new one to the south. The area allotted to the market
houses individual stalls used for market purposes, a
situation that has been encountered elsewhere but
remains unusual.

The unique feature of this plaza layout is that a
portion of the plaza has been formally and physically
designated as a rectangular corral for use in the rodeo/
bullfightlike activities of the *jaripeo* during the town's
festivals. As mentioned earlier, *jaripeos* in Oaxaca usually take place in the plaza, where a space is tempo-
rarily dedicated during the festival. However, here in
Villa Díaz Ordaz, the space allotted for the bullfight
has been made permanent.

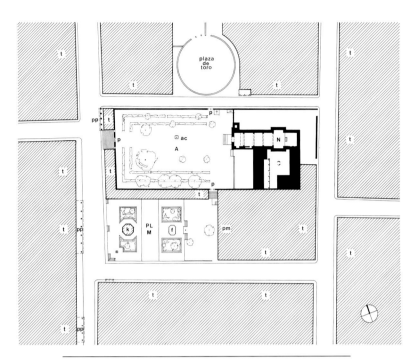

Tlanalapa, Hidalgo: San Francisco de Asís

Originally a Nahuatl-speaking community in the flat, pulque-producing maguey fields of the Apan meadows, San Francisco de Asís Tlanalapa was refounded as a *visita* church near Tepeapulco (Fig. 3.105). The word *tlanalapa* means "place of abundance" in Nahuatl, and its pictographic toponym is a body of water, like a lagoon, trimmed with flowers and *chalchihuitl*s, or jade beads (Fig. 3.106). The linguistic etymology reinforces the concept of water as a source of life, associated with the primordial sea.

Perhaps because of its proximity to Tepeapulco, Tlanalapa is another urban settlement that has a bullring built next to the convent in the sixteenth-century town, which supports the theory that some mendicant friars were substituting the animal-human sacrifice inherent in the Spanish bullfights for the human blood sacrifice that took place in the Mesoamerican ball game. In the case of Tlanalapa, the bullring is located immediately to the north of the *atrio* churchyard. Archaeological excavation within the bullring proper could shed some light on whether one structure did indeed supplant the other.

The orthogonal layout of the urban plan is very regular, and the city blocks are generous in size, following a consistent rectangular shape. A stairway leading from the street to the *atrio*-churchyard likely indicates the existence of a pre-Hispanic platform; additional staircases leading to the main doorway, to the

3.105. Tlanalapa, plan of town center. Courtesy of the School of Architecture Visual Resources Collection, The University of Texas at Austin (Box-Wagner Collection).

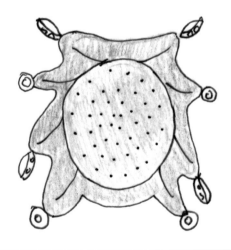

3.106. Tlanalapa, toponym depicted as source/body of water trimmed in flowers and jade beads. Redrawn by Logan Wagner.

church nave, and to a separate but adjacent staircase to the convent suggest an additional terraced platform of pre-Hispanic origin (Fig. 3.107). Small commercial establishments of narrow proportions located at street level along the *atrio*'s west and south walls imply a later invasion of these two narrow strips of land.

The *atrio* open space of rectangular proportions exhibits a processional route, outlined by low masonry

3.107. Tlanalapa, *atrio*, cross, church, and convento.
Courtesy of J.B. Johnson.

walls. Trees lining both sides of the masonry sacred way reinforce, shade, and formalize the circuit. An *atrio* cross in the center is aligned with the triumphal arched entry to the *atrio* on one flank and entry to the church's nave on the other. The *mudéjar alfiz* that squares off and frames the arched doorway corroborates its sixteenth-century origins, as do the bands of rich ornament that are reminiscent of those on the *posa* chapels at Calpan (Fig. 3.108).[104] *Posa* chapels are nonexistent today, but a small chapel-like structure stands at the southeast edge of the *atrio*.

The civilian plaza at Tlanalapa is unusual in that it is located to the south of the *atrio* and divided by four shallow platform levels. The north side of the plaza is separated from the south wall of the *atrio* by a narrow strip of commercial establishments. The east side of the plaza is fronted by the town hall, or Palacio Municipal. Next to this is an open space marked by two large planters with a fountain between them. The next division of the plaza is a relatively narrow strip dedicated to market-day activities. The westernmost section of the plaza is similar to the easternmost section in size and proportion and has in its center a nineteenth-century kiosk flanked by two planters that echo the octagonal shape of the kiosk. On the other side of the street that limits the west side of the plaza are additional commercial establishments graced with *portales* offering pedestrians protection from inclement weather. The street is unusual in that it is wider in front of the *atrio* and the plaza.

3.108. Tlanalapa, façade of church with *alfiz* and bands of ornament. Courtesy of J.B. Johnson.

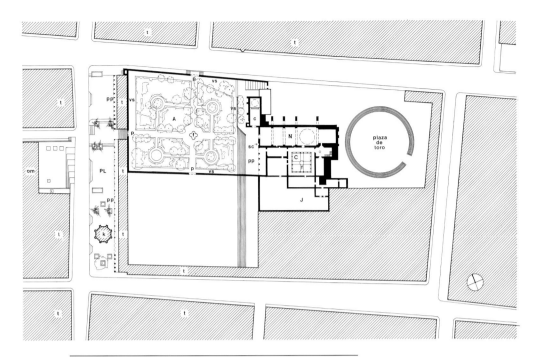

3.109. Tepeapulco, plan of town center. Courtesy of the School of Architecture Visual Resources Collection, The University of Texas at Austin (Box-Wagner Collection).

3.110. Tepeapulco, bullring. Courtesy of the School of Architecture Visual Resources Collection, The University of Texas at Austin (Box-Wagner Collection, VRC 91-9541).

Tepeapulco, Hidalgo: San Francisco

Tepeapulco is nestled between a volcano and a mountain in the heart of pulque country, the Apan Valley. Not far from the long-abandoned Mesoamerican power center of Teotihuacan, this early Franciscan foundation is generally associated with Fray Bernardino de Sahagún. It is also believed that Hernán Cortés maintained a residence here.

In addition to serving as a source of physical evidence for the practice of substituting bullfighting for the Mesoamerican ball game during the viceregal period, Tepeapulco exhibits several notable characteristics in its urban layout and open spaces (Figs. 3.109–3.110). Although heavily altered through the centuries, Tepeapulco's open spaces offer interesting features that have survived to this day. The monastic complex sits atop pre-Hispanic platforms. The *atrio*, or churchyard, is several steps higher than street level, while the monastery and church of San Francisco de Asís are even higher, reached by an imposing staircase, presumably pre-Hispanic, that leads from the *atrio* to the terrace level where the actual convent rests. Perpendicular to the church nave, a chapel frames the convent terrace. Although not unique, chapels on a perpendicular axis to the church nave are usually located some distance from the nave. Here the chapel sits right on the front north corner of the nave. The *atrio* itself has been heavily altered into an urban garden park (Fig. 3.111).

3.111. Tepeapulco, plaza. Courtesy of the School of Architecture
Visual Resources Collection, The University of Texas at Austin
(Box-Wagner Collection, VRC 91-9544).

3.112. Tepeapulco, Caja de Agua fountain in plaza.
Courtesy of the School of Architecture Visual Resources
Collection, The University of Texas at Austin (Box-Wagner
Collection, VRC 91-8329).

3.113. Tepeapulco, Caja de Agua drinking-water spouts.
Courtesy of the School of Architecture Visual Resources
Collection, The University of Texas at Austin (Box-Wagner
Collection, VRC 91-8222).

The town layout consists of the prescribed orthogonal street patterns, but the resulting urban blocks come in different sizes. Quite notable are two of the main streets, which are on axis with the north gate and the west main gate of the *atrio*. The street that lines up with the main *atrio* gate extends visually through the *atrio* to the entry to the church nave and continues through the interior of the nave to terminate at the altar.

Tepeapulco's plaza consists of a narrow strip on the western edge of the *atrio* where a long arcade of *portales* buffers the *atrio* from the new, highly reduced plaza. Equipped with some typical furnishings found in Mexican plazas, this strip includes a *kiosko*, numerous benches, and a few modern planters. Perhaps indicative of the earlier, much larger expanse of the original plaza is an aqueduct-fed carved-stone fountain with communal washbasins elaborated with carved lion heads as water spouts, a gem of colonial-period hydraulic engineering and an artistic masterpiece (Figs. 3.112–3.113). Presumably, this fountain would have been the crowning jewel at the center of the plaza that faces the *atrio*.

OPEN SPACE ENSEMBLES

As we learned in Chapter Two, the rigid urban layout dictated by the Laws of the Indies fortunately was altered by the incorporation of other open urban spaces not mentioned in the Laws' instructions. These "extra" urban spaces became integrated into the imposed urban layout and include the *atrio* churchyards, hospital chapel courts, marketplaces, and other open urban spaces that complement the central open space of the one stipulated plaza. Several communal open spaces form a melody culminating in a symphony of open volumes within the urban layout.

The examples that follow are not in any sense unique, for this same urban phenomenon is manifested in other categories we are presenting. It is in fact more common than not to experience several open spaces within the urban cores of Mexican towns, often urban settlements that were already inhabited at the time of the Spaniards' arrival. Some examples are preexisting spaces of Mesoamerican urban centers, but others are fortunate quirks caused by the irregular terrain when the urban grid was imposed by the Spaniards.

The delight of experiencing a series of open spaces within an urban layout provides pleasant hints and testimonial lessons for modern and future urban designers to heed when confronted with the job of creating new urban plans or renewing existing urban areas. Citizens and visitors to those towns will be grateful they did.

Tlaxiaco, Oaxaca: Santa María de la Asunción

The only hotel on the vast plaza is located on the high corner overlooking the central focus of the city. The evening we arrived, the market was just beginning to assemble, but we didn't pay much attention that night. The next morning we awoke to the view from our hotel balcony: a scene of the plaza transformed into a vast view of canvas tarps, mostly white. The ingenuity of the rope net systems that supported this "sea of shade" was intriguing to me as an architect, and I was reminded of an article I read many years ago entitled "The Native Genius of Indigenous Architecture."

Sinclair Black, July 1990

Tlaxiaco is situated in the Mixteca Alta, an extremely abrupt, mountainous, and now severely eroded area of the northern highlands in the state of Oaxaca. The Nahuatl name by which we know it today, Tlaxiaco, supplanted the original Mixtec name, a legacy from having been conquered by Aztec forces in the fifteenth century. Many Oaxacan towns suffered this fate, which is the reason they have Nahuatl rather than Mixtec names. Like most of Oaxaca, Tlaxiaco was evangelized by the Dominican Order. Founded in 1548 by Fray Gonzalo Lucero, the convent here is dedicated to Santa María de la Asunción (Fig. 3.114). Like many churches in Oaxaca, its low and squatty appearance is due to the precautionary measures taken by friar-builders in response to the strong seismic activity that has terrorized Oaxacan settlements from time immemorial.

At first glance, Tlaxiaco's central urban district displays a regular orthogonal plan. However, upon close inspection, we notice a proportional variety within the blocks. The city plan exhibits a long rectangular block shape at the periphery, which transitions to more square shapes at the center.

The Dominican Order is known to have had extensive landholdings, particularly in Oaxaca. Often land adjacent to the convent complexes was dedicated to specialized agricultural and animal husbandry activities brought from the Old World and implemented

3.114. Tlaxiaco, plan of town center. Courtesy of the School of
Architecture Visual Resources Collection, The University of
Texas at Austin (Box-Wagner Collection).

3.115. Tlaxiaco, plaza on market day, with the church of Santa María
de la Asunción in the background. Courtesy of the School of
Architecture Visual Resources Collection, The University of
Texas at Austin (Box-Wagner Collection).

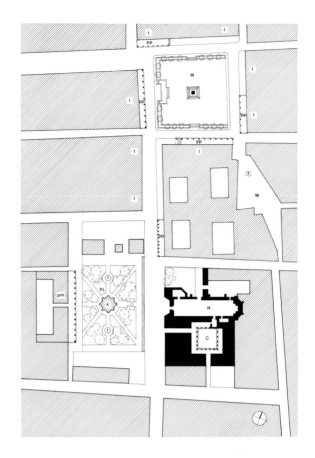

3.116. Tlaxiaco, empty market plaza. Courtesy of the School of Architecture Visual Resources Collection, The University of Texas at Austin (Box-Wagner Collection, VRC 90-9723).

3.117. Tlaxiaco, *portales* adjacent to the plaza. Courtesy of the School of Architecture Visual Resources Collection, The University of Texas at Austin (Box-Wagner Collection, VRC 90-9728).

by the Spanish friars in *huerta*, or orchard, land next to the convents. After the War of Reform (1857–1861), initiated by the first indigenous president of the Republic of Mexico, a Zapotec named Benito Juárez, the power of the church was curtailed almost to the point of extinction. During this period, the church lost many of its landholdings, causing drastic changes in urban central districts, especially around convents. Tlaxiaco is a dramatic case in point.

We notice the effects of the Reform because of the way it affects the nature of the urban open space. Immediately to the west of the church, a square that used to be a generous *atrio* has now been transformed into a nineteenth-century tree-studded park with a central kiosk flanked by two symmetrical fountains. Fronting this relatively new plaza is the Palacio Municipal (Town Hall). A handsome portal arcade between the plaza and the town hall serves as a welcome respite for pedestrians.

The dramatic loss of church land is illustrated here by the intervention of civilian construction abutting the cloister building block and even the apse of the nave. To the north of the church nave, an unusually shaped block unfolds until it reaches the presumably original civic plaza that is now dedicated to the market. The unusual geometry of the block to the north of the church suggests that it resulted from the church losing its landholdings. The haphazard nature of the eastern side of this city block creates an additional, albeit irregular, open space.

Market day in Tlaxiaco is a sight to behold (Fig. 3.115). The town is invaded by merchants arriving the night before, and the city is transformed by a sea of tarp-covered stalls. Empty, the market plaza is a bare slab except for a square outline of planters on three of its edges, with a lone monument punctuating the center (Fig. 3.116). The *portales* that surround the plaza on all four sides provide a dramatic perch from which to observe market activities (Fig. 3.117). Market day is a strong remnant of pre-Hispanic times; in Tlaxiaco it seems to have an especially powerful presence. The bareness of the central plaza on nonmarket days and the unusual irregular open space between the convent and the plaza pay tribute to the importance that Tlaxiaco gives to market activities. Market day is not confined to the civic plaza, but spills out onto the streets and open spaces of the extended vicinity.

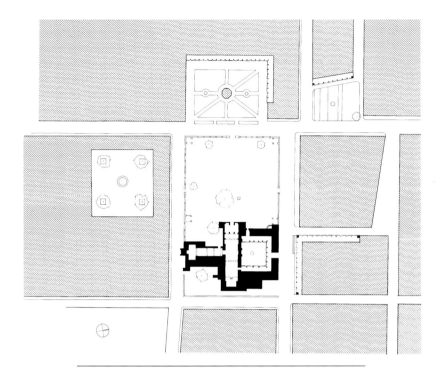

Tlacolula, Oaxaca: *Asunción de Nuestra Señora*

Every Sunday the town comes alive as one of the largest and oldest markets in the region spreads through the streets, the small plazas, and all but the most sacred *atrios*. This progression of *tianguis* starts with flowers and fine clothes and ends, after a mile or so, with permanent market buildings where charcoal is sold in the final stall. The Capilla del Señor de Tlacolula, a handsome domed space lined with tooled solid silver, is a deeply spiritual setting.

Hal Box, 1990

Located near the famous Mixtec site of Mitla in Oaxaca, Tlacolula de Matamoros has its origins in ancient times; the Zapotec language is still widely spoken here. The original Zapotec name is Guichibaa, which means "town of burials." In Nahuatl, "Tlacolula" has been translated as "place of branches." The name Matamoros was added after Mexico's independence from Spain, in honor of the hero Mariano Matamoros, who had distinguished himself in the War of Independence. Adding the surname of a hero of Mexican history to the town's original name is a common practice in Mexico (Fig. 3.118).

The Dominican convent church here was founded in the sixteenth century, although the church we see today probably dates from the seventeenth century (Fig. 3.119). The church is dedicated to the Virgin of the Assumption, one of many variations on titles for the

3.118. Tlacolula de Matamoros, plan of town center. Courtesy of the School of Architecture Visual Resources Collection, The University of Texas at Austin (Box-Wagner Collection).

Virgin Mary. The side chapel that bisects the nave to the south is unusual in its length and location and has a highly decorated baroque interior (Fig. 3.120). The chapel's baroque altar guardrail is made of solid silver, which was painted black so as to avoid being looted during the Mexican Revolution of 1910. The silver railing was discovered recently by accident during an overzealous cleaning program.

Although Tlacolula is surrounded by mountains, the town itself is laid out on relatively flat land. Hence, the orthogonal grid is quite regular, although quirks are evident in places where some blocks are much bigger than others, or the widening of a street creates an unpredicted angle, or unexpected open spaces add to the town's delight.

Tlacolula may be best known to modern travelers for the Indian market that is held on Wednesday and Sunday of every week (Fig. 3.121). On market day, merchants take over the town market plaza and many of the streets, eliminating vehicular traffic, as they do in Tlaxiaco. The market activities bring in crowds of people from villages in the surrounding hills, as well as from other towns in the central valleys, and large numbers of foreign and national tourists that make the day trip from Oaxaca City.

3.119. Tlacolula de Matamoros, *atrio* of Virgen de la Asunción. Courtesy of the School of Architecture Visual Resources Collection, The University of Texas at Austin (Box-Wagner Collection, VRC 90-7237).

3.120. Tlacolula de Matamoros, chapel dome of Virgen de la Asunción with silver gilding. Courtesy of the School of Architecture Visual Resources Collection, The University of Texas at Austin (Box-Wagner Collection, VRC 90-9378).

3.121. Tlacolula de Matamoros on market day. Courtesy of the School of Architecture Visual Resources Collection, The University of Texas at Austin (Box-Wagner Collection, VRC 90-9444).

The church *atrio* and the small plaza west of it are two of Tlacolula's open spaces that are not affected by the onslaught of vendors, merchants, and shoppers. There is also another small *jardín* plaza on the next block to the north. On market day, it is teeming with people and pervaded by overall cacophony, so that the silence and calm one encounters upon entering the church *atrio* come as a pleasant surprise, presenting a remarkable contrast.

All in all, Tlacolula's town center boasts numerous open spaces: the tree-studded *atrio* with its four *posa* chapels and *atrio* cross; the more private cloister on the north side of the nave; the plaza proper, across the street to the west of the church *atrio* and lined on two sides with *portales* (Fig. 3.122); the small *jardín* to the north of the plaza with a portal on the west flank; and the vast open esplanade of the market.

The lack of land associated with the convent seems to indicate that the large expanse dedicated to the market, located directly south of the church, was built on lands confiscated from the church after the War of Reform. That such a large open space was dedicated to the market underscores the importance market activities have for the community of Tlacolula.

Save for a bank of restrooms fronted by *portales* and a small kiosk centered by four planters, this large open space is an empty concrete slab except on market days, when it fills with tarp-covered stalls and teems with people, sounds, colors, and aromas.

Otumba de Gómez Farías, State of México: Purísima Concepción

Otumba is located in the pulque-producing area of the Apan plains near Tepeapulco and the famous ruins of Teotihuacan. Otumba gets its name from the original inhabitants, the Otomi. Its *altepetl* displays the water mountain, here with a human head topped by an unusual hairdo typical of the Otomi people. Otomi-speaking communities can still be found scattered throughout the Mexican Central Highlands. The added name of Gómez Farías refers to a hero of Mexico's Reform Period in the 1860s.

Otumba is best known in Mexican history for the fierce battle that took place there in the summer of 1520 between Spanish conquistador Hernán Cortés's bedraggled army and pursuing Aztec warriors. Cortés and his men had just escaped from Tenochtitlan after losing their first attempt to conquer the Aztec capital, a defeat known in Mexican history as the *noche triste*. Legend says that Cortés lamented this loss under a shady tree. In a fateful turn of events, the Spaniards were able to survive the pursuing Aztec army and

3.123. Otumba, memorial erected in 1520 by Cortés and conquistadors. Courtesy of the School of Architecture Visual Resources Collection, The University of Texas at Austin (Box-Wagner Collection, VRC 91-11261).

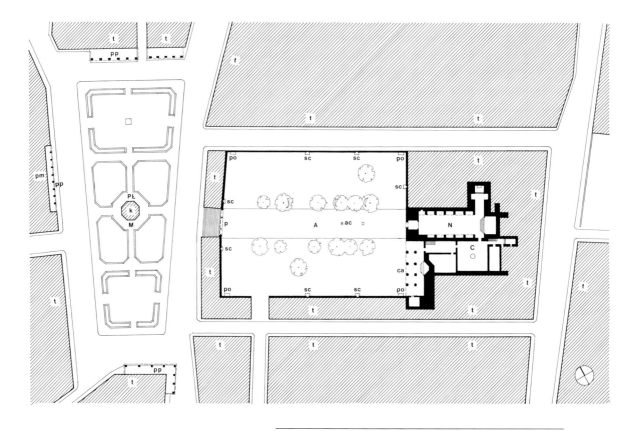

3.124. Otumba, plan of town center. Courtesy of the School of Architecture Visual Resources Collection, The University of Texas at Austin (Box-Wagner Collection).

3.125. Otumba, view of town center from market.
Courtesy of the School of Architecture Visual Resources Collection, The University of Texas at Austin (Box-Wagner Collection, VRC 91-9903).

kill the Aztec leader. The memorial they erected, an isolated cross on a round mound just north of town, survives from 1520 to this day (Fig. 3.123).

Otumba's site plan is unique, with several features that stand out, most noticeably the enormous main plaza shaped like a trapezoid (Figs. 3.124–3.125). This atypical form is bounded by streets set at an angle to the grid, probably due to original pre-Hispanic roads leading from the Otomi settlement. The plaza was remodeled in the nineteenth century in a classic French garden style with a kiosk in the center. More typically, three sides of the plaza look out onto covered arcades, or *portales*, although the *portal* on the south wraps around the corner, a rare occurrence.

Fronting the plaza on the fourth side facing east is a stairway up to the triple-arched triumphal entry that leads into the sacred open space of the church *atrio*. The presence of the stair suggests that the complex was built on a pre-Hispanic platform that elevates the *atrio* above street level.

Otumba's *atrio*, like so many others that lost land during the 1860s War of Reform, has been invaded by commercial establishments on the west and south sides. The convent's orchard lands suffered a similar fate. In spite of these losses, the tree-studded *atrio* has managed to preserve the characteristic elements of the architecture of conversion, including the *atrio* cross, all four *posa* chapels, and an open chapel embedded into the massive walls of the convent behind a *mudéjar* colonnade reminiscent of a Moorish mosque, all fronted by five arches of the portal (Figs. 3.126–3.128). Like many *atrios* in Mexico, the walls contain niches dedicated to the Stations of the Cross. Also, in concession to the importance of the church, the urban grid was modified so that a street leads directly to the south gate of the *atrio*.

3.126. Otumba, *portería* with larger central arch accentuating open chapel. Courtesy of J.B. Johnson.

3.127. Otumba, interior colonnade in proscenium of open chapel. Courtesy of J.B. Johnson.

3.128. Otumba, open chapel with half-hexagon flared apse that helps propel the sound of the mass. Courtesy of J.B. Johnson.

Tlacochahuaya, Oaxaca: San Jerónimo

Tlacochahuaya, located 21 kilometers to the southeast of Oaxaca City, means "humid place" in Nahuatl, suggesting that a swamp or bog used to lie nearby. A Zapotec-speaking community, Tlacochahuaya traces its origins to 1100 CE or earlier. Like many communities in Oaxaca, it was conquered by Nahuatl-speaking Aztecs in the fifteenth century.

The mission at Tlacochahuaya was established by

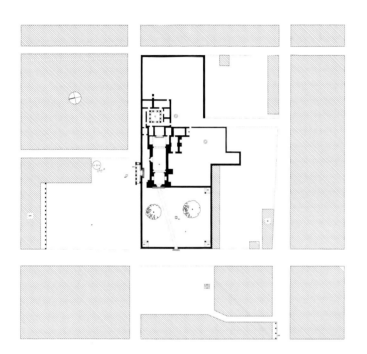

3.129. Tlacochahuaya, plan of San Jerónimo and surrounding spaces. Courtesy of the School of Architecture Visual Resources Collection, The University of Texas at Austin (Box-Wagner Collection).

3.130. Tlacochahuaya, *atrio*, portal, and *posa* chapel of San Jerónimo. Courtesy of the School of Architecture Visual Resources Collection, The University of Texas at Austin (Box-Wagner Collection, VRC 90-7267).

3.131. Tlacochahuaya, portal to plaza from San Jerónimo. Courtesy of the School of Architecture Visual Resources Collection, The University of Texas at Austin (Box-Wagner Collection, VRC 90-7273).

Dominican friars as early as 1546 and dedicated to San Jerónimo. Although the current church dates from the seventeenth century,[105] the original buildings served as a seminary for the Dominican friars. Two plazas and the Dominican church complex form the central element of the small town.

San Jerónimo de Tlacochahuaya's town and convent plan features a layout that deviates from the norm, suggesting that significant changes occurred over time (Fig. 3.129). One first notices architectural interventions in the southern half of the city block in which the convent-church-*atrio* complex is located. Also, the cloister of modest dimensions is located directly east of the church nave, behind it rather than in the usual south location. The three domed *posa* chapels (Fig. 3.130) in the *atrio* date from the seventeenth or eighteenth century and are augmented by a fourth at the end of a long walkway past a newer north portal that is elaborated with handsome cut-stone colonnaded *portales* (Fig. 3.131). The fourth *posa* was probably built

3.132. Tlacochahuaya, San Jerónimo *atrio*. Courtesy of the School of
Architecture Visual Resources Collection, The University of
Texas at Austin (Box-Wagner Collection, VRC 90-8537).

3.133. Tlacochahuaya, San Jerónimo *atrio*, façade, and portal prior to
recent landscape design. Courtesy of the School of Architecture
Visual Resources Collection, The University of Texas at Austin
(Box-Wagner Collection, VRC 90-7264).

3.134. Tlacochahuaya, *picota*, Spanish pillar in the plaza marking the center of town, here with added whipping posts.
Courtesy of the School of Architecture Visual Resources Collection, The University of Texas at Austin (Box-Wagner Collection, VRC 90-8913).

3.135. Tlacochahuaya, sundial or solar clock in the plaza.
Courtesy of the School of Architecture Visual Resources Collection, The University of Texas at Austin (Box-Wagner Collection, VRC 90-8550).

when the new portal was added. The main gateway into the *atrio*, a triumphal arch in the western wall, does not align with the church nave, so one approaches the church on the diagonal (Fig. 3.132).

A small plaza west of the *atrio* has recently been given a careful landscape design and a kiosk in an attempt to provide formal plaza trappings, but it is surrounded on three sides by the blank walls of residential buildings that do not engage the open space. On the north wall an arcaded portico leads to the major civic plaza. An awkward, narrow sliver of space between the portico and the north wall of the nave confirms that the nave was built later than the *atrio* and civic plaza (Fig. 3.133). The sum of all these anomalies indicates that major transformations occurred in the original layout of the convent in relation to the town.

The main plaza lies north of the convent, and across it the Palacio Municipal is flanked on its north side by an extensive arcaded portal that serves as an entry to municipal government offices. The east side of the L-shaped building block surrounding the plaza now houses the town's medical clinic.

The plaza has recently undergone extensive remodeling, but fortunately, two elements of early plaza furnishings survive: the *picota* and the solar clock. The *picota* is a Spanish plaza element, a masonry pillar that symbolically marks the center of the town (Fig. 3.134). It was usually placed during the founding ceremonies of a settlement, but soon thereafter it takes on a more draconian role, becoming the whipping post to which miscreants and criminals were tied to receive punishment by lashing in a public display of medieval judicial practices.

The second plaza element of colonial origin is the solar clock or sundial (Fig. 3.135). Here, the solar clock

3.136. Tlacochahuaya, decorated nave of San Jerónimo.
Courtesy of Sinclair Black.

consists of a stone block inscribed with gradations that indicate the time of day when the shadow produced by the gnomon is projected onto the inscribed stone. The survival of both of these plaza elements is rare in Mexican plazas of the sixteenth century.

The interior of the church is the jewel of Tlacochahuaya. Its richly decorated surfaces of colorful Christian scenes by native artists are overwhelming in their magnitude and style (Fig. 3.136). The elevated *coro*, or choir, at the west end of the nave has a shape that generates a lively sound from its choir and tracker-action organ.

Tepeaca, Puebla: San Francisco

Located on the plains south of the capital city of Puebla, Tepeaca was settled early in the contact period. Like Tepeapulco, Oaxaca, and Cuernavaca, Tepeaca claims that Hernán Cortés had a house here.

At first glance, the orthogonal grid is quite regular, like other sites in Puebla, with very large city blocks and a plaza of rather generous proportions (Fig. 3.137). The streets line up perfectly. The urban grid is very exact in the prescribed north–south and east–west orientation. This degree of precision is a rarity. The reason for this perfect layout is expressed in Tepeaca's Relación Geográfica, written in 1580, which indicates that the population of the town was dispersed and the "center" of town was located high in a canyon on top of the hill called Tlaitleque.[106] The new Tepeaca was founded at the foot of Tlaitleque on flat, level terrain that was perfect for a grid layout. Tepeaca is another example of a *reducción* foundation.

The Franciscan monastery consists of a cloister and a single-nave church dedicated to Saint Francis of Assisi. The nave terminates in a square apse. The walls of the nave are braced by rectangular buttresses, but at the main entry in the west façade, the buttresses protrude at an angle from the corners, seeming to embrace people entering the church from the *atrio*. A side chapel with a long narrow nave sits perpendicular to the main church and covers what used to be the *portería* arcade of the cloister.

Due to the War of Reform of the 1860s, which drastically constrained the church's power and property, the vast expanse of land that normally would be part of the convent has been invaded, including what would have been the convent's *huerta*. The *atrio* itself has been dramatically reduced to a fraction of its former grandeur. Today it consists of a narrow walkway from the street on the east side of the plaza (Fig. 3.138). In an interesting variation on *atrio* open space invasions, the space is dedicated to a cemetery, serving both religious and municipal uses, rather than being used as another city block for civic and residential buildings. The narrow walkway leading to the church

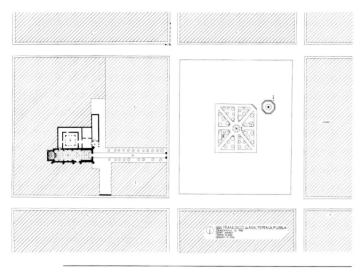

3.137. Tepeaca, plan of town center. Courtesy of the School of Architecture Visual Resources Collection, The University of Texas at Austin (Box-Wagner Collection).

Typical of plaza furnishings in Spain and Italy, the *rollo*'s origins date back to medieval times. The battlements of the crown testify to its military defensive purposes, since it was originally a lookout tower built to safeguard the town. Inside, a circular stairway leads to a vaulted room surrounded by a loggia arcade. The domed room was topped by a bell tower surrounded by a *chemin de ronde* walkway, its guardrail punctuated by stylized pinnacles. On the walls of the *rollo* we find interesting carved-stone features inserted into the masonry, among them shackles to imprison indigenous miscreants, pre-Hispanic zoomorphs, and what appears to be a stone-carved plaque of an eagle, perhaps a tribute to Tepeaca's original indigenous founder, Quauhtliztac, which means "white eagle." Guarding the *rollo* inside a metal knee-high fence are two stone-carved plumed coyotes of unmistakable pre-Hispanic origin.

3.138. Tepeaca, *atrio* and façade of San Francisco. Courtesy of the School of Architecture Visual Resources Collection, The University of Texas at Austin (Box-Wagner Collection, VRC 92-9721).

3.139. Tepeaca, El Rollo, c. 1559. Courtesy of the School of Architecture Visual Resources Collection, The University of Texas at Austin (Box-Wagner Collection, VRC 92-9717).

is formed by two parallel masonry walls that bisect the cemetery.

The most striking element of the site plan of Tepeaca's center is the enormity of the plaza space. The nineteenth-century tree-studded *jardín*, of geometric design, is a standard size with rectangular proportions and is located in the center of an immense open space. One could fit several *jardines* of this size into this vast plaza.

One of the most interesting aspects of the Tepeaca plaza is the existence of one of the few *rollos*, or towers, that has survived to this day (Fig. 3.139). The octagonal tower rises to the height of a three-story building.

SIXTEENTH-CENTURY COMMUNAL OPEN SPACES (FIVE HUNDRED YEARS LATER)

3.140. Etla, plan and section of town center. Courtesy of the School of Architecture Visual Resources Collection, The University of Texas at Austin (Box-Wagner Collection).

3.141. Etla, San Pedro y San Pablo atop a series of platforms. Courtesy of the School of Architecture Visual Resources Collection, The University of Texas at Austin (Box-Wagner Collection, VRC 90-9490).

3.142. Etla, plaza at the lower platform. Courtesy of the School of Architecture Visual Resources Collection, The University of Texas at Austin (Box-Wagner Collection, VRC 90-7325).

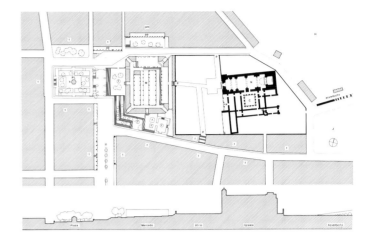

3.143. Etla, main street at plaza with the beginning of the series of platforms. Courtesy of the School of Architecture Visual Resources Collection, The University of Texas at Austin (Box-Wagner Collection, VRC 90-7324).

3.144. Etla, steps ascending to the *atrio* from the market. Courtesy of the School of Architecture Visual Resources Collection, The University of Texas at Austin (Box-Wagner Collection, VRC 90-7318).

Etla, Oaxaca: San Pedro y San Pablo

When we saw the complex at Etla for the first time in the bright cool sunshine of the Oaxaca Valley, we experienced the space-making quality of sunlight and its shadows. The contrast of bright light and deep shadow defined spaces as much as walls and roofs. The *atrio* was full of light; the sanctuary of the church was defined by darkness. The portal of the church reads as a maw, a mouth into the dark Underworld, emulating the ancient concept of a dark cave as a spiritual sanctuary. Progressing downhill from the dark sanctuary to the bright *atrio*, then through the dark market buildings and bright open plazas, we arrived at the *plaza mayor* at the bottom of the hill, tree shaded with dappled light and fragrant with the moist scent of flowers.

Hal Box, 1987

The *plaza mayor* of the town of Etla acts as a dramatic termination point for a series of four terraced communal spaces below the Dominican church of San Pedro y San Pablo on a gentle slope in the Oaxaca Valley (Fig. 3.140). Appearing much like the preconquest platform of a Zapotec or Mixtec sacred site, the series of terraces was in fact a 350 × 500 foot platform[107] built in the latter part of the sixteenth century above the site of an earlier church that had collapsed in 1575 due to its location in low wetlands, killing many townspeople.[108] The extra terrace space and market building that we see today are built on the site of the former church and the former *atrio*, now a broad terrace for pageantry. This creates a spectacular series of stepped open spaces perched on ascending hills that lead up to the sixteenth-century nave of the San Pedro y San Pablo monastery church (Fig. 3.141). The journey starts at the bottom in the tree-shaded *plaza mayor* (Fig. 3.142), moves to a higher grassy terrace, and then on a bit higher to a tree-lined park adjacent to the market (once probably open but now with a nineteenth-century stone structure; Fig. 3.143). Following the route of a procession, after climbing a few more steps, one enters the generous *atrio* through a triumphal cast-iron gateway (Fig. 3.144) and continues along the sacred way through the grand doorway, down the nave of the church, to arrive at the altar. Behind the church and cloister (another open space), the monastery block is backed by the *huerta*, which is watered from the still-extant colonial-era aqueduct. The *plaza mayor* sits just below the *atrio* of the former church and is bounded

3.145. Etla, cloister vault. Courtesy of the School of Architecture Visual Resources Collection, The University of Texas at Austin (Box-Wagner Collection, VRC 90-9084).

by the town's main market street, Independencia, which terminates at the Palacio Municipal on the far side of the plaza.

The present church at the top of the terraces was the ambitious undertaking of a community dedicated to rebuilding. The masonry vaulting and plaster ornamentation in the cloister walkways are of the highest-quality craftsmanship and design (Fig. 3.145). Close by, perched on a single hill just outside of town to the west, sits a chapel dedicated to El Señor de las Peñas (Lord of the Stones; Fig. 3.146). Known to grant good omens to people with building projects, El Señor de las Peñas is a favorite patron saint of masons, architects, and builders. Because the chapel is open for Mass only once a year, pilgrims to Las Peñas build miniature stone structures in the churchyard as offerings to this much-sought-after saint. Behind the chapel, the hill descends into a quadrangular Zapotec court formed by four temples. The court is punctuated with an altar in the center, completing the sacred quincunx form. This Classic period site has yet to be excavated and is covered in vegetation, but the outline is clear.

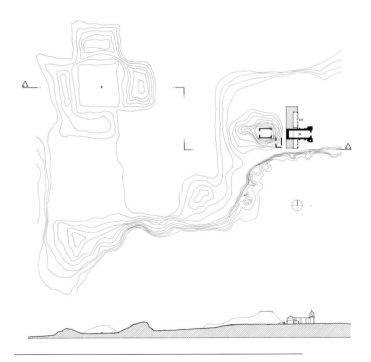

3.146. Etla, plan and section of Señor de las Peñas church and adjacent pyramids. Courtesy of the School of Architecture Visual Resources Collection, The University of Texas at Austin (Box-Wagner Collection).

3.147. Lake Pátzcuaro, primordial sea in Michoacán. Logan Wagner.

BISHOP QUIROGA'S UTOPIAS IN MICHOACÁN

In order to pacify these natives, and to attract and not frighten them, in my opinion we should not fight them but instead seek them out. More effective than the rigors and inhumanities of war, slavery, and ransom, would be the fodder of good works, once the natives had been sought out, and thereafter converted, cherished, and kept in the fold.

Bishop Vasco de Quiroga, quoted in McAndrew, *Open-Air Churches*

The area we now know as Michoacán, northwest of Mexico-Tenochtitlan, has been and still is inhabited by the Tarasco-Purépecha nation. A proud, independent, and fierce people, the Purépecha, called Tarascos by the Spanish, were never conquered by the imperialistic Aztecs. They exhibited several cultural traits that are unique to the region, such as the knowledge of advanced metallurgy, a preference for shaft tombs, and other practices not found elsewhere in Mesoamerica. Some linguists believe that the Purépecha language is more closely related to Andean Quechua than to any of the Mesoamerican language families.

The Tarasco-Purépecha area is a densely forested and picturesque locale in the mountains of present-day Michoacán, centered on Lake Pátzcuaro (Fig. 3.147). Lakes in Mesoamerica epitomize the terrestrial manifestation of the primordial sea. With four sacred sites around its edge and a central shrine on an island in the middle, Lake Pátzcuaro exhibits quincunxial centering and physically reinforces its identification with the primordial sea, here the center of the Purépecha sacred landscape.

After the fall of Tenochtitlan in 1521, the region was conquered by the cruel and ruthless conquistador Nuño de Guzmán. In 1531, Vasco de Quiroga arrived in Nueva España as an auditor with the Spanish Second Audiencia led by Sebastián Ramírez de Fuenleal. He was sent to Michoacán to deal with the indigenous population's complaints against the conquistador and *encomendero* Guzmán.[109]

Early on, Quiroga became concerned about the living conditions of the native population and imagined a solution in the form of a network of hospital towns. Each town would be taught a useful craft and would trade their wares at each other's markets, partly as a way to integrate Spanish market culture into the native way of life. In the service of this vision, Quiroga founded Santa Fe de la Laguna in 1533 as a prototype for the hospital towns that would be built around the lake.

In 1534, his proposal was very favorably approved by Charles V, and in 1538, Vasco de Quiroga was named bishop, allowing him to pursue his humanistic social vision unencumbered. His ideas about urban planning were embraced by both the Franciscan and Augustinian Orders under his direction, the two mendicant orders that had evangelized the indigenous groups in the Michoacán area. As the first bishop for the province of Michoacán, Quiroga was the major influence on the unique urban forms that towns would take in this bucolic land. Versed in the humanistic philosophies popular in literary circles of Europe at the time, such as the ideas of Erasmus and Thomas More, Quiroga saw an opportunity to implement the utopian ideas espoused by these humanists in helping the people of Michoacán.

Although providing health services to the native population was a major concern of the Spanish Crown, the inability of the Native Americans to cope with European diseases, which had been evident from the initial stages of the Spaniards' arrival in the New World, underscored the need to build hospitals. The native population of New Spain suffered three major epidemics—in 1520–1521, 1545, and 1576—that decimated them. Interestingly enough, during these tragic phases, the bishopric of Michoacán increased in population instead of sustaining the big drops experienced elsewhere in New Spain, perhaps because of the many hospitals built in Michoacán, thanks to the vision of Vasco de Quiroga.

These early hospital towns are important to our study because their construction typically includes types of open spaces not found in other new towns in New Spain. In general, the hospitals in these villages consisted of two batteries of rooms with *portales*, one for patients with contagious diseases and the other for patients with noncontagious diseases. The two wings were separated by a court or *atrio* fronted by a small chapel. Tzintzuntzan, as we shall see in the description, includes a separate stand-alone open chapel.

Most of the villages founded by Vasco de Quiroga are properly categorized as *reducciones*. Also known as *congregaciones*, *reducciones* resulted from a settlement policy that created "new towns" in which to gather indigenous populations that had scattered into the forests to avoid the approaching Spaniards. Devised to socialize and acculturate the natives, *reducciones* were described by reports of the period as "vivir en policía," which roughly translates as a means to gather, organize, control, and convert the population.

In addition to serving the health needs of the community, the hospitals and their patios or open spaces were instrumental in the socialization process. They served as settings for instruction, proselytizing, and the assignment of community labor tasks, as well as for the formation of *cofradías*, or church-related brotherhoods. Organizing communities in this fashion was readily accepted by the Purépechas, since it reminded them of precontact communal tribute labor practices.

The following is a chronological sampling of some of the early hospital settlements in the Tarasco-Purépecha area of Michoacán.

Tzintzuntzan, Michoacán: San Francisco

Michoacán is without doubt one of the privileged areas of evangelization in New Spain. As early as 1526, the Franciscans had established a base in Tzintzuntzan, the capital of the Purépecha nation (Figs. 3.148–3.149). The native ceremonial center buildings were left basically intact and are known as *yácatas*. The main structure consists of a pyramidal platform with five distinct round altars, which presumably allude to quincunx symbolism. Four of the ceremonial shrines represent the four lake settlements, while the fifth stands for the center of Lake Pátzcuaro, the axis mundi. Usually, when existing urban centers were refounded by the Spaniards, their ceremonial centers were destroyed and the stone reused to build the church and monastery or integrated into platforms for the church and *atrio*, thereby becoming part of the new town. In the case of Tzintzuntzan, the native cer-

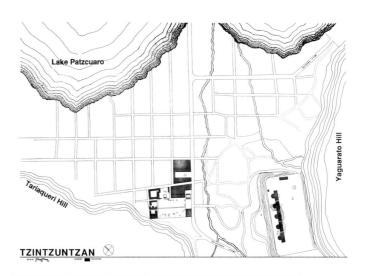

3.148. Tzintzuntzan, plan of area, plan of ancient *yácatas* once at the edge of the lake and the new town grid layout. Courtesy of the School of Architecture Visual Resources Collection, The University of Texas at Austin (Box-Wagner Collection).

emonial center was allowed to remain relatively intact. It still overlooks the town, commanding a view of the Franciscan conventual complex, the new grid layout of the Spanish town below, and sacred Lake Pátzcuaro beyond.

With the ceremonial center perched on the terraced hill to the east, the Franciscan convent, its contiguous hospital chapel, and the new urban grid were established in the alluvial flat land between the hill

3.149. Tzintzuntzan, ancient platform of Purépecha capital showing *yácata* rising on right, the town below, and Lake Pátzcuaro in the distance. Courtesy of the School of Architecture Visual Resources Collection, The University of Texas at Austin (Box-Wagner Collection).

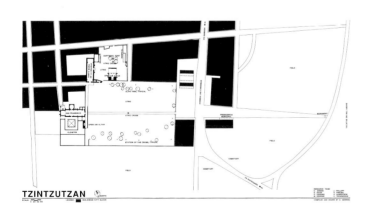

3.150. Tzintzuntzan, plan of church, *atrio*, hospital, and plaza. Courtesy of the School of Architecture Visual Resources Collection, The University of Texas at Austin (Box-Wagner Collection).

and Lake Pátzcuaro (Fig. 3.150). The town plan itself seems to have come along after the convent and hospital chapel were built. Instead of forming the nucleus of the community, the conventual complex lies at the edge of the urban grid, a peculiar layout repeated at Pátzcuaro and Erongarícuaro. For Tzintzuntzan, the space that is termed "the plaza" seems to be no more than an after-the-fact widening of the street.

Several aspects that are still evident today make Tzintzuntzan unique: the generous size of its rectangular *atrio*, the uncharacteristic presence of olive trees lined up in rows within it, and the existence of two separate church naves and an open chapel fronting the *atrio* (Fig. 3.151). The main church is dedicated to Saint Francis, and the other, once dedicated to the Third Order of the Franciscans, is now dedicated to La Soledad.[110]

Posa chapels, if they ever existed, are no longer in evidence. The Renaissance-style open chapel, on axis with the centuries-old olive trees, survives embedded in the west cloister wall, flush with the façade of the main church of San Francisco. At the northeast corner, on a perpendicular axis, is the church dedicated to La Soledad (Fig. 3.152).

What makes town centers in the Michoacán area different from their counterparts in the rest of sixteenth-century Mexico is the existence of an additional planned urban open space in the hospital chapel complex. Normally, the architecture of this complex consists of an enclosed patio, a room or rooms for the

3.151. Tzintzuntzan, *atrio* with main church and secondary church. Courtesy of the School of Architecture Visual Resources Collection, The University of Texas at Austin (Box-Wagner Collection).

3.152. Tzintzuntzan, church once dedicated to the Third Order of Franciscans, now to La Soledad. Courtesy of the School of Architecture Visual Resources Collection, The University of Texas at Austin (Box-Wagner Collection).

3.153. Tzintzuntzan, hospital open chapel. Courtesy of the School of Architecture Visual Resources Collection, The University of Texas at Austin (Box-Wagner Collection, VRC 91-217).

infirm, and an open chapel. The hospital *atrio* and its open chapel are located outside the north wall of the convent's majestic *atrio*. Nothing remains of the hospital structure per se. The entry to the hospital is on the north side of the urban block; however, from the main church *atrio* one can enter La Soledad and then the hospital *atrio* from the east door of the nave.

The detached hospital chapel is all that remains of the original hospital complex (Fig. 3.153). The sanctuary is enclosed by a three-arched portico. There is evidence that carved stone was salvaged from the native ceremonial center and used in the walls of the chapel. Like all the other hospital chapels, it is dedicated to the Virgen de la Concepción.

From the ramparts of the sacred Purépecha ceremonial center of *yácatas*, down to the splendid church *atrio*, spilling over into the hospital *atrio*, and culminating in the ad hoc civic plaza, Tzintzuntzan offers a series of separate but continuous communal open spaces. These unify the inhabitants in spaces sacred and secular, healing and educational, and

provide places where they could engage in labor and tribute endeavors. This approach would be refined in the new communities founded throughout the land.

Pátzcuaro, Michoacán: San Francisco

Vasco de Quiroga undertook to create actual communities in New Spain modeled on Thomas More's *Utopia*, with communally owned property, communally performed labor, representative government, and a variety of other features of More's ideal society. It would not be an exaggeration to say that America in the second quarter of the sixteenth century exhibited a phase of the European Renaissance that transcended European terms, one in which Christian-humanist programs, inapplicable and "utopian" in European society, came to be realities.

Charles Gibson, *Spain in America*

Pátzcuaro is the symbolic center, the place of power, the axis mundi, of a group of five towns on the edges of Lake Pátzcuaro, towns that form a quincunx on the primordial sea. Today its magical quality is heightened at the all-night celebration of Día de los Muertos, when the townspeople go by boat to visit the graves of their dead, who are buried on islands in the lake, carrying armsful of marigolds, favorite foods to tempt the spirits home, and huge candles to light their way. The original name of Pátzcuaro, Tzacapu-Arocutin-Pátzcuaro, means "the entrance to paradise," in other words, the entrance to where the dead go, where you live and are happy, Lake Pátzcuaro being the gate to this place.

After becoming the first bishop of Michoacán, Vasco de Quiroga learned that Pátzcuaro was the ancient sacred center of Purépecha and decided to establish the ecumenical center over the ancient sacred temple that perched on the hilly slopes overlooking Lake Pátzcuaro.

Quiroga, who realized the importance of locat-

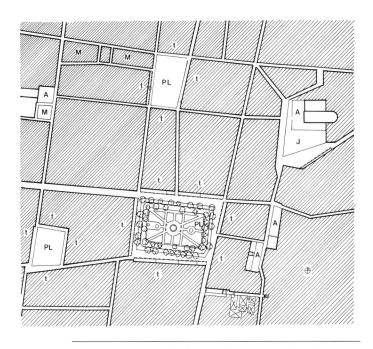

3.154. Pátzcuaro, town plan showing Plaza Quiroga, Plaza Chica, market, and Basílica de la Salud. Courtesy of the School of Architecture Visual Resources Collection, The University of Texas at Austin (Box-Wagner Collection).

ing his fabled five-nave cathedral over the most sacred center of the Purépecha world, embarked on the refounding of Pátzcuaro as the new capital of Michoacán Province (Fig. 3.154). As in Tzintzuntzan, the cathedral was located high on the edge of the new urban grid. From this elevated setting, in the most sacred spot in the Purépecha world, the unfinished cathedral, now known as the Basílica de la Salud, overlooks the new town below, the lake beyond, and the villages surrounding Lake Pátzcuaro.

Before the Spanish refounding of Pátzcuaro, roads emanated from the Purépecha shrine in a radial fashion, in strong contrast to the orthogonal grid laid out by Quiroga's architect and urban designer, the talented Toribio de Alcaraz. Traces of these radial streets are detectable today at the edge of town and in streets running diagonally on the square grid.

The new Spanish town epitomizes the beauty and order that are possible with an elegantly designed and executed urban grid layout. At the center and heart of the rectangular communal open space is the splendid *plaza mayor*. Now renamed Plaza Quiroga, the open space here is pleasantly shaded with majestic poplar trees and visually enriched by colorful flowering gardens (Fig. 3.155). Fronted by a diverse assortment of arcades forming the two-story *portales* that surround it, Plaza Quiroga was designed for the enjoyment and relaxation of the user (Figs. 3.156–3.157). It has the furnishings that every good Spanish plaza should have—stone-carved benches, colorful and textured pavers laid in splendid patterns, a *kiosko* bandstand, a fine bronze

3.155. Pátzcuaro, Plaza Quiroga from surrounding *portales*. Courtesy of the School of Architecture Visual Resources Collection, The University of Texas at Austin (Box-Wagner Collection, VRC 92-13381).

3.156. Pátzcuaro, streets intersecting Plaza Quiroga showing *portales* at the northwest corner. Courtesy of the School of Architecture Visual Resources Collection, The University of Texas at Austin (Box-Wagner Collection).

3.157. Pátzcuaro, *portales* at southeast corner of Plaza Quiroga. Courtesy of the School of Architecture Visual Resources Collection, The University of Texas at Austin (Box-Wagner Collection).

statue of "Tata" Vasco, and at its core, the source of life itself, the water fountain.

Two blocks north is Plaza Chica. Dedicated to the town's market, this open space is bustling with cacophonous sounds and aromas on the weekly market day, or, as it is still called today, *día de plaza*. Plaza Chica is where the Augustinian Order built their church, and just as at Plaza Quiroga, pedestrians are treated to the refuge and shade of heavy timber-and-stone *portales*.

Santa Fe de la Laguna, Michoacán

The exciting thing about arriving at Santa Fe de la Laguna for the first time was to see an idealized town plan designed by Bishop Quiroga built and intact after four hundred years. The form of the original Purépecha town, called Ueameo, was unchanged, and the original building materials of adobe and wood looked just as they would have when first built. The sequence of open spaces led from the generous walled plaza to the church *atrio* and beyond to the patio of the hospital, all handsomely detailed in simple forms. The paseo around the square gave ample shade. The town's people were gathered in the plaza at the town well for water.

Hal Box, 1988

Due to the fact that native populations were dispersed in the forested mountains,[111] most sixteenth-century mendicant establishments in the Michoacán area fall into the category of settlements known as

reducciones. To facilitate conversion, mendicant friars, with encouragement from the Spanish Crown, set about laying out new towns as places to gather scattered Amerindian populations. The need to create new towns for the vast local Purépecha nation gave Vasco de Quiroga an unprecedented opportunity to express his utopian ideals of society in physical form. Don Vasco, keen on the opportunity that was presented, designed and built into the urban grid of the new towns a synthesized vision of the utopian villages espoused in the teachings of Thomas More and Erasmus. Towns were created, and soon a vast network of villages dotted the forested and mountainous landscape, unifying the numerous Purépechas. Once founded, each village would then develop a unique craft and meet at marketplaces to trade with villagers from other towns with different crafts. Santa Fe de la Laguna was the first new town to be founded for this vision, serving as a model for a network of *reducciones* that Don Vasco founded and that other friars who were evangelizing in Michoacán emulated (Fig. 3.158).

Sick villagers were cared for in the medical courts, usually adjacent to the monastery and *atrio* block. Managed as labor and tribute co-ops, these first community clinics were serviced and maintained on a rotating basis by members of the village. Each consisted of an open court, a slender rectangular block of rooms with a covered porch, and the chapel proper. By far the most elegant structure of the hospital complex was the chapel. In some cases, as at Tzintzuntzan, it consisted of a bonafide open chapel, but in most cases it was actually a small covered nave.

The unconventional orientation of the urban layout of Santa Fe de la Laguna presents a chain of interconnected but decidedly distinct open spaces, like many Michoacán towns with hospital chapels. As identified in the historiography, at Santa Fe, as at most mendicant establishments in the diocese of Michoacán, a triad of interconnected open spaces was created: a civic plaza, a spiritual court, and a space for healing and barrio tributary labor organization (Fig. 3.159).

The town plaza is flanked on all four sides by comfortable, protective *portales*, but the north *portales* are backed only by a single south *atrio* wall instead of the front of assorted commercial and civic architecture (Fig. 3.160). Near the center of the public plaza is a fountain, which to this day is the source of potable water for the town's inhabitants. To see the local women

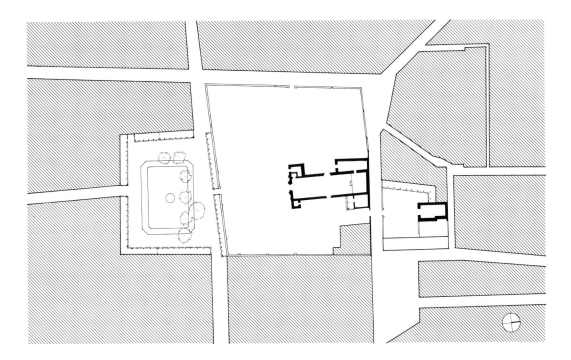

3.158. Santa Fe de la Laguna, plan of town plaza, church *atrio*, and
hospital with its *atrio*. Courtesy of the School of Architecture
Visual Resources Collection, The University of Texas at Austin
(Box-Wagner Collection).

3.160. Santa Fe de la Laguna, *atrio* wall *portales* on east side of plaza.
Courtesy of the School of Architecture Visual Resources
Collection, The University of Texas at Austin (Box-Wagner
Collection, VRC 2007-4382).

3.159. Santa Fe de la Laguna, street leading into civic plaza. Courtesy
of the School of Architecture Visual Resources Collection, The
University of Texas at Austin (Box-Wagner Collection).

fill their clay vessels with water today is a window into a way of life that has not changed much since Santa Fe was founded in 1533 (Fig. 3.161).

From the *plaza mayor* one enters the sacred church *atrio* through the triumphal gateway located at the center of the north portal. The road entering Santa Fe from Lake Pátzcuaro becomes the central urban street bisecting the rectangular plaza and the fountain near its center. The alignment continues through the fountain and to the triumphal gateway of the church *atrio*, creating a processional axis that projects into the realm of the sacred from outside the town proper. Upon crossing the threshold, one has entered the sacred realm (Fig. 3.162).

Entry to the *atrio* reveals continuing alignment with the church doorway. After crossing the deeply shaded portal of the Christian temple, the axis continues down the central aisle of the nave to culminate in the sanctuary altar of the main *retablo*.

The processional walkway leading to the church's entry bisects the open volume into east and west courts. The open space of the west *atrio* and east *curato* court form a total open volume nearly twice as large as the plaza. The west doorway of the church nave lines up with the west *atrio* door, which, in turn, faces the east nave door, effectively dividing the length of the nave in two halves. At twice the size of the east esplanade, the western portion of the open volume suggests ceremonial assemblies. The east or *curato* court is delimited by the courts used as residences

for the friars. This entire complex occupies two city blocks.

From the *curato* court, a doorway on the north wall faces the entry to the *atrio* of the hospital chapel dedicated to the Virgen de la Concepción, an *atrio* more delicate in scale than the main one (Fig. 3.163). The hospital *atrio* gateway in turn aligns with the door-

3.163. Santa Fe de la Laguna, looking from church *atrio* through portal to hospital. Courtesy of the School of Architecture Visual Resources Collection, The University of Texas at Austin(Box-Wagner Collection).

3.164. Santa Fe de la Laguna, *portales*. Courtesy of the School of Architecture Visual Resources Collection, The University of Texas at Austin (Box-Wagner Collection, VRC 91-588).

way to the chapel and culminates at the altar at the end of the chapel nave. The infirmary rooms delimit the west end of the hospital *atrio*. Lined with crude heavy timber columns supporting wood lintels, the *portales* continue, offering protection to the infirm (Fig. 3.164).

As sacred as the regular church *atrio*, the hospital chapel *atrio* is used for prayer and ministry to the infirm. The smallest and most delicate of the three open volumes of Santa Fe de la Laguna is also bisected by the processional pathway leading to the chapel doorway. A similarity in proportion to the open volume of the church *atrio* is visible.

The three pearls of open space in the village of Santa Fe de la Laguna epitomize the community spirit and ancestral bonding that is encouraged to permeate daily life through the ages by connecting the town's organization to the sacred cosmos; bonding with the community in outdoor civic, recreational, and market activities; and providing healing and solace. Don Vasco's vision did indeed crystallize.

Erongarícuaro, Michoacán: Nuestra Señora de la Asunción

In the time it took to drive from Santa Fe de la Laguna to the other side of the lake, I learned how to pronounce Erongarícuaro. The most active place we found in town was a woodworking shop that manufactures furniture painted by the town's artisans and shipped to expensive shops in the United States. The church itself is reached through a narrow street and series of handsomely proportioned communal open spaces. Boys were playing soccer in the *atrio*.

Hal Box, 1988

Vasco de Quiroga set up a network of villages administered from the ecclesiastical capital in Tzintzuntzan, which was later moved to Pátzcuaro. This network consisted of refounded existing Tarasco towns as well as new towns. After Pátzcuaro and Tzintzuntzan, the largest of these towns was Erongarícuaro. Located opposite Pátzcuaro on the northwest shore of the lake, Erongarícuaro is a name in the Purépecha language meaning "place with a view," and the convent here does indeed have a splendid view of the lake. Dedicated to Our Lady of the Assumption, Eronga, as it is affectionately called by the locals, sports a handsome stone façade in the plateresque style and, inside, a *mudéjar* ceiling of coffered wood known as *artesonado*.

As in Tzintzuntzan and Pátzcuaro, the convent-church complex does not sit directly by the civic plaza

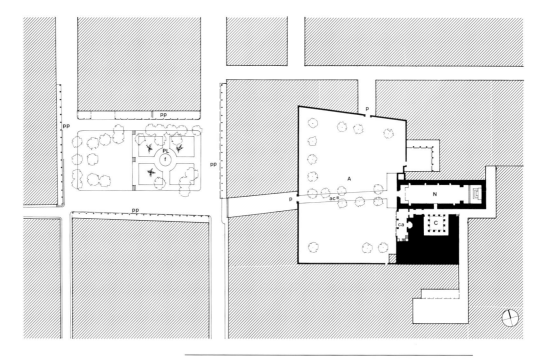

at the center of town but rather is half a block away (Fig. 3.165). Again, one assumes that this irregularity is due to the sweeping changes resulting from the War of Reform in the 1860s. Drastic transformations to the urban layout surrounding the convent are evident from an analysis of the plan of Erongarícuaro's center.

The civic plaza is still surrounded by wood-and-stone *portales* on all four sides, while the *atrio*-church-convent complex is located a city block west of it (Fig. 3.166). The plaza, which has a generous rectangular proportion, has now been divided in two: one half is a French-influenced geometric design with a fountain at its center, and the other, a tree-studded *jardín*. As testimony to the influence that the founding friars had on the urban layout of Erongarícuaro, the street flanking the south side of the plaza continues directly to the former *atrio* entrance and becomes a pathway leading to the main west entry of the *atrio* (Fig. 3.167). The *atrio*'s north door is likewise approached by an alley perpendicular to the street that flanks the *atrio*'s north side. Surrounded by civic buildings, the current form and size of the *atrio* reflects the nineteenth-century transformation of the convent's landholdings.

In addition to the *atrio*, the complex has two smaller courts, one accessible from the *atrio* (Fig. 3.168) and the other from the convent. The one north of the nave is what is left of the original hospital chapel, with two sides outlined by colonnaded *portales*. Curiously, another alley leads from the south side of

the nave to a small rectangular open space that probably used to be a loggia or portal fronting the *huerta* of the convent. A truncated rectangle, Erongarícuaro's *atrio* still retains an *atrio* cross in the center and the remains of one *posa* chapel at the southeast corner. Rows

3.167. Erongarícuaro, *atrio* of Nuestra Señora de la Asunción. Courtesy of the School of Architecture Visual Resources Collection, The University of Texas at Austin (Box-Wagner Collection, VRC 91-559).

3.168. Erongarícuaro, interior courtyard of church accessible from *atrio*. Courtesy of the School of Architecture Visual Resources Collection, The University of Texas at Austin (Box-Wagner Collection, VRC 91-51).

of trees line both the processional way and the central walkway within the *atrio*. On the south *atrio* wall next to the *posa* chapel is a south entry to the *atrio*, now blocked off by the walls of the buildings that invaded the original conventual complex space.

While documenting the convent at Erongarícuaro, we asked the presiding *cura* (priest) why he had located a basketball court within the historic and sacred *atrio*. His response, revealing the practical measures the church must take nowadays, was that locating the basketball court in the *atrio* at least brought the town's youth into the churchyard and thus under the church's influence.

Angahuan, Michoacán: Santiago Apóstol

As we entered the town, Angahuan seemed like some other part of the world. The houses are built like *trojes* of squared wood logs covered by wood shingle roofs, all more or less the same size and pitch, and smoke was coming out of the chimneys on this cool morning. The grid of the streets is consistent among the small wooden houses except for the church with its elegant façade, which sits at an assertive 45-degree angle to the rest of the town.

Hal Box, 1988

Founded as early as the 1530s, Angahuan has an urban plan with certain unusual features. All of the elements of a typical hospital chapel village of the sixteenth century exist; however, for unknown reasons, the church and its irregularly shaped *atrio* are skewed in relation to the orthogonal urban grid (Fig. 3.169). Angahuan is known to those interested in architectural history for the spectacular triple Moorish *alfiz* of the façade of Santiago Apóstol (Figs. 3.170–3.171).

The sacred hill in the middle of town serves as a cemetery (Fig. 3.172). There a back path leads from the top of the cemetery hill to the rear entry of the church through the sacristy. Was this concealed path used as a theatrical prop for religious illusion? It is reminiscent of Mesoamerican ceremonial centers like Cerros in Belize or Palenque in Chiapas, where hidden passageways within pyramid structures permitted officiating

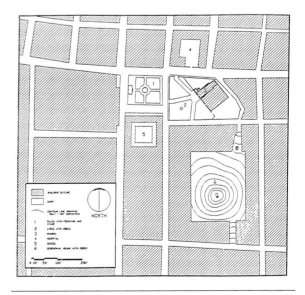

3.169. Angahuan, town plan. Courtesy of the School of Architecture Visual Resources Collection, The University of Texas at Austin (Box-Wagner Collection). Drawing by Brian Lang.

3.170. Angahuan, Santiago Apóstol *atrio* and façade. Courtesy of the School of Architecture Visual Resources Collection, The University of Texas at Austin (Box-Wagner Collection, VRC 2007-4876).

high priests to be in one location, and then, as if by magic, appear elsewhere, the hidden passageway concealing the priests' movements.

The hospital chapel takes up the block north of the church. Built of volcanic stone, it displays a handsome doorway framed by a Moorish *alfiz* (Fig. 3.173). The *alfices* and primitive *alfarjes* in Angahuan underscore the strong *mudéjar* influence here.

Angahuan is also known for its picturesque assortment of wood-plank houses, *trojes*. Built by master woodworkers, the *trojes* of Angahuan are constructed by mortise-and-tenon joining of hand-hewn planks for walls, and wood shakes on wood trusses for roofs, veritable masterpieces of wood craftsmanship (Fig. 3.174). As if the previous reasons weren't enough, Angahuan has also gained fame as the last village on the way to Paranguaricutirimícuaro, the village covered by lava during the eruption of Paricutín Volcano in 1948. One can still see, and even hike around, the steeple of the church that pokes out of the sea of hardened lava.

3.171. Angahuan, Santiago Apóstol Moorish portal with triple *alfiz*. Courtesy of the School of Architecture Visual Resources Collection, The University of Texas at Austin (Box-Wagner Collection, VRC 91-190).

3.172. Angahuan, cemetery. Courtesy of the School of Architecture
Visual Resources Collection, The University of Texas at Austin
(Box-Wagner Collection, VRC 2007-5549).

3.174. Angahuan, *troje* houses. Courtesy of the School of Architecture
Visual Resources Collection, The University of Texas at Austin
(Box-Wagner Collection, VRC 2007-5550).

3.173. Angahuan, San Lorenzo Capilla de Hospital.
Courtesy of the School of Architecture Visual Resources
Collection, The University of Texas at Austin (Box-Wagner
Collection, VRC 91-540).

VISIBLE OVERLAYS AND DELIBERATE ALIGNMENTS

When surveying sixteenth-century churches, one often finds evidence that a pre-Hispanic structure once existed where the church now stands. Without having to perform archaeological excavations, this evidence can be interpreted in a number of ways: the most obvious, of course, is when the church, or at times just the churchyard, or *atrio*, is at a significantly higher level than the general ground level of the town in question. In the cases where this occurs, the church and convent floor level has been built up to match the pre-Hispanic platform level. This change in elevation can be as low as a foot or two in some cases, or a dozen feet or more, as we shall see in some the following examples.

Spanish friars were faced with several conditions that promoted the practice of overlaying their towns on existing Mesoamerican sites rather than finding an empty site. In most cases the existing pyramid structure that defined a town center was so massive that removing it would be highly impractical. Furthermore, placing the church-convent complex at a higher level would enhance the presence of the new house of worship in the existing community. More importantly, locating the church over an existing native religious structure maintained a sense of the continuity of sacred space. This practice was not new. Roman temples were often built over Greek ones, just as Christian shrines, chapels, and churches were later built over pagan Roman temples. To Mesoamericans, this practice was customary as well. Many pyramid temple structures are actually a series of temples built one on top of another. When Spanish friars built their churches and temples over existing native platforms, it must have seemed natural and expected to the native inhabitants.

In some towns, the plazas and various open spaces are excessively large, much greater than the dimensions and proportions specified in the Laws of the Indies. This condition generally indicates that they were built on vast pre-Hispanic plazas, which the Spanish city planners used to create multiple generous urban open spaces.

At other times, usually in the ceremonial centers of smaller towns, the inverse is evident. This condition is by and large encountered when the original ceremonial center was located on abrupt mountainous terrain, which requires the normal layout and orientation of the church-convent-*atrio*-plaza complex to be altered to fit the topography.

An additional way to detect a possible overlay is when the church is built with stone that was utilized on a pre-Hispanic structure. Many times native carvings are in evidence. In many early churches from this period one can discover, upon close scrutiny, stones depicting pre-Hispanic motifs. Charles V himself ordered that stone from existing native temple structures be reused in building the Christian churches,[112] a labor-saving policy to say the least. In many cases, carved native stone is placed in strategic locations of the church, alluding perhaps to the certain reverence an indigenous mason would give to the motifs on the stone to be mortared in place.

Finally, pre-Hispanic urban planning might be evident in other structures that are now part of the new Spanish town, or in roads leading to particular urban settlements that seem deliberately aligned toward the main doorway of the church. This alignment penetrates the doorway and continues down the center of the main aisle of the nave and culminates at the most sacred spot of the town, the church's altar.

The examples shown below are only a handful of those we surveyed that allude to these design phenomena.

Mitla, Oaxaca

Rather than creating sacred space with pyramids, the builders of Mitla formed ceremonial courts with elegant low buildings. The town is thought to have been occupied at least as early as 100 CE and was active when the Spanish arrived in the 1520s. The perfection of the stone fretwork of the walls, breathtaking in photographs, is even more so when viewed in person, and the extent of the fine craftsmanship shows the reverence placed on the buildings. The town now weaves around the archaeological area with tourist markets in the streets. Fortunately, the Oaxacan archbishop who ordered the place destroyed in 1553 was unsuccessful, and Mitla has become a showplace of pre-Hispanic Mexico.

Hal Box, 1990

One of the most visible examples of friars incorporating existing native open courts into their building projects can be seen in the church of Santo Domingo in Mitla. The original layout of the ceremonial center

3.175. Mitla, palace patio. Courtesy of the School of Architecture Visual Resources Collection, The University of Texas at Austin (Box-Wagner Collection, VRC 2008-2528).

consists of several architectural groupings that create U-shaped courts and totally enclosed quadrangular courts that presumably began as U-shaped courts, that is, the prototypical Mesoamerican court and building sequence discussed in the first chapter (see Fig. 1.38 for plan of Mitla).

Perhaps because of the fine quality of the existing stone construction, the Dominican friars constructed the church and *atrio* in the open U-shaped court without destroying the Mixtec temples. The admiration of the Spaniards for the Mixtec architecture reached unprecedented levels.

The text of the Relación Geográfica of Mitla makes a very elaborate architectural description of the existing temples there, describing their use in idol worship, burial of nobles (*entierro*), administrative activities (*para tratar del gobierno de su república*), and rituals in which psychotropic plants were ingested and "peculiar activities" performed (*y también se ayuntaban a emborracharse y tener otros pasatiempos de su gentilidad*).

The Mitla RG is the most comprehensive and detailed architectural description of pre-Hispanic architecture of any Spanish document from the contact period. Careful measurements were taken, reporting accurate dimensions for all scales and providing valuable insight into ancient Spanish dimensioning: the distance of the temples from the settlement as the length of one crossbow shot (*un tiro de arcabus*); the length of courts as measured in human bodies (*huecos tres estados de hombre*); the distance between temples measured in paces (*diez pasos*); the platform height on which temples were placed,described in feet (*suben todos en un peso de treinta pies*); the dimension of the dressed stone placed over wood lintels (*vara y media*);[113] the thickness of wood beams as equivalent to the width of a man of medium girth (*gruesos como de un hombre de mediana corpulencia*); and even the size of the stones used in the architectural ornamentation in finger widths (*cuatro dedos*).[114]

The RG architectural account includes descriptions of materials like wood and stone. Stones in particular are described as white (*piedra blanca*) or marble (*marmoles*), and techniques used for finishing them are described as dressed (*de canto*) or carved (*labrados*). Admiration was expressed for joints described as mortarless (*sin ninguna mezcla de cal ni otra cosa*). Even the style of ornamentation was compared to Roman examples (*labores extrañas al modo romano*; Fig. 3.175).

Of particular interest to this study is that the colonial residential settlement was located beyond the sacred ceremonial center, allowing the architectural integrity of the temples to remain relatively intact to this day. The Dominican church and *atrio*, however, were located within a U-shaped court enclosure (Fig. 3.176). The absence of a Spanish cloister indicates that the Dominican friars utilized the quadrangular and U-shaped court arrangement just north of the church-*atrio* complex as their cloister. Presumably the Dominican friars chose this particular temple complex over all other temples at Mitla based on both the orientation and temple arrangement of this particular section of the pre-Hispanic Mitla site.

3.176. Mitla, San Pablo built in U-shaped courtyard.
Courtesy of the School of Architecture Visual Resources Collection, The University of Texas at Austin (Box-Wagner Collection, VRC 90-7212).

3.177. Hacienda Xaaga, walled courtyard. Courtesy of the School of Architecture Visual Resources Collection, The University of Texas at Austin (Box-Wagner Collection, VRC 90-6449).

3.178. Hacienda Xaaga, portal. Courtesy of the School of Architecture Visual Resources Collection, The University of Texas at Austin (Box-Wagner Collection, VRC 90-9206).

3.179. Hacienda Xaaga, entrance to Mixtec tomb. Courtesy of the School of Architecture Visual Resources Collection, The University of Texas at Austin (Box-Wagner Collection, VRC 90-6450).

Hacienda Xaaga, Oaxaca

Unplanned malfunctions are normal occurrences in expeditions of this nature, but they can lead to interesting discoveries. While exploring the countryside of Oaxaca in search of early towns, our trusted steed, the old Jeep Cherokee, broke down on us—again—in what seemed like the middle of nowhere. While we struggled to restart the car, a campesino told us he could fix it, and as he started work, Logan and I wandered over to see the large hacienda on the hill. As we were looking into the patio through a crack in the wooden gate, a man approached us to ask if we would like to look at an ancient tomb and unlocked the gate. We climbed down the stone stairs to enter the tomb, which had a typical Roman cross plan, with a long nave that had niches on its walls, an altar at the end, and a cross axis transept. Our discovery of Hacienda Xaaga, a most unusual early colonial hacienda with a patio built to include an ancient tomb, led us to dedicate a whole semester studio class to its documentation and adaptive reuse design three years later.

Hal Box, 1993

Apparently, the practice of including tombs in hacienda buildings continued well into viceregal times. Haciendas are Spanish America's version of southern plantations in the United States. As private enterprises, haciendas could be dedicated to a variety of economic endeavors: agricultural plantations, mining, or large cattle operations, just to name a few. Hacienda Xaaga, an agricultural complex, was dedicated to the cultivation and milling of wheat; the complex of residential buildings, stables, wheat mill, and the customary chapel are contained within a walled compound surrounding two courtyards or patios (Figs. 3.177–3.178).

Elaborate multichambered tombs of stone, many with colorful mural paintings, are evidence of architectural funerary practices at Oaxacan pre-Hispanic sites like Monte Albán, Huitzo, and many others, pointing to a long tradition of ancestor worship in Mesoamerica. Typically, tombs were built in the palace courts of the ruling elite. Archaeologists have found, through excavation and scientific analysis, that tomb chambers were visited regularly by living descendants, making that a common practice in pre-Hispanic times.

The Mixtec tomb located in Hacienda Xaaga's residential court is ornamented with typical Mitla-style *greca* stone fretwork (Fig. 3.179). Why would a Spanish enterprise such as a civilian hacienda be centered on a pre-Hispanic tomb? Closer architectural inspection coupled with historic archival research determined that some of the rooms in the otherwise colonial-era hacienda had been built in pre-Hispanic times. These earliest rooms were built using a technique reminiscent of rammed-earth construction, as opposed to the rest of the hacienda's construction of common adobe brick. The two rooms in front of the tomb are the remains of an ancient Mixtec palace. Archival material affirmed that the first owners were local Mixtec caciques, or lords, establishing the Indian origins of this viceregal hacienda.

As Spanish ways took hold, the original Mixtec palace evolved and grew into a typical walled hacienda with all the assorted rooms surrounding the two courtyards. The royal tomb of the ancestors of the contact period, lords of the chiefdom of Xaaga, continued to manifest its central architectural and symbolic sacred role.

Teposcolula, Oaxaca: San Pedro y San Pablo

Function alone cannot explain the amazement and awe one feels on discovering Teposcolula. In large part, this amazement is a response to unexpected juxtapositions: finding a massive walled urban complex, clearly intended for use by large numbers of people, in the rugged and sparsely populated mountains of the Mixteca Alta; or discovering a Renaissance dome in a remote village with dirt streets. Amazement is accompanied by a feeling of privilege, a sense of being singled out for a special experience. "Except for the villagers, I'll bet we're the first people to see this place in centuries," one says aloud.

Susan Kline Morehead, 1991

The Dominicans moved to Teposcolula in 1538 from Yanhuitlán, where they were in conflict with the *encomendero*, and in the ten years before returning to Yanhuitlán, they began the first of several building programs.[115] The town was relocated to the well-drained lower slopes from its original place on a hilltop and laid out on the standard grid plan of New Spain (Fig. 3.180). The friars introduced raising silkworms and mining salt, expanded the local industry of making cochineal dye, and established trading partners throughout the area. By midcentury, Teposcolula was the most populous and wealthy town in the Mixteca Alta.[116]

An account of a visit by Viceroy Mendoza in 1550 indicates that the current church was not yet in existence,[117] but the magnificent open chapel was begun in 1549 and completed by 1555 (Fig. 3.181).[118] Dominican architect Fray Francisco Marín designed both the church, dedicated to San Pedro and San Pablo, and the splendid Renaissance open chapel, dedicated to John the Baptist, which is a masterpiece.[119] He also designed the other two major Dominican houses in the Mixteca Alta, Yanhuitlán and Coixtlahuaca. San Pedro y San Pablo began as a single-nave, barrel-vaulted space, the typical plan in sixteenth-century New Spain. In 1692, it was enlarged to include a transept and apse, and the wooden ceiling was replaced with vaults over the bays.[120] Research in the 1990s by James Kiracofe suggests that a *retablo* for the church was created in 1578 by Simón Pereyns and Andrés Concha, European artists active in Mexico.[121] Unfortunately, no sixteenth-century *retablos* are still extant in the Mixteca Alta. One can find *tequitqui* sculptural elements similar to images in the Mixtec codices built into the façade of the church, such as the feathered Ionic capitals with native angel faces that support the sculptures of Saints Peter and Paul. Robert Mullen notes that this blending of symbols from two cultures is one of the earliest examples of *tequitqui* in New Spain.[122] The open chapel, however, far exceeds the church façade in sophistication and artistry.

Sited north of the church and monastery, facing west toward the *atrio*, the open chapel was built to house an altar (Fig. 3.182). In form, it consists of a central hexagonal dome flanked by lateral bays that terminate in the north *atrio* wall and the church. It is not centered on the main axis of the *atrio*, an axis reserved for the church, but it has its own centralizing dome and it aligns with the Mixtec Casa de la Cacica to the west. These basic elements, a dome-covered hexagon with flanking bays, are elaborated into a scheme rich with movement, the play of shadow and light, and the tension between inside and outside.

The dome, damaged by earthquakes in 1949 and restored by the end of the twentieth century, is a spherical form that centers the composition both literally and symbolically. A dome focuses on the center of the space below, calming existence, providing a sense of enclosure and safety. At the same time, its rising quality makes reference to the sky. At Teposcolula, the dome symbolically re-creates the sky in its star-ribbed pattern. The Indians had not developed arches or domes; their architecture was all based on post-and-lintel construction. This physical expression of security and serenity in the chapel made expressly for their

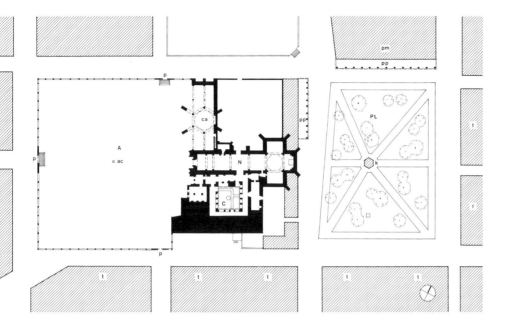

3.180. Teposcolula, plan of town center. Courtesy of the School of
Architecture Visual Resources Collection, The University of
Texas at Austin (Box-Wagner Collection).

3.181. Teposcolula, San Pedro y San Pablo. Courtesy of Sinclair Black.

3.182. Teposcolula, San Pedro y San Pablo open chapel and later church. Courtesy of the School of Architecture Visual Resources Collection, The University of Texas at Austin (Box-Wagner Collection, VRC 90-9244).

3.183. Teposcolula, portal to *atrio*. Courtesy of Sinclair Black.

use must have been reassuring as well as uplifting. McAndrew claims that no more skillful vault had been built in the Americas, adding that it "would have been notable in Spain, and it appears as phenomenal as a comet in New Spain."[123]

When one faces the open chapel, as the congregation of natives of Teposcolula would have done, one sees an overall pattern of lacy arches with a strong center that focuses the view to the interior and the altar. Like a foreshortened perspective drawing or the narrowing field of a zoom lens, the architectural elements combine to channel attention. Its pull is so strong that the altar seems magnetic. This visual centralizing and channeling is accomplished in several ways. One is the use of two arcades: the one in front rises 40 feet to the crowns of the arches, while the inner arcade is much lower, just half as high as the front. The effect is to lower the line of sight as one looks inside. In addition to creating this visual effect, the lower arcade carries a second story with two rooms, creating a wall with windows above the inner arcade. The function of these rooms is not known for certain, but one connects with the choir balcony of the church and may have been used for storage of musical instruments, or perhaps as a sacristy. Both are reached by stairs in the thickness of the back wall. In addition, open wooden mezzanine floors are tucked behind the back wall and open only onto the central domed space, completely hidden from viewers in the *atrio*. Edgerton, in his study of the use of theater in the conversion effort, suggests that these were probably used to create special effects, making objects or people appear "miraculously" on the center stage by ropes and pulleys.[124]

Another centralizing element is the front pair of flying buttresses that support the dome. They flare out and project 30 feet into the *atrio* like a pair of welcoming arms. In combination with the diminishing height of the arcades, they convey the illusion of a much deeper vista. Their angle coincides with the direction of the outward radial thrust of the dome, making them efficient both structurally and visually. The effect of depth is heightened by the rhythm of the arches supporting the dome. The space contracts as one moves through the open wings of the buttresses, opens again as the hexagon projects like a front bay, contracts again, and then stops as the opposite bay reaches the wall. This rhythmical contraction of space on the path to the altar contributes to its magnetic quality, visually urging the congregation closer.

Adding to the drama, the brilliant sunlight of southern Mexico bounces off the lacelike stone surface of the arcades and when it penetrates the screenlike façade, it contrasts dramatically with the shadows inside. The contrast is even more intense on the *atrio* wall, whose scalloped edge throws exaggerated shadows across the grass in late afternoon. The play of light, the movement in and through the spaces, and the balance between interior and exterior spaces are integral to the design of the open chapel and form the basis of one's lasting impression of it. The theater performed in the conversion effort was given a stage set by the architecture.

The standard elements at Teposcolula are civic plaza, church and convent, *atrio*, open chapel, and remnants of the *atrio* cross. No *posas* exist today, and it is possible none ever did. The walls of the *atrio* are simultaneously massive, as they protect and isolate the space, and open, with deep scallops between tall piers to a depth that invites those outside to see in and vice versa. The walls are pierced by three generous gates, one on axis with the cross and church door (Fig. 3.183).

Teposcolula's *atrio* is considered average in size, measuring 300 by 250 feet, and it sits to the west of the church and open chapel façades. Behind the open chapel to the east is a garden 120 feet square that is accessible from the church nave and through the outer wall. The city plaza, which is not quite rectangular, lies east of the complex and is about 200 by 280 feet. Altogether, this area constitutes a substantial amount of urban open space, bearing no resemblance to medieval European towns.

On axial alignment with the open chapel and slightly higher up a slope to the west is a building known as the Casa de la Cacica, the residence of a Mixtec queen.[125] It was built contemporaneously with the Dominican establishment, probably by the same craftsmen who traveled around the Mixteca area working on Fray Marín's several projects. The residence is an example of precolonial high-status architecture such as can be found in various codices, particularly the Codex Osuna of 1565, which shows the Tecpan of Mexico, a municipal seat of government, with both European arched openings and a precontact disk frieze. This blending of cultural elements rendered in the Osuna Codex created "a building intended to be a lasting architectural expression of the legitimate power and authority of the indigenous leaders, demonstrating not only their continuing role as transmitters of the tra-

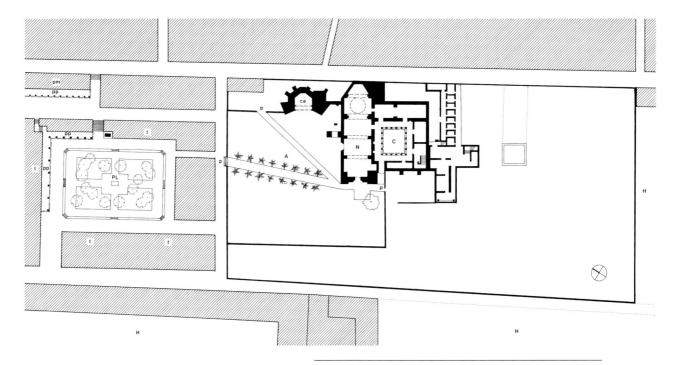

ditional culture but also their new role as interpreters and traducers of the new culture."[126] The compound is separated from the *atrio* by a large open space, but the congregation in the *atrio* could easily see across the space and up to the symbols of indigenous power in the disks of the frieze.

The plague of 1576–1578 that decimated the population also stopped work on both the convent complex and the Casa de la Cacica compound, which may then have ceased to be a residence and become a governmental building.[127]

Coixtlahuaca, Oaxaca: San Juan Bautista

Only the combination of local wealth, skill, and plentiful labor can explain the scale and splendor of such monasteries as Coixtlahuaca, Yanhuitlán, or Santo Domingo Oaxaca.

John McAndrew, *The Open-Air Churches of Sixteenth-Century Mexico*

Coixtlahuaca was a principal city of the Mixtecs, who had lived since the seventh century in city-states in the mountain valleys of Oaxaca and were known for their arts, especially illustrated codices and gold work inlaid with precious stones. When the area was conquered by the Aztecs in the fifteenth century, Coixtlahuaca paid tribute to Moctezuma in gold—twenty-five gourds of gold dust annually—and more cochineal red dye than all other towns together.[128]

3.184. Coixtlahuaca, plan of town center. Courtesy of the School of Architecture Visual Resources Collection, The University of Texas at Austin (Box-Wagner Collection).

As at Yanhuitlán, the *atrio* was sited north of the church rather than in the usual placement on the west, to accommodate the steep slope that drops toward a river west of the church (Fig. 3.184). The town, built on three levels to fit the topography, is north of the *atrio*, and *portales* line the main plaza (Fig. 3.185).

The Dominican *convento* at Coixtlahuaca has a 30-foot-high dramatic open chapel once covered with a Gothic star vault and built by the same friar-architect as Teposcolula and Yanhuitlán, Fray Francisco Marín (Fig. 3.186). As at Teposcolula, three pairs of buttresses flare at the rear, sides, and front of the chapel, the front pair reaching toward the congregation in a welcoming gesture, although they are in ruins today. As planned, they would have been flying buttresses, touching the ground with freestanding columns supporting a light and airy arcade. Earthquakes may have required that the arches be filled in. The chapel sits at the rear of the north side of the church but does not connect to it. Inside are two doorways, one large and the other small, with a third opening high above it, all leading into enclosed rooms rather than into the nave of the church. Edgerton suggests these rooms were used for theatrical events, allowing actors to emerge "miraculously" into the lower or upper space of the chapel.[129]

3.185. Coixtlahuaca, *portales* of plaza. Courtesy of the School of
Architecture Visual Resources Collection, The University of
Texas at Austin (Box-Wagner Collection, VRC 90-11439).

3.186. Coixtlahuaca, open chapel. Courtesy of the School of
Architecture Visual Resources Collection, The University of
Texas at Austin (Box-Wagner Collection, VRC 90-11441).

3.187. Coixtlahuaca, distant view showing siting on platform.
Courtesy of the School of Architecture Visual Resources
Collection, The University of Texas at Austin (Box-Wagner
Collection, VRC 90-11443).

3.188. Coixtlahuaca, north door. Courtesy of Sinclair Black.

barrel-vaulted spaces. Traces of murals can be found on the walls. The church has four shallow chapels on each side of the nave, demarcated by buttresses that support rib vaulting. The portal, also set between massive buttresses or towers like the one at Yanhuitlán, has a double stripe of niches flanking it that could have been influenced by Serlio.[131] The arched doorway has a delicate pediment enclosing an escutcheon emblazoned with the Hapsburg eagle, and above it is a dramatic scalloped rose window into the choir.

As Renaissance as the west portal is, the north door is equally handsome and dramatic, but here decorated in *tequitqui* (Fig. 3.188). Reached by a tree-lined diagonal walkway across the *atrio* from the north gate, past the open chapel, the north door was the main processional entrance during colonial times. Figures of John the Baptist flanked by Saints Peter and Paul stand on pedestals in the middle tier of the portal, above a high coffered triumphal arch. The rose window above them is surrounded by rosettes, a symbol of the Dominican Order based on the legend of a string of roses thrown to Saint Dominic when he asked the Virgin for a sign, the roses becoming the rosary. On either side of the window are reliefs in native style displaying the instruments of Christ's Passion. Among the ladder, the crown of thorns, and the nails are Mesoamerican versions of the stars, moon, and sun, and two human heads with speech scrolls curling from their mouths.

Fray Marín came to Coixtlahuaca in 1546; spent a year and a half designing and working on the platform, church, and monastery; and then left for another assignment. Work was completed about 1570. The stonemason in charge of the carvers who created the fine reliefs was named Tomás Ramírez; according to Perry, he is the only sixteenth-century native stone carver whose name is known to us.[132]

Epazoyucan, Hidalgo: San Andrés

Epazoyucan means "place of epazote," that subtle but essential herb used in the cooking of the popular frijoles of Mexican cuisine. Epazoyucan originally was an Otomi-speaking village near the obsidian mines that made Teotihuacan famous. Obsidian, a volcanic glass, was highly esteemed as a material for making very sharp blades used as weapons or cutting tools and was exported throughout Mesoamerica during the early Classic period. In the Postclassic period, from the mid-fourteenth century until the arrival of the Spaniards,

The whole complex was built on a huge platform the size of the one at Yanhuitlán (Fig. 3.187); the chapel floor is raised even higher, up a broad stair that extends beyond the central opening on either side and makes the chapel a stage. The arch above is decorated with *tequitqui* in a fascinating design of criss-crossed snakes, their tongues flickering and their tails ending in feathers. The town was once called Yodzo Coo in its original Mixtec language, meaning "plain of the snake," probably giving rise to the feathered-snake design decorating the chapel and naming the place. In a combination of symbols from two cultures, a Christian symbol of a pelican piercing its side in emulation of Christ's wound is carved between each loop of the writhing pairs of serpents.

Traces of gray stucco pavement on the *convento* platform were still visible to McAndrew when he visited before 1964.[130] The huge monastery building has three levels connected by massive staircases, walled gardens, an elegant cloister, and numerous

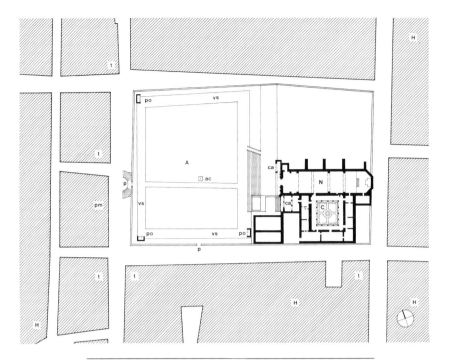

Epazoyucan was a dependency of the Mexica of Tenochtitlan, the Aztec capital.

After the arrival of the Spaniards, Epazoyucan initially became a Franciscan establishment, but by 1540 it had been ceded to the Augustinian Order. The monastery here is dedicated to San Andrés. The cloister walls of the convent of San Andrés are famous for the extensive and high-quality mural program that still survives to this day. During viceregal times, most of the available workers would inevitably have ended up laboring in the rich silver mines of nearby Pachuca, some 40 kilometers away.

Although nestled between the hills, volcanic formations, and outright mountains of the Central Highlands, Epazoyucan itself is located on relatively flat land. The regularity of the gridded urban plan testifies to the small pocket of level terrain in this otherwise abrupt land (Fig. 3.189).

The core of the town is the Augustinian convent. The open spaces are limited to the *atrio* and what was presumably the convent's *huerta*. A civic plaza is nowhere to be found. The otherwise large and rectangular city blocks of the grid are interrupted by a string of narrow blocks running north–south directly west of the *atrio*. One of those small blocks is where the Palacio Municipal is located, on axis with the convent's *atrio* (Fig. 3.190).

The convent complex is a strong example of an *atrio*-church-convent complex built over ascending pre-Columbian platforms. The lowest platform is ac-cessed by a semicircular staircase leading to a triumphal arch that opens onto the *atrio* on its west side. The *atrio* still has three of its rectangular *posa* chapels, each approached by the sacred way that leads processions in a counterclockwise direction (Fig. 3.191).

The *atrio* cross is located in the center and to the side of the central pathway that leads to a massive staircase rising to a second, higher pre-Hispanic platform (Fig. 3.192). Stairs that lead into the nave and also

3.191. Epazoyucan, San Andrés *posa*. Courtesy of the School of Architecture Visual Resources Collection, The University of Texas at Austin (Box-Wagner Collection, VRC 91-10614).

3.192. Epazoyucan, San Andrés *atrio* cross and church façade. Courtesy of the School of Architecture Visual Resources Collection, The University of Texas at Austin (Box-Wagner Collection, VRC 91-10613).

up to the portal of the cloister indicate the possibility of a third original platform. The barrel-vaulted open chapel is located in front of the bell tower at the north corner of the nave (Fig. 3.193). The single-aisle nave with five bays ends at the sanctuary and altar within a half-hexagon apse. It is supported on the north side by buttresses and on the south side by a square-shaped cloister. The conventual complex, consisting of *atrio*, church, cloister, and *huerta*, forms an entire large city block and, as such, determines the size of the adjoining blocks to the north and to the south.

3.193. Epazoyucan, San Andrés open chapel. Courtesy of the School of Architecture Visual Resources Collection, The University of Texas at Austin (Box-Wagner Collection, VRC 91-10610).

THE YUCATÁN EXPERIENCE

If the number, grandeur and beauty of its buildings were to count toward the attainment of renown reputation in the same way as gold, silver and riches have done for other parts of the Indies, Yucatán would have become as famous as Peru and New Spain have become. So many in so many places, and so well built are they, it is a marvel; the buildings themselves, and their number, are the most outstanding thing that has been discovered in the Indies.

Fray Diego de Landa, *Yucatan Before and After the Conquest*

Although it was the early Spanish explorers' first point of contact with Mesoamerica, the densely populated Maya-speaking area of the Yucatán Peninsula was viewed only as spoils in the initial round of conquests. The challenge to explore, conquer, convert, and colonize Yucatán was not initiated in earnest until the 1540s, two decades after the conquest of Tenochtitlan by Hernán Cortés and his men. Was there a reason for this delay? Yucatán does not have the mineral and natural riches of other areas of New Spain, nor even fertile land for agriculture or ranching. However, Yucatán did have people, the only resource it could offer, and as Landa admiringly affirms, Yucatán had architecture.[133]

In 1526, Francisco de Montejo was granted a Spanish royal charter for the exploration and conquest of Yucatán.[134] A veteran captain who had sailed on the Grijalva expedition of 1517, Montejo also accompanied Cortés on the conquest of Tenochtitlan. The actual conquest of Yucatán took some time and had to be accomplished by the father, the son, and the nephew, all named Francisco de Montejo. Francisco de Montejo, the father, attempted an *entrada* along the Caribbean coast and managed to establish primitive bases at Xelha in 1527 and Bacalar in 1544.[135] However, due to stiff resistance by the ancestors of the Cruzob Maya[136] of eastern Quintana Roo, the campaign had to be abandoned.[137] In 1540, Montejo, the son, entered the peninsula through the west coast of Yucatán, at modern-day Campeche on the Gulf of Mexico. After skirmishes and a major battle in 1542, Montejo, the son, conquered the much-decayed city of Tihoo, once the provincial capital of the region. He renamed it Mérida, and it became the first permanent Spanish settlement on the Yucatán Peninsula.

The Franciscan Order was given the nod to evangelize the Yucatán and, as early as 1535, had already established a monastery on the coast at Champotón near Campeche.[138] However, the friars had to await Spanish military control of parts of the interior before they could venture into the heart of Yucatán. Following the military triumphs of Montejo, the son, in 1545 and 1546, Franciscans established monasteries at Mérida and Campeche. Fray Bernardo de Lizana describes the initial construction strategy used by the friars in Mérida: "The place that was chosen was a Cu or tall hill handmade of stone which served as a house or temple for the Indians' idols."[139]

With an abundance of temples to choose from in Tihoo, friars selected the largest as the site on which to build the monastery of Saint Francis and its church, which they dedicated to Our Lady of Assumption. Spanish friars regularly used pyramid platforms as a base on which to build their churches, but here at Tihoo, as in Mitla, actual rooms in native temples were remodeled and reused as part of the convent.[140] At one point, the sprawling conventual complex of the Franciscans in Tihoo/Mérida was surrounded by a battlement wall for protection, not only against an uprising from the native population, but from marauding English and Dutch pirates, who posed an even bigger threat.

As is often the case, the center of town was established elsewhere. The cathedral, the *cabildo*, and other buildings that surrounded the new plaza were estab-

lished on unbuilt flat land. Flat land is the norm in Yucatán, in contrast to the mountainous regions of the Central Highlands and Oaxaca. Except for a low-hill area in the south known as the Puuc Hills, the Yucatán Peninsula consists of a flat limestone shelf a few meters above sea level. The flatness of Yucatán made the layout of the checkerboard urban grid very regular. Mérida's urban layout is a nearly perfect checkerboard. A city map from 1875 shows it as a perfect grid, interrupted only by the sprawling fortified Franciscan monastery complex (Fig. 3.194). Sadly, not a trace of the original Franciscan house survives today.

After founding their base in Mérida, the Franciscan friars set out to evangelize the Maya of Yucatán, establishing four major convents in Maní, Izamal, Motul, and Sisal, now a barrio of Valladolid. From these monasteries, friars were able to branch out and found hundreds of *visita* chapels throughout the land. As in other areas of the New World, many towns began as existing population centers with temple complexes. In other cases, similar to many in Michoacán, new town *reducciones* were founded by the friars in order to congregate native inhabitants who had fled and were dispersed in the low but dense brush thicket of the Yucatecan forest.

With almost three decades of experience in establishing towns in other areas of New Spain, Franciscan friars had developed a standardized architectural and urban layout for their new communities in Yucatán. Recent scholarship proposes that a three-phase construction sequence was used to establish mission churches in Yucatán. The first phase consisted of building a temporary primitive structure with ephemeral materials like poles and thatch. The second phase consisted of building a more permanent masonry chapel, usually in the form of a massive arched vault with one or two rooms on either side for a sacristy and friars' living quarters. A thatched structure open at the sides, called a *ramada*, was extended from the arch of the open chapel to provide much-needed shade for the congregation assembled in the makeshift nave. The third phase, generally built many years later, involved finishing an actual masonry nave. In this scheme, the open chapel eventually becomes the sanctuary. The vast majority of churches established in sixteenth-century Yucatán follow this pattern, and the second phase of the construction sequence can often be easily detected today, embedded in the much later third phase of the permanent nave.

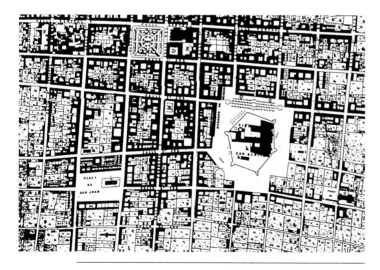

3.194. Mérida 1864–1865, map detail of fortified Franciscan monastery. Commissioned by José Salazar Ilarregui, the Comisario Imperial de la Península de Yucatán.

Chapels, Yucatán

The church noted for having the most elaborate *espadaña* in Mexico, at the village of Yotholín near the Puuc Hills, started out as the standard Yucatecan *atrio* and open chapel complex of the sixteenth century; the original open chapel is evident today at the east end of the church. If one looks closely, its original single-bell *espadaña* can be seen (Figs. 3.195–3.196). Functionally, *espadañas* supported the bells that rang to mark canonical hours before clocks were invented. Financially, they cost less to build than bell towers, important in the Yucatán, an area poor in resources. Aesthetically, they resemble the *cresterías*, or roof combs, of local Maya architecture. Their name comes from the old Spanish verb *espadañar*, meaning "to spread the tail feathers."[141]

A cenote to the south of the church, whose underground pool is about the same size as the plaza, is the original reason for building a town and church there. Today, the community is working to make the cenote more accessible so as to attract tourists.

In Sudzal, south of Izamal, a substantial level change from the open chapel to the newer nave allowed for the construction of a circular clerestory that allowed the sun's afternoon rays to fall on the gilded *retablo*, adding a dramatic visual effect that enhanced the theatrical nature of the liturgy.

For various reasons, some of the communities that were founded reached only the second phase of building and then were abandoned. One of the most famous of these is the open chapel at the archaeological site of Dzibilchaltun, just north of Mérida (Fig. 3.197). The site has Preclassic origins and was continuously

3.196. Yotholín, *espadaña*. Courtesy of the School of Architecture Visual Resources Collection, The University of Texas at Austin (Box-Wagner Collection, VRC 96-02878).

3.195. Yotholín, original chapel, now apse on east end of nave. Susan Kline Morehead.

3.197. Dzibilchaltun, Phase Two open chapel. Courtesy of the School of Architecture Visual Resources Collection, The University of Texas at Austin (Box-Wagner Collection, VRC 95-06015).

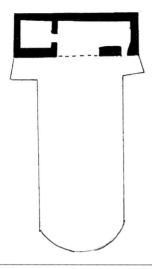

3.198. Tecoh, plan of Phase Two open chapel. Courtesy of the School of Architecture Visual Resources Collection, The University of Texas at Austin (Box-Wagner Collection, uncataloged).

inhabited until Mérida was established by the Spaniards. Others have been uncovered by archaeological excavation on the Caribbean coast. Our teams were able to document examples of villages abandoned after building Phase Two open chapels at Tecoh (Figs. 3.198–3.199), Uitzil, and Tok Batz Ka (Fig. 3.200), which, with guidance from archaeologist Luis Millet Cámara, we located in the overgrown brush forest of central Yucatán.

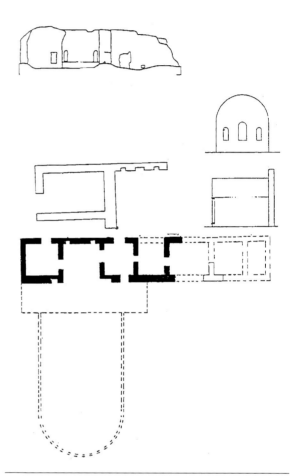

3.200. Tok Batz Ka, plan and elevation of Phase Two open chapel. Courtesy of the School of Architecture Visual Resources Collection, The University of Texas at Austin (Box-Wagner Collection, uncataloged).

3.199. Tecoh, Phase Two open chapel. Susan Kline Morehead.

Tibolón, Yucatán

Tibolón, located in central Yucatán, is a village lost in time. It seems that life here has not changed in centuries. From its appearance, the urban layout remains virtually untouched since the Franciscans resettled the town in the sixteenth century. The urban plan depicts a somewhat regular checkerboard pattern that incorporates at least five different temple platforms. The largest was used as the base on which to build the open chapel and the subsequent Phase Three nave (Figs. 3.201–3.202). As can be seen in the site plan, the sizable platform served as the *atrio* as well.

Each urban block consisted of several long, skinny lots running from the street to the center of the block, a typical configuration of lots in the urban plans of New Spain. This scheme allows a dense, contiguous construction at the street edge, leaving ample room on the lot to create courtyards, *huertas*, and small corrals on the portion of each lot that extends toward the center of the urban block. In the initial phase of urbanization on the Spanish grid, Yucatecan village dwellers erected vernacular housing at the street edge.

The Casa Maya, as the indigenous single-family dwelling is known, is among the defining traits of Yucatán. The typical rural house of a Maya peasant has been in existence since the earliest dwellings found in archaeological excavations: it is an oval-plan, apsidal structure with a thatched gabled roof. In Mesoamerican times, the Maya house was honored by being carved in stone on lintels found at the Nunnery Quadrangle in Uxmal (Fig. 3.203) and at the famous monumental arch at Labná (Fig. 3.204). The Tibolón plan shows Maya vernacular dwellings on a Spanish urban plan. The apsidal Maya houses (Fig. 3.205) form a continuous plane at the street's edge, leaving the majority of each urban block as one large open space. Privately owned, the narrow strips of each residential lot that create the street front extend into the center of the urban block. Houses create a solid protective wall fronting the street's public domain, while behind this solid barrier, family-scale open spaces such as patios and *huertas* are prevalent.

The shape of the apsidal Maya house is rectangular with rounded walls on the two short sides. Laid out with a cord still today, the design and building of the Maya house is a symbolic reenactment of the creation ritual performed by the primordial gods who created the Maya universe.[142] The proportions of the rectangu-

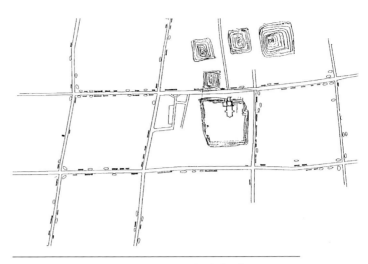

3.201. Tibolón, town plan. Courtesy of the School of Architecture Visual Resources Collection, The University of Texas at Austin (Box-Wagner Collection, uncataloged).

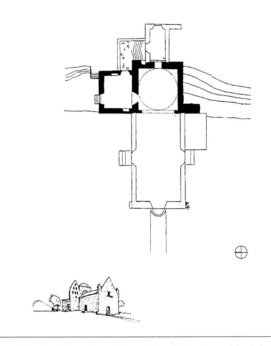

3.202. Tibolón, plan and rendering of church. Courtesy of the School of Architecture Visual Resources Collection, The University of Texas at Austin (Box-Wagner Collection, uncataloged).

lar plan are that of a golden or phi rectangle (1:1.618), and it is created using a cord. This plan is achieved by first outlining a square using the cord, then extending the cord from the midpoint of one side to an opposing corner and drawing it in an arc to extend the original side.[143] The ends of the rectangle thus created are rounded by the addition of semicircular apses. Planting four tree trunk posts in the corners manifests the

3.203. Uxmal, Casa Maya carved on lintel of Nunnery Quadrangle.
Susan Kline Morehead.

3.204. Labná, Casa Maya carved on arched gate.
Susan Kline Morehead.

3.205. Typical Casa Maya. Courtesy of the School of Architecture
Visual Resources Collection, The University of Texas at Austin
(Box-Wagner Collection, VRC 96-02919).

3.206. Tibolón, church and *espadaña*. Susan Kline Morehead.

four-sided directionality of the Tzuc partition evoked by the gods. The center of the dwelling is marked by the three-stone hearth, which creates a quincunx with the four posts. In some indigenous villages the custom still survives today of burying a newborn child's umbilical cord in a hole dug under the ashes of the hearth. The houses in Tibolón are replicated throughout Yucatán.

Clearly distinguishable from the later church, built with more massive masonry walls, the domed open chapel at Tibolón eventually became the sanctuary of the nave we can appreciate today (Fig. 3.206). The crested *espadaña* at Tibolón, reminiscent of the Maya *cresterías* of nearby Uxmal's Dovecote, proudly stands guard next to the domed open chapel, creating the west wall of the sacristy. The more recent masonry nave, of thinner caliber, is fronted by a massive but plain wall with a triangular pediment that is flanked on both sides by pointed merlons.[144]

Tibolón is a small fraction of the size of Izamal; however, the urban layout and architectural engagement of existing native ceremonial structures suggest that Tibolón used Izamal as a model. Among the similarities are that both settlements adapt the urban grid to existing structures, deforming its regularity; both engage the largest temple platform to create an *atrio* and base for the church/convent; at both, the eastern edge of the platform becomes the ledge for the open chapel, and the *subsequent* structure is built from the ground up to meet the level of the original Maya platform. Also at both sites, a *camarín*, a small room for private presentations of the patron saint's image as well as a place for robing it and storing its adornments, is built abutting the apse.

Izamal, Yucatán: San Antonio de Padua

After a day in Mérida, our small caravan of cars and trucks drove into Izamal at dusk and into a time warp. We seemed to be the only cars on the street; everyone was on bicycles or on a modified bicycle with a bench between two wheels in the front. Men were pedaling large pieces of freight or families of six or seven small people, who were sitting on the platform with children hanging on their backs. As we approached the center of Izamal, horses and horse-drawn carriages were moving about the broad streets. We began to sense the grand scale of the ancient city as it might have been in its best days.

Hal Box, 1993

Historical Background

Perhaps due to the sheer monumentality of its Maya temples, Izamal, in contrast to other early colonial sites, did not suffer the total destruction of native architectural fabric that was the order of the day. Instead, it became what may be the most sophisticated and articulate example of urban overlay and integration of native architectural fabric into the standardized Spanish urban plan. In all of New Spain, Izamal is the urban community that best demonstrates, at a colossal scale, the Spaniards' incorporation of native ceremonial centers into their own religious and civic urban layout.[145]

Miguel A. Bretos expresses it this way:

> In no other Franciscan work is the friars' motivation to build more evident than at Izamal. More than just a simple base to evangelize a district, Izamal was conceived as a symbol of the new faith, raised in this case not only symbolically, but dramatically and literally as well, over the ruins of the ancient beliefs. Its objective was to reclaim for Christianity the immemorial prestige of a sanctuary whose temples and massive platforms extended in all directions and from whose pinnacle one could glimpse the glimmer of the bluish waters of the Caribbean.[146]

Located in central Yucatán, the legendary Izamal has withstood the passage of time. Dating to at least the Early Classic, 300 CE, Izamal has always been the most important pilgrimage site in Yucatán, and it still is, even today. In ancient times, the sacred center of Izamal was dedicated to the sun god Kinich, in cosmic counterpoint to the shrine of the moon goddess Ixchel located on the island of Cozumel. Today, Izamal continues to be a pilgrimage shrine dedicated to the Catholic patroness, the Virgin of the Immaculate Conception, simply known as "La Virgen de Izamal."

In native settlements in the abrupt terrain of mountainous areas, the Spaniards had to adapt the orthogonal urban grid plan they were systematically implementing in the New World by distorting the grid's regularity to circumvent natural obstructions. In the case of Izamal, the urban grid had to be adapted to human-built mountains.

Inga Clendinnen captured the essence of the motivation behind the Franciscan friars' impressive building campaigns in Yucatán, and she hinted at what Diego de Landa might have been thinking when he and Juan de Mérida conceived the master plan for Izamal:

> Despite his intense engagement with the Indians, Landa took more than his share of administrative and political duties within the order. In 1553 he was charged with replacing the huts of the monastery at Izamal with a permanent stone structure. Details of the construction were left to the architect, the friar Juan de Mérida. It was the design and the overall layout which interested Landa. The whole was to be set out on a vast Maya platform—Izamal had been one of the most important Maya religious centres. The structures were not to be especially massive, and were in fact economical in their use of materials and labour. The design derived its undoubted grandeur from the scale and distribution of its great spaces for processions and collective ceremonial. The structure was flung across the land like the grandiose gesture it was: a most material testament of Landa's vision of the Church he and his brothers were building in Yucatan.[147]

Important to our study here is the recognition by scholars of the crucial role that the existence and use of open space played in Mesoamerican religious ritual, and how mendicant friars acknowledged this importance by continuing the practice of open space ritual as a strategy for conversion. Going well beyond simply implementing European-based urban design ideals, mendicant friars incorporated, reshaped, and selectively modified the ritual open space and made it part of the overall urban plan. The vast urban open spaces of Izamal, located both at ground level and on the terraced esplanades of the human-made mountains of the temple pyramids, were masterfully incorporated by Landa and his architect, Juan de Mérida, into what Sam Edgerton has termed "Theaters of Conversion." Clendinnen states this fact in unequivocal terms when talking about the vision Landa and Mérida made real, employing the power of spatial theatrical setting for ritual to occur:

> The friars saw their world very differently, and here the influence of Landa is crucial. It was he who had conceived and laid out the magnificent structures of the monastery of Izamal—the monastery which Toral, judging conventionally, declared "a splendid thing to see and a scandal to permit, and that certainly Saint Francis would condemn", especially as it would house at most one or two friars. Landa understood the declamatory power of structures: their capacity to mark and order the landscape. He also knew the power of properly orchestrated ritual action.[148]

Although all but abandoned, Izamal had remained an important Maya pilgrimage site at the time of contact. The Franciscan friars recognized the shrine's importance as they planned the evangelizing campaign in Yucatán. To Landa and his architect fell the challenge and the opportunity to create an epic transformation of a major Mesoamerican religious center.

Izamal is mentioned early by a variety of archival sources, including the books of Chilam Balam, Diego López de Cogolludo, and Diego de Landa.[149] Using a wealth of architectural detail, Landa describes several structures.[150] In the nineteenth century, Desire de Charnay excavated a human-made tunnel he had found on the east side of Kinich Kak Mo pyramid, only to abandon the enterprise in favor of digging in Chichén Itzá instead. Other viceregal-era archival material survives that makes reference to Izamal, including Lizana, Ciudad Real, and the *Relación de Yucatán*. In the nineteenth century, Izamal was rediscovered, romanticized, and forever immortalized in the Western world by text and drawings in the classic travel

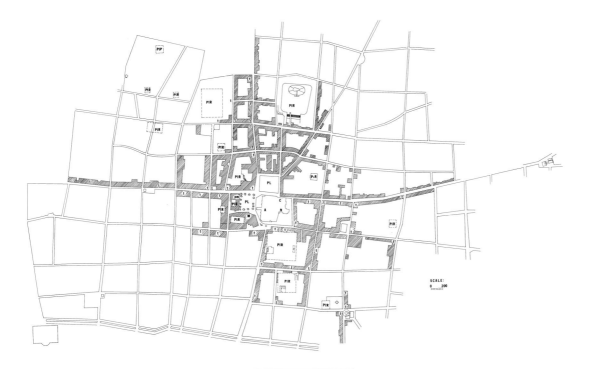

3.207. Izamal, current site plan. Courtesy of the School of Architecture Visual Resources Collection, The University of Texas at Austin (Box-Wagner Collection, VRC 2007-4832).

adventure book by John Lloyd Stephens and Frederick Catherwood, *Incidents of Travel in Yucatán*. In the twentieth century, archaeological work was done in the sixties and seventies by archaeologist Victor Segovia Pinto. In the nineties, restoration and consolidation work was undertaken on selected pre-Hispanic and colonial architecture under the direction of archaeologist Luis Millet Cámara. In his writings, Diego de Landa identifies the existence of twelve native temples at the time of initiating construction of the monastery at Izamal. More than three centuries later, in an 1895 treatise by Yucatán's Bishop Carrillo y Ancona, Landa is corrected in the number of existing structures he identified. In what appears to be an interpretation of Maya numerology the bishop states:

> If they weren't exactly twelve, the number of these great monuments, they probably were thirteen rather than eleven, because we observe that thirteen was the number that was used by the Maya for everything that had any importance. It was the sacred and symbolic number found in the archaeological investigations of the calendar and astronomy, in historical classifications, in cultural rituals, devotion of deities, of heroes, etc.[151]

The number of temples is vastly reduced in 1895, Carrillo y Ancona's time: "And now, three and half centuries after Father Landa located eleven or twelve, today only five or six remain. Surely these were the principal ones, and how many have not gone to ruins in the last forty years!"[152]

The first surface archaeological survey of pre-Hispanic structures was undertaken by Charles Lincoln and reported in his 1980 master's thesis. Lincoln's survey identified and documented at least twenty-five structures within the modern city limits of Izamal. A survey undertaken by Earthwatch volunteers under our direction in 1993 and 1994 confirmed the location of the structures identified in Lincoln's survey. Extensive stabilization was performed on the Kinich Kak Mo and Itzamatul pyramids in the nineties under the direction of Luis Millet Cámara, and he also accomplished minor consolidation work on Structure 24, also known as "El Conejo" (The Rabbit).

The overall plan of Maya Izamal indicates three large temple masses forming a triadic group. The largest three structures in Izamal, Kinich Kak Mo, Ppap Hol Chac, and Itzamatul, are grouped to form and shape a vast plaza. The plaza was of such grand scale that it was later transformed into a Spanish grand plaza, with a seemingly endless arcade of shady *portales*, a sprawling market, and two large city blocks (Figs. 3.207–3.208).

3.208. Izamal, aerial photo. Logan Wagner.

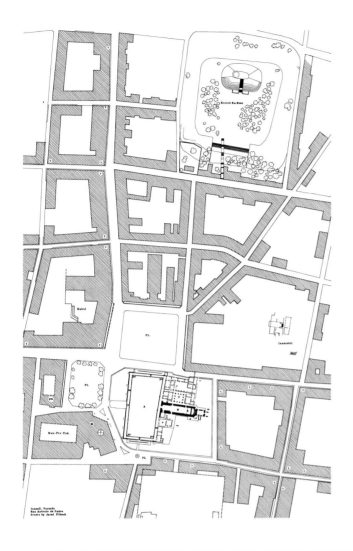

3.209. Izamal, downtown plan showing San Antonio de Padua convent at the bottom and Kinich Kak Mo at the top. Courtesy of the School of Architecture Visual Resources Collection, The University of Texas at Austin (Box-Wagner Collection, VRC 2007-4834).

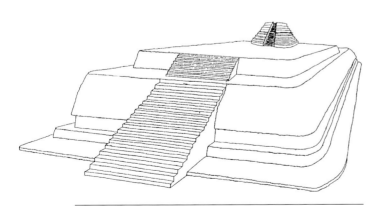

3.210. Izamal, Kinich Kak Mo rendering. Courtesy of the School of Architecture Visual Resources Collection, The University of Texas at Austin (Box-Wagner Collection, uncataloged).

Kinich Kak Mo

We know through various ethnographic sources that the Ppap Hol Chac pyramid was the largest in Izamal at the time Diego de Landa selected it as the pyramid upon which to build the monastery of San Antonio de Padua. However, after all the remodeling necessary to accommodate the monastery, it diminished in size. Today the Kinich Kak Mo pyramid is the largest and tallest structure in Izamal. The Kinich, as it is affectionately known, epitomizes an *izamaleño* architectural style (Fig. 3.209).

Description and admiration of the Kinich starts early with entries by Diego de Landa, including the first surviving sketch from 1566;[153] the local *encomendero* Juan Cueva Santillán;[154] and Fray Antonio Ciudad Real in 1588.[155]

Historic accounts admire the height and monumentality of the Kinich, and all describe the rounded-off corners, the monumental but eroded steps, and the original pagan shrine. They also refer to the replacement of the pagan shrine by a thatch-covered chapel, and later to the eventual disappearance of a Christian chapel dedicated to Mount Tabor after the original Mass held there on the day of the Transfiguration. By the time Ciudad Real described the scene in the 1570s, only three wooden crosses remained. Today, at the summit of Kinich Kak Mo, nothing remains but faint masonry traces of a foundation (Fig. 3.210).

Some of the narratives describe what must have been monumental stucco masks adorning the sides of the pyramid, similar, no doubt, to the Catherwood drawing from the mid-nineteenth century. Impressed by the size of the masks, the early chroniclers attributed the construction of the temples to a race of giants, by then long gone.[156]

In the 1990s, during restoration interventions, archaeologist Luis Millet Cámara described how ancient *izamaleño* builders experimented with innovative techniques, at times pushing the structural envelope. At the Kinich and other temples of Izamal, native builders tried creating a cantilevered cornice. At one point, however, the cornice had to be shored up by additional dressed boulders in order to support its massive weight.[157]

Of particular interest is the way the second platform level of the Kinich forms a large elevated plaza, with an additional smaller third platform at the north end, its monumental stairway leading to the summit (Fig. 3.211). A source of admiration in all the archival

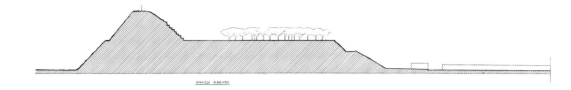

3.211. Izamal, section of downtown. Courtesy of the School of
Architecture Visual Resources Collection, The University of
Texas at Austin (Box-Wagner Collection).

narratives, the elevated plaza with its monumental
dimensions served as a spectacular perch for open-air
ritual. By 1588, Ciudad Real writes that the elevated
plaza had been taken over by trees and vegetation.
Today, the elevated plaza of the Kinich serves as a
delightful city park with stunning views.

Millet Cámara affirms that Kinich exhibits three
layers of construction phases. Speculation abounds
about the existence of a tomb chamber. Today the
rubble-filled tunnel discovered by Desire de Charnay
in the nineteenth century awaits exploration.

The platform plaza levels, the rounded corners,
the monumental stucco masks, the use of megalithic
stone, and the cantilevered cornice together form what
could be considered an Izamal architectural style.

The Convent of San Antonio de Padua and Its Atrio

The tightly knit historic fabric of Izamal is well known
for its beauty and abundance, making the town a jewel
of colonial architecture and a UNESCO-sponsored
World Heritage site. The convent of San Antonio,
with its majestic monumentality, constitutes the crown
jewel of Izamal's colonial architectural legacy. The
convent was envisioned by Fray Diego de Landa and
executed by architect-friar Juan de Mérida. The vision
entailed reshaping the largest pyramid of Izamal's ancient ceremonial center, the Ppap Hol Chac structure.

Dedicated to a version of the sun god Itzamna,
the Ppap Hol Chac pyramid was leveled down to its

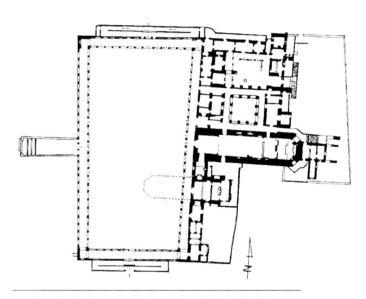

3.212. Izamal, plan of convent. Courtesy of the School of Architecture
Visual Resources Collection, The University of Texas at Austin
(Box-Wagner Collection, VRC 2007-4833).

bottom terrace, which is still more than 20 feet above
ground level. This monumental engineering task created the largest sixteenth-century *atrio* of the Spanish
New World. When completed, the *atrio* had a trap-
ezoidal shape, punctuated at each of the four corners
with large *posa* chapels (Fig. 3.212). The extensive arcade that connects the *posa* chapels was constructed in
the seventeenth century (Fig. 3.213). Massive, elegant
ramps were constructed on the north, west, and south
sides to ascend to the *atrio*, church, and convent from
the plaza below (Fig. 3.214).

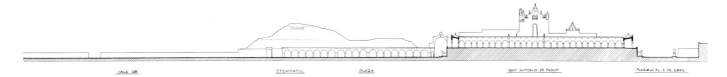

CORTE NORTE-SUR
IZAMAL, YUCATAN
1993

POR JIM FRAERMAN

3.213. Izamal, *atrio* with Linda Schele and Peter Mathews in the
shaded arcade. © Macduff Everton.

3.214. Izamal, ramp to *atrio* of San Antonio de Padua.
Susan Kline Morehead.

3.215. Izamal, *camarín* and flying buttresses at apse of San Antonio de
Padua. Susan Kline Morehead.

3.216. Labná, *sacbe*. Susan Kline Morehead.

As in the miniature example of Tibolón described above, the eastern edge of the monumental platform supports the open chapel, two patio cloisters, and the church. The length of the nave and the massive size of the cloister located to the north in the shade of the nave forced the decision to build these massive structures from the ground level at the east side of the *atrio* platform esplanade. The size of the nave was again increased when a unique and impressive *camarín* chamber was built at the east end to engage the apse of the church. To support the *camarín*, massive flying buttresses that rival Gothic examples found in Europe were constructed (Fig. 3.215). The original open chapel, with its attached palm-thatched *ramada* that is now nonexistent, was also located on the east edge of the *atrio*. The outline of the thatched nave *ramada* is shown on the site plan of the convent and *atrio*.

Sacbeob

Sacbeob, plural for *sacbe*, literally means "white roads" in Mayan, named for their appearance when plastered. These are elevated sacred ceremonial causeways and roads built by the ancient Maya. Usually *sacbeob* connect important structures within a ceremonial center, as in Labná (Fig. 3.216); sometimes they provide a link between architectural groupings or urban nodes, as in Tikal; and many times, they connect close and distant Maya cities. The longest *sacbe* uncovered to date connects the Postclassic sites of Yaxuna in Yucatán and Coba in Quintana Roo, a distance of nearly 100 kilometers (60 miles). At Izamal, up to five *sacbeob* have been detected.

The *sacbeob* of Izamal vary in height from 30 centimeters to 2 meters. The width can vary from 5 to 13 meters. Built with rubble masonry consisting of alternate layers of limestone and lime mortar, the *sacbeob* at Izamal were contained within retaining walls of carved dressed stone, and the walking surface was finished in a polished white lime stucco plaster.

Based on historic reports, interviews, and field observations, Charles Lincoln accounts for five *sacbeob* emanating radially from the center of town. Three lead in the cardinal directions, and one heads to the southwest. This was customary for ancient Maya cities, ethnographer Ralph Roys informs us:

> Every town had four ceremonial entrances at the cardinal points marked by a stone mound on both sides, and a road led from each of these to the center, where the more important inhabitants resided.[158]

The west *sacbe* leads to the site of Aké; the east to Structure 25; and the south to the town of Kantunil,

14 kilometers away. The north *sacbe* has not been located, and it is only mentioned in Lincoln's work because it was reported to nineteenth-century explorers.

The east, south, and southwest *sacbeob* seem to emanate from Ppap Hol Chac pyramid, site of the monastery, while the west *sacbe* begins at the Kabul pyramid (Structure 12). The central location of both of these structures affords a radial quality to Izamal's *sacbeob* as they emanate from the center of both Maya and colonial Izamal (Fig. 3.217).

To overlay Mesoamerican causeways and *sacbeob* with colonial grid streets is not without precedent. At least two of the main thoroughfares in downtown Mexico City are laid over ancient Tenochtitlan causeways that lead to the central sacred precinct of the Aztec capital. Reutilizing existing native *sacbeob* and causeways had at least two benefits to the Spanish town builders: first, it was an extremely economical and practical labor- and material-saving device; second, it highlighted the sacred processional importance of the temple pyramid. These same avenues would accentuate the new Christian shrine as well.

Throughout viceregal Mexico, examples are encountered of country roads that not only lead to the center of town, but literally and visually bisect the plaza, traverse the *atrio*, and head down the central aisle of the nave of the church to terminate at the altar *retablo*.

We propose that Spanish Izamal's street layout was influenced by the *sacbeob* of the Maya. From the north, south, east, and west, the main streets of Izamal that still exist today lead to the central plaza; a fifth street to the northeast became Calle 26a and the road to Tekal, not conforming to the Spanish grid. We

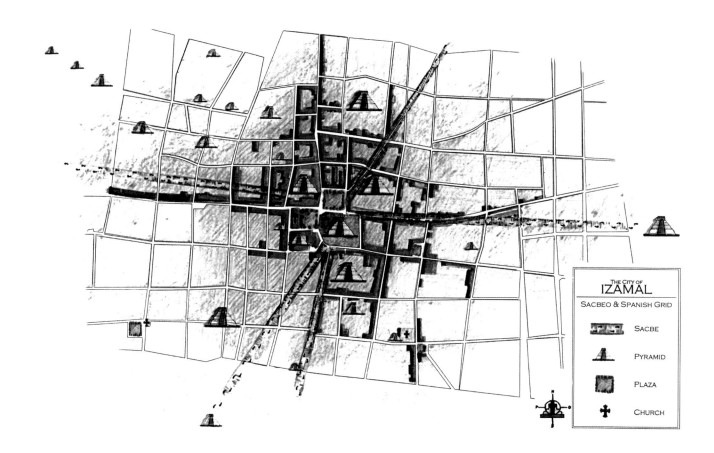

3.217. Izamal, site plan showing *sacbeob*.
Courtesy of the School of Architecture Visual Resources Collection, The University of Texas at Austin (Box-Wagner Collection). Drawing by Dayna Finley.

3.218. Izamal, Native Americans in traditional dress gathered in the *atrio* of San Antonio for Mass conducted by Pope John Paul II in 1993. Logan Wagner.

3.219. Izamal, Pope John Paul II celebrating the discovery of America in San Antonio *atrio* with image of the Virgin of Izamal beside him. Logan Wagner.

propose here that Calle 26a, at an angle to the square grid, exists because it once was the north *sacbe*. The northeast *sacbe* completes a quincunx arrangement.

Of all the places we examined, Izamal best illustrates the survival of indigenous sacred space and monuments beneath the overlay of Spanish ideals of urban design. In 1993, in commemoration of the five-hundredth anniversary of the discovery of America, Pope John Paul II celebrated Mass under a scorching summer Yucatecan sun, before a jam-packed *atrio* filled with indigenous groups in full native regalia (Figs. 3.218–3.219). The Mass, specifically for the native population, could not have been held in a more appropriate setting: a Christian sacred space built over a Maya temple.

CHAPTER FOUR

ORIGINS AND EVOLUTION

The discovery and subsequent colonization of the continent of America by Europeans, two conceptually different cultures, began a process of acculturation that transformed both. The dialogue that ensued was initiated within the Mesoamerican open urban space, space that would be transformed by the overlay of the conquering culture's own ideas of urban design and the incorporation of plazas. As the two cultures began to integrate, both were changed and a new culture emerged. As that happened, new volumes of open space began to emerge in the urban fabric of the sixteenth-century New World.

On one hand, the building of Mesoamerican urban centers alludes to, reenacts, and reinforces the mythical origins of that world, whose civilization came into existence from a void, a primordial sea, the source of life itself. Equating open urban space, shaped by the architecture that defines it, to the mythical primordial sea, Mesoamericans designed and developed urban centers inspired by nature's creation and evolutionary process. Their mastery at shaping and orienting the void, that is, creating open space within the urban setting, is evident in the harmonious integration of the built environment of voids and solids with the surrounding natural terrain, the skies above, and the universe beyond.

On the other hand, Europeans brought to the New World rediscovered urban design ideas and forms that have their origins at least as early as ancient Greece and Rome. These forms emanate, in orderly, organized, orthogonal grid fashion, from a central urban open space to create a setting that expressed the highest intellectual accomplishments of European civilization.

From the field of anthropology, we learn that different cultures think in different ways and develop their own worldviews, each culture tied to its own separate reality defined in terms of time and space.[1]

Mesoamericans believed that time runs in cycles and were obsessed with keeping track of time in this way. Major events involving rulers and dignitaries were carefully and accurately recorded and pegged to several time cycles. Based on keen observation of astronomical cycles of the sun, moon, Venus, and other celestial bodies, coupled with sacred numerology within their advanced mathematical system based on the number 20 (vigesimal system) and a deep understanding of the cycles of nature and agriculture, Mesoamericans developed a highly sophisticated calendrical system in which time, from its mythic origins, runs in cycles. For European-based cultures, time is a linear, never-ending continuum.

Just as time can be understood differently by one culture, so space can be understood differently by another. The Mesoamerican culture is a case in point: by using masses to shape space in which to manifest artistic scenarios of religious myth, Mesoamericans provided sacred settings where rituals were enacted.

The celebration of the highly sacred rituals induced alternate states of mind for participants, allowing them to experience a separate reality. The shaped open space allowed the ritual to unfold, which in turn led to the collective altered state. In this altered state, metaphorical portals opened, the conjuring of gods and spirits occurred, and the magical reality of liminal space was manifested, as still happens today in remote areas.

These are the open spaces Spanish friars encountered when they embarked on what was to become the largest building campaign in the world's history to that time. The Spaniards had their own ideas about urban open spaces and systematically implemented them throughout their vast domain in the New World. History reveals more each day the key role played by open space, especially in the critical first decades after the fall of Tenochtitlan during the conquest and colonization of the New World. Open space then became the initiating and propagating force that allowed for social integration of the two very different cultures. The vision and understanding of Fray Pedro de Gante and other early friars of the significance of incorporating native sacred open spaces and rituals into the new towns and church complexes facilitated the conversion efforts and helped fulfill the mandate of the Spanish enterprise.

A happy coincidence is that both cultures also used open space as a location for the trade and bartering of goods. Markets in Europe were located initially at the edges of villages, and as settlements grew, these impromptu, amorphously shaped market spaces were integrated into the urban fabric. In the urban centers of Mesoamerica, the *tianguis*, or market, played a major and specific role in the overall urban scheme. Generous, officially designated areas were dedicated to this communal activity; some of the grandest examples, found at Chichén Itzá and Tlatelolco-Tenochtitlan, are clear evidence of their importance to Mesoamerican societies. When the Spanish implemented their urban plan in the New World, as decreed in the Laws of the Indies, they specified that the central rectangular open space of the plaza, from which the grid emanates, be used as a setting for market activities, among others. The marketplace became the heart of the town for business and social purposes, separate from the sacred patio or *atrio* of the church, and it was surrounded by the secular institutions of the town: the Palacio Municipal or *cabildo*, residences of the afflu-

ent, banks, cafés, and stores. For centuries, we have called this communal open space that is the secular center of town "the plaza." Even today in the twenty-first century, market day, the most exciting day of the week, is still called by many indigenous communities *día de plaza*.

Another expression of open space originating in both cultures is the courtyard. Mesoamerican architecture is replete with courtyards, from quadrangular court layouts of ceremonial centers as described in Chapter One, to the densely populated residential open courts of Teotihuacan. Spanish rectangular courts reflected two antecedents: the agora and forum of ancient Greece and Rome, and the private walled garden and courtyard of Islamic architecture. Among the grand examples of courtyards in New Spain are the cloisters of the sixteenth-century convents. These interior patios with their familiar quadrangular shape held major religious significance for the Mesoamerican converts to Christianity. The coincidence of this shared architectural and cultural courtyard form, along with other symbolic architectural elements, proved pivotal in the early friars' efforts to convert the indigenous populations to Christianity.

Today, the enduring physical evidence of indigenous open space incorporated into the regular urban layouts implemented by the Spaniards in New World towns is vivid testimony of the syncretic role of open space as initiator and promoter of cultural integration and acculturation.

PLAZAS IN THE TWENTY-FIRST CENTURY

For the twelve years I lived in San Miguel, I visited the plaza almost every day for one
reason or another, at times for no reason other than to enjoy being in that special
communal open space, the place where something was always happening.

Hal Box, 2010

An important part of our study considers how plazas create the central meeting place or "living room"
for a neighborhood, town, or city. We wanted to find
out how these spaces actually work as social centers
and what particular ingredients and relationships are
necessary to give plazas the vitality we still see in them
today. There is a possibility that the plaza could be
used advantageously in new and restored neighborhoods in the United States as we adjust to new energy
restraints and changing social dynamics. To explore
these objectives, we first describe the way the Mexican plaza works in the twenty-first century, through
observations of the public spaces of San Miguel de Allende in the state of Guanajuato, a mainly eighteenth-
century town. We conclude with a discussion of ways
that variations of the plaza might be used to enhance
the evolving quality of urban and suburban life in the
United States.

THE SAN MIGUEL EXAMPLE

San Miguel de Allende, founded in 1542 on the Mexican high plateau by a Franciscan friar, became a secure stop for wagon trains transporting silver shipments
from one of the world's most prolific mines, in nearby
Guanajuato, to boats bound for Spain at the Gulf
city of Veracruz. This town has a population of about
80,000, 10 percent of whom are expatriates, and it is
a destination for many tourists, mostly Mexican but

some foreign, who come to visit the seat of Mexican
independence.[1] The town center moved several times
before it was formalized around its current *plaza mayor* in the eighteenth century (Fig. E.1). Locally known
as the Jardín, the *plaza mayor* started as a sloping patch
of earth in front of the church used for the main market. It was bounded on the north and south sides by
two-story residences belonging to the wealthy families
of the town, the ground floors of which held retail
shops, restaurants, banks, and bars behind arcaded
portales on both sides. The church with its small *atrio*
forms the east side, while the Palacio Municipal and

E.1.   San Miguel de Allende, central plaza, known as the Jardín.
Susan Kline Morehead.

residences form the west. The resulting architecturally enclosed space is the setting for the rituals of communal life in the town (Fig. E.2). The plaza was made level with formal walls and steps, and landscaped with shade trees and benches during the nineteenth century in the French manner that was the style of the time. It carried the many traditions of the Mexican people and enjoyed generations of familiarity.

Here we have all the ingredients for a plaza that can produce a vital place for business, social networking, and special occasions and is a part of everyday life. To describe how the plaza works, let's look at a typical day, starting around first light with the pleasant sounds of waking birds and church bells. Women sweeping the streets and walks with handmade brooms make way for a few people going to early Mass. The first businesses to open are the cafés under the *portales* and the shoeshine men staking out their favorite positions on the plaza. The newspaper vendor arrives with a load of papers from his car, lays them out on a low wall at the edge of the plaza, and soon begins to announce his wares in a strong, deep baritone. There are well-dressed people walking to work and beggars, mostly women, setting up their positions. A guitar is being

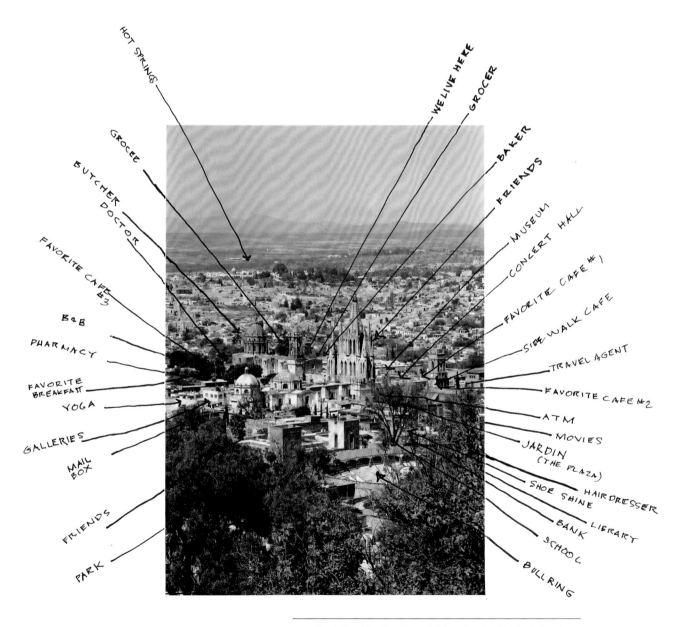

E.2. San Miguel de Allende, aerial view showing Hal Box's favorite locations. Hal Box.

played in the corner café, and locals come in to have their morning coffee, some reading newspapers on one of the dozens of cast-iron benches available, seeking sun or shade depending on the weather. Street venders of ice cream, *hamburguesas,* and tacos bring welcome smells later in the day.

Moving along one side of the plaza, late-model cars proceed in normal fashion along with a few donkeys loaded with bags of dirt or firewood being brought into town from the campo. The three sides of the plaza closed to cars are for pedestrians. Sometimes Indian dancers will perform here, or a marching band in uniform will play as prelude to a political speech, or a religious event will occur. Every couple of weeks there will be a parade of schoolchildren, or a bicycle race, or a horse parade, or a group of pilgrims on their way to a special pilgrimage site. Even *voladores* may set up a high pole in front of the church to perform their ancient flying ceremony. The best-attended parade is the Beginning of Spring parade, where hundreds of schoolchildren dressed as flowers attract multitudes of proud families. This is also the site for the Good Friday Pageant with its *flagelantes* and its many floats bearing statues of saints, each carried by seemingly dozens of men, all leading up to the major float with the cross and the principal characters and instruments of the Passion. A parade special to this town is the Locos parade, which involves thousands of residents dressed in crazy costumes of many colors representing cartoon characters, political figures, monsters, clowns, and fantasy figures, as well as many bands in the backs of trucks. Each of these parades fills the streets with crowds and lasts for several hours.

On a typical evening, the ambiance in the Jardín is filled with music, diners, walkers, and watchers. There will almost always be at least one mariachi band playing and several others standing on the corners hoping to be picked up and taken to a party, or to a loud and happy birthday surprise concert outside someone's bedroom at three in the morning. Large family parties in the Jardín bring out all ages at all hours. The once formal *paseo,* when young girls walked around the plaza in one direction while boys walked around in the other direction, chaperones watching from the benches, still happens on Sunday evenings, although in a less formal way. Often there are special concerts and movies open to the public on cool summer evenings. For special events like Christmas, New Year's Eve, or national and local holidays, the Jardín is the place to be—as it can be almost twenty-four hours a day.

QUALITIES OF SUCCESSFUL PLAZAS

The programmatic ingredients of a socially, financially, and architecturally successful plaza have the qualities embodied in the works of authors Camillo Sitte, Jane Jacobs, William H. Whyte, Spiro Kostof, and Setha Low, among others. A few details can be added, based on our observations.

- The location needs to have good pedestrian access and be located near the center of the neighborhood or city to establish a sense of *place.* A walking neighborhood can develop around it.
- There must be a public facility or gathering place such as a community center or concert hall. The Mexican church provides both of these ingredients. To build the sense of place in the plaza, a government building such as a city hall or public library should be included.
- There must be a sense of three-dimensional space created by the buildings and landscape that form it. The height-to-width ratio must give a sense of defining the space as walls enclose a room.
- There must be shelter from the elements—shade, windscreens, and *portales* around the edges in case of rain or scorching sun.
- The commercial ingredients, similar to those that would be required in a shopping center, include a selection of coffee shops, ice cream stores, cafés, gift shops, banks, newsstands/bookstores, and a hotel or bed and breakfast.
- The second and third floors of surrounding buildings should include residences and offices to provide occupancy and produce buildings high enough to shape the plaza space.
- An intensely used plaza is usually completely dependent on pedestrian access with remote parking down side streets, in nearby buildings, or possibly underneath the plaza, as in Barcelona and Querétaro.

A variation on the plaza is the pedestrian-dominated street. The street space that already exists in the United States has been dominated by traffic for the last fifty years. Most cities are desperately trying to re-create street life through a number of strategies: narrowing the streets by widening sidewalks, calming the traffic to make the pedestrian environment safe and accommodating, and encouraging rather than prohibiting sidewalk cafés. Canopies and trees provide the spatial definition as well as shelter, and parallel parking is an important factor in calming traffic. Circulation is linear and dependent on sidewalk cafés and display windows to make it lively.

The public parks serve vital functions as well, yet they exist for a different purpose, to provide a place of nature where one can get away from the crowd, a venue for amateur sports, and areas for general recreation. The plaza has a different role, supplying a place to be with other people in an urban setting while serving the social and business roles described above. The world has learned the names of the great plazas (squares) in the Middle East as they became the sites of pro-democracy rallies in 2011.

E.3. Chicago, Crown Fountain in Millennium Park. Susan Kline Morehead.

SPRAWL AND THE AMERICAN MYTH

As we continue to make U.S. cities more compact, connected, and walkable, retreating from suburban sprawl, the plaza can be a useful urban design prototype. The energy crisis may cause this to happen sooner rather than later. The sprawl prototype has only been dominant since World War II; seventy years is not long in the history of cities, so sprawl is not inevitable. It was a product of the American myth that living in the suburbs supplied individual freedom, provided a good place for children, and fostered the American Dream. Instead, the sprawl model produced isolation, created high infrastructure costs, used up good agricultural land, and made the country dependent on foreign oil.

The traditional U.S. ideal of the cabin in the woods has morphed into a house with a few feet of grass on each side surrounded by a forest of other houses, not trees. The car culture and investment in freeways support the idea of sprawl rather than community, yet there are many opportunities for the urbanizing strength of the plaza.

Having studied Mexican plazas and lived around them, we believe that communal open space in the urban fabric and suburban sprawl would enrich urban life in the United States today. We have lost the town square and the village green, and we have in their place regional shopping centers, strip developments, and sports-entertainment centers—which can only be accessed by car. Might the concept of the plaza— along with increased residential density—enable a life-style that fosters convenience and community with less dependence on energy for transportation and provides for a richer life experience?

The U.S. population lives in three different settings: urban, suburban, and rural. Already, people are moving back to the city from the suburbs, and communal open spaces are reappearing downtown in cities like Denver, Portland, Seattle, and Chicago. For example, Millennium Park in Chicago is many things: an extension of the vast open space on the edge of Lake Michigan, a covered concert hall for music venues, an active animated plaza, and a recently expanded art museum (Fig. E.3).

Detroit may be pointing the way. As of 2011, 40,000 acres of suburban sprawl lie abandoned, causing the city to cut municipal services to these areas. In response, Detroit is building rail transit to create density at the center and develop what are beginning to be called "huburbs," that is, concentrations of density on the rail lines.

The rural setting requires a car, but it also has communal spaces in meeting halls, churches, and markets that tie a community together. The suburbs are the no-man's land where you can walk to your neighbor's house but to nothing else, and where people too young, too old, or too poor to drive a car are trapped in their homes.

It may become necessary for the suburbs to become less dependent on the car. If that comes to pass, the tracts of thousands of individual houses will need to become more connected and dense enough to attract services and shopping, rather than requiring a car to drive ten or fifteen minutes to the nearest shops, cafés, services, or school.

In our investigations of the plaza in Mexico, we became aware of a major difference in the geometric fabric with the use of the plaza and the patio. Where a building in the United States is surrounded by open space, usually grass, in Mexico the geometry is the opposite: buildings surround the open space. Abstractly, the nine-square puzzle shows the difference (see Fig. 2.13). The gain in density, proximity, land use, and reduced infrastructure is significant—superficially it appears eight times more dense. It gives dimensions that are walkable rather than requiring a car and fuel. In the U.S. model, much of the open space is given to unusable front and side yards with grass, requiring precious and limited water, or worse, parking lots. The future may cause us to reconsider this diagram.

Throughout time, town patterns have changed to meet new conditions, even dramatically, as when the Spaniards occupied Mesoamerica and the Moors occupied Spain, as described in this book, or when economic catastrophes, war, or drought devastated a town. The spatial concept of the suburb is quite new and can be expected to adjust to cultural and economic changes. The example of the plaza may be useful in a reshaping of the suburbs. For example, the Domain, in Austin, Texas, has attempted to create the sense of an authentic street and has a great plaza with trees and children's activities near the center. In addition, there is a serious complement of apartments, offices, condos, and a hotel above the shops that line the street and plaza.

In the United States we have successful active plazas, in the tradition of Mexican plazas, in historic cities like Santa Fe, San Antonio, New Orleans, Savannah, Boston, Philadelphia, Los Angeles, San Francisco, Sonoma, New York, and Washington. The character of these vital centers has changed as major cities have grown up around them, yet they are still powerful centers of activity. A modern example like Mellon Square in Pittsburgh, built in the 1950s, provides an excellent special and functional lesson for the urban designer. Denver has made main downtown streets vibrant by removing cars, developing 16th Street into a bus/taxi-only pedestrian mall, and adding redevelopment and light rail lines. Lines cross this transit mall at several key points, ending at Union Station, which will once again be the nexus of all regional transportation.

Portland has at least three very vital, active plazas: Pioneer Square, Waterfront Park, and the central plaza of the new and exciting Pearl District. All three are served by either the east–west light rail or the north–south street car, and Pioneer Square serves as the symbolic hub for both systems.

Humanizing urban streets with shade trees and wide sidewalks for cafés brings people together where density already exists, animates the street life, and stimulates economic development.

Cities reconsolidate into connected and walkable compact developments related to existing corridors, rail transit, misused or disused institutional land, and downtowns. This is not an ideological position but an inevitable reality based not only on the environmental reality and the energy unsustainability of sprawl but on the economic reality of the end of oil.

The alternative is clear: only when we begin to base our growth on well-planned, well-designed concentrations of mixed-use, walkable, and connected communities with safe, active streets and great parks, all planned with town centers that are organized around public plazas and community activities, will we achieve a quality of life that is sustainable and that we deserve.

Mexico has provided us with the example we need. As tourists, we observe and experience the life and vitality of Mexican plazas. We are in awe and delighted; we want to be part of it. But does this contagious zest for urban life translate across cultures? Who uses the plazas we *do* have here in the United States?

Are a majority of the users members of Hispanic cultures, perhaps seduced by a subconscious nostalgia for the cultural urban roots permeating their DNA? Would our laws allow vendors, performers, and shoe shiners to ambulate through our communal open spaces, hawking their wares as they do in the plazas of Mexico and Latin America? Would our fast-paced schedules and our Calvinistic work ethic allow us to just sit in the plaza or in the surrounding open-air cafés and watch the world go by?

One can say that enjoyment of open urban spaces like plazas is more prevalent in the warmer climates, but even in the benign temperate climates of our country, one does not observe the same level of vigorous activity, social interaction, or personal contemplation that one sees in Mexican plazas. Does culture play a role here? In *The Hidden Dimension*, anthropologist Edward T. Hall illustrates how people from different cultures react differently to space and their proximity to others in public areas.[2] Nearness to the tropics seems to make people more relaxed, gregarious, and fun-loving, as if life were more enjoyable in temperate climates. Conversely, societies living in warmer geographical areas seem to be less productive than those living in colder climates. One wonders how climate change will affect these cultural differences.

What we do know is that plazas allow us the opportunity to stop and smell the flowers of life. We are encouraged by the fact that as society becomes more globalized, we are presented with ever-increasing opportunities for cultures to learn from each other. We believe that it is here, in our open-air living rooms—our plazas—that the equalizing social energy provided by open urban spaces can foment positive humanizing interaction (Fig. E.4).

Vamos pues, ¡a la plaza!

E.4.   The green living room created by a triangular Mexican plaza in Guanajuato. Susan Kline Morehead.

MEASURED DRAWINGS: PLANS OF TOWNS

1. Acatlan, Hidalgo: San Miguel Arcángel
2. Acatzingo, Puebla: San Juan
3. Ahuatepec, México: San Martín Caballero
4. Atipac, México: Santa María de Natividad
5. Axapusco, México: Templo de San Esteban
6. Cuatlazingo, México: Templo del Divino Salvador
7. Macuilxochitl, Oaxaca: San Mateo
8. Nopaltepec, México: Parroquia de la Asunción
9. Santa Clara del Cobre, Michoacán
10. Santa María Oxtotipac, México: San Nicolás
11. Tecamachalco, Puebla: San Francisco
12. Teotitlán del Valle, Oaxaca

13. Tepeyanco, Tlaxcala: San Francisco
14. Tezontepec, Hidalgo: San Pedro Apóstol
15. Xometla, México: San Miguel Arcángel
16. Zaachila, Oaxaca: Santa María Asunción
17. Zempoala, Hidalgo: Iglesia de Todos los Santos
18. Oaxaca, Oaxaca: Nuestra Señora de la Soledad and Nuestra Señora de San José
19. Cuautinchan, Puebla: San Juan Bautista
20. Tizatlán, Tlaxcala: San Esteban

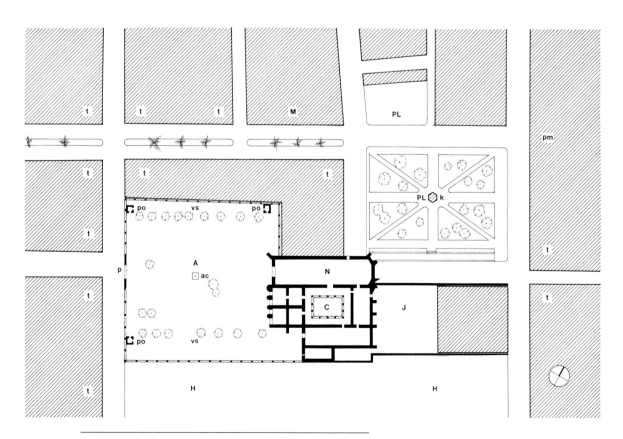

A.1.   Acatlan, Hidalgo: San Miguel Arcángel

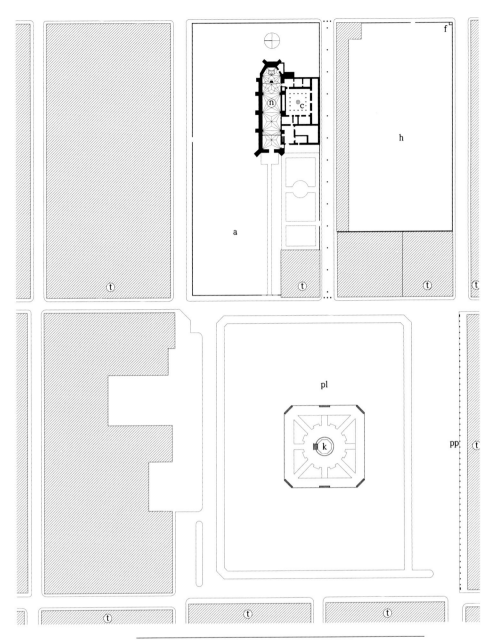

A.2. Acatzingo, Puebla: San Juan

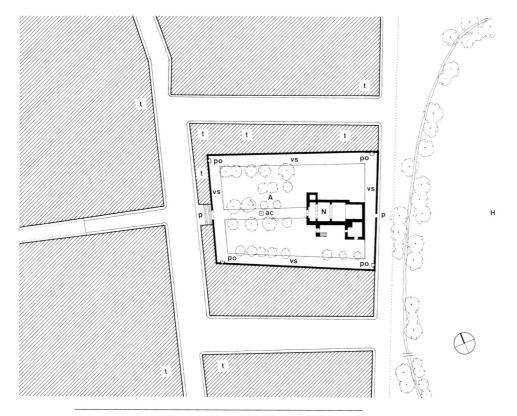

A.3. Ahuatepec, México: San Martín Caballero

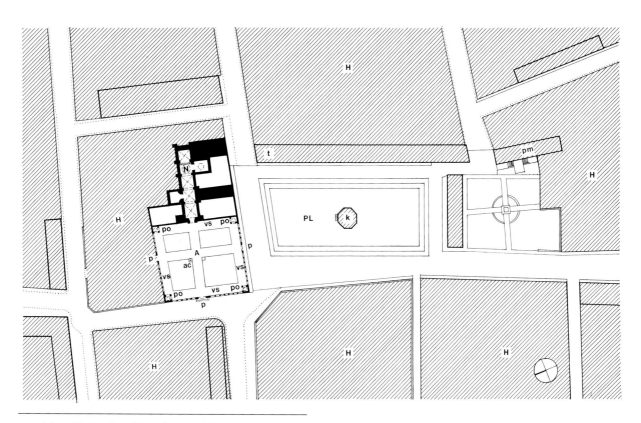

A.4. Atipac, México: Santa María de Natividad

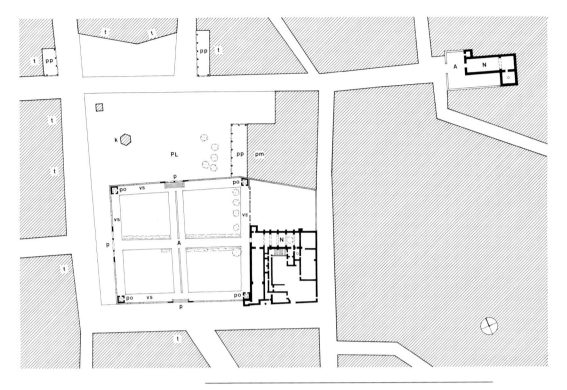

A.5. Axapusco, México: Templo de San Esteban

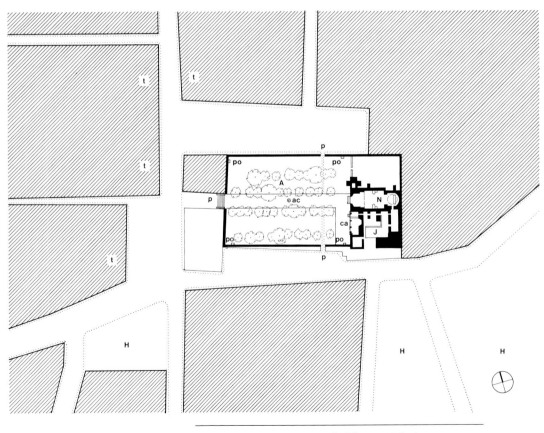

A.6. Cuatlazingo, México: Templo del Divino Salvador

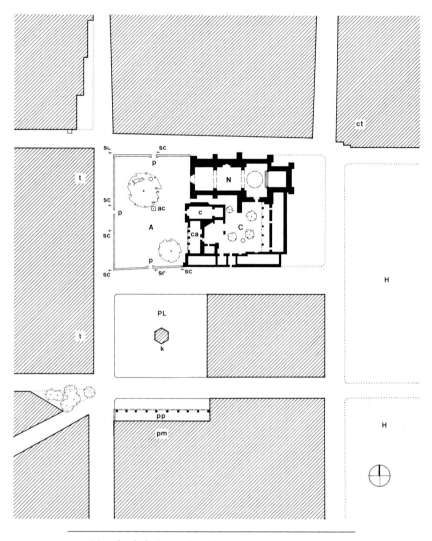

A.7. Macuilxochitl, Oaxaca: San Mateo

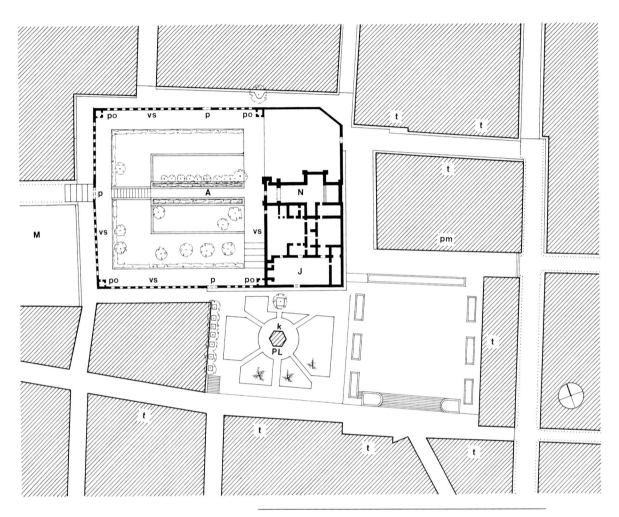

A.8.   Nopaltepec, México: Parroquia de la Asunción

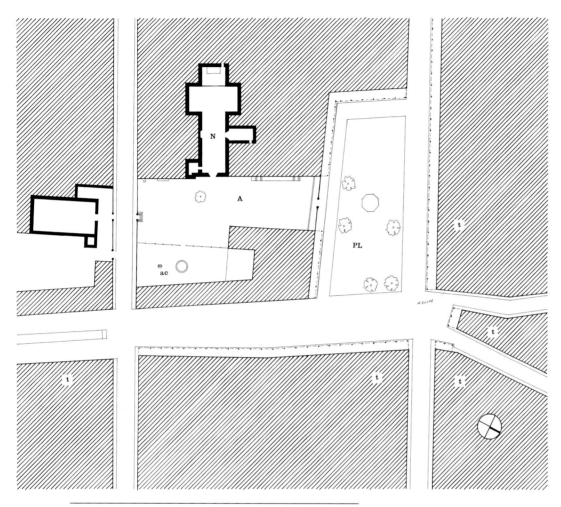

A.9. Santa Clara del Cobre, Michoacán

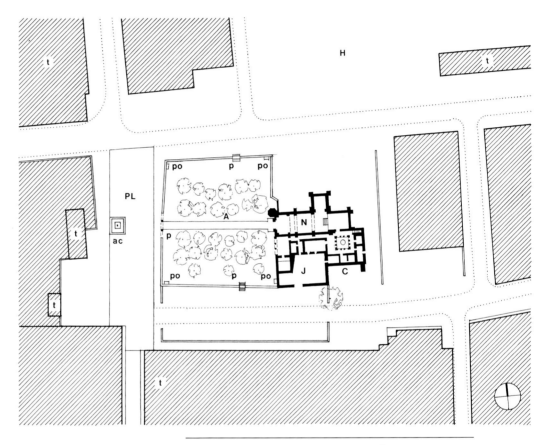

A.10. Santa María Oxtotipac, México: San Nicolás

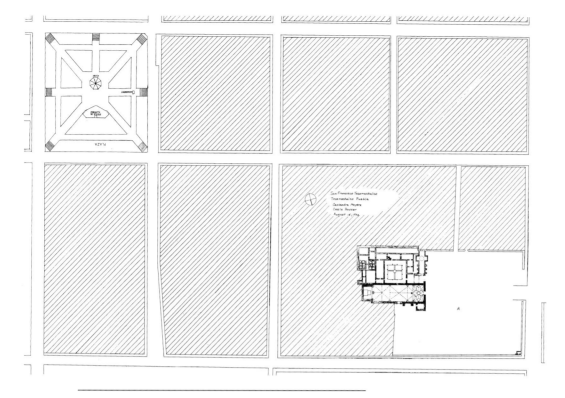

A.11.   Tecamachalco, Puebla: San Francisco

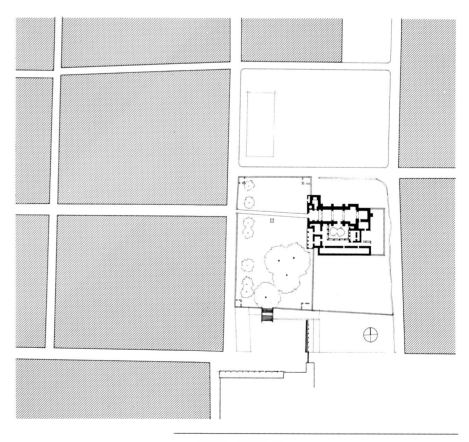

A.12.   Teotitlán del Valle, Oaxaca

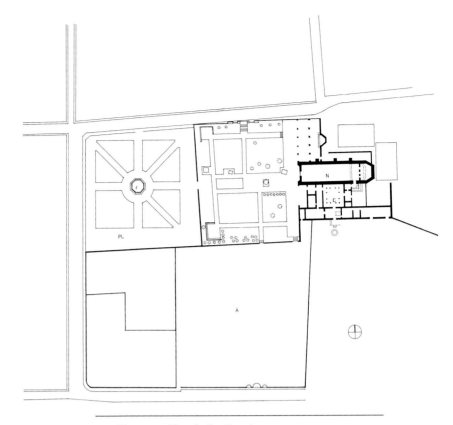

A.13. Tepeyanco, Tlaxcala: San Francisco

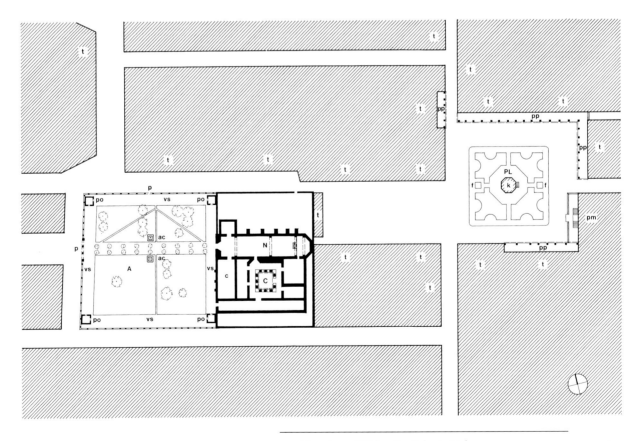

A.14. Tezontepec, Hidalgo: San Pedro Apóstol

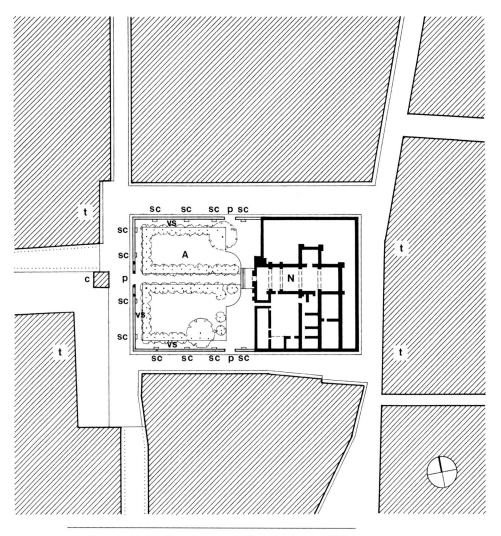

A.15. Xometla, México: San Miguel Arcángel

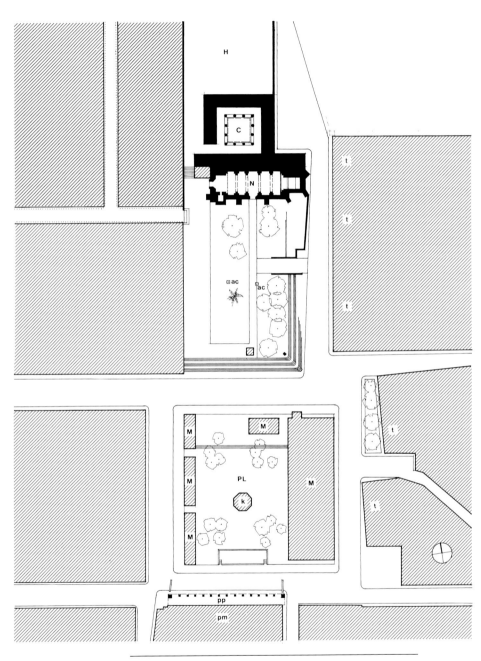

A.16. Zaachila, Oaxaca: Santa María Asunción

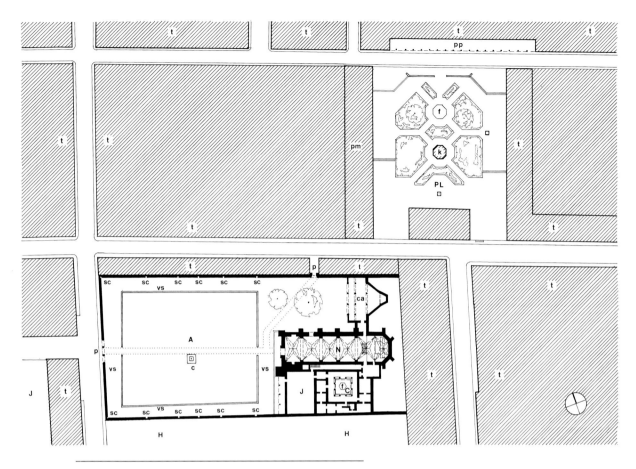

A.17. Zempoala, Hidalgo: Iglesia de Todos los Santos

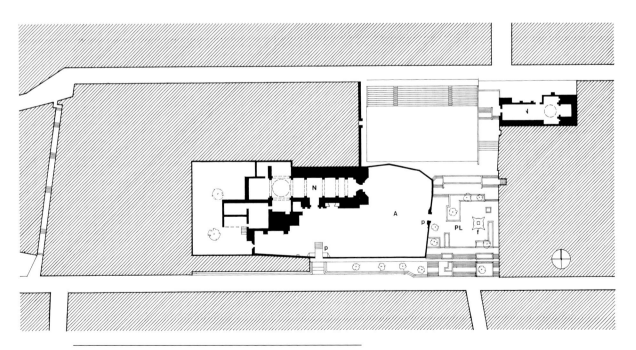

A.18. Oaxaca, Oaxaca: Nuestra Señora de la Soledad and Nuestra
Señora de San José

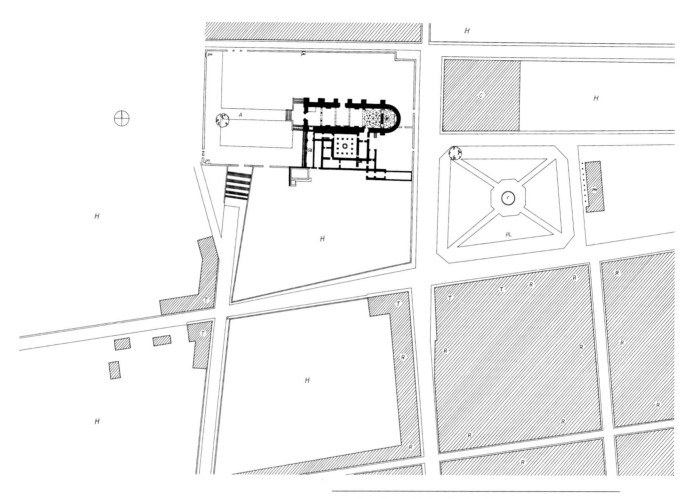

A.19. Cuautinchan, Puebla: San Juan Bautista

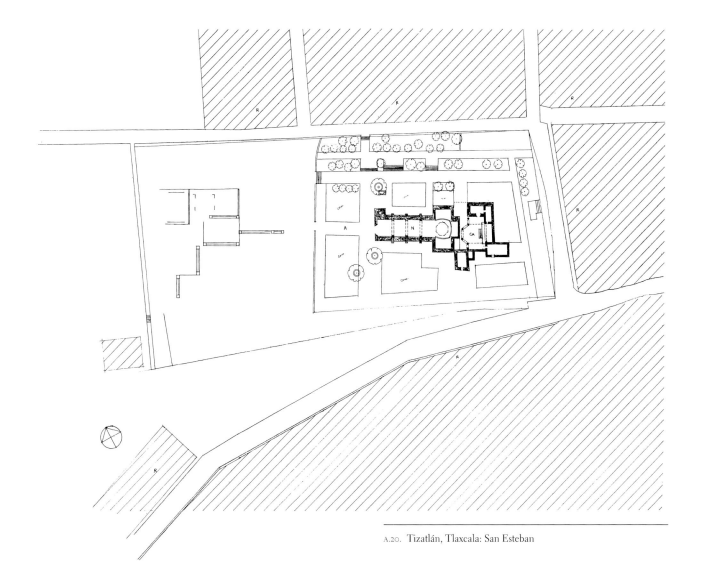

A.20. Tizatlán, Tlaxcala: San Esteban

NOTES

INTRODUCTION

1. Another name for plazas in Mexico is *zócalo*, a Spanish word meaning the base for the pedestal of a statue. It was coined in the nineteenth century when the base for a statue planned in honor of newly independent Mexico's president General Don Antonio López de Santa Anna was built in the Plaza Mayor of Mexico City in readiness for his triumphant return from the war in Texas. Because Santa Anna was captured at San Jacinto and Mexico lost half of its territory, the statue was never inaugurated, and a large square slab, the actual *zócalo*, remained in the plaza. With typical Mexican humor, residents of the capital began calling the plaza "the Zócalo," and the name stuck. Today many towns throughout Mexico call their plaza the Zócalo.
2. Betty Sue Flowers, personal communication to Hal Box, n.d.

CHAPTER ONE

1. Kirchhoff, "Mesoamérica," 94. "Mesoamerica" is a term coined by Paul Kirchhoff in 1943 to describe an area of Middle America with specific cultural traits in common not found in other areas of the American continent, including a system of mathematics based on the number 20 (vigesimal system); the use of a calendar; the triad of staple foods of corn, beans, and squash; and the existence of ballcourts. This geographic area is roughly delimited by a line from the Pacific Ocean in the modern Mexican state of Sinaloa to the southern limits of the state of Tamaulipas on the Gulf of Mexico as the northern edge, and a southern line in the middle of Central America from the Pacific side of northern Costa Rica to the Honduran Caribbean coast.
2. Linda Schele, personal communication to Logan Wagner, 1995.
3. Schele and Mathews, *Code of Kings*, 23.
4. Andrews, *Maya Cities*, 37.
5. Schele and Mathews, *Code of Kings*, 31.
6. Ibid., 40.
7. Freidel, Schele, and Parker, *Maya Cosmos*, 258.
8. M. E. Miller, *Maya Art and Architecture*, 170–179.
9. "Most cities in ancient Mesoamerica share two kinds of spatial patterns. First, public architecture is usually concentrated in one central district—the epicenter— and planning is almost always limited to buildings in the epicenter, with unplanned surrounding residential zones. . . . Second, most temples and other large buildings in Mesoamerican urban epicenters are arranged around formal rectangular plazas. These patterns suggest common concepts of urban design among the varied cultures of ancient Mesoamerica, from the Maya to the Aztec." Smith, "Form and Meaning," 27.
10. See "stela" in Miller and Taube, *Gods and Symbols*, 157. Epigrapher David Stuart first proposed that the Maya regarded their stelae as *te tun*, "stone trees," although he later revised his reading to *lakamtun*, meaning "banner stone," from *lakam* meaning "banner" in several Mayan languages and *tun* meaning "stone." See Stuart, "Kings of Stone," 153–154. Also see Martin and Grube, *Chronicle of the Maya*, 14.
11. *Popol Vuh*, 72–73.
12. Karl Taube states that the caiman was perceived and

portrayed as the earth in both Postclassic Yucatán and highland Mexico. "Itzam Cab Ain," 9. Also see "caiman" in Miller and Taube, *Gods and Symbols*; Bassie-Sweet, *At the Edge of the World*, 66.

13. "In Classic Maya texts, *nab* [*naab*] was the word both for 'plaza' and for large bodies of waters, including lakes, rivers and the ocean. The Maya conception of plaza as a 'watery' place through which spiritual communion with the Otherworld could occur was anchored in the precedent of the Olmec." Freidel, Schele, and Parker, *Maya Cosmos*, 139; also see fn 36 and p. 144. "*Naab*" and "*nab*" are interchangeable spellings, according to the *Dictionary of Maya Hieroglyphics* by John Montgomery (2002), updated by Peter Mathews (2003) and Christopher Helmke (2007) at www.famsi.org/mayawriting/dictionary.htm. Karen Bassie-Sweet (*At the Edge of the World*, 20) also confirms that *naab* means "plaza" and "lake."

14. Sahagún, *Historia general*, 25: "Era el patio del gran templo muy grande, tendría hasta 200 brazas en cuadro, era todo enlosado y tenía dentro de sí, muchos edificios y torres, la principal estaba en el medio y era la más alta y estaba dividida en dos capillas con sus insignias distintas" (translation by Logan Wagner). A fathom equals 6 feet. In old Spanish, a *braza* is the measurement obtained by extending arms from tip to tip. This measurement equals two varas. A vara is roughly equivalent to 85 centimeters (33 inches).

15. Andrews, *Maya Cities*, 11.

16. Ibid., 37–38.

17. Proskouriakoff, *Album of Maya Architecture*, 111–133.

18. Harrison, *Lords of Tikal*, 112.

19. Ibid., 167.

20. See "mountains" in Miller and Taube, *Gods and Symbols*, 120.

21. Lockhart, *Nahuas after the Conquest*, 14. Lockhart devotes Chapter 2, "Altepetl," to the concept, and he notes that Charles Gibson's *Aztecs*, although using the term *altepetl* only twice, is "essentially about the altepetl" (Lockhart, *Nahuas after the Conquest*, 478n5). Gibson uses the terms *tlatoani* (native ruler), *calpulli* (subdivision of a community), and *cabecera* (capital town of a local *tlatoani*) to describe native towns (*Aztecs*, 34).

22. For example, the *Diccionario de la lengua nahuatl*, by César Macazaga Ordoño, gives the meaning of *altepetl* in Spanish as "ciudad, villa o pueblo. Se forma de *atl*, agua y *tepetl*, montaña" (18).

23. D. Carrasco, *Religions of Mesoamerica*, 72–73.

24. Heyden and Gendrop, *Pre-Columbian Architecture of Mesoamerica*, 20.

25. García Zambrano, *Pasaje mítico*, 109.

26. In 1990, after photographing the murals, authors Wagner and Morehead and several colleagues, with a guide and lanterns, waded across the lake through stalagmites in water up to their necks; slithered through a long, tight channel; and climbed across massive boulders fallen from the cave ceiling before entering a room filled with crystal formations.

27. Tate, "Maya Cauac Monster's Formal Development," 33–54.

28. Reilly III, "Ecological Origins"; Schele and Mathews, *Code of Kings*, 45.

29. The convention called pars pro toto is like the poetic figure of speech called synecdoche and is employed frequently in Olmec art. A typical example is the depiction of the flame eyebrow of the Olmec Dragon to connote the full range of the dragon's powers, such as its ability to navigate land, air, and water, as well as its association with entrances to the Underworld. Aztec art similarly abbreviates the Earth Monster into a design band consisting only of its face. Peter David Joralemon employs the principle in his work *A Study of Olmec Iconography*. Also see Reilly III, "Art, Ritual, and Rulership," 27–45, and "Glossary of Olmec Motifs," 120–122.

30. David C. Grove (*Chalcatzingo*, 50) notes slight wearing at the base of the mouth, "as if people or objects had passed through . . . as part of rituals." Kent Reilly (personal communication to Logan Wagner, summer 1989) suggests rulers climbed through the mouth. Julia Guernsey confirms this reading in "Consideration of the Quatrefoil Motif," 78.

31. Tate, "Maya Cauac Monster's Formal Development," 33–54; Freidel, Schele, and Parker, *Maya Cosmos*, 215–216; and Stross, "Mesoamerican Cosmic Portal," 82–101.

32. Schele and Mathews, *Code of Kings*, 45, 193.

33. Ibid., 193.

34. "The sign [at Machaquilá] consists of a quatrefoil-shaped glyph that surrounds a darkened *imix* or HA ("water") glyph." Stuart and Houston, *Classic Maya Place Names*, 33.

35. Stross, "Mesoamerican Cosmic Portal," 82–101.

36. Guernsey and Love, "La Blanca in the Olmec World."

37. Michael Love describes Monument 3 as "an earthen sculpture . . . in the shape of a quatrefoil and formed of rammed earth, composed of a sandy loam . . . then coated with dark brown (nearly black) clay. The inner rim of the sculpture was painted with hematite red." He adds, "Our initial hypothesis is that the sculpture functioned as a locus of ritual in which water, or notions of fertility, were invoked. Such an idea is consistent with the quatrefoil shape, which in Classic period iconography symbolizes a watery portal to the supernatural realm. Dating to approximately 850 B.C., the La Blanca sculpture appears to be the earliest example of a quatrefoil known in Mesoamerica." http://www.authentic-maya.com/la_blanca.htm.

38. Mirrors were of pyrite in Mesoamerican times, and modern Tzetzal Indians in full costume regalia with modern mirrors hanging prominently from their chests celebrated in Izamal's plaza during the visit of the pope in 1993 (personal experience of Logan Wagner). On the role of mirrors in Mesoamerica, see Bassie-Sweet, *At the Edge of the World*, 103, 214n37, and "mirrors" in Miller and Taube, *Gods and Symbols*, 114.

39. García Zambrano (*Pasaje mítico*, 125) notes that the arrangement of burials, palaces, and courts in Mesoamerica takes advantage of depressions in the ground and is evidence of intentionality in organizing a composition around sunken courts, "as if they were the vestibules of the Underworld" (translation by Logan Wagner).

40. García Zambrano (*Pasaje mítico*, 43) highlights the importance of iconic markers on the landscape as natural indicators to the leaders of early migrating groups.

41. Freidel, Schele, and Parker, *Maya Cosmos*, 78–80, 85.

42. Schele and Mathews, *Code of Kings*, 26.

43. Linda Schele, personal communication, February 23, 1993.

44. Schele and Mathews, *Code of Kings*, 26; Freidel, Schele, and Parker, *Maya Cosmos*, 67.

45. Harrison, *Lords of Tikal*, 111, 173, 188, 189, 191.

46. Proskouriakoff, *Album of Maya Architecture*, 111–133.

47. Williams, "Scheme for the Early Monumental Architecture," 227–240.

48. Freidel, Schele, and Parker, *Maya Cosmos*, 113.

49. Ibid., 53.

50. Proskouriakoff, *Album of Maya Architecture*, 16.

51. See "Underworld" in Miller and Taube, *Gods and Symbols*, 177.

52. Freidel, Schele, and Parker credit Reilly in *Maya Cosmos*, 134–137.

53. Joralemon, *Study of Olmec Iconography*. Karl A. Taube (*Olmec Art at Dumbarton Oaks*, 113) says Elizabeth Benson, Joyce Marcus, and F. Kent Reilly concur.

54. Vogt, *Tortillas for the Gods*, 55.

55. Typical of Mesoamerican numerology, four *voladores* times thirteen spiral turns equals the number of years in the fifty-two-year calendar cycle.

56. Reilly III, "Cosmos and Rulership," 26; Joralemon, *Study of Olmec Iconography*, 14.

57. There seem to be no definitive dates that define "contact period," a term that for reasons of political correctness often replaces "conquest" and sometimes "colonial period." Two authors, Thomas H. Charlton and Patricia Fournier G., seem to suggest dates of 1521 to 1620 in the title of their paper "Urban and Rural Consequences of the Contact Period: Central Mexico, 1521–1620."

58. Kirchhoff, "Mesoamérica," 92–107. For a thorough study, see Scarborough and Wilcox, *The Mesoamerican Ballgame*.

59. Miller and Taube, *Gods and Symbols*, 42–44.

60. Schele and Mathews, *Code of Kings*, 207.

61. Miller and Taube, *Gods and Symbols*, 42–44.

62. Bunson and Bunson (*Encyclopedia of Ancient Mesoamerica*, 77) say a dozen ballcourts were constructed in Tajín.

63. Schele and Mathews, *Code of Kings*, 207.

64. Aurora McClain pointed out the figure-ground relationship of pyramid and ballcourt in a presentation to Hal Box's seminar at UT Austin.

65. Martínez Donjuán, "Teopantecuanitlán," 55–56.

66. Ibid., 77.

67. Karl Taube ("Olmec Maize God," 39–81) identifies elements representing Olmec Gods II, IV, and VI in David Joralemon's classification of Olmec gods and symbols and groups all three gods as aspects of the Olmec maize god.

68. Reilly III, "Cosmos and Rulership," 26; Joralemon, *Study of Olmec Iconography*, 14.

69. The Dallas Plaque is thought to be dated 900–500 BCE.

70. Gay, "Olmec Hieroglyphic Writing," 278–288.

71. Freidel, "Preparing the Way," 7, Catalogue Nos. 131, 234.

72. Sacred bundles, or god bundles, were in use in Mesoamerica as early as the fourth century CE and continued in use into the sixteenth century; much of Classic Maya art depicts sacred bundles during processions and other rituals; and, in contrast to merchant bundles, sacred bundles and the objects they enclose relate to gods and deities. Sacred bundles are usually round, with prominent, large knots, while merchant bundles are oblong and wrapped with rope and matting. Miller and Taube, *Gods and Symbols*, 47–48. Indigenous communities throughout Middle America continue to use sacred bundles today.

73. Schele, "Olmec Mountain," 108.

CHAPTER TWO

1. Mann, *1491*, 140.

2. Marcus Vitruvius Pollio's *De architectura* is the only surviving treatise from the Roman era.

3. Edgerton, *Theaters of Conversion*, 8.

4. Díaz del Castillo, *Historia verdadera*, 21; translation by Logan Wagner.

5. After the death of Moctezuma, Cuitláhuac was emperor for two months and died of smallpox in October 1520. Thomas, *Conquest*, 445.

6. Sherburne F. Cook and Woodrow Borah, in *Essays in Population History*, viii, estimate Mexico had a population of 25.2 million in 1518 that was reduced to 16.8 million by 1632, 6.3 million by 1648, 2.65 million by 1568, and 1.375 million by 1595. Alfred W. Crosby, Jr., in *The Columbian Exchange*, 37–38, notes that "the most spectacular period of mortality among the Ameri-

can Indians occurred during the first hundred years of contact with Europeans and Africans" and that there were about fourteen epidemics in Mexico between 1520 and 1600. In *The Aztecs*, 136, Gibson states, "Among all causes, epidemic disease is now recognized as paramount."

7. Among others, Hernán Cortés, Bernal Díaz del Castillo, Bernardino de Sahagún, Diego de Landa, Bartolomé de Las Casas, Alexander von Humboldt, George Kubler, and John McAndrew.

8. In England and France, a parvis is a court or enclosed space before a building, generally a church, or a portico or colonnade before a building (fourteenth century). The word is from Late Latin *paradisus* and Greek *paradeisos*, literally "enclosed park," and is of Iranian origin; it is akin to Avestan *pairi-daēza,* meaning "enclosure." These are also roots of the word *paradise*.

9. Cortés, *Letters from Mexico*, 103, 105.

10. Díaz del Castillo, *Conquest of New Spain*, 58.

11. Kubler, *Mexican Architecturey*, 112.

12. Ricard, *Spiritual Conquest of Mexico*, 2.

13. Kubler, *Mexican Architecture*, 116.

14. Ibid., 117 (Chávez), 128–129 (Mata); McAndrew, *Open-Air Churches*, 127.

15. Mullen, *Architecture and Its Sculpture*, 59, 66, 76.

16. Kubler, *Mexican Architecture*, 127.

17. McAndrew, *Open-Air Churches*, 127, 632.

18. Kubler, *Mexican Architecture*, 121–122.

19. Ibid., 123–124.

20. Ibid., 4.

21. Gibson, *Spain in America*, 69–70.

22. Gibson, *Spain in America*, 70. For details of friars' studies, see Ricard, *Spiritual Conquest of Mexico*, 39–60.

23. The modern-day dictionary of Nahuatl-English-Spanish is by Frances E. Karttunen, *An Analytical Dictionary of Nahuatl.*

24. McAndrew, *Open-Air Churches*, 69, 74.

25. Gibson, *The Aztecs*, 99–100.

26. McAndrew, *Open-Air Churches*, 29.

27. *The Tempest*, act 5, scene 1, lines 181–184, cited by Carrasco in *Religions of Mesoamerica*, 4. For elaboration of this idea in North America, see Mircea Eliade, "Paradise and Utopia," 88–111.

28. Zumárraga's personal copy of Thomas More's *Utopia* is in the Perry-Castañeda Library of the University of Texas at Austin, as noted and pictured in *Mexico: Splendors of Thirty Centuries*, 246.

29. As early as 1525, the firm of Jacob Cromberger in Seville won a monopoly for the book trade with Mexico from the emperor; in 1539, his son arranged for the first printing press to be set up in Mexico. By 1542, at least twelve rival booksellers in Seville were competing for the Mexican trade. Thousands of books are estimated to have been shipped to Mexico by 1539. Leonard, *Books of the Brave*, 95–99.

30. *Sixteenth-Century Architectural Books*, items 1, 3, 16, 20, and 21; and McAndrew, *Open-Air Churches*, 107, 603. Kubler says 1569 is the first citation of an architectural book in Mexico. *Mexican Architecture*, 104.

31. McAndrew, *Open-Air Churches*, 173.

32. San Miguel's *Qué cosa sea la arquitectura* and other titles are collected as Andrés de San Miguel Manuscripts, Benson Latin American Collection, General Libraries, University of Texas at Austin. Born in Spain, San Miguel sailed to New Spain in 1593, was shipwrecked, and vowed to join the Carmelite religious order if rescued. After a trip to Spain, he returned to New Spain in 1597, settling in Puebla and joining the Carmelites in 1598. His master work is the Convento de San Angel, 1615; he also built at least five other monasteries and a bridge over the Lerma River, and worked on draining the Valley of Mexico. He died in Guanajuato c. 1644.

33. McAndrew, *Open-Air Churches*, 173.

34. Murray, *Renaissance Architecture*, 72.

35. In 1996, the historic center of Pienza was made a UNESCO World Heritage Site, as it "represents the first application of the Renaissance humanist concept of urban design, and as such occupies a seminal position in the development of the concept of the planned 'ideal town' that was to play a significant role in subsequent urban development in Italy and beyond." whc.unesco .org/en/list/789.

36. *Paradise*, from its Iranian root, means a walled enclosure; the Garden of Eden refers to the Persian/Moorish paradise. Christopher Tadgell describes the fourfold Persian garden in India as a quincunx as he identifies it with Eden: "[I]n the Koran, Paradise is the Eden of Genesis whose definition is related to ancient Persian ideal order of an enclosed square divided by four rivers flowing in the cardinal directions from the source of the Waters of Life in the centre." *History of Architecture*, 153, 242.

37. Similar Islamic gardens were built in India by the Mughal rulers who migrated there from Persia, for example, Akbar's Tomb in Sikandra, the Taj Mahal in Agra, and the Shalimar Gardens in Lahore.

38. A thousand new towns were built between the early twelfth and mid-fourteenth centuries, more than doubling the number of European urban centers. Friedman, *Florentine New Towns*, 5.

39. Edgerton (*Theaters of Conversion*, 55) notes that the purpose of the early Christian atrium was to serve in the conversion of pagans during the first centuries after Christ, and it was an enclosed courtyard where crowds of newly converted adult catechumens should await confirmation. Prior to the use of such an atrium (actu-

ally a forecourt or parvis and different from the atrium of a Roman house), Christians met in houses, sometimes in the atrium or dining room of a Roman house. A house in Dura Europos, Syria, dated 231 CE is "the world's first definitely identified church," according to Warwick Ball in *Syria*, 42.

40. Edgerton, *Theaters of Conversion*, 32.

41. For more on this topic, see Low, *On the Plaza*, 84–95.

42. R. Miller, *Mexico: A History*, 134.

43. In 1500, the population of Tenochtitlan was 212,500, according to Michael E. Smith, "City Size," 411. Cholula was the second-largest city in Mesoamerica in 1500, estimated at 100,000. Various estimates put Paris at 200,000, London at 50,000 to 100,000, and Rome at 55,000 at that time; Milan, Venice, and Naples were about 100,000, and Beijing was the world's largest city in 1500. The ancient city of Teotihuacan is thought to have reached 200,000 in 600 CE, making it the sixth-largest city in the world at that time, according to Michael Coe, *Mexico*, 392.

44. Elman Rogers Service (1915–1996) formulated the nomenclature used to categorize primitive societies in *A Profile of Primitive Culture* and *Primitive Social Organization*.

45. A *siheyuan* is a communal open space formed by four houses that appeared in China as early as 1100 BCE and formed *hutongs*, or narrow streets.

46. It is interesting to know that our first Mesoamerican example, the Olmec site of Teopantecuanitlán, is contemporary with the entombment in 1323 BCE of King Tutankhamun in Egypt.

47. Webb, *City Square*, 30.

48. Michael Smith notes the high level of central planning suggested in cases of integrated orthogonal plans that exhibit a regular street layout, calling them "modular orthogonal" plans, noting the pattern is highly characteristic of Roman city planning, particularly military camps, in "Form and Meaning in the Earliest Cities," 16.

49. Kostof, *The City Shaped*, 49.

50. "The daily urban experience of Spaniards derived almost universally from tangled towns that, if of Roman origin, had lost their grid during the long Muslim occupation. None could show a planned monumental plaza in the center of the city-form." Kostof, *History of Architecture*, 445.

51. Shah Abbas I built Naqsh-e-Jahan (Image of the World) Square in Isfahan, Iran, starting in 1598, where he combined religion, commerce, and royal power in one setting. At one end is the mosque named for him, Shah Mosque, and at the other is the entrance to the Grand Bazaar, while facing each other on the sides are the gate to his palace compound, Ali Qapu, and the private Sheikh Lotfollah Mosque built for the royal court. The square was completed in 1629 and is 500 meters long, approximately 185 meters wide, and arcaded along its length.

52. "The [medieval] town piazza, which replaced the forum area of ancient times, was spatially, and in the size and quality of its buildings, a strongly marked feature, constituting, as it continued to do, the communal assembly area of the population." Hirons, *Town Building in History*, 89.

53. Collins and Collins, *Camillo Sitte*, 130–332.

54. Sitte quoted in Collins and Collins, *Camillo Sitte*, 154.

55. McAndrew, *Open-Air Churches*, 116.

56. Webb, *City Square*, 78.

57. Guzmán, *Territorio, poblamiento y arquitectura*, 160. López Guzmán identifies four types of settlements: Administrative Cities for the Spanish; Towns for Indians (Pueblos de Indios—here López Guzmán classifies both *reducciones* and existing native settlements into one category); Mining Enclaves (Enclaves Mineros); Frontier Towns (Poblaciones de Frontera).

58. According to Alberti, the church, which he calls a temple, "obviously the greatest and most important ornament of a city," requires open space to set it off from the urban fabric and to make it perfectly visible. It should "address a large, noble square and be surrounded by spacious streets, or better still, dignified squares, so that it is perfectly visible from every direction." Alberti, *De re aedificatoria*, Book 7, Chapter 2, 194.

59. Díaz del Castillo, *Historia verdadera*, 165. "Se puso una picota en la Plaza y fuera de la villa una horca"; translation by Logan Wagner.

60. Ibid., 175. "Nuestros corredores de campo que iban a caballo, llegaron a la plaza y patios donde estaban los aposentos"; translation by Logan Wagner.

61. Ibid., 227. "Acuérdame que tenían una plaza, adonde estaban unos adoratorios, puestos tantos rimeros de calaveras de muertos"; translation by Logan Wagner.

62. "Dejemos esto y digamos de los grandes y suntuosos patios que estaban delante del Huichilobos, donde está ahora Señor Santiago, que se dice Tlatelulco. Ya he dicho que tenían dos cercas de calicanto antes de entrar adentro, y que era empedrado de piedras blancas como losas, y muy encalado y bruñido y limpio, y sería de tanto compás y tan ancho como la Plaza de Salamanca" (Now let's leave this and talk about the sumptuous patios that were in front of Huichilobos, where now is Saint James, known as Tlatelulco. I've already mentioned that they [the patios] had two dressed-stone masonry walls before entering, that it was paved with white stones like slabs finely whitewashed and burnished and clean, and as long and as wide as the Plaza of Salamanca). Díaz del Castillo, *Historia verdadera*, 369; translation by Logan Wagner. In the sixteenth cen-

tury, Salamanca's plaza was "an irregular, unplanned void within the urban grid" (Kubler, *Mexican Architecture*, 98), not yet remade into the baroque plaza we see today.

63. McAndrew, *Open-Air Churches*, 116.

64. McAndrew quoting Doctor Cervantes de Salazar in *Open-Air Churches*, 116.

65. Fray Toribio de Benavente "Motolinía," *Memoriales o libro de las cosas de la Nueva España y de los naturales de ella* (Mexico: UNAM, 1971), 82, quoted by Ana Rita Valero de García Lascurian in "Plazas sagradas," 16; translation by Logan Wagner: "En toda esta tierra hallamos que en lo mejor del pueblo hacían un gran cuadrado, cerca de un tiro de ballesta de esquina a esquina, en los grandes pueblos y cabecera de provincia, y en los menores pueblos obra de un tiro de arco, y en los menores, menor patio; y este cercábenle de pared, guardando sus puertas a las calles y caminos principales, que todos los hacían que fueren a dar al patio del demonio; y por honrar más los templos, sacaban los caminos por cordel muy derecho, de una y dos leguas, que era cosa de ver desde lo alto como venían de todos los menores pueblos y barrios todos los caminos derecho al patio."

66. Díaz del Castillo, *Historia verdadera*, 130, 144.

67. Lockhart, *Nahuas after the Conquest*, 25.

68. In *The Aztecs*, 257, Gibson describes five classes of Aztec land: that belonging to the temples and gods, land of the community houses, land of the *tlatoque* (rulers), land of the nobles, and land of the community parceled out to individuals for their use. All these were substantially modified, with the result that "ultimately the greater part of the land passed from Indian possession and control altogether." Lockhart (*Nahuas after the Conquest*, 141–150) describes Aztec land tenure practices before and after the conquest. Both authors suggest that preconquest houses were scattered rather than organized densely. In *Conquest of Mexico*, 7, Serge Gruzinski describes the Nahua world as "rather a vague entity made up of a political, administrative, urban centre . . . , and of a series of villages and hamlets, and even scattered farms . . . [that] corresponded to . . . territorial units based on kinship. A relative hierarchy of lineages, a tendency to endogamy, communal ownership of land, material and military solidarity, and the cult of a tutelary god, the *capulteotl*, whose force resided in an image or a sacred bundle." Elizabeth Hill Boone describes how land records were kept: "Paintings kept record of *altepetl, calpulli*, and personal lands, identifying the boundaries and showing how the land was distributed. Such land documents were kept by the *altepetl* authorities, along with local tax and tribute lists, censuses, and other accounts of private property." "Pictorial Docu-

ments and Visual Thinking," 153. In response to question 30 of a Mérida *Relación Geográfica*, Gaspar Antonio Chi wrote in 1579, "In olden times all lands were communal and there were no property marks, except between provinces." Quoted by Frans Blom in "Gaspar Antonio Chi, Interpreter," 260. Online at http://onlinelibrary.wiley.com.

69. Exceptions include some towns in Yucatán, including Mérida and Valladolid, and some in Michoacán, where the town centers were built away from the monastic complexes.

70. ". . . y en el medio del pueblo . . . hermosas plazas . . . y que el conjunto de sus edificios, templos, palacios y pirámides . . . no estaban dispuestos a lo largo de las calles y avenidas como en ciudades europeas . . . sino alrededor de plazas y patios," Diego de Landa quoted by G. Sylvanus Morley in *La civilización maya*, 493, in Valero de García Lascurian, 16; translation by Logan Wagner.

71. The narrow pedestrian paths, mostly in an orthogonal grid layout, that have been found in Tenochtitlan and Teotihuacan separating residential compounds could be interpreted as streets within these two very dense urban built environments, although they are more like rectilinear paths or open-air hallways. See drawings 1 and 22 in Séjourné, *Arquitectura y pintura en Teotihuacán*, 18, 77–78.

72. We know that recent urban design antecedents were fresh in their minds. As described earlier, a similar urban layout for the Spaniards before their arrival in the Americas was the military camp set up in 1491 by King Ferdinand at the outskirts of the last remaining bastion of Moorish dominance in the Iberian Peninsula, the Caliphate of Granada. The military camp established during King Ferdinand's siege eventually became a town now known as Santa Fe de Granada in the province of Andalusia. Kubler, *Mexican Architecture*, 99.

73. Translation by Logan Wagner. *Plazas Mayores de México*, 118.

74. Fernández, *La Jerusalén indiana*, 75–88; Edgerton, *Theaters of Conversion*, 15.

75. Edgerton, *Theaters of Conversion*, 4.

76. Personal communication to Logan Wagner, 1995.

77. Klor de Alva, "Religious Rationalization," 233–245. He explains in more detail, "I believe the first phase represents a continuation of precontact state-level forms of ceremonialism and use of ritual space as well as precontact forms of state rationalization: widely disseminated abstract ideological ideals; well-articulated system of deities, rituals, and cosmological beliefs; and an abundance of generally phrased moral dicta. Because this is a time when interethnic, interaltepetl (the altepetl being the basic provincial sociopolitical unit) integra-

tion was still present, this period was characterized by the same large-scale, public ritual activities, covering great distances and making ceremonial use of extensive spaces, that were common in the precontact world." Ibid., 237.

78. McAndrew, *Open-Air Churches*, 216–217.
79. Edgerton, *Theaters of Conversion*, 2.
80. McAndrew, *Open-Air Churches*, 412–417.
81. The origins of the quincunx concept in Mesoamerica date to the "bar and four dots" symbol of Olmec iconography, in which the dots are at the corners of each directional plane, making these corners intercardinal points.
82. Fray Diego de Valadés published his engraving, the "idealized but garbled visual evidence" of the prototypical plan, in his *Rhetorica Christiana* in 1579 while living in Italy. McAndrew, *Open-Air Churches*, 293.

CHAPTER THREE

1. The alidade is an optical instrument for surveying along a line of sight to a movable stadia rod. Coupled with a compass, scale, pencil and paper, and the level surface of a plane table, it allows a team to make scaled drawings of open spaces delimited by architecture. The urban grid was documented using magnetic compasses and various measuring tapes, then drawn to scale.
2. Poole, *Our Lady of Guadalupe*, 26.
3. Karen Bassie-Sweet confirms that the earth goddess Tonantzin's home is a cave. *At the Edge of the World*, 45.
4. The major historians of Mexican architecture of the viceregal period, Toussaint, Kubler, McAndrew, and Weismann, do not mention the complex at Sacromonte, even though it is readily visible from the plaza of Amecameca that they do discuss. Trent E. Sanford, in *Story of Architecture in Mexico*, describes Sacromonte and makes the only mention we have found of the existence of an Aztec temple, Teteoinán, atop Sacromonte. D. Fortino Hipólito Vera, in *Santuario del Sacromonte*, a locally published monograph, provides a partial history of the complex. Mention is also made in several guidebooks.
5. In mid-July 1987, a chance discovery was made by Hal Box of a fresh clearing in the woods atop Sacromonte away from ritual routes and structures. The clearing was circular and centered on a trifurcated tree around which had been woven a circular platform of branches. Conjecture suggests that this was where hallucinogenic mushrooms, said by locals to be harvested at this time of year, were dried on the platform and consumed ritualistically within the circular clearing.
6. "Dos Palabras," 4.
7. Mentioned by Sanford in *Story of Architecture* (1947), 168. No other reference has been found.

8. "Dos Palabras," 4. Amequemecan (also spelled Amaquemecan) was at this time, 1519, a village of 20,000 people. Cortés describes his visit to "Amaqueruca" in *Letters from Mexico*, 80.
9. Díaz del Castillo, *Conquest of New Spain*, 123.
10. In Giovanni Bellini's painting *St. Francis in the Desert*, 1480, now in the Frick Museum, New York.
11. The date on Capilla de la Cueva is 1533; however, Kubler and Vera say 1534.
12. "Dos Palabras," 7. Other friars, such as Fray Toribio de Benavente (Motolinía), Fray Pedro de Gante, Fray Juan Rivas, and Fray García, are known to have visited Amecameca.
13. McAndrew, *Open-Air Churches*, 29.
14. Ibid., 30.
15. This legend is repeated at various sites in Mexico and seems apocryphal.
16. Vera, *Santuario del Sacromonte*, 35.
17. Ibid.
18. "Dos Palabras," 17; Escalada et al., *La ruta de los santuarios*, 104.
19. Kubler, *Mexican Architecture*, 524.
20. Toussaint, *Colonial Art in Mexico*, 41.
21. McAndrew, *Open-Air Churches*, 539.
22. Kubler, *Mexican Architecture*, 479.
23. Vera, *Santuario del Sacromonte*.
24. Ibid.
25. The Denominación de Santa Cruz was a small group of devoted followers of Fray Martín de Valencia.
26. "Dos Palabras."
27. Ibid.
28. Weismann, *Art and Time in Mexico*, 4.
29. Vera, *Santuario del Sacromonte*.
30. José Francisco Parra, the priest of the *parroquia* that supports Sacromonte financially, would like to replace the current sloped roof with a new flat roof.
31. Julio, the sacristan of Sacromonte (interview by Earthwatch team, July 22, 1987, Tape 2, Alexander Architectural Archives, School of Architecture, The University of Texas at Austin).
32. Vera, *Santuario del Sacromonte*.
33. "Dos Palabras."
34. Quoted in Austin, "Architecture for a New World," 28.
35. Edgerton, *Theaters of Conversion*, 62–64.
36. Phillips, "Processions through Paradise."
37. Hernando Toribio de Alcaraz, who arrived in Mexico in 1544, was the first on record. He was recommended in 1550 by Viceroy Mendoza as an architect and building inspector who could ensure that monasteries met the standard plan ordered in 1548 by Philip II. McAndrew, *Open-Air Churches*, 127.
38. "Authentic builders among the friars, to present knowledge, were few. Fray Juan de Alameda, OFM

(*obit* 1570) is probably one of them." Kubler, *Mexican Architecture*, 116-117. McAndrew concurs (*Open-Air Churches*, 334).

39. García Granados and MacGregor, *Huejotzingo*, 106; Moreno Villa, *Escultura colonial mexicana*, 24; Rojas, *Historia general*, 20; and Perry, *Mexico's Fortress Monasteries*, 93—these authors claim him as architect of all three. George Kubler, in *Mexican Architecture*, 117, claims only an early building at Huejotzingo and the church at Huaquechula. McAndrew (*Open-Air Churches*, 127, 334–339) also connects him with those two, Atlixco, and parts of Tula.

40. McAndrew, ibid., 334, citing Juan de Torquemada, *Monarquía indiana*, 1:319.

41. José Rojas Garcidueñas, in *Fray Juan de Alameda*, 11, says the advice was given by Juan de Tecto, theologian and one of the three Franciscans sent unofficially by Charles V in 1522; and the assessment of Fray Juan's language skills is from Mendieta, *Historia eclesiástica indiana*, bk. V, chap. 36. For more on Juan de Tecto, see McAndrew, *Open-Air Churches*, 30.

42. Ibid., 511.

43. The stair is fourteen steps high, one more than the thirteen levels of heaven in Mesoamerican ideology.

44. This "knotted cross," which was not the original *atrio* cross, had been the pinnacle of one of the *posas*. Fernández, *La Jerusalen indiana*, 110. Joseph Armstrong Baird, Jr. concurs, and he points out the similarity in form of the crown of thorns and Aztec serpents intertwined, in *Churches of Mexico 1530–1830*, 90.

45. The waters of earth are "pure, lifebearing," and the waters of the Underworld are "dark, fecund." Schele and Freidel, *Forest of Kings*, 66–69.

46. Reyes-Valerio, *Arte indocristiana*, 275–276.

47. Carrasco makes this point regarding "the power to give energy to the sun, which was sought in heart sacrifice of warriors" (*Religions of Mesoamerica*, 69), by quoting Alfredo López Austin, "Therefore, the ancients said that when they died, men did not perish, but began to live again almost as if awakened from a dream and that they became spirits or gods." *Human Body and Ideology*, 328.

48. Kubler, *Mexican Architecture*, 338. Phillips relates the *posas* to claustral corner altars, calling the *posas* an externalization of the cloister and its processional order. "Processions through Paradise," 149.

49. McAndrew, *Open-Air Churches*, 334.

50. Kubler, *Mexican Architecture*, 458.

51. Ibid., 524.

52. "The Emperor listened and asked questions about the Indians and the nature of the country. Cortés seized a sheet of parchment, rumpled it, and threw it upon the table. There was the map of New Spain—bristling with peaks, hollowed out into valleys, blistered with mountains, it was an inhuman land, but men had conquered it for the greater glory of His Catholic Majesty." Descola, *The Conquistadors*, 226.

53. McAndrew, *Open-Air Churches*, 224.

54. We have identified at least seventeen Mexican *espadañas*, in the states of Hidalgo (7), Morelos (4), Puebla (3), México (2), and Michoacán (1). Of those, ten were built by Augustinians, six by Franciscans, and one by Dominicans. These do not include those on the Yucatán Peninsula, where elaborate *espadañas* proliferate.

55. *Tequitqui*, a Nahuatl word meaning literally "one who pays tribute," is the art of native Mesoamericans, especially sculptors, working under Europeans in Mexico. It carries the same connotations as *mudéjar*, the art of Muslims working under Spanish Christians. The term *tequitqui* was coined by José Moreno Villa in *La escultura colonial mexicana*, 1942. McAndrew (*Open-Air Churches*, 201) says it is characterized by simplicity and directness of form, linearity, elaborate patterning in low relief, and a shorthand that combines horizontal and vertical planes into one.

56. Reilly III, "The Lazy-S," 413.

57. *Visita* refers to a second-tier town with its own church, attached to a larger "head town," or *cabecera*. *Visita* churches were usually smaller, and services were conducted by visiting clergy.

58. Father Bernabé Cobo to Father Alonso de Peñafiel, Puebla, March 7, 1630, *Obras II*, 467, as noted in Cook and Borah, *Essays in Population History*, 13.

59. McAndrew, *Open-Air Churches*, 244.

60. Mullen, *Architecture and Its Sculpture*, 60.

61. Ibid.

62. Toussaint, *Colonial Art in Mexico*, 106.

63. Perry, *Mexico's Fortress Monasteries*, 184.

64. McAndrew, *Open-Air Churches*, 124–125.

65. Mullen, *Architecture and Its Sculpture*, 66, quoting Dávila Padilla.

66. Ibid., 61.

67. Perry, *Mexico's Fortress Monasteries*, 186.

68. The goddess Mayahuel is the personification of maguey and is sometimes depicted with pulque flowing from her many breasts. Brundage, *The Fifth Sun*, 158.

69. Chase, *Mexico*; see Chapter 7, "Machineless Men—Their Food and Drink," 123–143.

70. Taylor, *Drinking, Homicide, and Rebellion*, 33, 39, 43.

71. Díaz del Castillo, *Conquest of New Spain*, 338.

72. Kubler, *Mexican Architecture*, 351, 164.

73. Ricard, *Spiritual Conquest*, 70.

74. Perry, *Mexico's Fortress Monasteries*, 141.

75. Ricard, *Spiritual Conquest*, 185.

76. McAndrew, *Open-Air Churches*, 225.

77. Kubler, *Mexican Architecture*, 415.

78. Adventures with Ruth, Episode 5, "Cocinar Mexicano" ("Gourmet: Video: Gourmet.com." Gourmet Magazine: Gourmet.com. Web. April 19, 2010. http://www.gourmet.com/video?videoID=64378014001).

79. Kubler, *Mexican Architecture*, 62.

80. Perry, *Mexico's Fortress Monasteries*, 113.

81. Ciudad Real, *Tratado curioso y docto*, 1:97.

82. García Granados, "Calpan," 370–374.

83. Of the five largest preindustrial buildings in the world, two are Egyptian pyramids and three are Mexican pyramids: two at Teotihuacan and one at Cholula. Linda Schele lecture to Mesoamerican Art and Architecture class, University of Texas at Austin, October 20, 1992.

84. A good source for archaeoastronomy is Anthony F. Aveni's *Skywatchers of Ancient Mexico*, in particular, "The Planning and Orientation of Mesoamerican Ceremonial Centers," 222–249.

85. Kubler, *Art and Architecture*, 34.

86. "In the sixteenth century, they [the Franciscans in France] favored scenes of the Last Judgment." Evans, *Monastic Iconography in France*, 40.

87. Mâle, *Religious Art in France*, 82–83.

88. Ibid., 99, 101.

89. Ibid., 104–106.

90. See the description of San Miguel Huejotzingo for more on the jade bead symbol, *chalchihuitl*.

91. García Granados, "Calpan," 373.

92. The columns are a naturalistic representation of the maguey cactus flower stalk. Small magueylike vegetation decorates the lower portion of the columns, marking the springline of the arch. García Granados ("Calpan," 373) suggests that the shields with the five wounds on these columns represent maguey flowers. The maguey motif may also have symbolic implications of maguey spines being used as bloodletters, especially in auto-sacrifice rituals, and maguey honey being the source for pulque, and today mescal and tequila.

93. Caso, *The Aztecs*, 45.

94. See "Rose," in Metford, *Dictionary of Christian Lore and Legend*.

95. Ibid., "Francis of Assisi."

96. Ibid., "Mary the Virgin." In Spanish, marigold is *caléndula* or *flamenquilla*.

97. Nahuatl was the language of the Aztecs and is in use in many parts of Mexico today.

98. Carrasco, *Religions of Mesoamerica*, 144–146. For a history of Day of the Dead and its celebrations today, including an interview with the guardian of San Martín Huaquechula, see Carmichael and Sayer, *Skeleton at the Feast*.

99. Rites such as Miccailhiuitontli and Miccailhiutl, or "Little Feast of the Dead" and "Great Feast of the Dead," which is alternatively called Tlaxochimaco, or "The Offering of Flowers," are discussed in Carmichael and Sayer, ibid., 28.

100. In ancient Mexico, *sellos* and *malacates*, spindle whorls, some with handles, were applied to damp pottery; stamps inked with various vegetable and mineral dyes were used to print skin, cloth, or paper. Designs of *sellos* are published in Enciso, *Design Motifs of Ancient Mexico*, and *malacates* are in his *Designs from Pre-Columbian Mexico*.

101. Identification of the sectioned heart at Calpan was made by Ignacio Cabral Pérez, Architecture Department, Universidad de las Américas, Cholula, in a seminar for Studio Mexico, University of Texas Architecture Department, March 5, 1992.

102. See shells on Temple of Quetzalcoatl, Teotihuacan, in relief band with serpent's body and rattles, indicating he is crossing between domains of earth and Underworld. Also see shells with other marine life in painted water band at Cacaxtla. G. E. Stuart, "Mural Masterpieces of Ancient Cacaxtla," 120–136.

103. Lyell, *Early Book Illustration*, 56, 59.

104. Kubler, in *Mexican Architecture*, 394, suggests Calpan is original and Tlanalapa a simplified version.

105. Ibid., 534.

106. López Guzman, "Territorio, poblamiento y arquitectura," 174–175.

107. McAndrew, *Open-Air Churches*, 271.

108. Kubler, *Mexican Architecture*, 527.

109. Simpson, *Encomienda in New Spain*, 84-85. Also see Ricard, *Spiritual Conquest*, 255.

110. The Friars Minor (1209), the Poor Ladies or Clares (1212), and the Brothers and Sisters of Penance (1221) are generally referred to as the First, Second, and Third Orders of St. Francis respectively.

111. "Two forces, dispersion and concentration, were constantly in tension: dispersion of population was the preferred mode of life of the Indians as opposed to concentration of population, the latter considered by the Spaniards as the only rational way for civilized men to live. Urbanized Indians were constantly returning to their cornfields in the montes or hills and the Spanish authorities constantly forcing them back into town." Markman, *Architecture and Urbanization*, 48.

112. McAndrew, *Open-Air Churches*, 181.

113. López Guzmán, *Territorio, poblamiento y arquitectura*, 353–355.

114. Ibid.

115. Kubler, *Mexican Architecture*, 532–533.

116. Perry, *Exploring Colonial Oaxaca*, 147.

117. Kubler, *Mexican Architecture*, 532–533.

118. Mullen, *Architecture and Its Sculpture*, 59.

119. Ibid., 76.

120. Ibid., 56.

121. Kiracofe, "Toward Reconstructing the Lost Retablo," www.interamericaninstitute.org.

122. Mullen, *Architecture and Its Sculpture*, 56.

123. McAndrew, *Open-Air Churches*, 547, 555.

124. Edgerton, *Theaters of Conversion*, 189.

125. Kiracofe, "Architectural Fusion," 70.

126. Ibid., 54.

127. Ibid., 72.

128. Early, *Colonial Architecture*, 32.

129. Edgerton, *Theaters of Conversion*, 191.

130. McAndrew, *Open-Air Churches*, 487.

131. Early, *Colonial Architecture*, 34.

132. Perry, *Exploring Colonial Oaxaca*, 131.

133. Landa arrived in Yucatán in 1549 and continued writing about it after he was called back to Spain in 1562.

134. Clendinnen, *Ambivalent Conquests*, 20.

135. Ibid., 21, 31.

136. New Spain's caste system included *peninsulares*, or officials born in Spain, at the top; criollos of Spanish descent next; then mestizos, or the mixed-race population; followed by native hidalgos, or descendants of the pre-Columbian nobility, who had collaborated with the Spanish conquest of Yucatán; and at the bottom, other native *indios*. During the seventeenth century, Maya lands were taken over by henequen and sugar plantation owners, and in 1847 the Maya *indios* rose up against these usurpers, beginning the Caste War. They established a remote stronghold at Chan Santa Cruz, rallied around a "speaking cross," and called themselves *cruzob*, "the people of the cross." They remained the most recalcitrant of the Maya, resisting "foreigners," including Mexicans and Westerners, as late as the 1960s.

137. It is possible that the forces encountered by Montejo off the coast of Quintana Roo were led by the first Spanish castaway, Gonzalo Guerrero, who organized the Maya of eastern Yucatán to fight against the Spanish.

138. Perry and Perry, *Maya Missions*, 26.

139. Lizana, quoted in González Cicero, *Perspectiva religiosa*, 87.

140. Perry and Perry, *Maya Missions*, 99.

141. Ibid., 54.

142. As described in the beginning of the *Popol Vuh*, 72: "The fourfold siding, fourfold cornering, / measuring, fourfold staking, / halving the cord, stretching the cord / in the sky, on the earth, / the four sides, the four corners, . . ."

143. Powell, in " Shapes of Sacred Space," describes the creation of a phi rectangle (50) and ties it to the *Popol Vuh* description of creation (422).

144. In 1998, the structure of the chapel was stabilized, and an overhanging metal roof replaced the traditional thatch, using funds from the World Monuments fund, according to Richard Perry on the Espadaña Press website, http://www.colonial-mexico.com/Yucatan/tibolon.htm.

145. Artigas, "Arquitectura a cielo abierto," 31–37.

146. Bretos, *Iglesias de Yucatán*, 71; translation by Logan Wagner.

147. Clendinnen, *Ambivalent Conquests*, 70.

148. Ibid., 114–115.

149. The books of Chilam Balam (the books of the "jaguar priest") are handwritten manuscripts of traditional knowledge (history, prophecy, myth, medicine, agriculture, etc.) collected in the contact period, written mostly in the eighteenth century, and named for the towns in which they were kept, the most important being those of Chumayel, Maní, and Tizimín. See, among others, Roys, *Book of Chilam Balam of Chumayel*; Edmonson, *Ancient Future of the Itza*; Craine and Reindorp, *Codex Pérez*. Diego López de Cogolludo was a Spanish Franciscan historian of Yucatán whose *Historia de Yucatán* was first published in Madrid in 1688.

150. Landa, *Yucatan Before and After the Conquest*, 85–90.

151. Carrillo y Ancona, *El obispado de Yucatán*, 285; translation by Logan Wagner.

152. Ibid., 285.

153. Landa, *Yucatan Before and After the Conquest*, 86.

154. Cueva Santillán, "Relación de Izamal y Santa María," 2:305, 2:303–308.

155. Ciudad Real, *Tratado curioso y docto*, 332.

156. Cueva Santillán was one of those early chroniclers. "Relación de Izamal y Santa María," 305.

157. Luis Millet Cámara, personal communication to Logan Wagner, 1993.

158. Roys, "Conquest Sites," 20.

CHAPTER FOUR

1. According to an anthropological theory based on linguistics, known as the Sapir-Whorf hypothesis, language is an additional determinant of reality. Based on the premise that reality is defined—or at least reflected—by language, this theory posits as an example the Hopi of the Uto-Aztecan language family, who have no words for past, present, or future time, suggesting that they view time quite differently from the rest of the world.

EPILOGUE

1. Nearby Dolores Hidalgo is the official site of the beginning of the war with Spain; San Miguel is on the Ruta de la Independencia.

2. Hall, *Hidden Dimension*, Chapters 11 and 12.

GLOSSARY

alameda—cottonwood grove; also, when capped, the name of a famous park in Mexico City.

alfiz (pl., *alfices*)—rectilinear frame, usually around an arched doorway or window, from Moorish and *mudéjar* architecture.

alidade—a device that allows one to sight a distant object and use the line of sight to draw a line on a plane table in the direction of the object or to measure the angle to the object from some reference point. A plane table is used in surveying to provide a solid and level surface on which to make field drawings, charts, and maps.

altepetl—Nahuatl for "community," literally "water mountain."

artesonado—a *mudéjar* ceiling of coffered wood; as distinct from an *alfarje*, a *mudéjar* wood-pieced ceiling with an interior timber frame decorated with carved moldings and interlacing laths that create geometrical patterns known as *lacería*.

atrio—the large, walled forecourt of a Mexican church, called a patio in the sixteenth century.

axis mundi—central point or axis of the world; in Meso-american cosmology, it connects the earth with the heavens and the Underworld, and it is also known as the World Tree.

Aztec—originally the Mexica from Aztlan settled Tenochtit-lan and in the late Postclassic formed the most powerful force in Mesoamerica as the Triple Alliance.

bar and four dots—a motif in Mesoamerican art describing the four-cornered universe with its axis mundi; also referred to as a quincunx.

barrio—Spanish for "neighborhood."

cabildo—Spanish for the building where the municipal council meets.

cacique (fem., *cacica*)—chief of a native town.

calpulli—Nahuatl for "neighborhood"; specifically one of the four quadrants of a town.

camarín—special small room for private viewings of an image and for robing it and storing its adornments.

capilla abierta—open chapel; also called *capilla de indios*.

capilla de indios—open chapel, a roofed altar built in a Mexican *atrio* for outdoor services; also called *capilla abierta*.

cartouche—a scroll-like tablet used either to provide space for an inscription or for ornamental purposes; also used to describe Mayan glyph enclosures.

castrum (pl., *castra*)—Roman military camp town: walled, foursquare, and bisected by streets that terminate in gates.

cenote—Mayan for "freshwater sinkhole"; in the Yucatán Peninsula, they connect to subterranean water bodies.

chalchihuitl—Aztec symbol for jade, preciousness, precious water, and precious blood, shaped like a round bead with a hole in the center.

chancel—the space reserved for the officiating clergy, often called the sanctuary, in front of the apse and altarpiece, and separated from the nave, usually by a chancel arch and/or a chancel rail.

chemin de ronde—(French for "round path") a raised, protected walkway behind a castle or church; a battlement.

cloister—an interior courtyard surrounded by a covered, colonnaded walkway in a monastery, similar to a peristyle.

coatepetl—Nahuatl for "snake mountain," one name for Sustenance Mountain.

cofradía—lay religious brotherhood.

convento—one- or two-story residence for friars.

cresteria—pierced and decorated wall that rises above a Maya building: a roof comb sits over an interior longitudinal wall, while a flying façade rises over the front wall.

cu—native temple or pyramid; a *teocalli*.

curato—the small room housing the priest in a *visita* church, built opposite the sacristy; also called *casa cural*.

double merlon—in Mesoamerica, a motif that stands for a portal into a mountain or the Underworld. The term *cleft* describes the motif, and the two terms are sometimes used interchangeably.

encomendero—a Spaniard who has been granted an *encomienda*.

encomienda—a royal grant of native labor to a Spanish settler and the tract of land where these natives are settled.

espadaña—bell wall, usually rising above the façade of a church.

feria—a feast day with markets, originally from Latin for "free day."

friar—a brother in one of the mendicant orders: Franciscan, Augustinian, or Dominican in early sixteenth-century Mexico.

hacienda—a landed estate, usually a plantation dedicated to agriculture or a ranch dedicated to cattle-raising or mining.

hospedería—guest quarters in a *convento* or monastery.

huerta—orchard.

Isabelline—style of ornamented architecture also known as Spanish Gothic and named after Isabella and Ferdinand, the Catholic Monarchs of Spain (1479–1504); it is characterized by lavish surface decoration of medieval character around doorways and windows.

jardín—garden; sometimes the name given to a landscaped *plaza mayor*.

maidan—Persian for "square" or "open field."

Manueline—style of ornamented architecture named after King Manuel I (1495–1521) of Portugal, characterized by marine and exotic motifs, twisted piers, and "wildly overdecorated" doorways and windows.

maw—mouth of a voracious beast.

Maya—Mesoamerican civilization from Preclassic (c. 2000 BCE–250 CE) to Classic (c. 250–900 CE) and Postclassic (900 CE–arrival of Spanish).

mendicant order—religious order of monks who have taken vows of poverty; also called a regular order, since the friars live by the rule, in contrast with priests of the secular orders who live in the world.

mercado—market.

merlon—the solid portion of a crenellated parapet wall.

Mesoamerica—a region and cultural area in Middle America, from North Central Mexico to Honduras. See note 1 in Chapter One.

mestizo/mestizaje—refers to racial and/or cultural mixing of Amerindians with Europeans.

Mixtec—indigenous inhabitants of the modern states of Oaxaca, Guerrero, and Puebla, an area known as the Mixteca. The high mountains of the area are called the Mixteca Alta.

mudéjar—the art of Moors working in Spain under Christian rule.

naab—Mayan for "lake," "lagoon," "sea," "plaza," and possibly "water lily"; also spelled *nab*.

Nahuatl—the language of the Aztecs, and the most commonly understood of the native languages in the Triple Alliance commonly known as the Aztec Empire of the Mexica.

noria—a vertical wheel outfitted with scoops to bring water up from a well or other source, usually for irrigation; commonly used to mean the well itself.

observants—a reformed branch of the Franciscan Order that followed Saint Francis's strict rule of poverty.

Olmec—the earliest civilization in Mesoamerica, c. 2000 BCE until c. 400 BCE. The Olmec heartland was in the lowlands of the Gulf coast, but other sites are found toward the Pacific.

open chapel—roofed altar used as a Mexican church with the *atrio* as nave; also *capilla de indios* and *capilla abierta*.

Otomi—a group of indigenous tribes inhabiting the central altiplano, or high plateau, of Mexico.

pars pro toto—artistic convention of allowing an abstracted part of an image to represent the whole, like the poetic figure of speech called synecdoche.

paseo—a walk around the perimeter of a plaza; also a promenade.

patio—Spanish word for an inner courtyard without a roof, similar to the peristyle of a Roman house. The *atrio* is a sacred patio.

picota—the stone pillar placed in the center of the plaza by Spaniards on creating a town—their first official act.

plateresque—style of architecture and ornament combining late Gothic and Renaissance elements, with some *mudéjar* features; named for its similarity to the overall patterning of the work of silversmiths.

plaza de armas—military parade ground.

plaza de toros—bullring.

plaza mayor—the main plaza in a town or city.

plaza—an urban communal open space defined by buildings and centering the community; a public square or similar open area in a town or city.

plazuela—small plaza.

porciúncula/portiuncula—north doorway of a mendicant church.

portales—covered walkways: porticoes, arcades, or colonnades facing or surrounding plazas or cloisters.

portería—the entrance to a monastery, usually an arcaded porch at the side of the church façade.

posa—a processional oratory or chapel at each of the four corners of some Mexican *atrios*, their openings indicating movement in a counterclockwise direction.

Purépecha (or Tarasco)—indigenous inhabitants of the modern state of Michoacán. The natives call themselves Purépecha; the term "Tarasco" is Spanish.

quatrefoil—a four-lobed shape that in Mesoamerica represents a cave, the open mouth of the Earth Monster, a portal to the Underworld.

quincunx—in Mesoamerican usage, a cosmic concept represented by a four-cornered space with an axis mundi or altar in its center; as a motif in art, it is known as "bar and four dots."

ramada—a covering of pole and thatch.

reducción (pl., *reducciones*)—new towns for the resettlement of dispersed native groups.

Relaciones Geográficas—texts and/or maps created to inform Philip II about his holdings in New Spain.

retablo—a retable; a large set of decorated panels of painting and/or sculpture rising above the back of an altar.

rollo—cylindrical or polygonal watchtower in a New World town plaza; judicial sentences were announced at the *rollo*.

sacbe (pl., *sacbeob*)—Mayan term meaning "white road"; a built-up and plastered ceremonial walkway connecting Maya sites or buildings.

sello—a clay seal or stamp used for printing designs on pottery, cloth, or bark paper.

stoa (pl., stoae)—a Greek building consisting of two rows of columns supporting a roof, sometimes with a wall on one side; also called a colonnade. Stoae often lined the edges of the agora, an open space used as a marketplace.

te tun—Mayan for "stone tree," "stela."

tequitqui—Nahuatl word meaning literally "one who pays tribute"; invented to describe the uniquely Mexican character of sculpture that resulted when European designs were translated into art by Indians. Like *mudéjar*, *tequitqui* alludes to art created in a postconquest culture by the subjugated peoples. It is characterized by simple direct forms, linearity, patterning in low relief, and the combination of horizontal and vertical planes into one.

testera—a niche, usually decorated with devotional objects, in the cloister wall at each of the corners; the focal point as one approaches on a counterclockwise path.

tianguis—Nahuatl for "market."

tienda—a small store.

tlacuilo—Mesoamerican artist/scribe.

troje—Spanish for "corn silo"; also used to describe all wood structures typical of Tarasco-Purépecha construction in Michoacán.

tzompantli—skullrack.

via sacra—sacred way or processional path; in Mexican *atrios*, the path connecting the four *posas*.

visita—a second-tier town with its own church, attached to a larger "head town," or *cabecera*; together the *cabecera* and its *visitas* formed a geographical jurisdiction called a *doctrina*, administered by friars.

volador (pl., *voladores*)—a flyer in a native religious ceremony performed by men (usually four) whirling outward, upside down, in descending spirals on ropes attached to the top of a tall central pole; a fifth man plays music from a platform atop the pole.

Witz—Earth Monster, in Mayan.

yácata—truncated cone-shaped pyramid found in the Purépecha/Tarasco area.

Zapotec—indigenous inhabitants of the Valley of Oaxaca.

zócalo—Spanish for "base," sometimes the name of a town's *plaza mayor*, coming from nineteenth-century Mexico City, when a gigantic base for an unfinished statue honoring Santa Anna was built in the center of the *plaza mayor* and the place was nicknamed the Zócalo.

BIBLIOGRAPHY

Alarcón, Hernando Ruiz de. *Treatise on the Heathen Su-
perstitions That Today Live Among the Indians Native to
This New Spain.* Translated and edited by J. Richard Andrews and Ross Hassig. Norman and London: University
of Oklahoma Press, 1987.

Alberti, Leon Battista. *De re aedificatoria/On the Art of
Building in Ten Books.* Translated by Joseph Rykwert,
Neil Leach, and Robert Tavernor. Cambridge: MIT
Press, 1988.

Alcalá, Jerónimo de. *Relación de Michoacán.* Mexico: El
Colegio de Michoacán, Gobierno del Estado de Michoacán, 2000.

Alexander, Hartley Burr. *The Mythology of All Races.* Vol. 11,
Latin-American. Boston: Marshall Jones, 1920.

Andrews, George F. *Maya Cities: Placemaking and
Urbanization.* Norman: University of Oklahoma Press,
1975.

Angulo Íñiguez, Diego. *Historia del arte hispanoamericano.*
Vol. 2. Barcelona: Salvat Editores, 1950.

Argan, Giulio C. *The Renaissance City.* Translated by Susan
Edna Bassnett. Planning and Cities Series, ed. George R.
Collins. New York: George Braziller, 1969.

Artigas Hernández, Juan Benito. "Arquitectura a cielo abierto, parte III. Ciudades: Izamal." *Cuadernos de Arquitectura Virreinal* 14 (1994): 31–37.

———. *Capillas abiertas aisladas de México.* Mexico City:
Universidad Nacional Autónoma de México, 1983.

———. *Metztitlán, Hidalgo: Arquitectura del siglo XVI.* Mexico City: Facultad de Arquitectura, Universidad Nacional
Autónoma de México, 1996.

Austin, Ann. "Architecture for a New World." *Earthwatch* 7,
no. 5 (April 1988): 28.

Aveni, Anthony F. *Skywatchers of Ancient Mexico.* Austin:
University of Texas Press, 1980.

Bacon, Edmund. *Design of Cities.* New York: Viking Press,
1967.

Baird, Ellen T. *The Drawings of Sahagún's* Primeros Memoriales: *Structure and Style.* Norman and London: University of Oklahoma Press, 1993.

Baird, Joseph Armstrong, Jr. *The Churches of Mexico 1530–
1830.* Berkeley and Los Angeles: University of California
Press, 1962.

Ball, Warwick. *Syria: A Historical and Architectural Guide.*
New York: Interlink Books, 1998.

Bassie-Sweet, Karen. *At the Edge of the World: Caves and
Late Classic Maya World View.* Norman: University of
Oklahoma Press, 1996.

Baxter, Sylvester, Bertram Grosvenor Goodhue, and Henry
G. Peabody. *Spanish-Colonial Architecture in Mexico.* 9
vols. Boston: J. B. Millet, 1901.

Beacham, Hans. *The Architecture of Mexico Yesterday and
Today.* New York: Architectural Book Publishing, 1969.

Bernal, Ignacio. *100 Great Masterpieces of the Mexican
National Museum of Anthropology.* Photographs by Constantino Reyes. New York: Harry N. Abrams, 1969.

Bernal, Ignacio, and Rubén Cabrera. *Teotihuacán: Official
Guide.* Mexico City: INAH-SALVAT, 1985.

Bierhorst, John. *The Mythology of Mexico and Central America.* New York: William Morrow, 1990.

Blom, Frans Ferdinand. *The Conquest of Yucatan.* New York:
Houghton Mifflin, 1936.

———. "Gaspar Antonio Chi, Interpreter." *American Anthropologist* 30, no. 2 (1928): 250–262. Online at http://
onlinelibrary.wiley.com.

Boone, Elizabeth Hill. "Pictorial Documents and Visual Thinking in Postconquest Mexico." In *Native Traditions in the Postconquest World*, ed. Elizabeth Hill Boone and Tom Cummins, 149–199. Washington, D.C.: Dumbarton Oaks, 1998.

Box, Hal. *Think Like an Architect*. Austin: University of Texas Press, 2007.

Boyd, Carolyn E. *Rock Art of the Lower Pecos*. College Station: Texas A&M Press, 2003.

Brady, James E., and Keith M. Prufer, eds. *In the Maw of the Earth Monster: Mesoamerican Ritual Cave Use*. Austin: University of Texas Press, 2005.

Braunfels, Wolfgang. *Urban Design in Western Europe: Regime and Architecture, 900–1900*. Translated by Kenneth J. Northcott. Chicago: University of Chicago Press, 1988.

Bretos, Miguel A. *Iglesias de Yucatán*. Photographs by Christian Rasmussen. Mérida, Yucatán: Producción Editorial Dante, 1992.

Brundage, Burr Cartwright. *The Fifth Sun: Aztec Gods, Aztec World*. The Texas Pan American Series. Austin: University of Texas Press, 1979.

Bunson, Margaret R., and Stephen M. Bunson, eds. *Encyclopedia of Ancient Mesoamerica*. New York: Facts on File, 1996.

Cabral, Ignacio. *Arquitectura religiosa en San Andrés Cholula, Puebla*. Puebla: Universidad de las Américas-Puebla, 1993.

———. *Arquitectura religiosa en San Pedro Cholula, Puebla*. Puebla: Universidad de las Américas-Puebla, 1994.

———. *Las capillas posa de San Andrés Calpan, Puebla*. Puebla: Universidad de las Américas-Puebla, 1991.

Camón Aznar, José. *La arquitectura plateresca*. Madrid: Instituto Diego Velázquez, Consejo Superior de Investigaciones Científicas, 1945.

Carlson, John B. "Rise and Fall of the City of the Gods." *Archaeology* 46, no. 6 (November/December 1993): 58–69.

Carmichael, Elizabeth, and Chloë Sayer. *The Skeleton at the Feast: The Day of the Dead in Mexico*. Austin: University of Texas Press for Trustees of the British Museum, 1991.

Carmona, Matthew, Tim Heath, Taner Oc, and Steve Tiesdell. *Public Places—Urban Spaces*. Oxford: Architectural Press, 2003.

Carrasco, Davíd. *Quetzalcoatl and the Irony of Empire: Myths and Prophecies in the Aztec Tradition*. With a new preface. Chicago and London: University of Chicago, 1992.

———. *Religions of Mesoamerica: Cosmovision and Ceremonial Centers*. San Francisco: Harper and Row, 1990.

Carrasco, Pedro. "The Civil-Religious Hierarchy in Mesoamerican Communities: Pre-Spanish Background and Colonial Development." *American Anthropologist* 63 (1961): 483–497.

Carrillo y Ancona, Crescencio. *El obispado de Yucatán: Historia de su fundación y de sus obispos desde el siglo XVI hasta el XIX*. Mérida: Imprenta de Ricardo B. Caballero, 1895.

Caso, Alfonso. *The Aztecs: People of the Sun*. Illustrated by Miguel Covarrubias. Translated by Lowell Dunham. Civilization of the American Indian series. Norman and London: University of Oklahoma Press, 1958.

Cervera Vera, Luis. *Plazas mayores de España*. Vol. 1. Madrid: Espasa-Calpe, 1990.

Chamberlain, Robert S. *The Conquest and Colonization of Yucatan, 1517–1570*. New York: Octagon Books, 1996.

Charlton, Thomas H., and Patricia Fournier G. "Urban and Rural Consequences of the Contact Period: Central Mexico, 1521–1620." Chapter 12 in *Ethnohistory and Archaeology: Approaches to Postcontact Change in the Americas*, ed. J. Daniel Rogers and Samuel M. Wilson, 201–216. Interdisciplinary Contributions to Archaeology series. Papers from a conference held in 1988 at the Society for American Archaeology meetings in Phoenix. New York: Plenum Press, 1993.

Chase, Stuart. *Mexico: A Study of Two Americas*. In collaboration with Marian Tyler. Illustrated by Diego Rivera. Electrotyped and published 1931; reprinted by Macmillan, 1935; paperback by Lancour Press, 2007.

Childs, Mark C. *Squares: A Public Place Design Guide for Urbanists*. Albuquerque: University of New Mexico Press, 2004.

Ciudad Real, Antonio de. *Tratado curioso y docto de las grandezas de la Nueva España: Relación breve y verdadera de algunas cosas de las muchas que sucedieron al padre fray Alonso Ponce en las provincias de la Nueva España siendo comisario general de aquellas partes*. 2 vols. Mexico City: Universidad Nacional Autónoma de México, 1993.

Clendinnen, Inga. *Ambivalent Conquests: Maya and Spaniard in Yucatan, 1517–1570*. Cambridge Latin American Studies 61. Cambridge: Cambridge University Press, 1987.

———. *Aztecs: An Interpretation*. Cambridge: Cambridge University Press, 1991.

Los códices de México. Mexico City: INAH, SEP, and Museo Nacional de Antropología, 1979.

Coe, Michael. "The Iconology of Olmec Art." In *The Iconography of Middle American Sculpture*, ed. Ignacio Bernal et al., 1–12. New York: The Metropolitan Museum of Art, 1973.

———. *The Maya*. 4th ed. London: Thames and Hudson, 1987.

———. *Mexico*. 3rd ed. rev. and enl. New York: Thames and Hudson, 1984.

Coe, Michael D., et al. *The Olmec World: Ritual and Rulership*. Princeton: The Art Museum, Princeton University, 1995.

Coe, Michael D., and Richard A. Diehl. *In the Land of the Olmec*: Vol. 1, *The Archaeology of San Lorenzo Tenochtitlán*; Vol. 2, *The People of the River*. Austin: University of Texas Press, 1980.

Coe, Michael, Dean Snow, and Elizabeth Benson. *Atlas of Ancient America*. Oxford: Equinox, 1986.

Collins, George R., and Christiane C. Collins. *Camillo Sitte: The Birth of Modern City Planning*. New York: Rizzoli, 1986.

Cook, Sherburne Friend, and Woodrow Wilson Borah. *Essays in Population History: Mexico and the Caribbean*. Berkley and Los Angeles: University of California Press, 1971. Online at books.google.com.

Cortés, Hernán. *Letters from Mexico*. Translated and edited by Anthony Pagden. Introduction by J. H. Elliott. New Haven and London: Yale University Press, 1986.

Cortés, Hernando. *Five Letters 1519–1526*. Translated and with an introduction by John Bayard Morris. New York: W. W. Norton, 1969.

Covarrubias, Miguel. *Indian Art of Mexico and Central America*. New York: Knopf, 1957.

Craine, Eugene R., and Reginald C. Reindorp, trans. *The Codex Pérez and the Book of Chilam Balam of Maní*. Norman: University of Oklahoma Press, 1979.

Crosby, Alfred W., Jr. *The Columbian Exchange: Biological and Cultural Consequences of 1492*. Contributions in American Studies series. Westport, CT: Greenwood Press, 1972.

Crouch, Dora P., Daniel J. Garr, and Axel I. Mundigo. *Spanish City Planning in North America*. Cambridge and London: MIT Press, 1982.

Cueva Santillán, Juan. "Relación de Izamal y Santa María." In *Relaciones histórico-geográficas de la gobernación de Yucatán (Mérida, Valladolid y Tabasco)*, ed. Mercedes de la Garza et al., 303–308. 2 vols. Fuentes para el Estudio de la Cultura Maya 1. Mexico City: Centro de Estudios Mayas, Universidad Nacional Autónoma de México, 1993.

Cullen, Gordon. *Townscape*. New York: Reinhold, 1961.

Cusi de García-Pimental, Carmen, and J.B. Johnson. *Churches of the Mayas: Religious Building of the Yucatan Peninsula from the Sixteenth Century*. Irvine, CA: JBJ Press, 2009.

Descola, Jean. *The Conquistadors*. Translated by Malcolm Barnes. New York: Viking Press, 1957; reissued New York: Augustus M. Kelley, 1970.

Diamond, Jared. *Guns, Germs, and Steel: The Fates of Human Societies*. New York: W. W. Norton, 1999.

Díaz del Castillo, Bernal. *The Conquest of New Spain*. Translated by J. M. Cohen. London: Penguin Books, 1963.

———. *Historia verdadera de la conquista de la Nueva España*. Mexico City: Editorial del Valle de México, 1976.

Díaz, Gisele, and Alan Rodgers, eds. *The Codex Borgia: A Full-Color Restoration of the Ancient Mexican Manuscript*. Introduction and commentary by Bruce E. Byland. New York: Dover Publications, 1993.

"Dos Palabras." Photocopy of typed manuscript of history of Amecameca and its churches given to author by Padre José Francisco Parra, July 24, 1987.

Durán, Fray Diego. *The History of the Indies of New Spain*. Translated, annotated, and with an introduction by Doris Heyden. Civilization of the American Indian series. Norman and London: University of Oklahoma Press, 1994.

Early, James. *The Colonial Architecture of Mexico*. Albuquerque: University of New Mexico Press, 1994.

Edgerton, Samuel Y. *The Mirror, the Window, and the Telescope: How Renaissance Linear Perspective Changed Our Vision of the Universe*. Ithaca and London: Cornell University Press, 2009.

———. *Theaters of Conversion: Religious Architecture and Indian Artisans in Colonial Mexico*. Albuquerque: University of New Mexico Press, 2001.

Edmonson, Munro S., trans. *The Ancient Future of the Itza: The Book of the Chilam Balam of Tizimin*. Austin: University of Texas Press, 1982.

Eliade, Mircea. "Paradise and Utopia: Mythological Geography and Eschatology." In *The Quest: History and Meaning in Religion*, by Mircea Eliade, 88–111. Chicago: University of Chicago Press, 1969.

———. *The Sacred and the Profane: The Nature of Religion*. Translated by Willard R. Trask. San Diego: Harcourt Brace Jovanovich, 1957.

Enciso, Jorge. *Design Motifs of Ancient Mexico*. New York: Dover Publications, 1953.

———. *Designs from Pre-Columbian Mexico*. New York: Dover, 1971.

Escalada, José Xavier, et al. *La ruta de los santuarios en México*. Mexico City: CVS Publicaciones, 1994.

Escobar, Jesús. *The Plaza Mayor and the Shaping of Baroque Madrid*. Cambridge and New York: Cambridge University Press, 2003.

Evans, Joan. *Monastic Iconography in France from the Renaissance to the Revolution*. Cambridge: Cambridge University Press, 1970.

Fagan, Brian M. *Kingdoms of Gold, Kingdoms of Jade*. London: Thames and Hudson, 1991.

Farris, Nancy M. *Maya Society under Colonial Rule: The Collective Enterprise of Survival*. Princeton: Princeton University Press, 1984.

Feraboli, Maria Teresa, and Angela Arnone. *City Squares of the World*. Vercelli: White Star, 2007.

Ferguson, William M., and Arthur H. Rohn. *Mesoamerica's Ancient Cities: Aerial Views of Precolumbian Ruins in Mexico, Guatemala, Belize, and Honduras*. Photographs by John Q. Royce and William M. Ferguson. Foreword by R. E. W. Adams. Niwot: University Press of Colorado, 1990.

Fernández, Miguel Ángel. *La Jerusalen indiana: Los conventos-fortaleza mexicanos del siglo XVI*. Edición privada, Smurfit Cartón y Papel de México, 1992.

Fernández Christlieb, Federico, and Ángel Julián García Zambrano. *Territorialidad y paisaje en el altepetl del siglo XVI*. Mexico City: Fondo de Cultura Económica, 2006.

Fifteenth-Century Engravings of Northern Europe. Exhibition catalogue by Alan Shestack. Washington, D.C.: National Gallery of Art, 1968.

Fifteenth-Century Woodcuts and Metalcuts from the National Gallery of Art. Catalogue prepared by Richard S. Field. Washington, D.C.: National Gallery of Art, 1965.

Finamore, Daniel, and Stephen D. Houston, eds. *Fiery Pool: The Maya and the Mythic Sea*. Salem, MA: Peabody Essex Museum, 2010.

Florescano, Enrique. *Memory, Myth, and Time in Mexico: From the Aztecs to Independence*. Translated by Albert G. Bork. Translations from Latin America series. Austin: University of Texas Press, 1994.

Flores Guerrero, Raúl. *Las capillas posas de México*. Introduction by Manuel Toussaint. Enciclopedia mexicana de arte, 15. Mexico City: Ediciones Mexicanas, 1951.

Folan, William S. "Sacbes of the Northern Maya." In *Ancient Road Networks and Settlement Hierarchies in the New World*, ed. Charles D. Trombold, 222–229. Cambridge: Cambridge University Press, 1991.

Foster, George McClelland. *Culture and Conquest: America's Spanish Heritage*. Chicago: Quadrangle Books, 1960.

Foster, Lynn V. *Handbook to Life in the Ancient Maya World*. Introduction by Peter Mathews. Oxford: Oxford University Press, 2002.

Foundation for the Advancement of Mesoamerican Studies, Inc., www.famsi.org.

Freidel, David. "Preparing the Way." In *The Olmec World: Ritual and Rulership*, by Michael D. Coe et al., 3–9. Princeton: The Art Museum, Princeton University, 1995.

Freidel, David, Linda Schele, and Joy Parker. *Maya Cosmos: Three Thousand Years on the Shaman's Path*. New York: William Morrow, 1993.

Friedman, David. *Florentine New Towns: Urban Design in the Late Middle Ages*. Cambridge: MIT Press, 1988.

Fuentes, Patricia de, ed. and trans. *The Conquistadors: First-person Accounts of the Conquest of Mexico*. With a foreword by Ross Hassig. N.p.: Orion Press, 1963; reprint with foreword, Norman: University of Oklahoma Press, 1993.

García, Casiano. *Vida del comendador Diego de Ordaz, descubridor del Orinoco*. Mexico City: Editorial Jus, 1952.

García Granados, Rafael. "Calpan." *Universidad de México* 1, no. 5 (March 1931): 370–374.

García Granados, Rafael, and Luis MacGregor. *Huejotzingo:*

La ciudad y el convento franciscano. Mexico City: Talleres Gráficos de la Nación, 1934.

García Valadés, Adrián. *Teotihuacan: The City of the Gods*. 10th ed. Mexico City: Ediciones Orto, 1979.

García Zambrano, Ángel Julián. *Pasaje mítico y paisaje fundacional en las migraciones mesoamericanas*. Cuernavaca: Universidad Autónoma del Estado de Morelos, 2006.

Garza, Mercedes de la. *The Mayas: 3000 Years of Civilization*. Translated by Amanda Mazzinghi. Florence: Bonechi, and Mexico City: Monclem Ediciones, 1992.

Gatje, Robert F. *Great Public Squares: An Architect's Selection*. New York and London: W. W. Norton, 2010.

Gay, Carlo T. E. "Olmec Hieroglyphic Writing." *Archaeology* 26, no. 4 (October 1973): 278–288.

Gehl, Jan, and Lars Gemzoe. *New City Spaces*. Copenhagen: Danish Architectural Press, 2000.

Gendrop, Paul. *A Guide to Architecture in Ancient Mexico*. Mexico City: Minutiae Mexicana, 1974.

Gibson, Charles. *The Aztecs under Spanish Rule: A History of the Indians of the Valley of Mexico, 1519–1810*. Stanford: Stanford University Press, 1964.

———. *Spain in America*. New American Nation series. New York: Harper and Row, 1966.

———. *Tlaxcala in the Sixteenth Century*. Stanford: Stanford University Press, 1952; reissued 1967.

Gómara, Francisco López de. *Cortés: The Life of the Conqueror by His Secretary*. Translated and edited by Lesley Byrd Simpson. Berkeley: University of California Press, 1964.

González Casanova, Pablo. *Estudios de lingüística y filología nahuas*. Mexico City: Universidad Nacional Autónoma de México, 1989.

González Cicero, Stella María. *Perspectiva religiosa en Yucatán, 1517–1571: Yucatán, los franciscanos y el primer obispo fray Francisco de Toral*. Mexico City: Colegio de México, 1978.

González Galván, Manuel. "Influencia, por selección, de América en su arte colonial." *Anales del Instituto de Investigaciones Estéticas* 13, no. 50 (1982): 43–54.

Grieder, Terence. *Origins of Pre-Columbian Art*. Austin: University of Texas Press, 1982.

Grove, David C. *Chalcatzingo: Excavations on the Olmec Frontier*. London: Thames and Hudson, 1984.

Gruzinski, Serge. *The Aztecs: Rise and Fall of an Empire*. Discoveries series. New York: Harry N. Abrams, 1992.

———. *The Conquest of Mexico: The Incorporation of Indian Societies into the Western World, 16th–18th Centuries*. Translated by Eileen Corrigan. Cambridge, UK: Polity Press, 1993.

———. *Painting the Conquest: The Mexican Indians and the European Renaissance*. Translated by Deke Dusinberre. Paris: Flammarion, 1992.

Guernsey, Julia. "A Consideration of the Quatrefoil Motif in

Preclassic Mesoamerica." *RES: Journal of Anthropology and Aesthetics* 57/58 (2010): 75–96.

Guernsey, Julia, and Michael Love. "La Blanca in the Olmec World." Lecture presented at the Olmec Conference, University of Texas at Austin, November 20–21, 2008.

Guernsey, Julia, and F. Kent Reilly, eds. *Sacred Bundles: Ritual Acts of Wrapping and Binding in Mesoamerica.* Barnardsville, NC: Boundary End Archaeology Research Center, 2006.

Hall, Edward T. *The Hidden Dimension.* New York: Random House, 1966.

Hammond, Norman. *Ancient Maya Civilization.* New Brunswick, NJ: Rutgers University Press, 1988.

Hardoy, Jorge E. *Pre-Columbian Cities.* New York: Walker, 1973.

Harrison, Peter D. *The Lords of Tikal: Rulers of an Ancient Maya City.* New York: Thames and Hudson, 1999.

Hedgemann, Werner, Elbert Peets, and Alan J. Plattus. *The American Vitruvius: An Architect's Handbook of Civic Art.* New York: Princeton Architectural Press, 1922.

Hernández de León-Portilla, Ascención. *Bernardino de Sahagún: Diez estudios acerca de su obra.* Mexico City: Fondo de Cultura Económica, 1990.

Hertzog, Lawrence A. *Return to the Center: Culture, Public Space, and City Building in a Global Era.* Austin: University of Texas Press, 2006

Heyden, Doris, and Paul Gendrop. *Pre-Columbian Architecture of Mesoamerica.* Translated by Judith Stanton. History of World Architecture series. New York: Electa/Rizzoli, 1980.

Hiorns, Frederick R. *Town-building in History: An Outline Review of Conditions, Influences, Ideas, and Methods Affecting "Planned" Towns through Five Thousand Years.* London: George G. Harrap, 1956.

Humboldt, Alexander von. *Political Essay on the Kingdom of New Spain.* The John Black Translation [Abridged]. Edited with Introduction by Mary Maples Dunn. Norman and London: University of Oklahoma, 1972.

Hunter, C. Bruce. *A Guide to the Ancient Maya Ruins.* Norman: University of Oklahoma Press, 1977.

Jacobs, Allan B. *Great Streets.* Cambridge: MIT Press, 1993.

Jacobs, Jane. *The Death and Life of Great American Cities.* New York: Random House, 1961.

Jenkens, Eric J. *To Scale: One Hundred Urban Plans.* New York: Routledge, 2007.

Joralemon, Peter David. *A Study of Olmec Iconography.* Studies in Pre-Columbian Art and Archaeology Number Seven. Washington, D.C.: Dumbarton Oaks, Trustees for Harvard University, 1971.

Karttunen, Frances E. *An Analytical Dictionary of Nahuatl.* Austin: University of Texas Press, 1983.

———. *Between Worlds: Interpreters, Guides, and Survivors.* New Brunswick, NJ: Rutgers University Press, 1994.

Keleman, Pál. *Art of the Americas: Ancient and Hispanic.* New York: Bonanza Books, 1969.

———. "Religious Sculpture of Colonial Mexico." *Art in America* 32 (1944): 109–117.

Kilham, Walter H[arrington]. *Mexican Architecture of the Vice-Regal Period.* New York, 1927; reprint, New York: AMS Press, 1971.

Kiracofe, James B. "Architectural Fusion and Indigenous Ideology in Early Colonial Teposcolula: The Casa de la Cacica: A Building at the Edge of Oblivion." *Anales del Instituto de Investigaciones Estéticas* (Mexico City: Universidad Nacional Autónoma de México) 17, no. 66 (1995): 45–84.

———. "Toward Reconstructing the Lost Retablo of Teposcolula." Unpublished manuscript ©1995, posted on www.interamericaninstitute.org, September 27, 2000.

Kirchhoff, Paul. "Mesoamérica: Sus límites geográficos, composición étnica y caracteres culturales." *Acta Americana* 1 (1943): 92–107.

Klor de Alva, J. Jorge. "Christianity and the Aztecs." *San José Studies* 5, no. 3 (1979): 6–21.

———. "Religious Rationalization and the Conversions of the Nahuas: Social Organization and Colonial Epistemology." In *Aztec Ceremonial Landscapes*, ed. Davíd Carrasco, 233–245. Niwot: University Press of Colorado, 1991.

———. "Spiritual Conflict and Accommodation in New Spain: Toward a Typology of Aztec Responses to Christianity." In *The Inca and Aztec States: 1400–1800,* ed. G. Collier et al., 345–366. New York and London: Academic Press, 1982.

Klor de Alva, J. Jorge, H. B. Nicholson, and Eloise Quiñones Keber, eds. *The Work of Bernardino de Sahagún, Pioneer Ethnographer of Sixteenth-Century Aztec Mexico.* Studies on Culture and Society, Vol. 2; Institute for Mesoamerican Studies, The University at Albany, State University of New York. Austin: University of Texas Press, 1988.

Knab, Timothy J. *A War of Witches: A Journey into the Underworld of the Comtemporary Aztecs.* New York: Harper Collins, 1995.

Koontz, Rex, Kathryn Reese-Taylor, and Annabeth Headrick. *Landscape and Power in Ancient Mesoamerica.* Boulder, CO: Westview Press, 2001.

Kostof, Spiro. *The City Assembled: The Elements of Urban Form Through History.* Boston: Little, Brown, 1992.

———. *The City Shaped: Urban Patterns and Meanings Through History.* Boston: Little, Brown, 1991.

———. *A History of Architecture: Settings and Rituals.* New York and Oxford: University of Oxford, 1985.

Kubler, George. "Architects and Builders in Mexico: 1521–1550." *Journal of the Warburg and Courtauld Institutes* 7, nos. 1–2 (1944): 7–19.

———. *The Art and Architecture of Ancient America: The Mexican, Maya and Andean Peoples.* 3rd ed. Pelican History of Art. New Haven and London: Yale University Press, 1990.

———. "The Design of Space in Maya Architecture." *Miscellanea Paul Rivet octogenaria dicata* 1 (1958): 515–531.

———. "Iconographic Aspects of Architectural Profiles at Teotihuacán and in Mesoamerica." In *The Iconography of Middle American Sculpture*, by Ignacio Bernal et al., 24–39. New York: Metropolitan Museum of Art, 1973.

———. *The Iconography of the Art of Teotihuacán.* Studies in Pre-Columbian Art and Archaeology Number 4. Washington, D.C.: Dumbarton Oaks, Trustees for Harvard University, 1967.

———. *Mexican Architecture of the Sixteenth Century.* 2 vols. New Haven: Yale University Press, 1948.

———. "Mexican Urbanism in the Sixteenth Century." *Art Bulletin* 34 (1942): 160–171.

———. "On the Colonial Extinction of the Motifs of Pre-Columbian Art." In *Essays in Pre-Columbian Art and Archaeology*, by Samuel K. Lothrop et al., 14–34. Cambridge: Harvard University Press, 1961.

Kubler, George, and Martin S. Soria. *Art and Architecture in Spain and Portugal and Their American Dominions, 1500 to 1800.* Pelican History of Art. Baltimore: Penguin Books, 1959.

Landa, Diego de. *Yucatan Before and After the Conquest.* Translated with notes by William Gates. Baltimore: Maya Society, 1937; reprint, New York: Dover Publications, 1978.

Lara, Jaime. *City, Temple, Stage: Eschatological Architecture and Liturgical Theatrics in New Spain.* Notre Dame: Notre Dame Press, 2004.

Las Casas, Bartolomé de. *A Short Account of the Destruction of the Indies* [1542]. Edited and translated by Nigel Griffin. Introduction by Anthony Pagden. London: Penguin Books, 1992.

Leipziger-Pearce, Hugo. *Architecture in the Americas: Its Significant Forms and Values.* Inter-American Intellectual Exchange. No. 282 Offprint Series. Austin: University of Texas at Austin Institute of Latin American Studies, 1943.

Leonard, Irving A. *Books of the Brave: Being an Account of Books and of Men in the Spanish Conquest and Settlement of the Sixteenth-Century New World.* Cambridge: Harvard University Press, 1949; reprint with a new introduction by Rolena Adorno, Berkeley: University of California Press, 1992.

León-Portilla, Miguel. *Aztec Thought and Culture: A Study of the Ancient Nahuatl Mind.* Translated by Jack Emory Davis. Norman: University of Oklahoma Press, 1963.

———, ed. *The Broken Spears: The Aztec Account of the Conquest of Mexico.* Expanded and updated. Boston: Beacon Press, 1992.

Lewis, Oscar. *Life in a Mexican Village: Tepoztlán Restudied.* Urbana: University of Illinois Press, 1963.

Leyenaar, Ted J. J. "*Ulama*, the Survival of the Mesoamerican Ballgame *Ullamaliztli*." *KIVA: The Journal of Southwestern Anthropology and History* 58, no. 2 (1992): 115–153.

Lincoln, Charles Edward. "A Preliminary Assessment of Izamal, Yucatan, Mexico." Master's thesis, Tulane University, 1980.

Lockhart, James M. *The Nahuas after the Conquest: A Social and Cultural History of the Indians of Central Mexico, Sixteenth through Eighteenth Centuries.* Stanford: Stanford University Press, 1992.

———. *Nahuas and Spaniards: Postconquest Central Mexican History and Philology.* Stanford: Stanford University Press, 1991.

———. "The Social History of Colonial Spanish America: Evolution and Potential." *Latin American Research Review* 7, no. 1 (Spring 1972): 6–45.

Lockhart, James, and Enrique Otte, eds. and trans. *Letters and People of the Spanish Indies, Sixteenth Century.* Cambridge Latin American Studies 22. Cambridge: Cambridge University Press, 1976.

López Austin, Alfredo. *The Human Body and Ideology: Concepts among the Ancient Nahuas.* Translated by Bernardo Ortiz de Montellano. Salt Lake City: University of Utah Press, 1988.

López Guzmán, Rafael. *Territorio, poblamiento y arquitectura: México en las relaciones geográficas de Felipe II.* Granada: Editorial Universidad de Granada, 2007.

Love, Bruce. *The Paris Codex: Handbook for a Maya Priest.* Introduction by George E. Stuart. Austin: University of Texas Press, 1994.

Love, Michael, and Julia Guernsey. "Monument 3 from La Blanca, Guatemala: A Middle Preclassic Earthen Sculpture and Its Ritual Associations." *Antiquity* 81 (2007): 920–932.

Low, Setha M. *On the Plaza: The Politics of Public Space and Culture.* Austin: University of Texas Press, 2000.

Lyell, James P. R. *Early Book Illustration in Spain.* London, 1926; reprint, New York: Hacker Art Books, 1976.

Lynch, Kevin. *The Image of the City.* Boston: MIT and Harvard, 1960.

Macazaga Ordoño, César. Diccionario de la lengua nahuatl. Mexico City: Editorial Innovación, 1979.

MacGregor, Luis. "Cien ejemplares de plateresco mexicano." *Archivo Español de Arte y Arqueología* 31 (1935): 31–45.

Madsen, William. "Religious Syncretism." In *Handbook of Middle American Indians* 6, Robert Wauchope, general editor, and Manning Nash, volume editor, 369–492. Austin: University of Texas Press, 1967.

Mâle, Emile. *Religious Art in France: The Late Middle Ages.*

A Study of Medieval Iconography and Its Sources. Edited by Harry Bober. Translated by Marthiel Mathews. Bollingen Series XC 3. Princeton: Princeton University Press, 1986.

Mann, Charles C. *1491: New Revelations of the Americas Before Columbus.* New York: Random House, 2006.

Markman, Sidney David. *Architecture and Urbanization in Colonial Chiapas, Mexico.* Memoirs series 153. Philadelphia: American Philosophical Society, 1984.

Martin, Simon, and Nikolai Grube. *Chronicle of the Maya Kings and Queens: Deciphering the Dynasties of the Ancient Maya.* London and New York: Thames and Hudson, 2000.

Martínez Donjuán, Guadalupe. "El sitio olmeca de Teopantecuanitlán en Guerrero." *Anales de Antropología* 22 (1985): 215–226.

———. "Teopantecuanitlán." In *Primer Coloquio de Arqueología y Etnohistoria del Estado de Guerrero,* 55–80. Gobierno del Estado de Guerrero: Instituto Nacional de Antropología e Historia, 1986.

———. "Teopantecuanitlán, Guerrero: Un sitio olmeca." *Revista Mexicana de Estudios Antropológicos* 28 (1982): 123–132.

Mayernik, David. *Timeless Cities.* Boulder, CO, and Oxford, UK: Westview Press, 2003.

Maza, Francisco de la, Felipe Pardinas, et al. *Cuarenta siglos de plástica mexicana: Arte colonial.* Mexico City: Editorial Herrero, 1970.

McAndrew, John. *The Open-Air Churches of Sixteenth-Century Mexico: Atrios, Posas, Open Chapels, and Other Studies.* Cambridge: Harvard University Press, 1964.

Mendieta, Jerónimo de. *Historia eclesiástica indiana.* Mexico City: Editorial García Icazbalceta, 1870.

Merriman, Roger Bigalow. *The Rise of the Spanish Empire in the Old World and the New.* Vol. 4, *Philip the Prudent.* New York: Cooper Square Publishers, 1962.

Metford, John C. *Dictionary of Christian Lore and Legend.* London: Thames and Hudson, 1983.

Mexican Wall Paintings of the Maya and Aztec Periods. Introduction by Ignacio Bernal. A Mentor-Unesco Art Book. New York: New American Library of World Literature by arrangement with UNESCO, 1963.

Mexico: Splendors of Thirty Centuries. Introduction by Octavio Paz. New York: Metropolitan Museum of Art, 1990.

Miller, Mary Ellen. "The Architectural Backdrops of the Murals of Structure 1, Bonampak." In *Fourth Palenque Round Table,* 1980, Vol. 6, ed. Merle Greene Robertson and Elizabeth P. Benson, 185–192. San Francisco: Pre-Columbian Art Research Institute, 1985.

———. *The Art of Mesoamerica from Olmec to Aztec.* World of Art series. London: Thames and Hudson, 1986.

———. *Maya Art and Architecture.* World of Art series. London: Thames and Hudson, 1999.

Miller, Mary Ellen, and Karl A. Taube. *The Gods and Symbols of Ancient Mexico and the Maya: An Illustrated Dictionary of Mesoamerican Religion.* London: Thames and Hudson, 1993.

Miller, Robert Ryal. *Mexico: A History.* Norman: University of Oklahoma Press, 1985.

Montgomery, John. *Dictionary of Maya Hieroglyphics.* 2002; updated by Peter Mathews (2003) and Christopher Helmke (2007) at www.famsi.org/mayawriting/dictionary.htm.

More, Thomas. *Utopia.* Pitt Press series. Cambridge: Cambridge University Press, 1879; reprint, 1956.

Morehead, Susan Kline. "An Iconology of Architectural Ornament at the Sixteenth-Century Mexican Monastery of San Andrés Calpan." Master's thesis, University of Texas at Austin, 1997.

Moreno Villa, José. *La escultura colonial mexicana.* Mexico City: El Colegio de México, 1942; reprint, Fondo de Cultura Económica, 1986.

Morley, G. Sylvanus. *La civilización maya.* Mexico City: Fondo de Cultura Económica, 1965.

Morris, A. E. J. *History of Urban Form: Before the Industrial Revolutions.* 3rd ed. London: Prentice Hall, 1994.

Motolinía, Toribio. *History of the Indians of New Spain.* Translated and edited by Elizabeth Andros Foster. Berkeley: The Cortés Society, Documents and Narratives Concerning the Discovery and Conquest of Latin America, New Series Number 4, 1950; reprint, Westport, CT: Greenwood Press, 1973.

Mullen, Robert J. *Architecture and Its Sculpture in Viceregal Mexico.* Austin: University of Texas Press, 1997.

Mumford, Lewis. *The City in History: Its Origins, Its Transformations, and Its Prospects.* New York: Harcourt, Brace and World, 1961.

Murray, Peter. *Renaissance Architecture.* New York: Abrams, 1971.

Neumeyer, Alfred. "The Indian Contribution to Architectural Decoration in Spanish Colonial America." *The Art Bulletin* 30, no. 1 (March 1948): 104–121.

Nicholson, H. B. "The Late Pre-Hispanic Central Mexican (Aztec) Iconographic System." In *The Iconography of Middle American Sculpture,* by Ignacio Bernal and Elizabeth Kennedy Easby, 72–97. New York: Metropolitan Museum of Art, 1973.

———, ed. *Origins of Religious Art and Iconography in Preclassic America.* Los Angeles: UCLA Latin American Center Publications, 1977.

Nicholson, H. B., with Eloise Quiñones Keber. *Art of Aztec Mexico: Treasures of Tenochtitlan.* Washington, D.C.: National Gallery of Art, 1983.

Nuttall, Zelia, ed. *The Codex Nuttall: A Picture Manuscript from Ancient Mexico. The Peabody Museum Facsimile* edited by Zelia Nuttall. New introduction by Arthur G. Miller. New York: Dover Publications, 1975.

Ortiz Lajous, Jaime. *Ciudades coloniales mexicanas*. Mexico City: Secretaría de Turismo, 1994.

Palladio, Andrea. *The Four Books of Architecture*. Introduction by Adolf K. Placzek. London: Isaac Ware, 1738; reprint, New York: Dover Publications, 1965.

Pasztory, Esther. *Aztec Art*. New York: Harry N. Abrams, 1983.

Pérez-Embid, Florentino. *El mudejarismo en la arquitectura portuguesa de la época manuelina*. Sevilla: Laboratorio de Arte de la Universidad de Sevilla, 1944.

Perry, Richard D. *Blue Lakes and Silver Cities: The Art and Architecture of Western Mexico*. Santa Barbara: Espadaña Press, 1977.

———. *Exploring Colonial Oaxaca: The Art and Architecture*. Santa Barbara: Espadaña Press, 2006.

———. *Mexico's Fortress Monasteries*. Santa Barbara: Espadaña Press, 1992.

———. *More Maya Missions: Exploring Colonial Chiapas*. Santa Barbara: Espadaña Press, 1994.

Perry, Richard D., and Rosalind Perry. *Maya Missions: Exploring the Spanish Colonial Churches of Yucatan*. Santa Barbara: Espadaña Press, 1988.

Peterson, Jeanette Favrot. "The *Florentine Codex* Imagery and the Colonial *Tlacuilo*." In *The Work of Bernardino de Sahagun, Pioneer Ethnographer of Sixteenth-Century Aztec Mexico*, ed. J. Jorge Klor de Alva, H. B. Nicholson, and Eloise Quiñones Keber, 273–293. Studies on Culture and Society. Albany, NY: Institute for Mesoamerican Studies, State University of New York, 1988.

———. *The Paradise Garden Murals of Malinalco: Utopia and Empire in Sixteenth-Century Mexico*. Austin: University of Texas Press, 1993.

Phelan, John Leddy. *The Millennial Kingdom of the Franciscans in the New World*. 2nd ed. rev. Berkeley and Los Angeles: University of California Press, 1970.

Phillips, Richard England. "Processions through Paradise: A Liturgical and Social Interpretation of the Ritual Function and Symbolic Signification of the Cloister in the Sixteenth-Century Monasteries of Central Mexico." 3 vols. Ph.D. diss., University of Texas at Austin, 1993.

Plazas Mayores de México: Arte y Luz. Mexico City: BBVA Bancomer, 2002.

Poole, Stafford. *Our Lady of Guadalupe: The Origins and Sources of a Mexican National Symbol, 1531–1797*. Tucson: The University of Arizona Press, 1995.

Popol Vuh: The Mayan Book of the Dawn of Life. Translated by Dennis Tedlock. New York: Simon and Schuster, A Touchstone Book, 1985.

Porter, Eliot, and Ellen Auerbach. *Mexican Celebrations*. Essays by Donna Pierce and Marsha C. Bol. Albuquerque: University of New Mexico Press, 1990.

———. *Mexican Churches*. Albuquerque: University of New Mexico Press, 1987.

Powell, Christopher. "The Shapes of Sacred Space: A Proposed System of Geometry Used to Lay Out and Design Maya Art and Architecture and Some Implications Concerning Maya Cosmology." Ph.D. diss., University of Texas at Austin, 2010.

Pre-Columbian Art. Foreword by Hasso von Winning. N.p.: Stendahl Art Gallery, [1963?].

Prescott, William H. *Conquest of Mexico*. Garden City, NY: Blue Ribbon Books, 1943.

Proskouriakoff, Tatiana. *An Album of Maya Architecture*. New ed. London and Norman: University of Oklahoma Press, 1963. First edition by Carnegie Institution of Washington, 1946.

———. *Maya History*. Edited by Rosemary A. Joyce. Austin: University of Texas Press, 1993.

Rasmussen, Steen Eiler. *Experiencing Architecture*. Cambridge: MIT Press, 1959.

Reese, Thomas F., ed. *Studies in Ancient American and European Art: The Collected Essays of George Kubler*. New Haven and London: Yale University Press, 1985.

Reilly III, F. Kent. "Art, Ritual, and Rulership in the Olmec World." In *The Olmec World: Ritual and Rulership*, by Michael D. Coe et al., 27–45. Princeton: The Art Museum, Princeton University, 1995.

———. "Cosmología, soberanismo y espacio ritual en la Mesoamérica del Formativo." In *Los olmecas en Mesoamérica*, coordinated by John Clark, 239–259. Mexico City: Citibank, 1994.

———. "Cosmos and Rulership: The Function of Olmec-style Symbols in Formative Period Mesoamerica." *Visible Language* 24, no. 1 (January 1990): 12–37.

———. "The Ecological Origins of Olmec Symbols of Rulership." Master's thesis, University of Texas at Austin, 1987.

———. "Enclosed Ritual Spaces and the Watery Underworld in Formative Period Architecure: New Observations on the Function of La Venta Complex A." In *Seventh Palenque Round Table, 1989*, ed. Merle Greene Robertson and Virginia M. Fields, 125–135. San Francisco: Pre-Columbian Art Research Institute, 1994.

———. "Glossary of Olmec Motifs." In *The Olmec World: Ritual and Rulership*, by Michael D. Coe et al., 120–122. Princeton: The Art Museum, Princeton University, 1995.

———. "The Lazy-S: A Formative Period Iconographic Loan to Maya Hieroglyphic Writing." In *Eighth Palenque Round Table, 1993*, ed. Merle Greene Robertson, Martha J. Macri, and Jan McHargue, 413–424. San Francisco: Pre-Columbian Art Research Institute, 1996.

———. "Olmec Iconographic Influences on the Symbols of Maya Rulership: An Examination of Possible Sources." In *Sixth Palenque Round Table, 1986*, ed. Merle Greene Robertson and Virginia M. Fields, 151–166. Norman: University of Oklahoma Press, 1991.

Reps, John W. *The Making of Urban America: A History of City Planning in the United States.* Princeton: Princeton University Press, 1965.

Reyes García, Luis. *Cuauhtinchan del siglo XII al XVI: Formación y desarrollo histórico de un señorío prehispánico.* Weisbaden: Franz *Steiner* Verlag GMBH, 1977; Puebla: Fondo de Cultura Económica USA, 1988; Mexico City: Centro de Investigaciones y Estudios Superiores en Antropología Social, 1988.

Reyes-Valerio, Constantino. *Arte indocristiana: Escultura del siglo XVI.* Mexico City: Instituto Nacional de Antropología e Historia, 1978.

Ricard, Robert. *The Spiritual Conquest of Mexico: An Essay on the Apostolate and the Evangelizing Methods of the Mendicant Orders in New Spain, 1523–1572.* Translated by Lesley Byrd Simpson. Berkeley: University of California Press, 1966; California Reprint Series edition, 1974; first paperback printing, 1982.

Robertson, Donald. *Pre-Columbian Architecture.* New York: George Braziller, 1963.

Robertson, Merle Greene, ed. *Third Palenque Round Table, 1978, Part 2.* Austin: University of Texas Press, 1980.

Robicsek, Francis, and Donald M. Hales. *The Maya Book of the Dead.* Norman: University of Oklahoma Press, 1981.

Rojas, Pedro. *Historia general del arte mexicano: Época colonial.* Mexico City: Editorial Hermes, 1963.

Rojas Garcidueñas, José. *Fray Juan de Alameda: Arquitecto franciscano del s. XVI.* Mexico City: Ábside, 1947.

Romero de Terreros, Manuel. *El arte en México durante el virreinato.* Mexico City: Editorial Porrúa, 1951.

Rosenau, Helen. *The Ideal City in Its Architectural Evolution.* London: Routledge and Kegan Paul, 1959.

Roys, Ralph L., trans. *The Book of Chilam Balam of Chumayel.* Norman: University of Oklahoma Press, 1933; 1967.

———. "Conquest Sites and the Subsequent Destruction of Maya Architecture in the Interior of Northern Yucatan." *Contributions to American Anthropology* 11, no. 54. Washington, D.C.: Carnegie Institution of Washington, 1952.

———. *The Indian Background of Colonial Yucatan.* Norman: University of Oklahoma Press, 1972.

Sabloff, Jeremy A. *The Cities of Ancient Mexico: Reconstructing a Lost World.* London: Thames and Hudson, 1989.

Sahagún, Fray Bernardino de. *Historia general de las cosas de la Nueva España.* Mexico City: Porrúa, 1946.

Sánchez de Carmona, Manuel. *Traza y plaza de la Ciudad de México en el siglo XVI.* Mexico City: Universidad Autónoma de Azcapotzalco, 1989.

Sanford, Trent Elwood. *The Story of Architecture in Mexico.* New York: W. W. Norton, 1947.

San Miguel, Andrés de. *Qué cosa sea la arquitectura.* Andrés de San Miguel Manuscripts. Benson Latin American Collection, General Libraries, University of Texas at Austin.

Sartor, Mario. *Arquitectura y urbanismo en Nueva España: Siglo XVI.* Mexico City: Grupo Azabache, 1992.

Scarborough, Vernon L. "Ecology and Ritual: Water Management and the Maya." *Latin American Antiquity* 9, no. 2 (June 1998): 135–159.

Scarborough, Vernon L., and David Wilcox, eds. *The Mesoamerican Ballgame.* Tucson: University of Arizona Press, 1991.

Schele, Linda. "The Olmec Mountain and Tree of Creation in Mesoamerican Cosmology." In *The Olmec World: Ritual and Rulership,* by Michael D. Coe et al., 105–117. Princeton: The Art Museum, Princeton University, 1995.

Schele, Linda, and David Freidel. *A Forest of Kings: The Untold Story of the Ancient Maya.* New York: William Morrow, 1990.

Schele, Linda, and Peter Mathews. *The Code of Kings: The Language of Seven Sacred Maya Temples and Tombs.* New York: Simon and Schuster, 1998.

Schele, Linda, and Mary Ellen Miller. *The Blood of Kings: Dynasty and Ritual in Maya Art.* New York: George Braziller in association with the Kimbell Art Museum, 1986.

Séjourné, Laurette. *Arquitectura y pintura en Teotihuacán.* Mexico City: Siglo Veintiuno, 2002.

Serlio, Sebastiano. *The Five Books of Architecture: An Unabridged Reprint of the English Edition of 1611.* New York: Dover Publications, 1982.

Service, Elman Rogers. *Primitive Social Organization: An Evolutionary Perspective.* New York: Random House, 1962.

———. *A Profile of Primitive Culture.* New York: Harper and Row, 1963.

Simeon, Remi. *Diccionario de la lengua náhuatl o mexicana.* Mexico City: Siglo Veintiuno, 1981.

Simpson, Lesley Byrd. *The Encomienda in New Spain: The Beginning of Spanish Mexico.* Berkeley and Los Angeles: University of California Press, 1950; first paperback printing, 1982.

Sixteenth-Century Architectural Books from Italy and France. Introduction by Peter A. Wick. Cambridge: Harvard College Library, 1971.

Smith, Michael E. "City Size in Late Postclassic Mesoamerica." *Journal of Urban History* 31, no. 4 (May 2005): 403–434.

———. "Form and Meaning in the Earliest Cities: A New Approach to Ancient Urban Planning." *Journal of Planning History* 6, no. 1 (February 2007): 3–47.

Soustelle, Jacques. *The Olmecs: The Oldest Civilization in Mexico.* Norman: University of Oklahoma Press, 1985.

Spinden, Herbert J. *A Study of Maya Art: Its Subject Matter and Historical Development.* New introduction and bibliography by J. Eric S. Thompson. New York: Dover Publications, 1975.

Stierlin, Henri, ed. *Ancient Mexico*. Architecture of the World Series 11. Lausanne: Benedikt Taschen, n.d.

——. *The Art of Maya*. Köln: Evergreen of Benedikt Taschen Verlag, 1994.

——. *Art of the Aztecs and Its Origins*. New York: Rizzoli, 1982.

——. *Art of the Maya: From the Olmecs to the Toltec-Maya*. New York: Rizzoli, 1981.

——, ed. *Mayan*. Architecture of the World Series 10. Lausanne: Benedikt Taschen, n.d.

Stocker, Terry, Sarah Meltzoff, and Steve Armsey. "Crocodilians and Olmecs: Further Interpretations in Formative Period Iconography." *American Antiquity* 45 (1980): 780–759.

Stross, Brian. "The Mesoamerican Cosmic Portal: An Early Zapotec Example." *RES: Journal of Anthropology and Aesthetics* 29/30 (1996): 82–101.

Stuart, David. "Kings of Stone: A Consideration of Stelae in Ancient Maya Ritual and Representation." *RES: Journal of Anthropology and Aesthetics* 29/30 (1996): 148–170.

——. "Ten Phonetic Syllables." Chapter 26 in *The Decipherment of Maya Writing*, ed. Stephen Houston, Oswaldo Fernando Chinchilla Mazariegos, and David Stuart, 194–206. Norman: University of Oklahoma Press, 2001.

Stuart, David, and Stephen D. Houston. *Classic Maya Place Names*. Studies in Pre-Columbian Art and Archaeology No. 33. Washington, D.C.: Dumbarton Oaks Research Library and Collection, 1994.

Stuart, David, and George Stuart. *Palenque: Eternal City of the Maya*. London: Thames and Hudson, 2008.

Stuart, Gene S., and George E. Stuart. *Lost Kingdoms of the Maya*. Washington, D.C.: National Geographic Society, 1993.

Stuart, George E. "Mural Masterpieces of Ancient Cacaxtla." *National Geographic* 182, no. 3 (September 1992): 120–136.

Tadgell, Christopher. *The History of Architecture in India*. London: Phaidon Press, 1990.

Tate, Carolyn E. "Art in Olmec Culture." In *The Olmec World: Ritual and Rulership*, by Michael D. Coe et al., 47–67. Princeton: The Art Museum, Princeton University, 1995.

——. "Landscape and a Visual Narrative of Creation and Origin at the Olmec Ceremonial Center of La Venta." In *Pre-Columbian Landscapes of Creation and Origin*, ed. John Edward Staller, 31–66. New York: Springer, 2008.

——. "The Maya Cauac Monster's Formal Development and Dynastic Contexts." In *Pre-Columbian Art History: Selected Readings*, ed. Alana Cordy-Collins, 33–54. Palo Alto, CA: Peek Publications, 1982.

——. "Patrons of Shamanic Power: La Venta's Supernatural Entities in Light of Mixe Beliefs." *Ancient Mesoamerica* 10, no. 2 (1999): 169–188.

——. *Yaxchilan: The Design of a Maya Ceremonial City*. Austin: University of Texas Press, 1992.

Taube, Karl A. *Aztec and Maya Myths*. The Legendary Past. Austin: University of Texas Press in cooperation with British Museum Press, 1993.

——. "Itzam Cab Ain: Caimans, Cosmology, and Calendrics in Postclassic Yucatan." *Research Reports on Ancient Maya Writing* 26/27 (August 1989): 1–12.

——. *Olmec Art at Dumbarton Oaks*. Washington, D.C.: Dumbarton Oaks Research Library and Collection, 2004.

——. "The Olmec Maize God: The Face of Corn in Formative Mesoamerica." *RES: Journal of Anthropology and Aesthetics* 29/30 (1996): 39–81.

Taylor, William B. *Drinking, Homicide, and Rebellion in Colonial Mexican Villages*. Stanford: Stanford University Press, 1979.

Tedlock, Dennis. *Breath on the Mirror: Mythic Voices and Visions of the Living Maya*. New York: Harper Collins, 1993.

Teotihuacan: The National Museum of Anthropology. 3rd ed. Mexico City: GV Editores, 1988.

Three Centuries of Mexican Colonial Architecture. Mexico City: Secretaría de Educación Pública, 1933.

Thomas, Hugh. *Conquest: Montezuma, Cortés, and the Fall of Old Mexico*. New York: Simon and Schuster, A Touchstone Book, 1993.

Thompson, J. Eric S. *Maya Hieroglyphic Writing: An Introduction*. Norman: University of Oklahoma Press, 1960.

Toscano, Salvador. *Arte precolombino de México y de la América Central*. 4th ed. Mexico City: Universidad Nacional Autónoma de México, Instituto de Investigaciones Estéticas, 1984.

Toussaint, Manuel. *La arquitectura religiosa en la Nueva España durante el siglo XVI*. Iglesias de México series, ed. Manuel Toussaint, Dr. Atl, and José R. Benítez, VI. Mexico City: Secretaría de Hacienda, 1927.

——. *Colonial Art in Mexico*. Translated and edited by Elizabeth Wilder Weismann. Austin and London: University of Texas Press, 1965.

——. *Oaxaca y Tasco*. Lecturas Mexicanas 80. Mexico City: Fondo de Cultura Económica, Cultura SEP, 1985.

——. *Paseos coloniales*. 2nd ed. Mexico City: Imprenta Universitaria, 1962.

Tunnard, Christopher, and Boris S. Pushkarev. *Man-Made America*. New Haven: Yale University Press, 1963.

Valero de García Lascurain, Ana Rita. "Plazas sagradas del México Antiguo." In *Plazas Mayores de México: Arte y Luz*. Mexico City: BBVA Bancomer, 2002.

Vázquez Benítez, José Alberto. *Las capillas posas de Calpan*. Lecturas Históricas de Puebla 55. Puebla: Secretaría de Cultura, Comisión Puebla V Centenario, 1991.

———. *Historia de un convento.* 2nd ed. Puebla, Mexico: Centro de Estudios Históricos de Puebla, 1990.

Vera, D. Fortino Hipólito. *Santuario del Sacromonte.* Amecameca: Tipografía del "Colegio Católico," 1888.

Vitruvius Pollio, Marcus. *Vitruvius: The Ten Books on Architecture.* Translated by Morris Hicky Morgan. Cambridge: Harvard University Press, 1914; reprint, New York: Dover Publications, 1960.

Vocabulario arquitectónico ilustrado. Mexico City: Secretaría del Patrimonio Nacional, 1976.

Vogt, Evon. *Tortillas for the Gods: A Symbolic Analysis of Zinacanteco Rituals.* Cambridge: Harvard University Press, 1976.

Wagner, E. Logan. "Open Space as a Tool of Conversion: The Syncretism of Sacred Courts and Plazas in Post Conquest Mexico." Ph.D. diss., University of Texas at Austin, 1997.

———. "The Sunken Court of Teopantecuanitlán." Unpublished paper, University of Texas at Austin, 1994.

———. "Urban Spatial Continuity as a Tool of Conversion: The Case of Izamal." Paper presented at conference, "Cultural Transmission and Transformation in the Ibero-American World, 1200–1800," Virginia Tech, 1995.

Webb, Michael. *The City Square: A Historical Evolution.* London: Thames and Hudson, 1990.

Webb, Michael, and Francisco Asensio Cerver. *Redesigning City Squares and Plazas: Urban Landscape Architecture.* New York: Hearst Books International, 1997.

Weckmann, Luis. *The Medieval Heritage of Mexico.* Translated by Frances M. López-Morillas. New York: Fordham University Press, 1992.

Wedel, Waldo R. "Structural Investigations in 1943." In *LaVenta, Tabasco: A Study of Olmec Ceramics and Art: Smithsonian Institution Bureau of American Ethnology,* no. 153. Edited by Philip Drucker. Washington, D.C.: USGPO, 1952.

Weismann, Elizabeth Wilder. *Art and Time in Mexico: From the Conquest to the Revolution.* Photographs by Judith Hancock Sandoval. New York: Harper and Row, 1985.

———. *Mexico in Sculpture, 1521–1821.* Cambridge: Harvard University Press, 1950.

Westheim, Paul. *The Art of Ancient Mexico.* Translated by Ursula Bernard. Garden City, NY: Doubleday Anchor Books, 1965.

Westheim, Paul, et al. *Cuarenta siglos de plástica mexicana: Arte prehispánico.* Mexico: Herrero, 1969.

Whyte, William H. *City: Rediscovering the Center.* New York: Doubleday, 1998.

Wilder, Elizabeth, ed. *Studies in Latin American Art: Proceedings of a Conference Held in the Museum of Modern Art New York, 28–31 May 1945, under the auspices of the Joint Committee on Latin American Studies of the American Council of Learned Societies, the National Research Council and the Social Science Research Council.* Washington, D.C.: American Society of Learned Societies, 1949.

Williams, Carlos. "A Scheme for the Early Monumental Architecture of the Central Coast of Peru." In *Early Ceremonial Architecure of the Andes,* ed. Christopher B. Donnan, 227–240. Washington, D.C.: Dumbarton Oaks, 1985.

Yanes Díaz, Gonzalo. *Espacios urbanos del siglo XVI en la región Puebla-Tlaxcala.* Gobierno del Estado de Puebla, 1991.

Yoffee, Norman. *Myths of the Archaic State: Evolution of the Earliest Cities, States and Civilizations.* New York: Cambridge University Press, 2005.

Zucker, Paul. *Town and Square.* New York: Columbia University Press, 1959.

INDEX

quizoquipan, 72, 76; *76*
Augustinian Order, 35, 38, 93, 150, 174
Austin, Texas, 201
"Avenue of the Dead," Teotihuacan, 49
Axapusco, town plan, *206*
axis mundis, 2, 13, 26, 52; *26*
Aztec Empire, 35–38, 47, 49, 224n68
Aztec poem, 71
The Aztecs under Spanish Rule (Gibson), 224n68

ballcourts, 28; *28*; as axis mundis, 31; banned and destroyed, 119; bullfights as substitute for, 119–121, 126, 128; as inverse pyramids, 28; *29*; as portals, 28, 119
baroque city plan, 43
"Basic Plaza Grouping" (Andrews), 22
Basílica de la Salud, Pátzcuaro, 153
basin, quatrefoil, 16; *17*
basketball, 159
bastides, 40, 43
Becerra, Francisco, 39, 107
Beginning of Spring parade, 199
Benavente, Toribio de, 38, 46, 47, 51, 124
Black, Sinclair, 77
blood scroll, 97
Bonampak murals, 5; *6*
book trade, 222n29
Boone, Elizabeth Hill, 224n68
Brady, James E., 12
Bretos, Miguel A., 183
Brunelleschi, Filippo, 33
bullfights: construction of bullring, 121; *122–123*; as substitute for ball games, 119–121, 126, 129; temporary bullrings, 79, 121; *79, 122–123*
Burgoa, Francisco de, 101

caiman/crocodile symbol, 6–7, 49; *7*
calendrical systems, 195
Calpan, 111–119; church, *112*; Constantino Reyes-Valerio on, 111; façades, *112, 114, 115*; Last Judgment scene, *118*; medallion of Saint John, *119*; *posa*, 115–118; stairs to *atrio*, *113*; town center plan, *111*
calpullis, 53–54
camaríanes, 183
Campo de' Fiori, 45
cantilevered cornice, 187
Capilla de la Cueva, Sacromonte, 65–66
Capilla del Señor: Sacromonte, 71; *67, 68, 71*; Tlacolula, 134; *135*
Capilla Real, Cholula, 51; *52*
car culture, 200
Carrasco, David, 12–13
Carrillo y Ancona, Crescencio, 185
carving tools, preconquest, 113
casa cural, 124
Casa Maya, 180; *181, 182*
caste system in New Spain, 228n136

Caste War, 228n136
castrum grid, 40, 43
Catherwood, Frederick, 185
Catholic Church: liturgy, 48; post-Reform loss of land, 133, 137, 139, 144; veneration of saints, 72. *See also* Augustinian Order; Dominican Order; Franciscan Order; friar-architects; friars
Cauac Earth Monster, 14
causeways, 21, 49, 65, 191–192
caves: cave chapel, Sacromonte, 68; cave formations, Sacromonte, 65; churches built over, 62–63; C shapes as, 23; European views of, 68; rituals performed in, 68; as supernatural portals, 13–14, 62, 68, 103; *15*; Teotihuacan, 13, 103
cemeteries: Achiutla, 99; Angahuan, 159; *161*; Calpan, 111, 119; *112*; Tepeaca, 144–145
Cempoala, 46; *55*
cempoalxochitl (marigold), 116–117; *117*
cenotes, 77–79, 178; *78*
center tree (*wakah-chan*), 23
Chalcatzingo: hills forming double merlon, 16–18; *18*; monuments with quatrefoils, 14; *16*
chalchihuitl (jade beads): and religious syncretism, 87, 115–116; in Tlanalapa toponym, 126; *126*
chalchiumomozco (cave on a hill), 64
Chalma, Señor de, pilgrimage site, 63; *63*
Cham Bahlum, 21
Champotón, 36
Chapultepec (Grasshopper Hill), 13
Charles V, 36, 61, 149, 162
Chase, Stuart, 103
Chávez, Diego de, 38
Chicago, Illinois, 200; *200*
Chichén Itzá: ballcourt, 28; heart motif, 117–119; market plaza, 196; *Tzompantli* (skullrack), 47; *47*
Chilam Balam, 184, 228n149
China, 42
Cholula: Capilla Real interior, 52; Plaza Mayor, 45; population, 223n43; Relación Geográfica, 58; *60*
Christian-humanist programs, 152. *See also* More, Thomas
church naves, 48, 69, 129–131; *83, 99, 144*
Churriguera, Alberto de, 42
Citlateptl, *altepetl* sign for, 13
City Square (Webb), 42–43
Ciudad Real, Antonio de, 111, 187–188
Clendinnen, Inga, 184
clinics/infirmaries, 154, 157. *See also* hospital towns
cloisters, 40, 48; Etla, *148*; Huaquechula, 89; Tochimilco, *110*; Yanhuitlán, *102*
coastal towns, 46
coatepetl (snake mountain), 12
Coatzintla, Veracruz, atrio, 50
cochineal dye, 166, 170
The Code of Kings (Schele & Mathews), 26, 28
Codex Osuna, 53, 169; *52*
cofradías, 150
Cogolludo, Diego López de, 184

Ixmiquilpan mural, 51
Izamal, 183–193; aerial photo, 186; *atrio, 189, 190, 192; ca-marín* and flying buttresses, *190*; convent plan, *188*; current site plan, *185*; downtown plan, *187*; downtown section, *189*; Kinich Kak Mo pyramid, 7, 184–185, 187–188; *8, 187*; Pope John Paul II, 193; *193; sacbeob,* 191–193; *192*; San Antonio de Padua convent, 188–191
izamaleño architecture, 187
Iztapalapa, Relación Geográfica, 55

Jacobs, Jane, 199
jade symbol (*chalchihuitl*), 87
Jardín, San Miguel de Allende, 197–199; *197, 198*
jaripeos, 121, 125
Jilotepec, 51
Johnson, J. B., 63
Joralemon, Peter David, 26
Juárez, Benito, 133
Judgment Day motif: Calpan, 114, 117–119; *118*; Huaquechula, 114; Huejotzingo, 86, 114; *86*
Juxtlahuaca Cave, 13; *14, 15*

Kabul pyramid, 192
kan tzuk, kan xuc (four sides, four corners), 23
Kinich Kak Mo pyramid, 7, 184–185, 187–188; *8, 187. See also* Izamal
kiosks: Huejotzingo, 85; *85*; Huequechula, 89; Molango, 97; Otumba, 139; Pátzcuaro, 153; Tepeapulco, 131; Tepoztlán, 106; Tlacochahuaya, 143; Tlacolula, 137; Tlanalapa, 128; Tlaxiaco, 133
Kiracofe, James, 166
Klor de Alva, Jorge, 50–51
Kostof, Spiro, 199
Kubler, George: friars as "spiritual militia," 39; on Maya architecture, 3; on Molango, 93; on Tochimilco, 108; on Topoztlán, 106–107; on Villa Díaz Ordaz, 124

La Blanca quatrefoil basin, 16; *17*
Labná, 191; *181, 191*
lakamtun (stone banners), 6; *6*
Lake Pátzcuaro, 149; *149*
Landa, Diego de, 48–49; design of Izamal, 184, 185, 187–188; *Yucatan Before and After the Conquest,* 176
Las Casas, Bartolomé de, 38
Last Judgment: Calpan, 114, 117–119; *118*; Huaquechula, 114; Huejotzingo, 86, 114; *86*
La Venta, 16
"La Villa," 63
Laws of the Indies, 46; adaptations to native layout, 49–50, 131, 162; plaza to be used as market, 196; prototype town, *49*
lazy-S shape, 97
legend for measured drawings, 62
Léon, 45
Lincoln, Charles, 185, 191
Lizana, Bernardo de, 177
Lockhart, James, 12, 224n68

Locos parade, 199
lookout towers, 145; *145*
Low, Setha, 199
Lucca city plan, *44*
Lucero, Gonzalo, 131
Luschner, Johann, 119
Luther, Martin, 33

Machaquilá, 16; *16, 17*
Machuca, Pedro, 33
Macuilxochitl, town plan, *207*
Madrid Plaza Mayor, 42, 45
maguey motifs, 227n92
maize deities, 18, 31; *31*
Making of Urban America (Reps), 41
Mâle, Emile, 114
Malinalco, 15
Malinche, 36
maps. *See* Relaciónes Geográficas
marigolds, 116–117, 152; *117*
Marín, Francisco, 38, 101, 166, 170, 173
market day, modern, 196; origin of, 149; Otumba, 139; Pátzcuaro, 154; Tlacolula de Matamoros, 134; *136*; Tlaxiaco, 133; *132*
market square: importance in Europe and Mesoamerica, 196; secular plaza as, 48; Tlatelolco plaza, Tenochtitlán, 35, 47
Martínez Donjuán, Guadalupe, 29
Martin of Tours, 89–90
Mass, 47
Mata, Andrés de, 38
Matamoros, Mariano, 134
Mathews, Peter, 26, 28
Maya civilization: creation myth, 6–7; decline of, 35; importance of plazas, 5; Maya vase, 22
McAndrew, John, 2; *The Open-Air Churches of Sixteenth-Century Mexico,* 170; on Teposcolula, 169; on Tepoztlán and Calpan, 106; on Yanhuitlán, 100; on Zoquizoquipan, 93
measurements, Spanish, 163
Mellon Square, Pittsburgh, 201
Memoriales (Motolinía), 47
Mendoza, Antonio de, 101, 166
Mérida (Tihoo), 176; *177*; map of monastery, *177*
Mérida, Juan de, 38, 77, 184, 188
merlons, double, 16–18, 31, 72; *18, 19, 75*
Mesoamerica, 219n1(ch1); communal open spaces, 2; concept of space, 3–9; cyclical time, 195; native crops, 41. *See also* Spanish invasion of Mesoamerica
mestizos, 36, 64, 66
metallurgy, 149
metaphorical plaza, 23; *23*
Mexica civilization, 35
Mexican Architecture of the Sixteenth Century (Kubler), 124
Mexican terrain, 90
Mexico City, 38, 51, 192, 219n1. *See also* Tenochtitlan

Rocky Point, Belize, 21
rollos (towers), 145; *145*
Rome, architectural influence of, 33–35, 40, 43, 45–46, 50
roses, 116
Rossellino, Bernardo, 33, 40
Roys, Ralph, 191
rulers: identified with mountains, 124; and quatrefoil symbols, 16; *17*

sacbeob (white roads), 26, 44, 48, 191–193; *192*
sacred bundles, 32, 221n72
sacred patio. See *atrio*
sacred river, 63
Sacromonte: aerial photo, *66*; Capilla de la Cueva, 68; Capilla del Señor, 66; *67, 68, 71*; cave formations, 65; chronological progression, 64–67; cultural progression, 68–70; earthquakes, 65–66; mule legend, 65; plans, *67*; Sacred Way, 69, *70*; spatial progression, 70–71
Sahagún, Bernardino de, 7, 38, 129
Saint Francis, 114–116
Saint Gabriel's horn, 58; *60*
Salamanca, 42, 45, 47
salt mining, 166
San Antonio de Padua convent, 188–191; *188–190*
San Bernardino de Siena de Sisal, 77–81; *77, 78*; plan, *77*
San José de los Naturales chapel, 51
San Martín, 89–90
San Miguel, Andrés de, 40, 222n32
San Miguel, Huejotzingo, 84
San Miguel Achiutla, 97–100; church, *98, 99*; siting on east-west axis, 99; town plan, *98*
San Miguel de Allende, 197–199; aerial view, *198*; Jardín plaza, *197*
Santa Clara del Cobre, town plan, *209*
Santa Fe de Granada, 40, 43
Santa Fe de la Laguna, 149, 154–157; *atrio*, *155, 157*; church, *156, 157*; plaza, *155, 156*; *portales*, *155, 157*; town plan, *155*
Santa María Oxtotipac, town plan, *210*
"SANT IVAN" mirror image, 119; *119*
Sapir-Whorf hypothesis, 228n1
Schele, Linda: on Dallas Plaque, 32; on importance of open space, 5; on maize-deity symbolism, 28, 31; *31*; on quincunx symbol, 26; on superimposed temples, 50; on Teopantecuanitlán, 31; *31*; on triad centering, 18, 21
Second Audiencia, 149
Segovia Pinto, Victor, 185
Seibal quatrefoil-shaped glyph, 16
seismic activity: Coixtlahuaca, 170; Parcutín eruption, 160; Sacromonte, 65–66; Teposcolula, 166; Tlaxiaco, 131
sello of marigold, 117
Señor de Chalma church, 63; *63*
Señor de las Peñas church, 148; *148*
Serlio, Sebastiano, 40, 173
Serna, Antonio de, 101
seven, significance of number, 116
shaft tombs, 149

Shakespeare, William, 39
shared forms, 196
shell motif, 117–119, 227n102; *118*
silkworms, 166
silver, 134, 174; *135*
site visit procedures, 61–62
Sitte, Camillo, 44, 199–200
Sixtus V, 43
smallpox, 36, 221n5. *See also* epidemics
smudging, 103
snakes: and crown of thorns, 226n44; feathered snake design, 173; plumed serpent image, *14, 15*; snake mountain (*coatepetl*), 12
solar clocks, 143; *143*
solstices, 31, 64, 80; *31*
space: European sense of, 42–43, 45; experiencing, 1; use of, 195. *See also* open space ensembles
Spain in America (Gibson), 152
Spanish invasion of Mesoamerica: chronology, 35–36; notable persons involved in, 38–39; opinions of natives, 41; purposes of, 35; reaction to city plans, plazas, 37; town founding campaign, 41, 49; under Vatican control, 50; use of slave labor, 41, 44–45
Spanish measurements, 163
Spanish towns, 46
speech glyphs, 86
"spiritual militia," 39
sprawl, 200–202
square, tied to creation, 23
stairs: circular, 93; with volute, 18; *19*
Stations of the Cross, 69–71, 87; *70*; Otumba, 139; Tochimilco, 109
steel, 41
stelae: representing banners, 6; *6*; *te tun* (trees), 6; of Zapotec ruler (Monte Albán), 16; *17*, 54
Stephens, John Lloyd, 185
stigmata: Calpan, 114–115, 227n92; *115*; Huejotzingo, 85–87, 89; *87*; Mexican version of, 86–87
stones: Aztec craftsmanship, 47; reuse for later buildings, 61, 100, 150, 162; "stone trees," stelae as, 6
streets: alignment of, 162; *beh*, 26; European vs. Mesoamerican, 43–44, 48–49; *sacbeob* (white roads), 26, 44, 48, 191–193; *192*
stucco monumental masks, 187
Studio Mexico, ix, 29, 77; *11, 30*
suburban sprawl, 200–202
sun: movements of, 31, 80; *31*; sundials, 143; *143*; sun gods, 184, 188
sunken courts, 16, 103; Calpan, 111, 119; *113*; Teopantecuanitlán, 18, 28, 29–31; *19, 31*; Tepoztlán, 106; *107*; Tochimilco, *108*; 109
surveying, 61–62
sustenance mountain, 12, 116

Tadgell, Christopher, 222n36
Tarasco, 149–154, 157